NEW WOMAN FICTION, 1881–1899

CONTENTS OF THE EDITION

NEW WOMAN FICTION, 1881–1899

General Editor
Carolyn W. de la L. Oulton

Volume 3
Mona Caird, *The Wing of Azrael* (1889)

Edited by
Alexandra Warwick

Routledge
Taylor & Francis Group

LONDON AND NEW YORK

First published 2010 by Pickering & Chatto (Publishers) Limited

2 Park Square, Milton Park, Abingdon, Oxon OX14 4RN
711 Third Avenue, New York, NY 10017, USA

Routledge is an imprint of the Taylor & Francis Group, an informa business

First issued in paperback 2017

BRITISH LIBRARY CATALOGUING IN PUBLICATION DATA

New woman fiction, 1881–1899.
Part 1, Volumes 1–3.
1. Women – Social conditions – Fiction.
I. Oulton, Carolyn, 1972–. II. Fothergill, Jessie, 1851–1891. Kith and kin. III.
Lee, Vernon, 1856–1935. Miss Brown. IV. Caird, Mona. Wing of Azrael. V.
Ayres, Brenda, 1953– VI. Yuen, Karen. VII. Warwick, Alexandra.
823.8'08-dc22

ISBN-13: 978-1-85196-641-7 (set)
ISBN-13: 978-1-138-75553-6 (hbk)
ISBN-13: 978-1-138-11309-1 (pbk)

Typeset by Pickering & Chatto (Publishers) Limited

CONTENTS

INTRODUCTION

In 1888, Mona Caird was probably the most famous feminist in Britain. Her notoriety came from her publication of an article entitled 'Marriage' in the *Westminster Review* in August 1888. In response to her assertion that 'the present form of marriage ... is a vexatious failure',[1] the *Daily Telegraph* posed the question 'Is Marriage a Failure?' and the ensuing correspondence was huge; some 27,000 letters were received between 9 August and 29 September from men and women of all classes and occupations. The anonymized signatures indicate the range of opinions expressed: 'One Who Has Suffered'; 'A Contented Young Spinster'; 'Married and Contented'; 'A Matrimonial Failure'; 'A Happy Husband and Father'.[2] Although few of the letter-writers agreed to the full extent with Caird's radical opinions, many expressed unhappiness with their married lives and it is significant that so many people considered marriage to be in question at all.

The Victorians were intensely self-conscious and self-scrutinizing of their society. 'Questions' had frequently been posed – the 'Condition of England Question'; the 'Eastern Question', 'The Irish Question', the 'Woman Question' – suggesting a willingness to interrogate existing social and political conditions, but against this was an increasing recourse to ideas of the 'natural': to permanent, unchanging states validated by biology and particularly by the post-Darwinian translations of scientific theory to social conditions. The Woman Question and its successors in the New Woman debates of the end of the century were especially bound up in such issues of the 'naturalness' of femininity and motherhood and assumptions, both radical and conservative, that biology determined society, morality and destiny.

It is one of the dreadful coincidences of history that the intense interest in the social and legal relations of men and women expressed in the pages of the *Telegraph* was displaced by speculation on a more dramatically horrible example of the treatment of women: the Whitechapel murders. By 27 September the mutilated bodies of two women had been found and the perpetrator had a name: Jack the Ripper. The journalist George R. Sims remarked on the celebrity of the current suspect and listed 'Mrs Mona Caird' as one of those other celebrities whom the public would push aside in order to meet him.[3] Although some feminists such as Florence Fenwick Miller and Frances Power Cobbe attempted to use the Whitechapel murders to draw attention to the issue of violence against women, they were a tiny minority in the great tide of newspaper reporting which showed little regard for the female victims. The desperately poor East End prostitutes were easily made 'other' and the resistance to considering them within a continuum of attitudes to all women proved strong and enduring even into the twentieth century.[4]

Caird had clearly articulated the continuum in her *Westminster Review* article: 'We see now completed our own way of settling the relations of the sexes. The factors of our system are: respectability, prostitution, strict marriage, commercialism, unequal moral standard for the two sexes, and the subjection of women'. She describes the present form of marriage as 'the worst, because the most hypocritical, form of woman-purchase' and suggests that '[w]e are also led to conclude that modern "Respectability" draws its life-blood from the degradation of women in marriage and in prostitution'.[5]

Caird was not the first to suggest the relationship between marriage and prostitution and by the time of the 'Marriage' article there were many people writing and campaigning on a wide range of issues concerning women. The term feminism is contentious in relation to these women, and some men, of the late nineteenth century and it is important to think of their work and ideas within their own context, as well as drawing comparisons with second- and third-wave feminism.[6] Victorian feminism was complex and certainly not a single set of beliefs and aims that were shared by all those working towards political and social change for women. Almost a hundred years earlier Mary Wollstonecraft in *A Vindication of the Rights of Woman* (1792) had argued that women existed in a state of ignorance, vanity and idleness created by their enforced exclusion from education and citizenship. Wollstonecraft also suggested (and this was later echoed by Caird) that women were the least fitted to bring up children because of their own stunted intellectual growth. Early nineteenth-century radical groups, such as the socialist group around Robert Owen in the 1820s and 1830s, included reference to women in their programmes, linking the freedom of women to wider social emancipation. The campaigns for the abolition of slavery at this time also lent a rhetorical device that continued throughout the century: the analogy between British women and slaves and between marriage and slavery is made in John Stuart Mill's book *On the Subjection of Women* (1869). Caird knew this text and the influence of Mill's arguments about the cultural construction of femininity, as opposed to the supposedly 'natural' character of women, can be seen in her own work.

Although the Reform Act of 1832 reorganized to some extent the inequalities of the old electoral system to recognize the changed conditions of industrialized Britain, women continued to be excluded.[7] This prompted the first petition to Parliament asking for the enfranchisement of women and although the petition was rejected, small groups continued to campaign. While the second Reform Act of 1867 was being debated John Stuart Mill and Henry Fawcett presented another petition demanding that female suffrage be considered. It was again rejected, but in every year from 1870 to 1878 and from 1884 to 1889 private members' bills were presented to Parliament calling for extension of the franchise to women.[8] Caird was active in the movement for the franchise: she belonged to a series of organizations, beginning with the National Society for Women's Suffrage in 1878. At the beginning of the twentieth century she was involved in the Women's Social and Political Union, the militant organization led by the Pankhursts, and she defended their controversial direct actions in her essay, 'Militant Tactics and Woman's Suffrage (1908), saying that 'when women possess full human and civic rights, they may justly be called upon to confine themselves to constitutional measures'.[9]

The campaign for women's suffrage, however, was not the central focus of social reformers during the nineteenth century. From about 1850 onwards, organized groups consisting mainly of middle-class philanthropists were working for change in areas such as education and employment.[10] Gradually, and on the prompting and agitation of campaigners, the state began to intervene in the 'private' matters of family and married life. The major challenges were to the legal non-existence of the married woman. The feminist campaigner Barbara Bodichon defines the state of the married woman in her *A Brief Summary, in Plain Language, of the Most Important Laws concerning Women* (1854):

> A man and wife are one person in law; the wife loses all her rights as a single woman, and her existence is entirely absorbed in that of her husband. He is civilly responsible for her acts; she lives under his protection or cover, and her condition is called coverture. A woman's body belongs to her husband; she is in his custody.[11]

Beginning with the Divorce and Matrimonial Causes Act in 1857, a series of new laws moved, in what seemed to some to be painfully small steps, towards some acceptance that women were independent beings, entitled to possession of themselves and their property. The 1857 Act made divorces slightly easier to obtain[12] and a second Act in 1878 provided for financial support for women granted judicial separations when in danger from violent husbands. The problems created by financial dependence were further addressed in the 1884 Matrimonial Causes Act, and in 1870 and 1882 two Married Women's Property Acts between them gave women the right to retain their own property and earnings after marriage.

There was also a strong movement initially grouped around the effort to gain the repeal of the Contagious Diseases Acts. Passed in 1864, 1868 and 1869 in an attempt to control sexually transmitted diseases in the military, they allowed for the compulsory detention, examination and treatment of women suspected of prostitution in garrison towns. The campaigns necessitated public discussion of matters of sexuality, but the direction of discussion was not towards a recognition or liberation of autonomous female sexuality. It was rather towards moral reform for all, and more particularly, men. A 'double standard' was seen to prevail, in which a greater moral (sexual) laxity in men was tolerated, while women were expected to conform to a higher ideal. The difference in expectation rested in part on a view summarized by William Acton's statement that 'women ... are not very much troubled by sexual feeling'.[13] Although this was by no means the only view and there were those, including men in the medical profession, who argued that women possessed sexual instincts of their own,[14] after the suspension (in 1883) and eventual repeal of the Contagious Diseases Acts in 1886, the majority of reformers coalesced around an idea of social purity. Broadly, this meant the regulation of sexuality and encompassed a number of different aims, including suppression of prostitution and pornography, cleaning up popular entertainments like the music halls, raising the age of consent and instituting other protections for women in the public sphere. The coalition encompassed a wide range of motivating beliefs but, as Angelique Richardson notes, in the increasingly repressive atmosphere of the 1880s,

> the social purity campaigns which had set out to challenge the idea of the male sexual urge as a biological fact now began to privilege nature over nurture, arguing that men were essentially sexually reckless while (unfallen) women were innately moral and the nation's best chance of 'race regeneration.'[15]

This, then, is the legal and social context in which Caird published *The Wing of Azrael* in 1889. It was actually her third novel although the first two, *Whom Nature Leadeth* (1883) and *One That Wins* (1887), had been published under the pseudonym of G. Noel Hatton.[16] Despite her notoriety after the 'Marriage' article, *Azrael* did not sell in great quantity and was never reprinted. Her fourth novel, *The Daughters of Danaus* (1894), was much more successful[17] and remains better known since its republication by the Feminist Press in 1989. She continued to write fiction and non-fiction throughout her life and her last novel was published in 1931, the year before her death. Caird was not an isolated writer but was part of London literary society, where she knew many other authors including Thomas Hardy.[18] She also met other people concerned with issues of gender: the American feminist Elizabeth Cady Stanton recorded meeting her in 1888 when she was preparing the 'Marriage' article,[19] and she attended groups like the Men and Women's Club.[20] Among Caird's closest friends were two women poets, Mathilde Blind and Elizabeth Sharp (to whom she dedicated *The Wing of Azrael*). Sharp's husband was also a well-connected writer who wrote, unusually, under a female pseudonym: Fiona McLeod. Caird's own husband is a rather sketchy figure in what is known of her life; they were married in 1877 but Caird seems to have travelled abroad and spent a good deal of time in London while he remained on his estate in Scotland. Their only child, Alister, was born in 1884. What either of the couple thought about their own marriage is not known,[21] but the wider topic is the central focus of all of Caird's novels.

Given Caird's dedication to the subject of marriage, the position that she takes in the preface to *Azrael* is perhaps unexpected, in that she identifies herself primarily as a novelist and states her belief in the weakness of didactic fiction: 'there is no intention on the writer's part to make it serve a polemical "purpose" or to advocate a cause. Its object is not to contest or to argue, but to represent' (below, p. 4). She appears to be extending to her characters something of the same right to self-determination that she wished to see for real people: there is no justification for treating fictional beings as 'puppets' and denying their 'will' and 'personality' (below, p. 3). Caird sees humans as narrative creatures and suggests that the 'truth' is best achieved by producing narratives that can compete with received wisdom. By presenting a 'true' narrative the appeal should be to the reordering of the inner narratives, and hence the beliefs, of others. It is a method that works not by didactic argument but by creation of a sympathetic resonance; what Richardson calls a homeopathic principle.[22]

It is perhaps for this reason that Caird does not produce her novel in any experimental form but remains within a largely Realist framework, albeit one inflected with the legacy of the Gothic. The Gothic novels that dominated the late eighteenth and early nineteenth centuries already provided a blueprint for the story of female oppression within the home and family, although they were distanced chronologically, geographically and socially from the present by their settings in aristocratic or Catholic locations of a rather non-specific European past. In such novels, the home had frequently featured as at best an ambiguous space for women and at worst a place of imprisonment and terror. In the older Gothic it is most usually the father or the patriarch who represents the authoritarian, and sometimes murderous, threat to women, but the developments in the novel in the Victorian period begin to locate the threat more firmly in the present, in Britain and emanating from the lover or husband. The novels of the Brontë sisters are early and unusually direct examples of this: in their work the domestic spaces all oscillate between being secluded places of safety and protection and terrifyingly closed prisons dominated by whimsical and tyrannical rulers. Variations on the Gothic motifs of female oppression persist throughout the century and the sensation novels of the 1860s and '70s, such as Mary Braddon's *Lady Audley's Secret* (1862) or Wilkie Collins's *The Woman in White* (1860) weave them together with issues drawn directly from the present.

Caird draws very obviously on an existing repertoire of Gothic tropes in *The Wing of Azrael*. The isolated castle in which Viola is virtually imprisoned after her marriage provides a tangible metaphor for the condition of marriage itself: it is half-ruined but still inhabited. The castle is positioned on the edge of a cliff, but like that other man-made structure, marriage, it is still sturdy and, despite being gradually undermined by the sea and the weather, it will be many years before it collapses. There are a number of other familiar Gothic elements: Viola's vision of blood on the threshold; the 'bluebeard chamber' where an earlier Mrs Dendraith was murdered; the apparition that rises from the bed; the sinister housekeeper/prison warder; the dagger with the bloodstain; and although some of these are demystified (the apparition is Philip, the bloodstain is probably rust), many connect with one of the strongest themes of Gothic: the destructive return in the present of events of the past.

Gothic repetition had by this time accrued some associations with a post-Darwinian notion of heredity in which the returning curse is less to do with a metaphysical fate and more with the perceived inevitability of the biological recurrence of inherited traits. Thus Philip, whose physical resemblance to the family portraits is pointed out several times, can be seen as the latest in a line that includes the wife-murderer and the brutally stupid and jealous ancestors of the duel story. In some ways, Caird's use of the Gothic could be regarded as being at odds with her stated desire to represent realities: few of Caird's readers would have lived in haunted Norman castles. However, what the Gothic does allow Caird to do is to question the apparent biological inevitability of certain behaviour by placing it in something like a historical context.

Although the post-Darwinist appropriation of biology in ideas of inheritance was a cause taken up by many in the late nineteenth century, Caird was strongly opposed to it. Many other feminists and New Woman novelists espoused eugenic ideas of ensuring the future of the race through production of healthy children, seeing in them a way of asserting the equality and even primacy of women.[23] For a range of ideological positions including radical eugenicist feminists, social purity campaigners and conservatives wishing to defend a *status quo*, 'Nature' is taken as fundamental truth: an explanation of social structures and a justification for their continuance or for their reform along specific lines. Caird emphatically and repeatedly rejects such positions:

> [t]he 'Nature' argument is surely palpably ridiculous. It is almost incredible that it should be necessary to point out that fallacy and confusion that results from adopting this patent, moveable, double-action reversible premiss, which may be shifted at pleasure – brought forward or suppressed according to the conclusion at which one desires to arrive, or the practices which one desires to justify.[24]

In 'Ideal Marriage' she writes: '*Evolution!* the word awes us. We are like children frightened at our own shadows'[25] and emphasizes instead the potential of rational thought to resist being driven 'like dead leaves on a gale'.[26] She asserts that '*Belief in the power of man to choose his direction of change:* this is the creed of the future'[27] and argues that the deliberate choices to be made are not those of the eugenicists in breeding to refine the race, but intellectual decisions to change purposefully the structure of social life.

The argument of Caird's original 'Marriage' article is essentially a historical analysis in which she shows that the position of women and the condition of marriage are not inevitable products of biology or a more nebulous notion of 'human nature' but are profoundly historically determined. In the first paragraph she states that 'the particular form of social life, or of marriage ... has by no means existed from time immemorial' and goes on:

> it is necessary to clear the ground for thought upon this subject by a protest against the careless use of the words 'human nature', and especially 'woman's nature'. History will show us, if anything will, that human nature has apparently limitless adaptability, and that therefore no conclusion can be built upon special manifestations which may at any time be developed. Such development must be referred to certain conditions, and not be mistaken for the eternal law of being.[28]

Marriage practices in other cultures, past and present, were an important element of the developing disciplines of anthropology and ethnology, and Caird's ideas on the historical, and prehistorical, variations of marriage were strongly influenced by her reading in these fields. Her entry in *Who's Who* lists collecting antiquities among her recreations, and in her work she quotes from a range of sources, including E. B. Tylor's well-known *Primitive Culture* (1871), John Lubbock's *Prehistoric Times* (1869) and from Carl Starcke's *The Primitive Family*, which was published in the same year as *Azrael* and by her own publisher, Trübner. In *Azrael*, the proto-New Woman Sibella's room is described as having books and work lying about, as well as antique vases and 'prehistoric things in bronze' (below, p. 198). They link her to the past and to the possibility of human societies being other than they are in the present. It is also significant that while many anthropological texts were concerned with questions of evolution, Caird instead drew from them the focus on the construction of social relations. She had also read work by socialist thinkers[29] and the economic conditions of women are a fundamental part of her critique. She points out the lack of recognition of woman's labour in the household[30] and she represents marriage in starkly economic terms. In her essay she locates the present form of marriage as having developed in the Reformation (particularly under the malign influence of Luther), 'when commerce, competition, the great bourgeois class, and that remarkable thing called "Respectability" also began to rise'.[31] For her, the rise of capitalism has solidified the status of women as a form of currency, with the bourgeois values of respectability disguising the fact that women still exist in essentially feudal conditions analogous to those of slavery in which they possess neither themselves nor the products of their labour.

Azrael is much concerned with questions of property and ownership. Viola and Adrienne do not make simple romantic mistakes in their marriages, they are clearly objects of exchange, elements in transactions made to stabilize their families' precarious finances. On Philip's complaint that Viola's father has continued to ask his son-in-law for money, her rejoinder is that 'I, being not the seller but the thing sold, can scarcely be held responsible. The object of merchandise called to account for its owner's delinquencies? – surely that is very unbusiness-like!' (below, p. 269). Caird would have been aware of the passage of the Married Women's Property Act in 1882 and, even though after the Act a real Viola would have had the right to retain any earnings, her father's tirade in chapter IX makes it clear how unrealistic her desire to earn her own living still was. A legal right had been established but it was still practically beyond the reach of most.

Caird is also aware that the establishment of the right to material property has not been accompanied by a right to an assertion of selfhood. There are three distinct episodes in the novel that centre on this question, dramatized through the giving of gifts: Harry's present of the dagger before her marriage and Philip's gifts of the necklace of Dendraith diamonds and of the star ornament. The episodes are critical because they embody the questions of property, the woman's status as subject or object and her conversion from one to the other. The diamond star is offered to Viola as a 'reward' for her obedience (below, p. 186), and although she tries to refuse it Philip insists that as his wife she must take it and wear it as he directs. The parallel between marriage and prostitution is clear, even if the transactions of bourgeois marriage are carried out in diamond jewellery rather than small change. In the argument about the dagger Viola asserts: 'I accepted this gift, not as your wife, but as *myself*. I was not your wife then ... Am I always to be *your wife*, never myself?' (below, p. 149). In this she draws the distinct line between her independent existence and her disappearance as a subject upon marriage. Philip's reply is simple: 'The world regards and criticises you now as my wife, and nothing else. What else are you? You possess no other standing or acknowledged existence' (below, p. 149). In the journey home after the wedding ceremony the dagger is directly juxtaposed with the family diamonds, the gift that is not a gift to her, but to 'Mrs Dendraith', whoever it is that temporarily occupies that identity. Viola's mistaken hope that she can retain something of 'herself' is symbolized in the dagger, it is truly a double-edged weapon in that using it to 'free' herself from her husband she brings about her own destruction.

It is a very specific aspect of the right to self-possession that the gift episodes punctuate: the right to the possession of the body. The philosophical discussions of Caleb, Harry and Philip circle around questions of free will and although Viola lacks the education to articulate her thoughts in formal terms, she is clearly shown as asking them in more intuitive ways. Her first appearance at the opening of the novel shows her considering the issue of her identity, whether she has a separate and distinct self and whether that self has any continuity in time. In common with other agonized little girls of women's writing, like Jane Eyre, Catherine Earnshaw and Maggie Tulliver, readers are shown that problems of identity exist from an early stage in a woman's life. The integrity of Viola's identity is shown in the opening episode as grounded equally in body and mind and Caird goes on to demonstrate that they cannot be separated: a woman's right to her own body must be absolute for any free and independent self to exist. The first assault on Viola's body comes when she is still a small child and Philip demands that she open her eyes so that he can see their colour. The second is when Philip's father attempts to kiss her and she reacts violently against it. Although Lisa Surridge suggests that this incident draws attention to the difference in the legal rights of single and married women,[32] it seems rather to indicate that there is no real difference: the female child is already an object and the jocular sexual harassment of the little girl is simply part of the education that she must receive in order to become a wife. Although the age of consent had been raised from thirteen to sixteen shortly before the publication of *Azrael*,[33] Caird's point is not about Viola's age specifically, but the continuity of the unwanted sexualized attention directed at all girls and women. Caird shows in some detail the reactions of all those in the scene and we see the uncomfortable enforcement of the girl's social compliance through the varieties of embarrassment, surprise, laughter and innuendo that take place. Viola's own reaction is intense and explicit. As she thinks about the incident she feels that

> she had been treated with insolence, as a being whose will was of no moment, whose very person was not her own; who might be kissed or struck or played with exactly as people pleased, as if she were a thing without life or personality. (below, p. 30)

Philip later tries to kiss the child Viola again and, holding her, will not release her unless she kisses him and repeats a form of words that he gives her. She refuses and he lets her go. It is a horrible parody of their marriage ceremony in which she is obliged to repeat the words of the service even though she refuses to assent to them and after which she will not be released. In this episode when she is still a child she thinks to herself that 'the man had no right to interfere with her liberty' (below, p. 48), but we see clearly that the marriage ceremony gives him precisely that right. Although the text is reserved in its language, Caird makes it obvious that Viola suffers from Philip's insistence on his rights to her body. There are many references to the 'living hell' (below, p. 183) of undesired sex and Viola is continually distressed at the sexual gossip of the other women, as well as at the assumptions made about the arrival of children. Under the law, the wife was considered to have consented to sexual intercourse with her husband during the marriage ceremony and was not entitled to withdraw that consent at a later stage. Although a case in which the possibility of marital rape was in question was quite widely reported during 1888 and 1889,[34] it was not actually recognized in law until over a hundred years later.[35] Caird also suggests, as was argued by twentieth-century feminists, that rape is an expression of power rather than sexuality. In the murder scene she writes of Philip that: 'Overcoming her frantic resistance, he kissed her long and steadily on the lips, partly because it pleased him to do so, partly it seemed, because it tortured her' (below, p. 300). Viola has little fear of Philip's physical violence, but she is afraid of what was still only barely recognized in law: mental cruelty.[36]

Almost all of Philip's actions are of a sadistic nature: he ties Viola's dog's legs together and throws stones at it, he beats a horse and he breaks a cat's leg. As well as slavery, ill-treatment of animals is another important analogy that is drawn in many feminist writings. It was an analogy widely used and in mid-century it was often perceived as ironic that greater legal protection existed for animals than for wives and that offenders were far more vigorously pursued and prosecuted.[37] Philip's treatment of animals is an indication of his character but also an indictment of a more general culture. Caird was part of the anti-vivisection movement that was gathering strength at the end of the century and wrote several pieces in support of it. In those pieces she suggests that the partridge-shooting sportsman and the cook boiling a live lobster are only versions of the cruelty exhibited by vivisectors and argues that such cruelty arises from the existence and perpetuation of a hierarchical view of the value of living beings. There is an imaginary line, she says:

> Beneath this line would be placed all those beings in relation to whom the human moral code becomes non-effective: just above the line would be ranged those who had some slight, uncertain hold upon the sentiment of their fellows: above this, again, would come those possessing definite though meagre rights, and so on up the scale, till we arrive at the full complement of rights, and the full sense of moral responsibility on the part of mankind, towards this favoured class.[38]

She goes on to point out that despite historical variations in the position of the line of rights, women, black people, the poor and animals still largely fall below it.[39] There is an example of her linking of those for whom the moral code is non-effective in chapter IX. Viola has just been subjected to her father's humiliating speech on the uselessness of women and immediately afterwards she sees the gardener labouring in the rain despite his painful rheumatism and then finds her old dog close to death. All three are victims of 'dumb tragedies that nobody heeds' (below, p. 73) because their suffering is not significant in the scale of human values.

In her anti-vivisection writings Caird argues again that cruelty is not the result of natural impulses but historically contingent learned behaviour. As Richardson points out in her discussion of eugenics, Caird believed far more strongly in imitation than in inheritance.[40] In *Azrael* the reader can easily see the part played by men in the oppression of women, but the more dispiriting examples are those of the women. Viola's mother is the most immediate model, whom she is expected to imitate in order to learn womanhood, and Mrs Sedley carefully educates Viola in what she believes to be Christian ideas of duty and self-sacrifice. As with the other women, Caird does not criticize Mrs Sedley's actions as conscious and deliberate, she shows them instead as the result of social coercion and the inability to think clearly through the logical implications of her own feelings. Mrs Sedley is genuinely upset at the prospect of her daughter's marriage but she is unable to resist it or even to articulate what it is that troubles her. She feels a contradiction between sacred duty and mercenary marriage but can only reconcile them under a nebulous notion of sacrifice. In Mrs Sedley we see that 'sacrifice' is a delusion as her husband has only been rendered more brutal and coarse by her selfless behaviour. Caird shows that marriage, motherhood and self-sacrifice are not natural inheritances but are brought about by training, emotional blackmail and social pressure.

In *Azrael*, Viola, although central to the narrative, is only one of a range of female characters all of whom can be seen to be possible versions of a woman's existence. The other married women show alternative futures for Viola: the grotesquely wriggling and gossiping Mrs Courtenay, who Caird tells us is actually painfully shy, is a weak woman who joins the group of bullies to protect herself; Lady Clevedon is an ambitious woman who has managed to find satisfaction of her ambition in her grand marriage and, most painfully, Mrs Evans, who is a precise example of the figure described by Caird in her essays: married young, devoted to her duty as a wife and mother and becoming in the course of it weak, unhealthy, 'dim and petty in thought' (below, p. 163), charmless and ultimately unloved.

These women are all lost, but worse, they are participating in the perpetuation of their own oppression into future generations: 'Most women ... spend their energies in making all these time-honoured iniquities possible and successful, encouraging the repetition of these profitable old crimes apparently for all eternity!' (below, p. 221). Although men make the most obvious demands, it is clear that the women educate their daughters for the sacrifice and then police the behaviour of married women mercilessly through a vile combination of self-conscious 'morality' (as with Mrs Pellett) and salacious gossip. The saddest examples that Caird presents are the other young women: Adrienne and Dorothy. Like Viola, Adrienne is faced with a mercenary marriage to a man she does not like or respect in order to save her family's fortunes and she too is thoughtful, clever and attractive. Although she voices the familiar creed, 'It is not a hopeless struggle, dear Viola, if once we realise the beauty and the blessedness of *sacrifice*' (below, p. 181), she is conscious of the iniquity of the situation. Caird places her in direct debate with Sibella and their conversation offers what is not available to Viola: a clear description of the conditions under which she is undertaking a marriage. It almost succeeds and Adrienne later finds herself wondering what Sibella would make of her engagement to the ugly buffoon Bob Hunter. She achieves her peace, 'a life of smooth prosperity and domestic contentment' (below, p. 289), only at the price of denial of such rebellious thoughts. Although the youngest of the women in the novel, Dorothy Evans, remains unmarried at the end and is the only figure in whom Caird indicates the possibility of same-sex desire (below, p. 165), there is no optimistic suggestion for her future; the last mention of her is her turning aside in miserable silence when Viola's name is mentioned (below, p. 290).

The most important alternative for Viola is the example of Sibella, who has left her husband and lives as a single woman. Sibella is educated and clear-thinking: it is she who voices Caird's arguments against sacrifice and points out the historical trajectory of the treatment of women. She is able to sustain a friendship across gender lines with Harry when Viola's similar developing friendship with Dick Evans is denied. Sibella also echoes the revulsion that Viola feels against motherhood. The questioning of this fundamental assumption about women's relationship to children marks an important difference between Caird's work and that of other feminist and New Woman novelists. Caird believed that the radical appropriation of motherhood by eugenicists like Olive Schreiner and Sarah Grand had no more potential for liberation than the sentimentalized versions of mother and child found elsewhere in Victorian culture.[41] Women, through their lack of education, were the least suited to bring up children and children are, as she writes elsewhere, 'the means and method of a woman's bondage',[42] the hostages who ensure women's acquiescence to their situation. Sibella, however, is an outcast who is compromised in her actions. She is unable to save either Adrienne or Viola and is obliged to endure the attentions of Philip Dendraith, who assumes that because she belongs to no man in particular, she is available to all.

Nevertheless, Sibella's survival is important as it is one of the few rays of hope in the darkness that closes the novel. Margaret Morganroth Gullette, in her afterword to *The Daughters of Danaus*, suggests that it is a brave decision on Caird's part to let her heroine Hadria live, albeit in great loss and disappointment. Of the deaths of other heroines she says that at 'some level, such deaths accept the culture's determination that marriage be the only successful course for adult women. The authors' "acceptance" operates at that subterranean level at which alternative fates for transgressive women cannot be imagined, except for death.'[43] In 1889 Caird cannot imagine another fate for Viola. 'We cannot ask every woman to be a heroine and choose a hard and thorny path'[44] she writes in 'Marriage', and although Sibella does ask this of Viola, 'Are all women who come after you to be worse off, to be heavier-hearted, because of you?' (below, p. 221), at the end of the novel only Sibella is left on that path. Viola succumbs to a familiar end for the transgressive woman: madness and death. The reader assumes that Viola throws herself into the sea and, although there is perhaps some consolation in her absorption into the ecstatic elemental force with which she closely identifies, there is a crucial difference between the endings of *Azrael* and *The Daughters of Danaus*. At the end of the latter, we are told that Hadria 'turned away, as a flood of bitter grief swept over her, so that she felt as one drowning.'[45] Her drowning is only metaphorical and she will not perpetuate the cycle of sacrifice as Viola has. There are other differences between the two novels that suggest a hesitantly optimistic movement forward, for example in the myths that provide their titles. *Azrael* is prefaced by a passage from the bible on the origin of the scapegoat. There is no consciousness or possibility of resistance for the goat, it is simply driven out to be taken by death, and images of sacrifice and the punishment of the innocent recur throughout the novel. The daughters of Danaus, by contrast, offer resistance to their forced marriages, however slight and largely unsuccessful.[46] Lisa Surridge suggests that in *Danaus*, 'the novel's most striking scenes involve women's liberatory relationship with time and change. The text's temporal shifts, plot gap, and subjective rendering of time suggest what Caird saw as the radical potential of historical variation.'[47] *Azrael* demonstrates little sense of this. Indeed, the deployment of Gothic devices makes it harder to locate in the present, despite the many circumstantial details of late nineteenth-century life. The fate of the murdered Lady Dendraith, although 'fifty or a hundred years' ago, is joined to that of Viola and 'the empty phantom Time' (below, p. 189) is not liberating but imprisoning. By casting off the remnants of the Gothic, in *Danaus* Caird is able to show that the *ordinary* condition of marriage is one of oppression and misery. Harry Lancaster observes that the 'woman marries and gives no sign; no one knows how the unthinkable is worked out in daily detail' (below, p. 80), and Hadria's story is much closer to the daily working out of the unthinkable, at least to the middle-class readership of Caird's novels.

Through the overt violence of *Azrael*, though, Caird asks the question still unanswered in the late twentieth century: what actions can be construed as self-defence against violent or abusive husbands or partners?[48] Just as she did not wish for the perpetrators of violence against women, children or animals to undergo brutal punishments,[49] Caird would not have accepted that Viola's actions were right; understandable perhaps, but not to be condoned. She is the scapegoat constructed through the denial of the social, political and psychological selfhood of women. Viola is 'the child of her generation' (below, p. 200), 'a symbol of the troublous age in which she lived, a creature with weakened and uprooted faith, yet with feelings and instincts still belonging to the past, still responding to the old dead and gone dogmas' (below, p. 252), and it is telling that Caird can only sketch the hopeful precursor of the next generation in the minor figure of Sibella. Only a few years later, however, Sibella had a host of sisters and the New Woman carried the torch of feminism into the new century.

Notes

1. M. Caird, 'Marriage', *Westminster Review*, 130:2 (1888), pp. 186–201, on p. 197.
2. H. Quilter (ed.), *Is Marriage a Failure?* (London: Swann Sonnenschein, 1888).
3. G. R. Sims, in *Sunday Referee*, 16 September 1888; see the casebook site at http://www. casebook.org/press_reports/dagonet.html.
4. The Yorkshire Ripper enquiry of the late 1970s and early 1980s operated on very clear distinctions between 'respectable' and other victims. See also J. R. Walkowitz, *City of Dreadful Delight: Narratives of Sexual Danger in Late-Victorian London* (London: Virago, 1992).
5. Caird, 'Marriage', pp. 194, 195, 197.
6. For a discussion of this in relation to Caird, see A. Heilmann, 'Mona Caird (1854–1932) Wild Woman, New Woman and Early Radical Feminist Critic of Marriage and Mother-hood', *Women's History Review*, 5:1 (1996), pp. 67–95.
7. The Reform Act redrew electoral districts to bring about some representation from the new towns and cities that had previously not had representation. The franchise was slightly extended, but only to men who owned or leased land worth £10 a year.
8. It was not until 1918 that the vote was given to women aged over thirty who were house-holders or wives of householders and in 1928 to women aged over twenty-one.
9. M. Caird, 'Militant Tactics and Women's Suffrage', *Westminster Review*, 170:5 (1908), pp. 525–30, on p. 528.
10. See, for example, P. Levine, *Feminist Lives in Victorian England: Private Roles and Public Commitment* (Oxford: Blackwell, 1990); B. Caine, *Victorian Feminists* (Oxford: Oxford University Press, 1992); M. Vicinus, *Independent Women: Work and Community for Single Women 1850–1920* (London: Virago, 1985).
11. Quoted in L. Surridge, *Bleak Houses: Marital Violence in Victorian Fiction* (Athens, OH: Ohio University Press, 2005), p. 88.
12. The position of the wife was not equal to that of the husband. He could obtain a divorce by proving two counts of adultery; the wife had to provide, in addition to two counts of adultery, further grounds such as incest, bigamy or bringing a mistress into the marital home. She could obtain a judicial separation, by which she reverted to a single woman's status in relation to property.
13. W. Acton, *The Functions and Disorders of the Reproductive Organs* (London: John Churchill, 1871), p. 115.
14. See L. Bland, *Banishing the Beast: English Feminism and Sexual Morality, 1885–1914* (London: Penguin, 1995).
15. A. Richardson and C .Willis, 'Introduction', in A. Richardson and C. Willis (eds), *The New Woman in Fiction and in Fact* (Basingstoke: Palgrave Macmillan, 2001), pp. 1–38, on p. 8.

16. Some sources suggest that Caird was the author of *Lady Hetty* in 1875, but this appears to be a confusion arising from the names of the authors: *Lady Hetty* was written by C. M. Caird.

17. S. Ledger, *The New Woman: Fiction and Feminism at the Fin de Siècle* (Manchester: Manchester University Press, 1997), p. 24.

18. There is no biography of Caird, but for further biographical information see S. Forward, 'A Study in Yellow: Mona Caird's "The Yellow Drawing Room"', *Women's Writing*, 7:2 (2000), pp. 295–307; and Heilmann, 'Mona Caird'.

19. Cited in A. Heilmann, *New Woman Strategies* (Manchester: Manchester University Press, 2004), p. 162.

20. The Men and Women's Club was founded by Karl Pearson and Elizabeth Cobb in 1885 and included as members or guests Olive Schreiner, Annie Besant, Eleanor Marx and Emma Brooke. For Caird's involvement, see Bland, *Banishing the Beast*, pp. 126–7.

21. Heilmann, 'Mona Caird', p. 78.

22. A. Richardson, '"People Talk a Lot of Nonsense about Heredity": Mona Caird and Anti-Eugenic Feminism', in Richardson and Willis (eds) *The New Woman in Fiction and in Fact*, pp. 183–211, on pp. 198–9.

23. For further discussion of eugenics and the New Woman, see A. Richardson, *Love and Eugenics in the Late Nineteenth Century: Rational Reproduction and the New Woman* (Oxford: Oxford University Press, 2003).

24. M. Caird, *Beyond the Pale: An Appeal on Behalf of the Victims of Vivisection* (London: William Reeves, 1897), pp. 69–70.

25. M. Caird, 'Ideal Marriage' *Westminster Review*, 130:5 (1888), pp. 617–36, on p. 619.

26. Caird, 'Marriage', p. 200.

27. Caird, 'Ideal Marriage', p. 619.

28. Caird, 'Marriage', p. 186.

29. She quotes from Charles Fourier and St Simon, for example, and in her writings there are some echoes of Friedrich Engels's book *The Origin of the Family, Private Property and the State* (1884).

30. For example, Caird, 'Marriage', p. 198; Caird, 'Ideal Marriage', p. 634.

31. Caird, 'Marriage', p. 186.

32. Surridge, *Bleak Houses*, p. 197.

33. In the 1885 Criminal Law Amendment Act, the passage of which was due at least in part to the 'Maiden Tribute of Modern Babylon' articles published in 1885 in the *Pall Mall Gazette* by W. T. Stead. Stead's sensational articles described his purchase of a thirteen-year-old virgin for £5. A late amendment to the bill, the Labouchère Amendment, introduced a new offence of gross indecency between men, effectively criminalizing male homosexuality and was the law under which Oscar Wilde was convicted in 1895.

34. See Surridge, *Bleak Houses*, p. 202.

35. House of Lords ruling in the case of *R v R* in 1991.

36. See discussion in Surridge, *Bleak Houses*, pp. 179–84.

37. Ibid., pp. 86–90.

38. Caird, *Beyond the Pale*, pp. 64–5.

39. Ibid., pp. 65–8.

40. Richardson, '"People Talk a Lot of Nonsense about Heredity"', p. 189.

41. Heilmann, *New Woman Strategies*, pp. 160–1. Caird writes in *The Daughters of Danaus*, 'A woman with a child in her arms is, to me, the symbol of an abasement, an indignity,

more complete, more disfiguring and terrible, than any form of humiliation that the world has ever seen' ((New York: Feminist Press, 1989), p. 341).

42. Caird, *The Daughters of Danaus*, p. 341.

43. M. Morganroth Gullette, 'Afterword', in Caird, *The Daughters of Danaus*, pp. 493–534, on p. 513.

44. Caird, 'Marriage', p. 195

45. Caird, *The Daughters of Danaus*, p. 491.

46. For discussion of the use of the daughters of Danaus myth, see Heilmann, *New Woman Strategies*, p. 215.

47. L. Surridge, 'Narrative Time, History, and Feminism in Mona Caird's *The Daughters of Danaus*', *Women's Writing*, 12:1 (2005), pp. 127–41, on p. 127. See also her discussion in *Bleak Houses*, pp. 190–1.

48. In the 1990s there were three high-profile appeals by women imprisoned for the murder of their abusive husbands. The cases of Kiranjit Aluwalia, Sara Thornton and Emma Humphreys provoked much discussion of the issues of provocation and self-defence. See J. Knelman, 'Why Can't a Woman be More Like a Man: Attitudes to Husband-Murder 1889–1989', in J. Rowbotham and K. Stevenson (eds), *Behaving Badly: Social Panic and Moral Outrage, Victorian and Modern Parallels* (Surrey: Ashgate, 2003), pp. 193–206.

49. M. Caird, 'Punishment for Crimes against Women and Children', *Westminster Review*, 169:2 (1908), pp. 550–3, on p. 553.

BIBLIOGRAPHY

Acton, W., *The Functions and Disorders of the Reproductive Organs* (London: John Churchill, 1871).

Bland, L., *Banishing the Beast: English Feminism and Sexual Morality, 1885–1914* (London: Penguin, 1995).

Caine, B., *Victorian Feminists* (Oxford: Oxford University Press, 1992).

Caird, M., 'Marriage', *Westminster Review*, 130:2 (1888), pp. 186–201.

—, 'Ideal Marriage' *Westminster Review*, 130:5 (1888), pp. 617–36.

—, *Beyond the Pale: An Appeal on Behalf of the Victims of Vivisection* (London: William Reeves, 1897).

—, *The Daughters of Danaus*, (New York: Feminist Press, 1989).

—, 'Militant Tactics and Women's Suffrage', *Westminster Review*, 170:5 (1908) pp. 525–30.

—, 'Punishment for Crimes against Women and Children' *Westminster Review*, 169:2 (1908), pp. 550–3.

Forward, S., 'A Study in Yellow: Mona Caird's "The Yellow Drawing Room"', *Women's Writing*, 7:2 (2000), pp. 295–307.

Heilmann, A., 'Mona Caird (1854–1932) Wild Woman, New Woman and Early Radical Feminist Critic of Marriage and Motherhood', *Women's History Review*, 5:1 (1996), pp. 67–95.

—, *New Woman Strategies* (Manchester: Manchester University Press, 2004).

Knelman, J., 'Why Can't a Woman be More Like a Man: Attitudes to Husband-Murder 1889–1989', in J. Rowbotham and K. Stevenson (eds), *Behaving Badly: Social Panic and Moral Outrage, Victorian and Modern Parallels* (Surrey: Ashgate, 2003), pp. 193–206.

Ledger, S., *The New Woman: Fiction and Feminism at the Fin de Siècle* (Manchester: Manchester University Press, 1997).

Levine, P., *Feminist Lives in Victorian England: Private Roles and Public Commitment* (Oxford: Blackwell, 1990).

Morganroth Gullette, M., 'Afterword', in M. Caird, *The Daughters of Danaus* (New York: Feminist Press, 1989), pp. 493–534.

Quilter, H. (ed.), *Is Marriage a Failure?* (London: Swann Sonnenschein, 1888).

Richardson, A., "'People Talk a Lot of Nonsense about Heredity": Mona Caird and Anti-Eugenic Feminism', in A. Richardson and C. Willis (eds), *The New Woman in Fiction and in Fact* (Basingstoke: Palgrave Macmillan, 2001), pp. 183–211.

—, *Love and Eugenics in the Late Nineteenth Century: Rational Reproduction and the New Woman* (Oxford: Oxford University Press, 2003).

Richardson, A., and C .Willis, 'Introduction', in A. Richardson and C. Willis (eds), *The New Woman in Fiction and in Fact* (Basingstoke: Palgrave Macmillan, 2001), pp. 1–38.

Surridge, L., *Bleak Houses: Marital Violence in Victorian Fiction* (Athens, OH: Ohio University Press, 2005).

—, 'Narrative Time, History, and Feminism in Mona Caird's *The Daughters of Danaus*', *Women's Writing*, 12:1 (2005), pp. 127–41.

Vicinus, M., *Independent Women: Work and Community for Single Women 1850–1920* (London: Virago, 1985).

Walkowitz, J., *City of Dreadful Delight: Narratives of Sexual Danger in Late-Victorian London* (London: Virago, 1992).

CHRONOLOGY OF EVENTS IN MONA CAIRD'S LIFE

Year	Events
1854	24 May: Alice Mona Alison born in Ryde, Isle of Wight.
1877	19 December: Marries James Alexander Henryson-Caird.
1878	Joins National Society for Women's Suffrage.
1880	Portrait of Caird by John Everett Millais exhibited at Grosvenor Gallery.
1883	*Whom Nature Leadeth* published under pseudonym G. Noel Hatton.
1884	22 March: Son Alister James born.
1887	*One That Wins: The Story of a Holiday in Italy* published under pseudonym G. Noel Hatton.
1888	August: 'Marriage' published in *Westminster Review*. November: 'Ideal Marriage' published in *Westminster Review*.
1889	April: *The Wing of Azrael* published.
1890	March: 'The Morality of Marriage' published in *Fortnightly Review*. June: 'The Emancipation of the Family' published in *North American Review*. Joins Women's Franchise League.
1891	7 July: 'The Position of Women' published in *Manchester Guardian*. *A Romance of the Moors* published. Volume also contained two other short stories: 'For Money or for Love' and 'The Yellow Drawing Room'. Member of the first council of the Women's Emancipation Union.
1892	May: 'A Defence of the So-Called "Wild Women"' published in *Nineteenth Century*. October: 'Why Women Want the Franchise' read at Women's Emancipation Union conference.
1893	*A Sentimental View of Vivisection* published.
1894	February: 'Phases of Human Development' published in *Westminster Review*. *Some Truths about Vivisection* published. *The Daughters of Danaus* published.
1895	*The Sanctuary of Mercy* published.

Year	Events
1897	*Beyond the Pale: An Appeal on Behalf of the Victims of Vivisection* published.
	The Morality of Marriage and Other Essays on the Status and Destiny of Women published.
1898	*The Pathway of the Gods* published.
	Member of The Free Press Defence Committee.
1899	March: 'Does Marriage Hinder a Woman's Self-Development?' published in *Lady's Realm*.
1902	*The Logicians: An Episode in Dialogue* published.
1904	14 June: Joins Theosophical Society.
1905	July: 'The Duel of the Sexes' published in *Fortnightly Review*.
1906	*Romantic Cities of Provence* published.
	November: 'A Ridiculous God' published in *Monthly Review*.
1907	October: Joins Women's Social and Political Union.
1908	May: 'Punishment for Crimes against Women and Children' published in *Westminster Review*.
	June: Takes part in Hyde Park women's suffrage demonstration.
	November: 'Militant Tactics and Women's Suffrage' published in *Westminster Review*.
	The Inquisition of Science published.
1909	19 January: Resigns from Theosophical Society.
	Joins London Society for Women's Suffrage.
1910	July: 'The Lot of Women' published in *Westminster Review*.
1913	6 June: Delivers presidential address to the Personal Rights Society.
1915	'The Role of Brute Force in Human Destiny' published in *Quest*.
	The Stones of Sacrifice published.
1918	November: 'The Greater Community' published in *Fortnightly Review*.
1921	James Caird dies.
1931	*The Great Wave* published.
1932	4 February: Dies in St John's Wood, London, aged 77.

THE WING OF AZRAEL

by
Mona Caird

Yesterday, this Day's madness did prepare
To-morrow's Silence, Triumph or Despair.[1]

In THREE VOLUMES.

VOL. I

LONDON:
TRÜBNER & CO., LUDGATE HILL.
1889.
[All rights reserved.]

Ballantyne Press
Ballantyne, Hanson and Co.
Edinburgh and London

To
ELIZABETH A. SHARP,
THIS BOOK
IS
DEDICATED
WITH
GRATEFUL AND ADMIRING AFFECTION

PREFACE

Much has been said for and against the writing of 'novels with a purpose.'

As well might one argue for and against the finding of the Philosopher's Stone.[2] The work of fiction whose motive is not the faithful rendering of an impression from without, but the illustration of a thesis – though that thesis be the corner-stone of Truth itself – has adopted the form of a novel for the purposes of an essay, and has no real right to the name. So long as there is true consistency in the actions and thoughts of the characters, so long as they act and think because circumstances and innate impulse leave them no alternative, they cannot be fitted into exact correspondence with any view or made into the advocates of any cause. If the author preserve his literary fidelity, rebellion among the actors inevitably springs up. Far from being puppets, as they are so often erroneously called, they are creatures with a will and a stubborn personality who often drive the stage-manager to the brink of despair; and as for being ready to 'point a moral and adorn a tale'[3] at his bidding, they would sooner throw up their parts and leave him alone on the deserted stage to lament his own obstinacy and their insubordination.

Human affairs are too complex, motives too many and too subtle, to allow a small group of persons to become the exponents of a general principle, however true. An argument founded on this narrow basis would be without value, though it were urged with the eloquence of a Demosthenes.[4]

Certain selected aspects of a truth may be – indeed must be – presented to the reader with insistence; for the impressions made upon a mind by the facts of life depend upon the nature of that mind which emotionally urges upon the neutral vision one fact rather than another, and thus ends in producing a more or less selective composition, and not a photograph.

But this process – entirely purposeless – takes place in the mind of every one, though he be as innocent as a babe of any tendency to weave romances; the most strictly matter-of-fact person being, indeed, the arch-offender as regards deviation from the centre of general truth. His own faculties and prejudice, in this case, play the artist, selecting images of reality which group themselves after a certain inevitable fashion; and these represent for him what he is pleased to call real life, with its 'morals' and its 'lessons,' precisely corresponding, not to existence itself, but to the judgment and the temper of the unconscious dramatist.

'The eye only sees that which it brings with it the power of seeing,'[5] whether 'the eye' belong to one who describes his impression or to him who allows it to be written secretly on his heart. For in the heart of each man lies a recorded drama, sternly without purpose, yet more impressive and inevitable in its teaching than the most purposeful novel ever written.

To transcribe this invisible world so that the impress becomes revealed, is to write a novel; good, bad, or indifferent, as the case may be, but a novel *par excellence*,[6] and not an essay.

The writer of fiction has to present, as best he may, a real impression made upon him, including the effect of such impulse to the imagination as it may have given, and of all the art – if art there be – or exercise of fancy by which the record is faithfully conveyed to other minds.

To reveal that image with so much skill that the vividness of the representation is hardly less than that of the original, is to write a novel well, though even yet the image itself may not be of sufficient interest to make its record of extreme value.

These are, according to my view, the conditions of the novel: first, of its claim to the title at all; secondly, of its merit; and thirdly, of its greatness, which implies the fulfilment of the other two conditions, while demanding also that the impression recorded shall be fine enough and striking enough to appeal to those sympathies in human nature which are most noble and most generous, as well as to that mysterious sense of proportion and beauty which holds relation to the suppressed and ill-treated, but ever-present poetic instincts of mankind.

I have described these unattained ideals of the art of fiction in order to show as convincingly as possible that however much this book may be thought to deal with the question recently so much discussed,[7] there is no intention on the writer's part to make it serve a polemical 'purpose' or to advocate a cause.

Its object is not to contest or to argue, but to represent. However much it fails, that is its aim.

If anywhere temptation is yielded to and the action is dragged out of its course in order to serve any opinion of my own, if anywhere, for that object, a character is made to think or to speak inconsistently with himself and his surroundings, therein must be recognised my want of skill, not my deliberate intention, – the failure of my design, not its fulfilment.

INTRODUCTION[8]

AZRAEL or Azazel, according to Muhammadan and Jewish writings, was the Angel of Death, of Fate, of Destruction. Azazel or Zamiel is the Jewish name for this angel. He separates the soul from the body, and is associated with the idea of evil and malignant Fate. He has been identified with Typhon; his dwelling is in the desert or wilderness which is the emblem of immeasurable, all-devouring Time.

'Aaron shall cast lots upon two goats, one lot for Jehovah, and the other for Azazel. And Aaron shall bring the goat upon which the lot for Jehovah fell, and offer him for a sin-offering. But the goat on which the lot for Azazel fell, shall be presented alive before Jehovah, to make atonement with him, to let him go to Azazel in the wilderness.'

'And the goat shall bear upon him all their iniquities unto a land not inhabited; and he shall let go the goat into the wilderness.'

'And he that let go the goat for the scapegoat shall wash his clothes, and bathe his flesh in water, and afterwards come into the camp.'

'And Aaron shall lay both his hands upon the head of the live goat, and confess over him all the iniquities of the children of Israel, and all their transgressions in all their sins, putting them upon the head of the goat, and shall send him away by the hand of a fit man into the wilderness.'

CONTENTS

CHAPTER I

MIST

The great stable-yard clock was slowly striking the hour – midnight. Over the park hung a white and stealthy mist, touched by white and stealthy moonlight. Great elm-trees loomed through it heavy and still: they seemed to be waiting for something that never came.

The mist was thick, but one could see through it a large white house with innumerable majestic windows, very broad and very high. Even in this dim light it was evident that everything was falling into decay. Grass grew in the shrubberies, and weeds in the gravel-paths; it was a melancholy, forsaken old place, closed in, and silent as the grave. The house stood hushed in the moonlight, with blinds drawn, windows closed; all but one blind and one window on the first floor, on that side of the house which faced the garden, and beyond it a steep avenue of elm-trees.

At that open window a small figure was kneeling; a dark-haired little girl, who leant her elbows on the sill and gazed up the mystic avenue. The line of trees led the eye to the top of the hill, and there ending, created an unsatisfied longing to see over the other side. The child peered forth eagerly into the still, passionless mystery of the night. Throngs of bewildering thoughts were stirring the little soul to its depths: – what was it, and whence this strange world that does NOT come to an end at the top of the avenue, at the boundary of the park? – this world that goes on and on, field after field, till it comes to the sea, and then goes on and on again, wave after wave, till it comes once more to the land, and then – ? then the realms of the air, and the great cloud-regions, and beyond these – Nothing, a great all-embracing Nothing that *will* not stop; that goes on and on, and still on, till the brain reels at the thought of it – but it does not stop then; it never stops, or would stop, or could stop, even when God sounded the last trumpet and the worlds shrivelled up in the flames on the Judgment Day – how, even then, could it stop?

Could God Himself order that there should not be that great thought-confounding Emptiness? The child shuddered at the impious doubt, but her perplexed little mind staggered under the weight of the questions that came tumbling over one another in their haste.

The mystery of her own existence; –that was a terrible perplexity to the little metaphysician. Was this being, this *self* a reality in this strange, cold region of Nothingness? Was anything real and actual, or was it all a mistake, a shadow, a mist which would presently melt again into the void?

Yet if there were no reality, whence these thoughts? The child touched herself tentatively. Yes, she was, she *must* be real; a separate being called Viola Sedley, – with thoughts of her own, entirely her own, whom nobody in all this big world quite knew. *Viola Sedley*; – she repeated the name over and over to herself, as if to gain some clearer conception of her position in relation to the universe, but the arbitrary name only deepened the sense of mystery. Am *I*, this thought and feeling, Viola Sedley? Will the thought that I shall think, and the feeling that I shall feel to-morrow, be Viola Sedley too? It seemed awful to the child to be walking in the midst of 'eternal verities'[9] without knowing them; to be plunged in Infinite Nothingness, and not understand if it would some day swallow us up, or if we should be rescued by the living Thought that seemed to have so true an existence. How had Thought prevailed against that Nothingness, risen out of its heart, if it were not some real thing stronger than all?

Viola could not have expressed these questions in words; but her ideas, preceding language (though so intimately related to it), stretched out into regions where she could find no answer, and where no answer was to be found.

Conceptions of God, Nature, Destiny, were running riot in the child's consciousness, her strict religious training raising questions without giving solutions, and torturing her with a sense of inconsistency demanding double-faced belief. The doctrine of eternal punishment had already begun to haunt this lonely child with its terrors. From long association, the gloom of the great park and the giant trees seemed to her to speak warningly of what was to come. The place was full of voices and of symbols. The elm avenue led to the outer world beyond the park, the world where there was sunshine and a wide horizon, strong winds and liberty. Here at home a belt of dark trees shut out the far-away skies, here one seldom felt the open winds; it was stagnant and eventless. To go up that avenue and away into the world had been one of Viola's most passionate longings from her earliest childhood. From the summit one could catch a glimpse of the sea, the wonderful sea that spoke and sang all the year long, in winter and summer; through the warm days and through all the long dark nights – eternally speaking and prophesying and lamenting. Viola thought that if only she could reach the sea she would not be lonely any more. She would throw herself down beside it, and it would know everything: all the fear and the longing, and the love and pity that was in her; and then the pain would go, and the waters would creep up to her softly and tell her not to grieve, and she would fling herself into the beautiful waves, and then – Suddenly the child stretched out her arms and sank against the window, passionately sobbing.

Very white and very still was the mist to-night. Even in high midsummer it might often be seen hanging about that damp old park, and this was early in the spring, before the bursting of the leaf.

One might fancy that the mist lay as a curse upon the place, shrouding all things, chilling all things, bringing to all things rottenness and decay.

Was there some influence in the atmosphere of that old house that was like the still, penetrating mist without? – something that worked its stealthy way into the heart, shrouding all things, chilling all things, bringing to all things rottenness and decay?

CHAPTER II

A YOUNG MAN CALLED MOMUS

Viola Sedley, the youngest and the only girl among a family of boys, was a pale, dark-haired little creature, with large grey eyes and delicately cut features. People said that she exactly resembled her mother, but the resemblance was only superficial. Mrs. Sedley's hair was smooth and shining, while Viola's fell about her massively, for it was heavy and thick. Mrs. Sedley's eyes were brown and quiet; Viola's had the grey, shifting tint, that marks the nervous temperament, and the yearning look of a sensitive, bewildered soul. Her father saw only the likeness between mother and daughter, and he called the child, in impatient displeasure, 'a little Puritan.' He would have preferred to see her a robust, coarse-fibred creature of his own kind; a girl who would have no reserve or sensitiveness or subtleties of feeling. Mrs. Sedley, with her still, dutiful ways and religious principles, had irritated him from the first day of her meek reign at the Manor-House, and he was highly displeased to find that Viola promised to follow in her mother's footsteps.

Mr. Sedley, by nature, was blustering and self-indulgent, but on the whole well-meaning, with the fatal habit of so many people who mean well, of getting into debt. His wife's tendencies, on the other hand, were ascetic. Her conscience never let her rest until she had made things as unpleasant for herself as circumstances would permit, and by long practice in the art, she had now achieved a ghastly power of self-suppression. Her reward had been the approval of her own conscience and the half-contemptuous approbation of her lord. He regarded her, in the most literal and simple-minded manner, as his possession, and Mrs. Sedley piously encouraged him in an idea which she thought was amply confirmed by the Scriptures.

Happy the religion and happy the society that can secure beings of Marion Sedley's type for its worshippers, for the faith of such people remains as steady under 'conspiracies of tempest from without, and tempest from within,'[10] as it stands beaming with uplifted eyes on days of halcyon calm. Rooted beyond the farthest wanderings of the Reason, it lies securely out of reach of any attack that may be directed against it through that ungracious faculty.

Mrs. Sedley, following the dictates of her creed, had spent her life in the performance of what she called her wifely duty, and this unfailing submissiveness, this meek and saint-like endurance, had now succeeded in turning a man originally good-hearted into a creature so selfish, so thick-headed, and often so brutal, that even his all-enduring wife used to wonder, at times, if Heaven would give her grace to bear her heavy cross patiently to the end!

Nature – regardless, as usual, of motives – was taking her stern revenge upon the woman who had spent her whole virtuous life in drawing out her husband's evil nature, and in stunting what little good there was in him by her perpetual encouragement of his caprices and her perpetual self-effacement. Morbidly apt at self-reproach on all other points, she never even suspected that the wreck of this man's life was partly her own doing. She accepted the consequence of her acts not as their natural punishment, but as another Heaven-sent trial to be borne without murmuring.

Among her numerous 'Heaven-sent trials' was the behaviour of her three eldest sons, the first of whom had been obliged to leave the country after a detected attempt to cheat at cards. The other two were in the army, living royally beyond their means, and appearing to derive no benefit whatever from the heart-rending prayers offered up daily, almost hourly, by their anxious mother for their welfare, temporal and spiritual.

There had been many painful scenes at the Manor-House of late between Mr. Sedley and his sons; the father refusing to pay their ever-recurring debts, while the mother prayerfully interceded on their behalf. The times were very bad just now; rents were falling, farms being given up; if things went on like this much longer, Mr. Sedley declared, they would all be in the workhouse![11] His own debts were steadily accumulating, but of this he said nothing to his wife. Viola was not of marriageable age, and therefore unable as yet to retrieve the family fortunes. Retrenchments became necessary, but the burden of these Mrs. Sedley took first upon her own shoulders, and then laid small hardships on her daughter, Mr. Sedley being shielded till he could be shielded no longer.

Miss Gripper, a severe maiden, who lived and did needlework in the village, used to remark upon the shabbiness of Mrs. Sedley's garments when she appeared, with Viola and her youngest son Geoffrey, in church every Sunday morning. Miss Gripper added that when Providence placed people in a certain position, it expected certain things of them; and, in *her* humble opinion, it showed a thankless, not to say an irreverent, spirit to appear in the Lord's house Sunday after Sunday in a turned black silk,[12] – and not such very good quality, to begin with!

Miss Gripper's feelings were threatened, as time went on, with greater and greater outrage, for the young men were going from bad to worse; yet Mrs. Sedley loved and hoped on. It was still her sons who made the most irresistible appeal to her motherly affections: the girl, beloved as she was, must always be prepared to make sacrifices for her brothers. In order that they should have a college education and every social advantage, Viola had to go almost without education at all; to afford them means to amuse themselves stylishly, their sister must be stinted of every opportunity and every pleasure. The child of course accepted this without question; her whole training dictated subordination of self, above all when the welfare of her father or her brothers was concerned. She absorbed this teaching readily, for she was her mother's ardent worshipper, and promised to be a credit to that exemplary lady.

She seemed, indeed, less bright and happy than a child ought to be, but then Mrs. Sedley laid more stress on religious and moral qualities than on mere happiness. Possibly Viola's sex made happiness seem unessential; for the mother would certainly have been much concerned had she seen one of her boys wandering about with that wistful look in his eyes, that strange accustomed sadness which she scarcely noticed in her little girl. Yet Mrs. Sedley anticipated the troubles of her daughter's future with unspeakable dread. What had a woman to look for – a dutiful woman such as Viola must be – but sorrow and pain, increasing as her life's shadow lengthened on the dial? If not quite so heart-breaking as her mother's life had been, Viola's could not escape the doom that lurks in the air of this world for all women of her type. Indeed, for all kinds and conditions what sorrow and lamentation! For each type its peculiar miseries, but the cup for all!

There were times when Mrs. Sedley, forgetting for a moment the steadiness of her faith, felt that it might be better if the child were to pass away to another world before she had tasted the sorrows of this one. But already the childish heart had swelled with sorrowful emotion; already a dim threatening consciousness of the awful solitude of a human soul drowned in the deeps of life and eternity had raised a panic within her. She was cursed with that melancholy metaphysical consciousness of the Infinite and the Unknown with which the British mind is usually so entirely untroubled. Viola, however, was not a persistently gloomy child. When her brother Geoffrey (a boy a couple of years her senior) came home for the holidays, she plunged heart and soul into his occupations, and was as happy as only children (and possibly angels) know how to be.

Geoffrey was a long-legged, good-hearted schoolboy, with rosy cheeks, brown eyes, and a mop-like head of fair hair. He was at Eton, acquiring a mystic thing called 'tone,' which evinced itself when he came home, in lively practical jokes of a most harassing character, played upon everybody within reach, without respect for age, sex, or dignity; chiefly, however, upon the maids and gardeners, who might at such times have answered Mr. Mallock's question,[13] whether life is worth living, with a unanimous, and gloomy negative.

The head-gardener, Thomas, whose mowing-machine had been put out of order, whose tools had been lost beyond recall, whose watering-pots leaked consistently, was heard to threaten to speak to Mr. Sedley if this sort of thing went on much longer. The second gardener, 'Old Willum,' as his chief called him, was made of softer stuff, showing lenience towards the little escapades of youth, even when Geoffrey took occasion to substitute charlock[14] for cabbage-seed as soon as the old man's back was turned, causing the long suffering one to sow a fine crop of that pestiferous weed in the kitchen-garden. 'Old Willum,' with his rheumatism, his patient industry, his tender old heart, was incapable of resentment.

Viola had a passionate love and pity for this old man; her eyes used to soften at the sound of his voice, at the sight of his bent figure trundling a wheelbarrow, or digging up the everlasting weeds in the gravel-terrace before the house. 'Old Willum,' her mother, and Geoffrey were the beings on whom she expended the treasures of her affection; on these, and on Bill Dawkins, a handsome unclipped poodle named in affectionate memory of a departed under-gardener, who had been a great favourite with the children.

Bill Dawkins was indeed an enchanting animal, ridiculously intelligent for such a world as this; a creature full of life and enterprise, true to the core, and devotedly attached to his little mistress. He and Geoffrey used to treat her with a certain chivalrous condescension as 'a weaker vessel'.[15] Bill Dawkins, in his moments of wildest excitement, would turn and run back encouragingly to see that Viola was following.

What adventures those three used to have together in the woods and fields, in the beautiful rambling old gardens of the Manor-House! And what intoxication there was in this new-found liberty for the closely-watched, closely-guarded child!

The mere sight of the sunshine pouring down upon the open midsummer fields, the mere thrill of a bird's note, as the three companions set off together upon some wild ramble, would stir the little heart almost to bursting.

Only now and then in poetry would she find relief for this pent-up painful rapture, but books of poetry were not very plentiful at the Manor-House; besides, Mrs. Sedley did not think any poet, except Cowper,[16] safe reading for her daughter.

So there was nothing for it as regards expression but to run riot with Bill Dawkins over the fields, and to join in his wild, consciously fruitless chases after starlings, skylarks, or some old rook, who flapped his glossy wings in dignified retreat from the presumptuous assailant.

The child's whole heart went out in love towards the living creatures around her; and the sight of suffering among the least of these would bring hot tears of anguish to her eyes. Things that she saw in the fields – the preying of creature upon creature; the torture suffered and inflicted in the every-day game of life – caused her many a bitter pang, and induced her to ask questions when she went home, which Mrs. Sedley found very difficult to answer. She generally told Viola that all things were wisely ordered, and that we must not permit a questioning spirit to grow up in us, as that would lead to doubt and sin.

So Viola was silent; but when next she saw the piteous terror of a mouse, as it awaits, horror-stricken, the spring of its captor; when next she heard the almost human scream of the hare when its doom overtakes it, she wondered as painfully as ever at the strange conflict and struggle of Nature, though she closed her lips and let the problem eat deeper and deeper into her bewildered soul.

A lake on the park boundary was the favourite haunt of this happy trio. Here in spring they would watch the frog-spawn developing into masses of wriggling tadpoles, finding never-ending interest and joy to be found in watching these Protean[17] reptiles, who shed their frivolous tails and appeared suddenly as sedate and decorous young reptiles, wanting only size to give them that expression of unfathomable profundity, which in the full-grown frog seems to hint at wisdom greater than all the wisdom of the Egyptians.[18]

Viola used to keep some tadpoles in a water-butt behind one of the sheds in the garden, giving them romantic names, and secretly hoping that in course of time they would answer to them. She consulted Thomas on the subject, but he shook his head with a knowing wink, and said he didn't think tadpoles took, as one might say, much notice; – not tadpoles in a ordinary way, he didn't think.

Viola urged that Marmion,[19] the biggest of the tadpoles, used to swim to meet her when she appeared, but she observed that he did the same at the approach of Thomas, who had absolutely no sympathy with tadpole nature. To 'Willum,' who showed fondness for the creatures (as was only natural), they paid no special regard; they wagged their tails at everybody, and showed a great lack of discriminating power in their ceaseless exultation.

On the whole, one could enter into closer and more personal relations with their elder brothers down at the lake, only that here their vast numbers made strictly selective friendship a matter of difficulty. On one occasion, when the children were deeply engrossed in trying to persuade a green and juicy young frog to eat Albert biscuits,[20] they looked up and beheld a young man standing beside them laughing, and a little behind him a tall lady, also laughing.

The children started up in shy alarm.

'So this is the way you two wild young people amuse yourselves,' said the lady, who was no stranger, but the children's aunt Augusta, one of Mr. Sedley's sisters, who had married and settled at Upton, a village about twelve miles from the Manor-House.

She was an important, self-possessed-looking woman, tall and thin, with dark eyes, hair, and complexion, a long face, rather thin lips, and a neat compact brow.

Her face expressed her character pretty accurately.

Harry Lancaster, her present companion, used to say of her that she had enough will-power to drive a steam-engine, an unassailable self-confidence, and opinions of cast-iron.

She was an ambitious woman, whose ambitions had been gratified by her marriage with Lord Clevedon, a courtly person of the old school, with whom she had really fallen in love after a fashion, perhaps because he satisfied her innate desire for all that is dignified and grandiose.

Harry Lancaster was a slim, boyish-looking, brown-haired fellow, with a frank humorous face, whose charm lay chiefly in its expression. His dark bluish-grey eyes were brimming over with amusement and sympathy, as he stood with folded arms looking down upon the two shame-faced children.

'It seems ages since I saw you, my dears,' said Aunt Augusta, in her clear self-confident accents. 'Are you never coming to see me and your cousins again? Percy was asking after you only this morning, and little Augusta too. I think I must carry you off with me to-day after lunch, no matter what your mother says. My good sister-in-law thinks me too frivolous a person to trust her chicks to,' she added to Harry, with a laugh.

'And so you are,' said Harry. 'I have had serious thoughts of leaving your hospitable roof because I find your influence morally deleterious.'

'Impertinent boy! And before these children too! My dears, you must always put cotton-wool in your ears when this wicked cousin of mine speaks. He is a very dreadful young man, I must tell you – the most dreadful thing under the sun: a Radical!'[21]

'What is a Radical?' asked Geoffrey, looking up into the face of the 'dreadful thing,' which smiled amiably.

'A creature in the form of a human being, but with the soul of a demon,' answered Lady Clevedon. 'I don't know if he feeds upon little children, but he certainly devours widows' houses.'

The children stared.

'After dark,' pursued her Ladyship, 'he becomes phosphorescent, and emits from his mouth and nostrils green fire.'

Geoffrey laughed at this in a sceptical manner.

'It's all very well to laugh,' said his aunt, 'but you don't know what a dangerous young man it is! Let us stroll back together to the house, and I will try to get your mother's permission to take you home with me.'

A visit to Clevedon was like a visit to a fairy palace, and the children followed their aunt and her talkative companion across the park, with hearts beating high for pleasure.

Mrs. Sedley was inclined, as usual, to find some reason against their going, but her husband interposed. Through his sister he hoped some day to find a wealthy husband for his daughter.

'Take them, my dear, take them,' he said graciously.

The neighbouring estate to that of Lord Clevedon had just been inherited by a distant relation of the late owner, who was without sons or nephews, and this new Sir Philip Dendraith had a young son who would be just the right age for Viola when they both grew up, and who would also be one of the most eligible young men in the county.

'It will do the children a world of good to have a little outing,' said Mr. Sedley cheerfully.

He was a big, thick-set man, with a ruddy face, reddish hair, and rather bleared light blue eyes. There was a certain jauntiness about his manner, and he was a notorious flirt; though, as his sister very frankly remarked, 'no clever woman could ever be got to flirt with him; he was not amusing enough.'

'Have you seen anything of your new neighbours?' Mr. Sedley inquired, as the little party sat down to lunch in the big, dull, old-fashioned dining-room of the Manor-House.

'Sir Philip Dendraith and his family? No; at least I have seen Sir Philip and his son at a meet of the Upton hounds, but I have not yet called on his wife. He is an appalling creature; loud, pushing, altogether obnoxious. It is a sad pity that the main branch of the family died out; this man is not fit for the position.'

'And the son?' inquired Mr. Sedley.

'Ah! he is of quite a different stamp; a true Dendraith; handsome, polished, keen-witted. He reminds me of that portrait of Andrew Dendraith at the old castle on the cliff, the man in the last century who was said to have killed his wife because he discovered she was in love with another man.'

'Handsome, then?' said Mr. Sedley.

'Wonderfully handsome,' Lady Clevedon answered. 'Of course his parents are crazily fond of him.'

'Ah! I suppose you will call at once at Upton Court.'

Lady Clevedon shrugged her shoulders.

'My instinct is to put off the evil day.'

'Bad habit, putting off!' said Mr. Sedley, sagely, at which his sister gave a sardonic chuckle. Perhaps she was thinking of Mr. Sedley's debts!

After luncheon the two children were taken off to the 'Palace of Delight.'[22] Harry Lancaster entertained them during the twelve miles' drive with a running stream of fantastic talk. Lady Clevedon sat back in the carriage and quietly laughed at him, while Harry, on his side, seemed to be amusing himself in a sort of secret sub-fashion with the rest of the company, and with the entire situation.

He was one of those happy people to whom life is always more or less amusing, and this pleasant sensation became particularly keen when he was visiting his 'baronial cousin,' as he called her.

Most people were frightened of Lady Clevedon, who was noted for her powers of satire, but Harry bared his head to the storm, and its lightnings played about him harmlessly. She liked his audacity, even when he attacked her most cherished convictions. With all his boldness and freedom, he was what she was pleased to call a 'gentleman,' a title which she bestowed or withheld with a discrimination sometimes a little arbitrary.

'I wish I knew what you mean by "gentleman,"' Harry said, after some unoffending person had been consigned to the region of outer darkness, where there are no gentlemen, but only weeping and wailing and gnashing of teeth.[23] 'I think you are inclined (perhaps we all are) to make the word stand for a certain sublime something which we mix up in a glow of excitement with qualities purely social.'

'My dear boy, we are not all etymological dictionaries; we use words in their ordinary accepted sense, and leave definitions to – "the Unemployed."'[24]

'But,' persisted Harry, 'I want to know what is meant in common parlance by a "gentleman."'

'Ask me to express one of the 'ultimate elements' (which you are always prosily talking about) in terms of something else,' returned her Ladyship.

'Ah! that's an idea!' Harry exclaimed joyously. 'A gentleman is a social *element;* he can't be reduced to any lower terms; he is among the original bricks of which the universe is built; he is fundamental, indestructible, inconceivable, and' –

'Harry, is *nothing* sacred to you? Does this horrible Radicalism sweep away all the traditions that you learnt at your mother's knee?'

'Far from it,' said Harry. 'Although I have no respect for class, and no reverence for rank, I still realise that the house of Lancaster stands apart from and above all principalities and powers, and that it is more glorious in its fall than ever it was in the palmiest days of its prosperity.'

'You don't deserve to belong to it!' exclaimed Lady Clevedon. 'This virus of democracy has poisoned your whole system.'

'Democracy – what is democracy?' questioned Harry, pensively.

'The misgovernment of fools by madmen!' she returned.

He smiled. '"You murder with a definition!"'[25]

'I am sick of the nonsense that people talk now-a-days, calling themselves "advanced,"' Lady Clevedon pursued; – 'advanced in folly, let me tell them!

Every shallow idiot with a clapper in his head thinks himself entitled to get up and make a jangle like any chapel-bell that whitens one's hair on Sunday mornings!'

'Use Mrs. Allen's hair-restorer,'[26] suggested Harry frivolously.

Lady Clevedon's face changed.

'Harry,' she cried impressively, 'there was a young man in ancient mythology of very good position, but he succeeded in rendering himself so obnoxious to the gods by his inveterate habit of making fun of them, that he at last got turned out of heaven. That young man's name was Momus.'[27]

'Unhappy Momus!' said Harry. 'Do you chance to know any of the fatal jokes by which he lost his place among the Olympians?'

Lady Clevedon laughed.

'Much use it is to point a moral for *your* benefit, young man.'

'Perhaps he chaffed Jupiter about his love-affairs, by Jove!'

'I dare say; he was a vulgar god. But be good enough to suit your conversation to these children.'

'I am sure they are interested in Momus,' said Harry. 'The question you raise is one of extreme significance, is it not so, Viola? I am sure you feel with me that the first instance of vulgarity on record is a subject of reflection for a philosopher.'

'Harry, Harry!'

'One of the profoundest mysteries of the universe, my dear cousin; the bane of philosophy, the despair of religion, the insuperable obstacle to the doctrine of the soul's immortality, and the' –

'Harry, if you talk any more nonsense I shall stop the carriage, and leave you ignominiously on the road.'

'Well, well; – perhaps the day will yet come when I shall be taken at my true worth.'

'Heaven forbid!' exclaimed Lady Clevedon as they drove through the gates of her domain; 'that would be a punishment greater than you could bear!'

He made a grimace.

'To a woman I must not grudge the last word,' he said.

His cousin laughed.

'When a man begins to give points to his adversary on account of her sex, the adversary may hoist the flag of victory.'

'Take it,' he said, 'take it and be thankful!'

Clevedon was a large ugly block of building, standing upon a raised plateau, whence the land sloped majestically towards the park.

The faces of the two children grew eager as the great white house appeared in sight. The carriage having been dismissed, Aunt Augusta proposed a stroll till

Percy and his sister should return from their ride. Meanwhile the children might gather some hothouse flowers to take back to their mother.

'What a fine old place this is, in its own way!' Harry observed, as they wended their steps to the garden; 'it is so gentlemanly, so' –

'Harry! There was a young man in ancient mythology called' –

'Nay, so stately, so calm, so well-bred; so smooth and blandly expansive,' pursued Harry, in language which would have pleased Quintilian,[28] who always regarded as hopeful those pupils whose literary productions required pruning, rather than the young proficients whose style at the beginning showed the delicate reticence of maturity.

'I like the place; I am not going to have it scoffed at,' said Aunt Augusta.

'Scoffed at! I am admiring it. Scoffed at! Why, I have a friendly feeling towards every nook and corner of it. I like it, I love it; but – it amuses me!'

'An incorrigible Momus!' cried Lady Clevedon.

'It is perfect,' he broke out again. 'I am sure Geoffrey and Viola agree with me that it is perfect.'

'You bewilder these poor children, Harry.'

'Just run your eye round the four quarters of the heavens. Could anything be more dignified? I repeat my question, Viola – could anything be more dignified?'

She shyly shook her head.

'No; nothing could be more dignified! Look how the land spreads out round the mansion, in a sort of liberal manner, as if it would say: I am at your entire disposal; pray take as much of me as you please, there is no stint; be expansive; the more so the better; you have only to mention the quantity, and it is yours!'

'Then observe what a benign and courteous sweep leads the eye from the terrace-level to the park. No abrupt lines there; your very curves are baronial! And your cattle! What an air of conscious worth! what splendour of outline and richness of colour! what harmony of action! what a Highland fling of movement! what' –

'If you make fun of my husband's Highland cattle, he'll never forgive you: better make fun of ME than that. Come, don't dawdle so; you are getting too garrulous.'

But change of scene proved no check to his eloquence.

'There is nothing in the world to beat an old English garden,' he exclaimed, rhetorically. 'What sweet and lazy influences linger in the air by fern-fringed walls! what indolent joys exhale from flower-borders where violets and precocious primroses offer themselves to be cherished – it is as if one had found a new world!'

Viola looked up at him wonderingly, while Geoffrey, forgetting his shyness, suddenly began to talk – chiefly about rabbits and pistols and repeating rifles.

Then they all went into the hothouses, and came out laden with delicate sweetly-scented flowers, which Viola touched with ecstatic and reverent fingers.

The children were allowed to amuse themselves as they pleased, while Aunt Augusta and her talkative cousin strolled on together.

'Harry,' she said, after a few minutes of desultory conversation, 'have you given up that mad idea of yours yet?'

'About music?' His face changed and saddened. 'I cannot cure myself of the mad idea. Meanwhile, of course, I retain my commission,'[29] he added, rather bitterly.

'The sooner you cure yourself the better. As a musician you would starve. Besides, how do you know you have enough talent to' –

'I know nothing at all about my talents – (pardon me for interrupting); I only know that failure in that pursuit would be sweeter to me than success in any other.'

'Foolish boy!'

'Now, Augusta, what do you mean? How often have you preached to me against doing things by halves; how often have you pierced with ridicule men who "took up" a thing, and tinkled amiably upon some instrument, or made smudges on clean paper, – any one, in short, who tried to imitate the last stage of an art without laying the foundations. You said it was like the attempt of a builder to roof a house that wasn't built.'

'Well?'

'Well! why not build the house from the foundation?'

'Why not go and starve?' she inquired. 'Go and starve to slow music?'

Harry paused for a moment, looking at her; and then, with one of his sudden inconsistent actions, he lifted his stick on to the tip of his first finger, balanced it there for a moment skilfully, and shot it up far and swift towards the sky. It rose, like a rocket,[30] and came down again at a little distance into a gooseberry-bed.

'Take care that is not *your* fate,' said Lady Clevedon.

'It must have been splendid going up,' Harry returned; 'and what a "fine rapture"[31] when it had risen to its utmost and felt the heavens above, and the earth widen beneath it' –

'And how exhilarating when it felt itself in the gooseberry-bed!'

'There are many sticks rotting in the gooseberry-bed that have never known the upper air at all,' Harry observed; 'they have secured themselves against all risk of downfall by prudently taking the lowest place.'

'Like the Unjust Steward,'[32] suggested Lady Clevedon, whose Scripture was weak.

'Or the rebellious angels,'[33] added Harry, with a laugh. He picked up a mouldering apple-twig and held it out to his cousin to consider.

'Observe, it is damp and brittle; I can snap it anywhere, for it has not the toughness of life in it. Lichen grows upon it, and unwholesome moss, and it is teeming with crawling and creeping things; shall I show you?'

'Be good enough to keep away,' cried the lady hastily.

'They are skurrying about in great agitation; they can't imagine what has happened. They are telling one another, that they *knew* how it would be all along, and that if only *their* advice had been listened to' –

'D-a-m!' exclaimed Lady Clevedon, spelling the word (after her own fashion) as a concession to public sentiment, 'here are Sir Philip Dendraith and his incomparable son! What effrontery to come here before we have called at Upton Court! I shall make him pay for this!'

Sir Philip Dendraith was a tall, broad-shouldered man, with a hooked nose, high cheek-bones, sharp little blue eyes, and a grey beard, which retained signs of having once been reddish in tint. The younger Philip resembled his father scarcely at all; he was a slim, dark-haired youth, with face and figure almost faultless. Harry Lancaster, flinging away the decayed apple-twig, stood watching him with sudden intentness, while Lady Clevedon, donning her stiffest air, awaited the approach of the visitors. They raised their hats.

'Pardon our intrusion,' Sir Philip called out in loud self-confident tones; 'we were taking a walk across country and lost our way' –

'So I observe,' said her Ladyship.

'Got into your park through the bit of woodland by the roadside down yonder, and found ourselves in the gardens before we knew where we were. Lady Clevedon, I presume?'

She bowed.

'Not – ?' with an interrogative glance at Harry.

'Not,' she repeated conclusively.

'Ah!' observed Sir Philip, throwing himself back and looking round, 'charming garden you have here.'

'I am glad it pleases you.'

'Oh, vastly, vastly; fine old place altogether.'

Lady Clevedon stood waiting.

'Ah!' cried Sir Philip, descrying Viola and Geoffrey in the distance, 'your children, no doubt?'

'No,' she said, 'not my children.'

'Perhaps Lady Clevedon would be so kind as to mention which is the shortest way out of her domain,' interposed Philip Dendraith the younger; 'we have intruded long enough.'

'Allow me to come with you; it is not easy to find the road unassisted,' said Harry.

Sir Philip, apparently much against his will, was then hurried off by his son, under Harry's escort.

'I trust we shall shortly renew our acquaintance,' he said in parting; 'near neighbours, like ourselves, should make a point of being friendly.'

Again Lady Clevedon frigidly bowed.

As the three arrived at the end of the path they came upon Geoffrey and Viola peering curiously into some hot-beds.

'*Not* Lady Clevedon's children?' repeated Sir Philip.

'No; her nephew and niece,' said Harry.

'Nice little girl!' observed Philip the younger. 'Fine eyes.'

She flushed up, and took a step backwards.

'Let me see what colour they are.'

She shut the lids tightly and covered her face.

'Oh! unkind little girl! I shall tell your mamma,' said Philip teasingly.

'Oh! no, no, *no*!' she cried, with unexpected terror; '*please* don't tell her.'

'Is the mamma so formidable? Well, then, let me see your pretty eyes, and I promise not to tell how unkind you were.'

But at this Viola again fell back, with a look of strange distress, whereupon Harry took her hand and said soothingly, 'Never mind, Viola; this gentleman was only joking; he won't tell your mother, if you don't wish it.'

He was holding open the garden-door as he spoke.

On the threshold Philip stopped, looked over his shoulder, and kissed the tips of his fingers gallantly.

'Nut-brown maid,[34] farewell!' he said, and passed through with a laugh.

'Come on, Viola; let's go with them,' cried Geoffrey, taking her hand; 'he's rather a lark, that fellow.'

But Viola passionately flung him off, and before he realised what had happened the child had run to the farther end of the garden.

'Rum things girls!' was Geoffrey's comment as he pursued his new-found hero and philosophically left the eternal riddle to solve itself among the gooseberry-bushes.

When Harry returned after conducting the trespassers into the Upton road, he found his cousin in a very bad temper.

'Intolerable creature!' she broke out. 'Where can he have sprung from, with his voice and his manners? "Fine place" indeed! Impertinent upstart! You were asking what a gentleman is, Harry; well, I can tell you what a gentleman is *not*: – Sir Philip Dendraith.'

'Tactless person, certainly; and rather uncouth. The father and son are a curious contrast, are they not?'

'Most extraordinary! That boy is a Dendraith all over. Fine-looking lad.'

'A gentleman, I suppose?' said Harry.

'Every inch!'

'I thought so. Well, as a mere *man*, give me that "lumbering wain,"[35] his father; more qualities to rely upon there; more common but cosy humanness. There is something polished and cold-blooded about that young Adonis,[36] with his white teeth, that gives me a shiver all up my spine. It is astonishing how insolent polished people can be.'

'The Dendraiths always were a little cold-blooded,' said Lady Clevedon, 'and a little over clever. It is *not* human to be very clever; one cannot disguise that fact.'

CHAPTER III

PHILIP DENDRAITH

Sir Philip Dendraith, by a sudden turn of fortune's wheel, had been hoisted out of obscure and somewhat speculative spheres into the pure white light of what Harry Lancaster had called in his haste 'landed propriety.'

He was related to the last owner of the Dendraith estate through his mother's family, a fact which he had enjoyed and made much use of in his former existence, having a highly developed instinct of adoration for social pre-eminence, and a ferret's keenness in routing out unwilling relatives, lofty and far-removed, but profitable.

'My cousin, Sir John Dendraith,' might have fallen from his dying lips in those prehistoric days when he owned to the solid and simple name of Thompson, and used to wander with his wife and son from small furnished house to smaller furnished house, where crochet antimacassars and crystal lustres[37] gave the keynote to existence.

In those dark ages Mr. Thompson used to be always launching ideas which required capital and a company – brilliant ideas that only wanted carrying out, such as a method of blacking boots by machinery, patent umbrellas that opened automatically on being held upright, and folded up again when their position was reversed (facetious friends used to say that they even buttoned and unbuttoned themselves as occasion required). There were ingenious hooks and eyes that never came undone until their owner desired it, and then yielded without a struggle; coal-scuttles which made the putting on of coal a positive luxury to a sensitive invalid, – and other wonderful inventions, not to speak of the celebrated millennium double-action roller-blind, whose tassel could under no circumstances come off in the hand, and which never acquired the habit of rolling up askew and remaining blocked in a slanting and crazy position half-way up the window. As for his mowing-machine, and his instrument for putting out fires in their most advanced stages, a child might use them.

Philip Thompson was endeavouring to increase his small income by bringing some of these valuable ideas into notice, when one morning, to his infinite surprise, he awoke and found himself Sir Philip Dendraith; that is to say, he was informed that, by a most extraordinary series of events, he had become the next heir to the Dendraith estates, and it was hoped that he would assume the family name.

This he lost no time in doing, and with the name of Thompson he put away also things Thompsonian; his patent umbrellas and coal-scuttles; and now only his plump, simple-minded wife took any pride or interest in these once absorbing themes.

The social world was to this fortune-favoured man the only and the best of all possible worlds; to rise in it his sole ambition. With this object the family had always conscientiously kept *something* beyond their means, whether (said Lady Clevedon) it were a phaeton[38] or a footman, or merely a titled relative, stuffed and cured, to stand picturesquely in the middle distance and be alluded to. This, she added profanely, was of more value than many footmen.

Her inclination had been to remain unaware of the existence of the new baronet, but this idea was more easily conceived than carried out.

When a church-bell clangs loudly every Sunday morning close to your ears, philosophy counsels that you take no notice of the barbarism, but human frailty may nevertheless succumb.

Sir Philip had entered upon his new sphere in high good spirits, determined to enjoy all that it offered to the full, and to take his place among his peers with a dash and style that would make him known and respected throughout the country.

There was no escaping him. Like a teasing east wind that blows low, he met one round every corner, blustered against one at every turn, let one face north, south, east, or west in fruitless attempt at evasion. Perhaps Lady Clevedon, who could turn things social into ridicule cleverly enough, but to whom social laws were nevertheless indisputable, felt all along that there was no escaping the acquaintance of Philip Dendraith, be he mad, drunk, or a fiend in human shape; and she finally, in no very affable mood, drove over and called at Upton Court.

Lady Dendraith's plump good-nature much amused her visitor, and the latter came back disposed to be friendly towards the simple old person who was full of innocent pride in her husband and son, as well as brimming over with naïve astonishment at the sudden change in their fortunes.

'After lodgings and furnished houses, a place like this does seem wonderfully palatial; but my husband and son take to it as if they had been here all their lives, bless their hearts!'

'Bless *your* heart, old lady!' thought the visitor, who was forgiving to any one who amused her. 'If ever there was a good old soul you are that person, my dear!'

As for Lord Clevedon, he regarded his new neighbour with the highest disfavour, though he too recognised the duty of knowing a Dendraith, in whatever stage of mental or moral decomposition he might chance to be.

'The fellow has none of the real Dendraith blood in him,' he said; 'it was a sad pity that the old stock died out!'

'Have you seen the son?' asked Lady Clevedon.

Her husband straightened his thin figure, and drawing his head out of his necktie and collar, gave it a twist as if he had half a mind to unscrew the thing and take it down for closer examination – perhaps under the impression that the machinery wanted oiling.

'Yes, I have seen the son.'

'Not like either of his parents, I think. Did he not strike you as being very like that portrait at the old house on the cliff of Andrew Dendraith? – the man that had such an extraordinary story, you know. I think he used to take opium among other things, and was suspected of having murdered his wife – though nobody could ever prove it. He was a man of considerable power, but I don't fancy he minded the precepts he used to write in his copy-books as he might have done.'

'The fellow was no credit to his relations,' said Lord Clevedon, screwing his head on again as a hopeless case (the works required a thorough cleaning, and he didn't see his way to getting it done).

'Andrew Dendraith,' he continued, 'was one of the bad characters that seem to crop up in the family now and again, as if there were some evil strain in it not to be overcome.'

'It is curious that this young Philip should be so like Andrew,' said Lady Clevedon; 'the relationship is not very close, but the resemblance, to my mind, is striking. In figure they are alike; this boy is tall and slim and well put together, as Andrew was, and he has the same cold, keen, handsome face, with perfect, clean-cut features, and already there is plenty of control over the muscles. His manners are polished – too polished for his age, almost; though perhaps one fancies that, through seeing him beside his awful father, who really' –

'Who, upon my honour' – assisted Lord Clevedon.

'Is likely to give the county a severe fit of social indigestion,' concluded his wife.

However, the county gulped him down; and though it suffered from a pain in the chest, it did its duty to the new representative of the Dendraiths, calling upon his wife with exemplary punctuality.

Mrs. Sedley, among the rest, wearily set out to perform her task. She put on her best bonnet, provided herself with a card-case,[39] and ordered the carriage.

No one ever quite knew if that old vehicle would hold together for another drive, but the family seemingly meant to go on paying its calls in it, till the faithful servant 'died in harness,'[40] as Harry Lancaster used to say, with characteristic fondness for incongruous metaphors.

Geoffrey saw the old chariot at the door, and rushed in to ask if he and Viola might accompany their mother.

'And Bill Dawkins,' added Viola.

'What larks if we break down on the road!' cried Geoffrey.

However, no such lively calamity occurred; they rumbled respectably along the high-road and through the little villages, Bill Dawkins behaving with the utmost decorum on the back-seat beside Geoffrey; so much so, in fact, that Viola was afraid he would get tired – whereat her brother jeered.

'Bill Dawkins isn't a *girl*!' he cried scornfully. 'Are you, Bill?' at which compliment the poodle thumped his tail upon the carriage-cushion and cast down his eyes.

Sir Philip, coming down the avenue of Upton Court, met the carriage driving up. Viola and Geoffrey recognised him and looked at one another.

If Lady Clevedon or Harry Lancaster had been present, they would have derived much gratification from the sight of the meeting between Mrs. Sedley and her new neighbour.

Sir Philip raised his hat gallantly and gave a loud shout of welcome.

'How do you do, Mrs. Sedley? Going to call on the old lady? That's right; she's just having a nap, – rather a weakness of Lady Dendraith's – afternoon naps.'

'I fear we shall disturb her,' said Mrs. Sedley in her steady, shy, withdrawn tones.

'Dear me, no, not at all; she will be delighted, I assure you. We were wondering we hadn't seen anything of you before. However, better late than never. Family cares, I daresay. These your chicks? Halloa! why, these are the two children I saw at Clevedon! Lady Clevedon's nephew and niece, of course. Well, my boy, can you conjugate your ζυπτο or do you spend all your time and brains on old Father Thames?[41] You must make friends with *my* boy, though he is some years older than you; he can conjugate you anything you like, I can tell you. The young people are getting so clever nowadays, there's no holding them. I see the little girl has had the good taste to copy her mother,' Sir Philip continued, chucking Viola under the chin. 'Couldn't have had a better model, my dear. Will you give me a kiss?' he asked, bending down without waiting for permission.

'No, I won't,' said the child, shrinking away from him and squeezing Bill Dawkins uncomfortably close to the farther side of the carriage.

Sir Philip laughed.

'Ah! you don't care to kiss an old man like me!'

'No, I *don't* want to kiss you!' said Viola irately.

Bill Dawkins barked.

'Viola, dear!' remonstrated Mrs. Sedley, at which a look of intense trouble came into the child's face. If her mother's sacred wishes and her own feelings should now come into open conflict, there would blaze up a small Hell in that childish breast; for, trivial as the occasion seemed to grown-up consciousness, the intensity of feeling that it called out is impossible to represent, much more to exaggerate.

'Come now, I *must* have a kiss,' said Sir Philip in a playful manner, and going round to the other side of the carriage. 'If you give me a kiss, I'll give you a sweet-meat when we get up to the house; there's a bargain now!'

'I don't want sweetmeats – I don't want sweetmeats,' cried Viola, darting away again in increased dislike as Sir Philip's bearded face appeared beside her.

'She does not need any reward for behaving politely, I am sure,' said Mrs. Sedley. 'Viola, dearest, you will give this gentleman a kiss when he asks you to do so.'

The child's eyes fixed themselves in silent desperation on the ground. Her face became white and set.

'That's a good little girl,' said Sir Philip. 'I am sure we shall soon be excellent friends, for I am very fond of children. Now for my kiss.'

He bent forward to take it, when Viola, with a suppressed cry, wildly plunged off the seat to the bottom of the carriage and hid her face in the rug. Upon this Bill Dawkins became violently excited, alternately jumping down to thrust his nose against Viola's hair, and springing on to the seat to bark persistently in Sir Philip's face, getting more and more enraged as that gentleman threw back his head and laughed heartily, with the remark that he had never been treated so unkindly by a lady before.

'Well, I suppose I must give it up for the present,' he said. 'If you will drive on to the house, Mrs. Sedley, I will return with you.'

'Oh! please don't let us bring you in,' began the visitor, but Sir Philip drowned her remonstrance, and directed the coachman to drive on.

He met the carriage at the door, and helped Mrs. Sedley to alight.

Bill Dawkins sprang out with a yelp of joy, followed by Geoffrey. On the steps stood Philip Dendraith the younger.

'Now then, little woman,' said Sir Philip kindly enough, as Viola held back, with defiant eyes. 'Come along.'

'Come on, Ila, you young silly!' urged her brother. 'He doesn't want to kiss you now.'

Sir Philip leant across the carriage with a laugh, upon which the child, mak-ing a violent effort to escape, flung herself against the door at the farther side, and fell, hurting her head and arm. In falling she had moved the handle of the door, which suddenly burst open.

'Good heavens! save her!' cried Sir Philip.

Before the words were out of his mouth his son, with marvellous rapidity, had darted round just in time to rescue the child from a dangerous fall. Her body was half out of the carriage when he caught her in his arms and carried her quickly into the house, where he laid her on a sofa and summoned his mother to the rescue. Mrs. Sedley had, fortunately, not seen the accident.

'Poor dear little creature!' cried the good Lady Dendraith; who had just been roused from her 'nap', 'are you much hurt, my dear? I think not, for she doesn't cry at all.'

'She never cries,' said her mother, shaking her head; 'she is like a little woman when she hurts herself.'

'Dear, dear! – what would she like, I wonder? – some brandy and water to revive her, and perhaps she ought to see the doctor.'

But Mrs. Sedley thought that she could easily manage with the help of a few simple remedies. Viola appeared to have been rather startled than really hurt. She lay quite quiet, but with an anxious, watchful look in her eyes, which changed to something approaching terror when Sir Philip's loud voice was heard in the hall.

She started up.

'Don't let that man come in; don't let him come in!' she cried wildly.

Lady Dendraith looked surprised, and Mrs. Sedley naturally felt uncomfortable.

'Hush, Viola dear, nobody will disturb you; you should not speak so, you know; it is not like a little lady.'

'I don't want to be like a little lady!' cried Viola, who seemed to be in a strange state of excitement.

'I think,' said Mrs. Sedley, 'that I ought to take her home at once, though I am sorry to cut short my visit to you, Lady Dendraith; and I am most grateful for your kindness to my little girl.'

When Mrs. Sedley said she would go she always went without delay, and Viola having shaken hands with her hostess (she refused to kiss her, though without impolite remarks), returned to the carriage on foot, looking behind her in a frightened manner lest her *bête noire*[42] should be present.

He was standing in the entrance when they went out, and expressed much concern at the shortness of the visit. Viola shrank away to the other side of her mother.

'Well, young lady, I am glad to see you are all right again. Upon my honour, you sent my heart into my mouth when you burst that door open! What a fierce little maiden it is! I hope you won't treat your lovers in this fashion in the time to come, or you will have much to answer for.'

Mrs. Sedley, objecting to have Viola spoken to about lovers, cut the conversation short by shaking hands with her host once more and entering the carriage.

'No, I am not going to ask for a kiss now,' said Sir Philip, as Viola shrank away hastily, ' but I think my son, who saved you from a severe accident, deserves one; and you won't mind kissing *him*, though you are so unkind to his poor old father.'

'I don't want to kiss anybody as long as I live!' cried Viola. 'I hate everybody; I' – She broke down with sheer passion.

Father and son burst out laughing, and Philip, bending down, lifted her swiftly in his arms, quietly kissed her in spite of her violent resistance, and placed her in the carriage beside the poodle, who received her with acclamation. She struck her laughing enemy with her clenched fist, and then flinging herself against the cushions, hid her face, drawing up the rug over her head, and burst into low heart-broken sobs.

'Viola, Viola!' in tones of surprised remonstrance from Mrs. Sedley.

The carriage rolled away down the avenue and emerged into the bare down country, but the child did not stir. Mrs. Sedley was afraid that this unwonted excitement might be the precursor of some illness; and thought it wiser not to interfere except by a few soothing words.

Geoffrey showed a boyish inclination to laugh at his sister for making such a fuss about nothing, but his mother reproved him, as it seemed to make her more excited.

Bill Dawkins was greatly concerned about her. He searched her out among the rugs, as if he were hunting for rats, and expressed his sympathy with wistful eloquence. Once she put her arm round his neck and drew him to her passionately, and if it had not been for his thick coat, the good poodle might have felt some hot tears falling on his shaggy head.

Viola did not recover her spirits all that day. Mrs. Sedley watched her anxiously, and sent her to bed early, with compresses on her arm and a bandage on her head.

When all was quiet, and Viola found herself alone, she crept out of bed, went to the window and drew up the blind. There stood the avenue, stately and beautiful in the moonlight, wreathed with mists.

The vision brought the tears welling up again from the depths of the child's wounded soul. Her grief was all the bitterer because she could not express it in words even to herself; she could only feel over and over again, with all a child's intensity, that she had been treated with insolence, as a being whose will was of no moment, whose very person was not her own; who might be kissed or struck or played with exactly as people pleased, as if she were a thing without life or personality. Her sense of individual dignity – singularly strong in this child – was outraged, and she felt as if she could never forgive or forget the insult as long as she lived. The jocular good-natured way in which it had been offered made it only the more unbearable.

'I hate you; I *hate*,' cried Viola, mentally apostrophising her enemies, 'I hate everybody in the world – except mother and Bill Dawkins.'

CHAPTER IV

RELIGIOUS DIFFICULTIES

As soon as her children had acquired enough cohesion to sit upon a pew-seat, Mrs. Sedley had taken them to church. Sometimes, indeed, she had been too hasty and taken them almost before that epoch, so that the hapless little beings used to crumple up and slip to the ground, keeping their mother occupied in gathering and replacing them during the service.

Among Viola's earliest remembrances were these miniature declines and falls, which had generally been occasioned by her being painfully tired during the early part of the service through the dire necessity of sitting still, and by the sleepy exhaustion produced at last by an infinite number of suppressed desires; among them a very vivid longing to stroke the sealskin jacket of the former Lady Dendraith who used to sit in the pew just in front of her. Once, in fact, watching her opportunity with beating heart, she had actually realised her soul's ambition by drawing her little hand timidly down from Lady Dendraith's shoulders to her waist, and then leaving off in a panic on hearing a smothered chuckle from one of her too wide-awake brothers.

These delinquents took a special delight in leading her into mischief during service. The pew was large,[43] and ran in two directions at right angles to one another, so that there was one part of it quite out of Mrs. Sedley's range of vision, where unholy deeds might be wrought.

Here they would pelt one another with catapults, or build a Tower of Babel out of prayer-books; the stately edifice almost reaching to the top of the pew. (It was one of Harry Lancaster's wicked sayings, that Mrs. Sedley was going to mount into heaven upon a staircase of these volumes, and it must be admitted that the number of her books of devotion was exciting to the profane imagination).

Viola characteristically took all things connected with religion in grim earnest. Her after-pangs of remorse, if she had taken too much interest in the Tower of Babel, were very keen, and she often suffered indescribable terrors from the conviction that her sins would be punished in the fires of hell. Sometimes she experienced strange emotional upliftings, when she believed that she felt the very presence of Christ, and a passionate inspiration for a life devoted only to His service. And then would follow days of fruitless effort to keep up to the level of these moments of ecstasy.

On Sunday afternoons it was Mrs. Sedley's custom to read the Bible with the two children, taking them into her own sitting-room (*boudoir* is a term inconsistent with this lady),[44] and closing the door after her with a quiet solemnity which to Viola had something of awful sacredness.

Geoffrey, alas! had been known to whistle a secular melody after that ceremony of initiation, and it was a common amusement with him to secretly alter all the markers in his mother's Bible and 'Daily Meditations,'[45] or to place them against chapters in the Old Testament which consisted chiefly of proper names, because his mother found some difficulty in pronouncing them.

After the reading the children were allowed to express their ideas upon what they had heard, and to ask a few questions. Geoffrey always took a morbid interest in Satan, and (Satan being a biblical character) Mrs. Sedley could not consistently refuse to gratify it. His questions were of a nature to whiten the hair of an orthodox mother!

Viola's difficulties were of another kind. She could not understand the stories of holy treachery and slaughter related of the children of Israel, in whose wanderings she and her brother always took the keenest interest. It was an actual grief to her when her heroes suddenly broke away from a most well-ordered and respectable career to go forth, like a swarm of hornets, to injure and destroy. That 'the Lord commanded them' only made the matter darker. Mrs. Sedley could not enter into these difficulties. She herself would not have hurt the poor fly, which appears to be regarded as the last creature entitled to human mercy (unless, perhaps, it interrupted her prayers or distracted her attention from holy things); but she entirely approved of the wholesale massacres perpetrated by the chosen people in the name of the Lord, and considered that His name was greatly glorified thereby.

Viola was also disturbed by the strange story about Balaam[46] when he was sent for by Balak to come and 'curse him' the Israelites. 'God came unto Balaam at night, and said unto him: If the men come to call thee, rise up and go with them: but yet the word which I shall say unto thee, that shalt thou do.'

So Balaam naturally goes.

Then, to Viola's infinite bewilderment, 'God's anger was kindled because he went, and the angel of the Lord stood in the way for an adversary against him.'

The child's face of dismay at this apparent instance of Divine inconsistency would have been comic had it not been piteous.

'But why was God angry when He had told Balaam the night before to go with the men if they came to call him?'

Mrs. Sedley first said that 'the ways of Providence were past finding out,' but remembering that her sister-in-law had once burst into a fit of immoderate laughter at this reply, she suggested that the Lord had possibly meant to try Balaam's faithfulness.

She never noticed in her younger pupil the hungry desire to find something that she could worship, the piteous efforts of the tender-hearted child to adore the God who sent forth the Israelites to smite whole races with the edge of the sword, and to leave not one remaining of the people.

Fortunately the New Testament was read on alternate Sundays, and if to love Christ be the one thing needful for salvation, Viola certainly fulfilled the condition. She was an enthusiastic little Christian, though there were yet many flaws in her orthodoxy which her mother had to patch up as best she might.

Being made sound on one side, she was apt to give way on the other, causing poor Mrs. Sedley much trouble, and demanding more mental agility than she possessed. How God could be willing to accept the pain and grief of one divine being as a substitute for the pain and grief of other guilty beings was what Viola could not understand. If the guilt could pass away from the guilty at all, how should God let the burden of it rest on some one else, as if God were greedy of pain for His creatures, and could not forgive generously and entirely? It was like the story of the young prince who, when he was naughty, had a little slave beaten in his stead, quite to the satisfaction of the royal father.[47] Religious difficulties began early in Viola's experience, as probably they do in most essentially religious natures. Doctrine and dogma and commentary were provided for her so liberally, that, as Wilkins the coachman technically remarked, 'It was enough to give the poor child a surfeit.' Thomas, with his practical instincts, 'didn't see no sense in cramming a lot o' religion into a young lady with Miss Viola's prospects, *he* didn't – not a lot o' fancy stuff of Mrs. Sedley's makin' up, as drawed down the face till it was as long as a 'olly'ock: and never a smile or a "good-day" to a soul about the place – he didn't see what good come of such religion, *he* didn't.' And Thomas shoved his spade into the earth with a vigour corresponding to the vigour of his conviction that if *he* could see no use in a thing, use in it there could not possibly be.

When Geoffrey was away (and this, of course, was during the greater part of the year) Viola led a strange, lonely life. She had no companions, Mrs. Sedley being afraid to let her associate much with her cousins at Clevedon, because their training was, in her opinion, so godless.

Viola's education was of the simplest character. Her mother gave her lessons in history, geography, and arithmetic every morning after the usual Bible-reading and prayer, and as she grew older Viola had to practise her music for an hour every afternoon. Music being one of her passions, the hour, in spite of its drudgery, had its charms. The piano was in the drawing-room, a large dreary, dimly-lighted dungeon, which chilled the very marrow of one's bones. The furniture was set stiffly against the colourless walls, while the dreary ornaments under their glass shades seemed – as Harry Lancaster fantastically remarked – like lost souls that had migrated into glass and china bodies, and there petrified, entranced, were forced to stand in the musty silence till the crack of Doom.

Just for one hour daily that musty silence was broken. It was an enchanted hour, especially in autumn and winter, when the firelight made the shadows dance on the walls and ceiling, and threw a rosy glow over the whole colourless scene. And then the spirit of music arose and went forth, weaving spells, and calling from the shadows a thousand other spirits who seemed to fill the dull old room with tumultuous life and the air with strange sweet thrills and whispers from a world unknown. Then the lost souls would cast off the curse that held them, and become half-human again, though they were very sad, indeed quite heart-broken, for they knew they were imprisoned in these ridiculous bodies till time should be no more, and then what awaited them but the torments of the damned? Viola would be seized sometimes with a panic as she thought of it.

There were two glass lustres on the marble mantelpiece, which caught the firelight brilliantly, and in the centre an ormolu[48] clock with a pale blue face of Sèvres china, a clock whose design must have been conceived during a vivid opium dream of its author, so wild and unexpected were its outlines, so distracted and fantastic its whole being.

'A drunken beast,' Harry Lancaster had once called the thing after a state call at the Manor-House. As it had cost fifty pounds, Mrs. Sedley fondly hoped and concluded that it was exquisitely beautiful, and she would have been very much amazed, though but slightly offended, had any one presumed to doubt its loveliness.

If the imprisoned soul had a sensitive nature, how it must have suffered from the impertinent quirks and affected wrigglings of its domicile! How it must have hated being misrepresented to the world by so florid and undignified a body!

Perhaps Viola enjoyed her hour of practising so much partly because she was then certain to be alone. At no other time in the day could she count upon this. She would often remain in the drawing-room long after the practising was over, much to the astonishment of her mother.

There was something indescribably fascinating to the child in the silence that followed the music; it was quite unlike the silence that preceded it – unlike every other silence that one knew.

In autumn, when it grew dusk early in the afternoon, she could hear, between the pauses of the music, the sound of old 'Willum's' broom sweeping the dead leaves from the path before the window. This too fascinated her. The notes would pour out at times as if they were inspired by the roar of the wind outside, which was stripping the great trees of their foliage, – and suddenly they would cease – a pause – then always again, through the wind's tumult, the steady swish-swish upon the gravel, and the old man's bent, patient form moving slowly forwards along his path of toil.

The wild freedom of the wind, the wild sweetness of the remembered music – the dim room, the lost souls – what was it in the scene that stirred the childish heart to its depths? Nature, human toil, human possibilities, joys unutterable, and unutterable dooms, – even here, in this sheltered monotonous home, those spectres stood upon the threshold of a young life, to announce their presence to the soul.

CHAPTER V

BREAKING BOUNDS

If only she was let alone, Viola could make herself very happy in the gardens and quaint old surroundings of her home. She had the poetic faculty of drawing out the secrets of common things. The cucumber-frames, the old garden; the tumble-down red-roofed sheds where Thomas potted his geraniums, the apple-house smelling so deliciously, and the conservatory, with its warm sweet scents of earth and flowers; not one of these but gave her exquisite pleasure.

She had many favourite haunts and one secret retreat in the heart of a little wood whither she used to run at rare and ecstatic moments when she managed to elude the vigilance of her nurse.

Had it not been for Viola's loving reverence for her mother, she would have much oftener tasted the delights of liberty, for they were very sweet; poor little phantom of liberty as it was that she enjoyed, when for a brief half-hour she buried herself in her leafy hermitage, and felt that no human being in all the world knew where she was or could interfere with her, mind or body.

Viola had all sorts of treasures here, gathered in the woods and fields: plants, snail-shells, oak-apples, and insects which she kept in a large deal-box furnished forth with mould and greenery, much after the fashion of the poor tadpoles' home, – those tadpoles who, alas! had never thriven, and one morning, after a night of heavy rain, had been washed away, Heaven only knew whither. That had been a real tragedy to Viola, and now another was in store for her.

It was autumn; a mildly splendid day late in the season, but singularly warm for the time of year.

The nurse, happily, became languid with the heat, and sat down, while Viola was allowed to wander about by herself. She took the opportunity to visit her domain. The sunshine that filtered through the fretted beech-roof seemed different from any other sunshine that ever worked a forest-miracle; the wreaths of clematis and eglantine and the glossy-leaved briony flung themselves from branch to branch with wilder freedom than in any other spot in all the earth – so thought their little votary. The place corresponded to the vividly fresh and joyous side of the child's nature, as the chill drawing-room, with its lost and tortured souls, and its patient old patrol without sweeping dead leaves from others' pathways, answered to the more thoughtful and melancholy side of her character.

The bower was sacred to Life and Liberty; the drawing-room to servitude and death, in all the forms in which they attack humanity.

Across the lawn, with Bill Dawkins at her heels, along a flower-bordered walk behind the garden-wall, Viola hastened; then out by a wicket-gate into the park, and across the open, in the face of staring cows, to a little copse, the sacred grove wherein the temple stood. She plunged in and pursued her way along the path which she had worn for herself in struggling through the under-wood. She paused for a moment, thinking she caught an unusual sound in the solitude. There seemed to be a slight rustling and shaking among the leaves, as if the nerves of the little wood were thrilling. Viola's heart beat fast. What if her temple were discovered and desecrated? She hurried on breathlessly; the myste-rious tremor continuing, or rather increasing, as she came near. Her forebodings were only too true!

There, in the holy of holies, stood Thomas, pruning-knife in hand (he had always been a maniacal pruner), tearing and cutting down the magnificent sheets of clematis, – just then in the height of its glory, – crushing the berries of the briony beneath his heavy boots, and running his ruthless knife round the trunks of the trees where the ivy climbed too high.

'O Thomas, Thomas! what *have* you done?' exclaimed Viola piteously. Bill Dawkins barked aggressively at the destroyer with his tail erect, exactly as if he were saying, 'On behalf, sir, of this young lady, I demand an explanation.'

The old iconoclast turned slowly round and looked at Viola and her poodle, not in the least understanding.

'I'm a takin' the ivy off some of these 'ere trees,' he observed, dragging down a great network of greenery and flinging it on the ground.

'Why do you take down the pretty ivy?' asked the child tearfully.

'Explain yourself, sir,' barked Bill Dawkins.

'Why, because it'll kill the trees if I leaves it to grow,' said Thomas.

'But why do you pull down the clematis and the briony? Oh, why do you, Thomas?'

'Why, Miss,' said Thomas, puzzled, 'I thought as it looked untidy sprawling all over the place; I didn't know as you liked to see it, or I wouldn't have touched it; not on no account.'

Viola gave the old man a little sad forgiving smile, and the hot tears fell as she moved desolately away, like some lost spirit driven from its home.

What maniac was it who said that sorrow is the nurse of virtue?[49] Surely it is the inspirer of all rebellious sins. It is like a storm, destroying old landmarks. How petty, how unnoticeable to the great tempest must seem the little walls and fences marking the 'mine' and 'thine' of men! And great sorrow, whatever its occasion, has in it all the blindness and the passion of a tempest.

It was not merely the defilement of the consecrated spot that filled the childish heart with grief. In its destruction Viola dimly saw a type of the degrading of all loveliness, the crushing of all exquisite and delicate things. A lonely life had fostered in her this poetic tendency to read figurative meanings into outward objects; and these types were to her not mere shadows, but solid links that bound together all the world, material and spiritual, in an intimately related whole.

It had always been one of Viola's dearest ambitions to reach the sea, the vision of whose sparkling immensity had strongly moved her when she and Geoffrey used to go up to the top of the great avenue and look down upon it.

But she was strictly forbidden to wander beyond the garden when her nurse was not with her, and the sea was not only beyond the garden, but beyond the park! Yet the sight of the avenue, with the long afternoon shadows lying across it, its tempting perspective leading the eye toward the forbidden country, filled Viola with an overpowering desire to be on the verge of the great waters, to feel the sea-wind in her face and hear the boom of the waves upon the beach.

Her grief made ordinary rules seem petty, and she turned her steps towards the avenue, without pausing to consider consequences, causing Bill Dawkins to give a yelp of joy, and to run gaily after the cattle, who were staring with all their might at the intruders. And now the spirit of adventure began to stir in the child's breast, and she instinctively quickened her footsteps, thrilled with the sensation of her freedom and ready to buy it at almost any price.

Arrived at the top of the avenue, she stood breathless – Bill Dawkins by her side – and gazed at the brilliant scene before her. Wood and field and farmstead lay placidly dozing in the benedictory sunshine; these merging gradually into bare downs, and these again abruptly ending in the cliffs which reared their stately ramparts to the sea. The sea! Ah! there it lay stretched in a long gleaming line from farthest east to farthest west, hiding its mystery and its passion with a lovely smile.

Viola, climbing the locked park-gate, found herself upon the public road. She felt a faint thrill of awe as she saw it stretching before her, white and lonely between the clipped hedges.

It was poor upland country; quite different from the land about the Manor-House, which lay in the valley of a little stream. But so much the more wild and delightful!

How far away the sea might be, Viola did not know; she made straight for it, as if she had been a pilgrim bound for her shrine.

It was very lonely. For half an hour she had walked without meeting any one, and then the road ran through a little village where some children were playing, and an old woman crept along, with a bundle under her arm.

She stared at Viola, and the children stared. Bill Dawkins smelt at the bundle, and would have sniffed at the children, but they fled shrieking to their mothers.

Viola quickened her pace, vaguely feeling that human beings were menacing to her liberty. A turn of the road took her again into solitude, and with it came a strange intoxication. How marvellous was this sunshine pouring down over the wide cornfields! It seemed to confuse all reflection and to wrap the mind in an ecstatic trance. How madly the larks were singing this afternoon! The fields were athrill with the flutter of wings and the air quivered with song. Once Viola was tempted to leave the road and take a short cut by the side of a little copse, where Bill Dawkins went wild after game, and caused his mistress some delay by his misdeeds. The shadows were perceptibly longer when she and the dishevelled poodle (now distinguished by a mud-covered nose) emerged again upon the high-road.

Here the sea came clearly into sight, acting upon the heart of the little pilgrim as a trumpet-call. The country became more and more bare and bleak as it rose towards the cliffs; the crops grew thinner, and gradually cultivation fell off into little patches here and there, till at last it ceased altogether, and there was nothing but the wild down grass shivering in the sea-wind.

If inland, the sunshine had seemed brilliant and all-pervading, here on the open downs, with the gleaming of the sea all round, its glory was almost blinding.

Would they never reach the cliff-side?

Viola started into a run, and Bill Dawkins bounded madly in front of her, looking back now and then to make sure that she was following.

The saltness of the ocean was in the air; the fresh wind stung the child's cheeks to crimson. At last the end of the journey was reached; a little coastguard station marked the highest point, and then the land sloped with different degrees of abruptness towards the edge of the great cliff, which rose to a vast height above the sea, so that a boat rocking on the waves beneath had to be carefully sought for by the eye, and appeared as a tiny black speck upon the water.

There were a few streaks of smoke left far away on the horizon, in the wake of vanished steamers, and one or two fishing-boats lay becalmed; the sky line was lost in haze, a fine-weather haze, betokening heat. Viola sat down on the grass to rest, with her arm round Bill Dawkins. Oh the marvel of that sunshine! How the air thrilled and trembled with the splendour of it! The earth seemed as if it were swimming in a flood of light. Surely one could feel it reeling through the regions of space, a joy-intoxicated creature! Viola looked round, half in fear, half in rapture, at the thought of the world's mad dance through endless solitudes, and she actually believed that she felt the whirl of its motion as the breeze went by, and the wide horizon seemed to swim round her dizzily.

The swerving sensation was perhaps increased by watching the sea-gulls poising and wheeling in the air along the giddy cliff-side, and the jackdaws swarming and chattering about its clefts and crevices.

Sometimes the gulls would rise above the summit of the headland and come so close to Viola that she could hear the strange creaking of their wings as they swooped and swung and swept in a thousand graceful caprices of movement, to finish dramatically with a sudden dive or turn in the air, uttering their melancholy cry. Viola felt herself thrill from head to foot. These birds fascinated her, but she did not like them. They seemed cold, able, finished creatures, but they had no feeling, they were utterly pitiless – like Philip Dendraith, she thought. The little jackdaws were not so graceful or so perfect, but they were pleasanter and more human. They were like his kind old mother.

Ah! how sweet was the scent of the earth! how sweet the breath of the sea! Viola envied the family of the coastguardsman who dwelt in the little white-washed cottage, with its tar-blackened waterbutt outside the door, and the flag placidly curving over the roof in the faint sea-breeze. Two sea-gulls with flashing plumage were sweeping round it, grandly undulating, while on the bank outside the house lay a young child with round limbs bare to the sun and winds, a being almost as free as the wild sea-birds themselves.

Viola wished that she too had been a child of the coastguardsman, so that she might live always upon this cliff-side, in the fresh winds; always – sleeping and waking – have that sea-murmur in her ears, and the cry of the gulls thrilling her with sweet fancies. She was too excited to sit still. She rose presently and began to walk farther along the cliff, going near enough to the edge to see the scattered rocks at its foot, and to watch the gulls as they circled and swooped and settled in busy companies, intent upon their fishing.

At some distance farther along the coast another headland ran out into the sea, and upon it Viola could discern what looked like a ruined castle, standing desolate above the waves. Had she known the part which that castle was to play in her life she would have turned and fled back to her home instead of pursuing her adventure. She had heard her father speak of some old ruin on the coast: how once it stood far inland, but the hungry sea had gnawed at the cliffs till it crept up close to the castle, which now stood defiant to the last, refusing to yield to the besieger. As she drew near, Viola noticed that there was a belt of wind-shorn trees encircling the ruin at some distance inland, and that in a hollow of the downs lay what seemed to be the gardens and surroundings of a human habitation. A gate led into a short avenue, at the end of which stood a large gloomy-looking house, built of grey stone. The place appeared deserted and was falling into decay. On the steps moss was growing luxuriantly, the front-door gave the impression that it was never opened, and the windows had evidently not been cleaned for years.

Viola's curiosity was aroused, but with it an undefined sense of fear; the place was so strangely lonely, and had such a deadly look of gloom. It recalled to the child her own lonely position, and suggested vague and awesome thoughts which had not assailed her out in the sunshine. But she could not leave the vault-like old house without further explorations. It had for her a mysterious fascination.

She found that it possessed great half-ruined stables and a large yard at the back, – the weeds growing apace between the paving-stones. She ventured to try if she could enter the house by the back-door, but it was locked; so was the door of the stable.

The gardens, which lay sheltered from the wind in the hollow, were beautiful in their neglected state. There was a terrace on the higher ground with a stately stone palisade, and at either end an urn, round which climbing plants were wreathed in the wildest abandonment. Below, among the little pillars of the parapet, a fiery growth of flowers rushed up, flame-like, amid grasses and self-sown vegetation of all kinds. The house was joined to the ruin, which ran out upon the headland, and appeared to be almost surrounded by the sea. Part of the castle had been repaired and converted into a dwelling, and this had then been added to, till the habitable portion of the building attained its present gaunt appearance and great size.

Viola's next step was to explore the castle, which stood perilously balancing itself on the extreme verge of the land, striking roots, as it seemed, into the rock, and clinging on to the narrow wave-fretted headland for dear life. The limestone cliff had been worn to a mere splinter, which ran out into the sea, the neighbouring land being reft into narrow gorges, into which the waves rushed searchingly with deep reverberations. The ruin was wonderfully preserved considering its exposed situation. The walls were of immense thickness, and it seemed as if the rock on which they stood must itself crumble before they yielded to the long-continued assault of time and weather. Apparently the castle had once been a Norman stronghold, though now only a very small portion of it remained to tell the tale.

By this time the brilliancy of the day had begun to decline; and with the afternoon had come that pensive look that settles upon a landscape when the light ceases to pour down upon it directly from above. The voice of the wind, too, had grown melancholy as it wandered through the great ruined windows and stirred the sea-plants that had managed to establish themselves in the inhospitable soil.

Bill Dawkins of course had run wild, scampering hither and thither in breathless astonishment, poking his muddy nose into dark passages, scrambling helter-skelter to the top of a ruined staircase, where he would be seen standing with his comical alert-looking figure marked against the sky, tail high in the air, head well raised, and in his whole attitude an air of intelligent inquiry which would have convulsed with laughter anybody to whom animal life was a less serious affair than it was to Viola. The dog looked as if he ought to be scanning the horizon with a telescope to one eye.

Viola was just about to follow him up the steps, when she was startled, and for the moment terror-stricken, by a loud peal of laughter which rose above the ceaseless pulse-beat of the waves in the rock-chasms round about. She gave a low gasp and clutched a little tamarisk-bush beside the staircase, for she had almost fallen. She listened breathlessly. The laughter was renewed, and Viola now heard several men's voice, apparently coming from the farthest part of the ruin. If she were discovered here, these men might be angry with her for trespassing. Her ideas were vague and full of fear; the romantic strangeness of the place, with its hollow subterranean sounds, excited her imagination. Though prepared for almost anything, however, it did not occur to her that Bill Dawkins' scamper to the top of the ruined staircase at that particular moment was to determine the whole course of her future life; but so it proved!

CHAPTER VI

THE CUSTODIAN OF THE CASTLE

Viola crouched lower and lower in her hiding-place, for she fancied the voices were coming nearer. The tones somewhat reassured her, for they were quiet and pleasant.

'I *should* like to know where the little beast comes from,' one of the invisible beings remarked; 'I never saw anything to beat that attitude. It's not only human, it's classical.'

'Classical?' echoed a second voice, which Viola thought not quite so pleasant as the former.

'Our friend means that it possesses the attributes of a class,' said a third voice, this one quite different in tone and quality from the other two; there was a slight touch of cockney accent, and an evident struggle with the temptation to say *h*at-tributes.

'Quite so; you always know what I mean, Foster,' said the first voice; 'that poodle has the manners of the highest circles; quite clear that he mingles in good society. I must really introduce him to my cousin; she would be charmed with him.'

'Lady Clevedon is not without class-prejudices,' the man called Foster remarked in a judicial manner. 'Women of the upper ranks have much to contend with; we must look leniently upon their follies; it is the part of the philosopher to smile, not to rail, at human weakness.'

Viola thought this sounded promising for her. This tolerant person, at any rate, would be on her side, if she were found guilty of the human weakness of trespassing.

'We must not forget,' the philosopher pursued, 'that only a limited responsibility can be attached to the human being in his present relations with the universe. Without plunging into the vexed question of Free Will, which has set so many thinkers by the ears, we must admit that our freedom *can* only exist, if at all, in a certain very modified degree. We are conscious of an ability to *choose*, but our choice is, after all, an affair of temperament, and our temperament a matter of inherited inclinations, and so forth, modified from infancy by outward conditions.'[50]

'We are not compelled to do things, only we must,' some one interposed a little impatiently.

The philosopher laughed.

'Quite so, Mr. Dendraith; we are compelled by ourselves; the 'Ego'[51] constrains itself, and I don't see how we can logically retreat from that position.'

'Well, I for one am quite prepared to do it *il*logically!'

This idea seemed to stun the philosopher, who made no reply.

At the mention of the word *Dendraith* Viola's heart stopped beating. The memory of that visit to Upton Court still rankled, and her hands clenched themselves fiercely as she thought of it. Presently, to her horror and surprise, the enemy came into sight, followed by his companions. They could not see her, for she was hidden behind the flight of steps.

They had strolled on till they came to one of the great windows, and here they established themselves in a group, Philip Dendraith sitting in the deep embrasure, digging out weeds from between the stones with the end of his stick; Harry Lancaster leaning against the masonry with his head thrown back; while the philosopher, a small fair man with a little face and big forehead, sat huddled together on a large stone, amidst a tangle of weedy vegetation, the tips of his fingers joined; and his head meditatively on one side. His hands showed that he had been engaged in manual work. He was pale, and spare; and he wore a small, very fair beard and moustache. His eyes were light blue and exceedingly intelligent.

Against the background of gleaming sea the figure of Philip Dendraith, framed by the rough Norman window, stood out very strikingly. Every line was strong and flowing, and the face laid equal claims to admiration.

Yet, perfect as it was, it by no means lacked strength or individuality, as handsome faces often do. There was only too much strength in the thin delicate lips, and in the square jaw which gave vigour to the face, without heaviness. The eyes were rather small and close-set; keen in expression. Dark, sleek hair; closely cropped, harmonised with a smooth, brown and colourless skin; a laugh or smile displayed a set of miraculously white teeth, even and perfect as if they had been artificial. As often happens, this last perfection gave a singularly cold expression to the face; after the first shock of admiration (for it was nothing less), this became chillingly apparent, but the eye still lingered on the chiselled outlines with a sort of fascination. Philip Dendraith seldom smiled, but when he did the smile had always the same character. It was steely and brilliant, with a lurking mockery not pleasant to encounter. His manners, young man as he was, were very polished; he was by instinct a courtier.

'If the fellow were going to murder you,' Harry Lancaster used to say, 'he would bow you into an easy-chair, so that you might have it done comfortably.'

It would have been hard to find two men more unlike than Philip Dendraith and Harry Lancaster.

Cold, keen, self-reliant, fascinating, Philip compelled admiration, and to certain natures his personality was absolutely dazzling. Power of all kinds is full of attraction, and power this young man possessed in no common degree. Already he was beginning to exercise an almost boundless influence over women, whose education – the potent, unconscious education of their daily lives – tends to exaggerate in them the universal instinct to worship what is strong.

Harry Lancaster's charm, curiously enough, lay partly in the absence of certain qualities that made the other man so attractive. He had none of those subtle flatteries which were so pleasant even when they could not be supposed to proceed from real feeling, but he was genial, ready to help, quick to foresee and avoid what might wound another's feelings; daring, nevertheless, in the expression of unpopular opinion to the last extreme.

In Philip's suavities there often lurked a hidden sting – so well hidden that it could not be openly resented, yet full of the bitter poison of a sneer.

It was in his nature to despise men and women, and to rule them through their weakness for his own ends.

'As we were saying, then, before our friend's inordinate laughter interrupted our cogitations,' the philosopher remarked, taking up the lost thread of conversation with his usual pertinacity – 'as we were saying, Realism as opposed to Nominalism[52] is doomed to extinction under the powerful' –

'Paw,' suggested Philip.

'Paw of Science?' said Caleb Foster dubiously. 'The metaphor seems crude.'

'But powerful, like the Paw,' said Philip, sending a pebble spinning over the window-ledge into the sea.

'Science,' pursued Caleb, weighing his words, 'is the enemy of poetry and mysticism' –

'I doubt that,' said Harry; 'I think it has a poetry and mysticism of its own.'

'That point we must lay aside for after-discussion,' returned the clear-headed Caleb quietly.

'Better put that aside, certainly,' observed Philip.

'Science views Nature as a vast concourse of atoms constrained only by certain eternal vetos (if one may so speak), and out of the general co-ordination of these vetoed units arise the multiplex phenomena that we see around us.'

Viola bent forward eagerly, trying hard to understand.

'The vetos may be of the simplest character, but how ever simple and how-ever few, a complex result must arise from their grouping under the conditions. Given the alphabet, we get a literature. There you have the doctrine of Necessity in a nutshell.'

Philip turned his small eyes languidly on the speaker.

'And – what then?' he asked.

'What then?' echoed the philosopher. 'Having got rid of misleading concep-tions, philosophy migrates to new pastures. We no longer speak of life as if it were some outside mysterious influence that pours into dead matter and trans-forms it; we believe that there is no such independent imponderable, but only different states of matter arising from forces within itself.'

'And anything that goes on outside the pale of our cognition – ?' asked Philip, slightly raising his eyebrows.

'Such things,' said Harry, 'are, philosophically speaking, not 'in Society;' one doesn't hear about them; one doesn't call upon them; they are not in our set.'

The philosopher seemed a little puzzled. He smiled a melancholy smile and looked pensively out to sea.

Philip was still engaged in sending small stones spinning into the void, and he had gradually worked himself so far towards the outer edge that half his body appeared to be overhanging the sea, which lay immediately below the window.

'I say, you'll very soon be "not in our set" yourself if you don't look out,' said Harry.

Philip laughed, and swung himself round, so that now he was sitting with both legs over the farther edge of the embrasure. He seemed to revel in the dan-ger. Viola turned cold as she saw him lean half out of the window in the effort to descry a ship on the horizon.

'Instantaneous death is not, strictly speaking, a calamity,' observed the irre-pressible philosopher; 'the mind has no time to dwell upon the idea of its own destruction. Pain, mental or physical, is the sole misfortune that can befall a man, and this is incompatible with unconsciousness.'

'Well, then, Foster, suppose you give me the pleasure of treating you as I treat these pebbles; let me flick you dexterously into the ocean.'

But the philosopher laughed knowingly, and shook his head.

'Reason is not our ruling attribute,' he said; 'sentiment is the most powerful principle in the human breast.'

'Come out, will you?' cried Philip, apostrophising an obstinate pebble which had wedged itself tightly in between two blocks of stone. 'I *will* have you out; the thing imagines it is going to beat me!'

'Have you never been beaten?' inquired Harry.

'No; nor do I intend to be, by man, woman, or child,' Philip answered, with a screw of the lips as he at last forced out and flung away the refractory pebble.

His manner gave one the impression that so he would treat whomsoever should resist him. The mixture of indolence and invincible determination that he displayed was very singular.

Caleb Foster expressed an idea that was passing through Harry's mind when he said, disjointedly, as if thinking aloud, 'Given with this temperament, irresponsible power, absence of control – lessons of life artificially withheld – result, a Nero.'[53]

'Are you calling me a Nero?' asked Philip, with a laugh. 'Nothing like philosophy for frankness. What's my sin?'

'Ask your conscience,' returned Caleb. 'I know of none.'

'My conscience has struck work,' said Philip; 'I gave it so much to do that I tired it out.'

Caleb gave a thoughtful nod.

'I believe that it may indeed become obscured by over-exercise,' he said. 'The simple human impulses of truth and justice are, after all, our surest guides. Too subtle thinking on moral questions makes egoists and straw-splitters of us, and hands us over to the mercies of our fallible judgments.'

'And why not?' asked Harry.

He insisted – much to Viola's consternation – that goodness and intelligence are truths identical, and that one of them could never lag far behind the other.

'Granted their close affinity,' said Caleb, 'but it does not follow that the most reasonable man is also the most moral. Morality is not evolved afresh in each human being by a logical exercise. It is the result of a long antecedent process of experiment which has embedded itself, so to speak, in the human constitution, so that morality is, as it were, reason preserved' –

'Apt to have a bad flavour, and to be sometimes poisonous from the action of the tins,'[54] added Harry.

The philosopher thought over this for some seconds, with his head very much on one side.

Philip Dendraith had another definition of morality.

'I speak from observation,' he said, 'and from that I gather that it is immoral to be found out. I can conceive no other immorality.'

'Halloa! here's our friend the gentlemanly Poodle!' exclaimed Harry, as that intelligent animal appeared in sight.

Bill Dawkins paused in his headlong career, and stood staring at the group.

'I wonder who your master is,' Harry continued, re-doubling his blandishments; 'perhaps the name is on the collar. Hi! good dog – *rats!!*'

Bill Dawkins pricked up his ears and bore down upon the indicated spot. The philosopher found that his highly developed forehead had become the destination of a lively shower of earth and small stones, which the dog was grubbing up, sniffing and snorting excitedly. Caleb quietly removed his forehead out of range and stood looking on.

'If the beast hasn't almost upset the Philosopher's Stone!'[55] exclaimed Harry.

Caleb opened his mouth to speak.

'We might find in these efforts a type of the Realist's struggle to lay hold of the abstraction in his own mind, an *eidolon*[56] which he translates into objective existence,' he observed, calmly and persistently philosophic. But the young men were too much occupied in cheering on the deluded poodle to heed him.

'No name on the collar,' said Harry; 'but he's clearly a highly connected animal – well-bred too; and he's beginning to see it's a hoax; he's giving it up in despair and registering cynical vows not to the credit of mankind.'

'Come here, animal,' said Philip.

Bill Dawkins' nostrils moved inquiringly.

'I want some amusement, and I think you can give it me.'

As Bill Dawkins did not obey, Philip laid hold of him by the ear and compelled him to come; much to the creature's indignation.

Bringing a piece of string from his pocket, the young man then proceeded to tie the dog's legs together diagonally ; his right front paw to his left hind paw, and the other two in the same way.

The result, when he was set down again, was a series of agitated stumbles and a state of mind simply frantic. The sight seemed to afford Philip much joy; he looked on and laughed at the creature's struggles.

'This is a subtle and penetrating form of wit,' Harry remarked, with a frown; but Caleb Foster seemed amused at the animal's embarrassment, good-natured man though he was.

'He'd make a good target,' remarked Philip, taking aim at the poodle with a small stone, and following up with a second and a third in rapid succession. The last one hurt; for the dog gave a loud yelp, and Harry, flushing up, was springing to the rescue, when an angry cry rang through the air, and almost at the same instant the dog was encircled by a pair of small arms, and hugged and caressed as even that well-appreciated poodle had never been caressed in his life before.

'By the Lord Harry,[57] it's the little Sedley girl!'

CHAPTER VII

MURDER

Frantically Viola tore off the string that bound the creature's legs, and then turning fiercely to Philip, she said, with quivering lips, white with passion, 'How dare you ill-treat my dog? How dare you? You are a cruel, wicked man, and I hate you!'

'Well done, little virago,' said Philip, laughing. 'Now, tell one who has your welfare sincerely at heart, how did you get here all by yourself?'

'Why did you throw stones at Bill Dawkins? You are cruel – you are wicked; I think you are Satan.'

There was a shout of laughter at this.

'Well, I *have* had two good compliments this afternoon!' Philip exclaimed, still laughing; 'to be called Nero and Satan within half-an-hour is something to remember oneself by!'

'Poor, good dog! poor, poor dog!' cried the child, almost in tears, and stooping again to caress him.

'Your dog is not much hurt, little girl,' said Harry kindly. 'See, he is wagging his tail, quite cheerfully; he knows it is all right.'

'He always forgives very easily,' said Viola. '*I* wouldn't forgive that man if I were he.'

'Now, do you know, little lady, I believe you are mistaken,' said Philip, with one of his brilliant smiles; 'I wouldn't mind betting that the time will come when you would forgive me far greater offences than this one against your poodle. You belong to the forgiving sex, you know.'

'No, I don't,' cried Viola, fiercely.

'Do you mean to say, for instance, that you haven't forgiven me for kissing you that afternoon at our house? You were very angry at the time, but you are not angry about that now – are you?'

Viola's face was a study.

Philip threw back his head and laughed at the look of helpless passion which made the child almost speechless.

'There is some mettle here,' he said, addressing the others; 'a high-spirited young animal who would be worth breaking in when she grows up. Women of this type love their masters.'

'I wouldn't be too sure of that,' said Harry, as he bent down and tried to soothe the excited little girl, and to find out how she came to be here alone.

'Life,' said the philosopher, with amiable intent, 'is beset with inevitable disturbances of the mental equilibrium (perhaps the child does not understand the word *equilibrium* – let us therefore substitute *balance*). These, however, it is possible to reduce to a minimum by a habit of mind which – but I fear I fail to impress our little friend. No matter. In early years the human being is the creature of impulse; reason has not yet ascended the throne. We must be content to be the sport of circumstances. Are you content to be the sport of circumstances, my good child?'

Viola looked shy and shook her head.

'The little woman is a treasure!' exclaimed Philip, laughing. 'Now I want to make you say you forgive me,' he went on, unexpectedly stooping down and lifting her into the window embrasure, where he established himself in his old perilous position, with Viola struggling in his arms.

'I say, do look out,' cried Harry; 'a mere breath would send you into the sea.'

Philip treated these warnings with contempt.

'Now, listen to me,' he said quietly, as he quelled the child's struggles with a clever movement; 'it is of no use fighting, for I am stronger than you; but I don't want to make you stay here against your will; I want you to stay willingly, and to say that you forgive me, and that you like me very much.'

'I hate you,' said Viola.

'Oh! no, you don't,' cried Philip in a low, soft voice; 'you can't hate a poor man who thinks you a nice, dear little girl, and wants you to be fond of him. That wouldn't be fair, would it?'

Viola was silent: he had struck the right chord.

'If I had known the dog belonged to you, I wouldn't have tied his legs together or thrown stones at him; – (though they were very little stones, you know). Now won't you forgive me if I say I am very sorry?'

'No,' said Viola. 'Let me go.'

Philip gave a deep sigh.

'You pain me very much,' he said. 'What can a man do when he has offended but say he is sorry and will never do it again?'

'Let me go,' repeated Viola.

'I say, Philip, you are teasing the child,' remonstrated Harry.

'No, I'm not; I want to make amends to her, and see if she has a nice disposition.'

'You want to experiment with your diabolical power,' muttered Harry.

'Now, Viola,' Philip continued (his voice was very soothing and caressing), 'you see how repentant I am, and how anxious I am to be forgiven; I want you just to say these words after me, and to give me a kiss of pardon when you have said them. These are the words: "Philip Dendraith, though you have behaved very badly, yet because you are fond of me, and repent, I forgive you, and I kiss you in sign of pardon." When you have said that I will release you.'

'I won't say it,' said Viola.

'Oh! but I am sure you will. You know that it would be right and just to say it. I know your mother teaches you to be forgiving, and that you will forgive. See, I am so sure of it that I open my arms and leave you at liberty.'

He released her, and waited with a smile to see what she would do. She stared at him in a dazed manner. His arguments had bewildered her; she felt that she had been trusted, and that it would be dishonourable to betray the trust; and yet – and yet the man had no right to interfere with her liberty. There was a vague sense that his seemingly generous confidence had something fraudulent in it, though it placed him in a becoming light.

A look of pain crossed the child's face, from her certainty of this, and her utter inability to put it into words. Few people know how cruelly children often suffer from this inequality in their powers of apprehension and expression.

'It's not fair,' was all she could say. However, Philip had so far gained his point that she did not take advantage of her freedom to leave her tormentor; she only shrank away as far as she could, and sat with her head pressed against the stone-work of the window.

The partial victory made Philip's eyes glisten: it was delicious to him to use his power, and he already regarded Viola as an adversary worthy of his mettle, child though she was.

Harry, thinking she was reconciled to the situation, abandoned thoughts of interference, and Philip, with much tact, forbore to press his advantage. He began to talk about impersonal matters, cleverly spinning stories on the slenderest thread of suggestion, and so much did he interest the child that she forgot who was speaking, and forgetting that, forgot to be angry.

Philip smiled, and glanced over his shoulder at his companions.

'The forgiving sex!'

'Tell me some more, please,' said Viola, in a dreamy tone.

'Once upon a time,' Philip went on obediently, 'this old castle stood six miles inland, before the sea bit its way up to it and bombarded it as it is doing now. At that time it was one of the finest castles in England, and the barons who owned it, were very powerful. I fear they were rather a quarrelsome lot; we hear of them having endless rows with other nobles, and one of them, not content with his own wife, must needs take away the wife of one of his neighbours; and the neighbour was annoyed about it, and challenged him to single combat, and they hacked at one another for a whole afternoon in plate armour (electro-plate, you know, not real silver). It was a dreadful scene.'

'And what happened?' asked Viola breathlessly.

'Well, the other baron ran his lance through Lord Dendraith's arm, and he said, "A hit, a very palpable hit;" but the baron, putting his lance in his left hand, came on again, swearing diabolically, and this time he unhorsed my ancestor and smashed in his helmet, and then he gave him a deep wound in the leg, and soon the tilting-ring[58] was swimming in gore, for the two men were both wounded. The bystanders noticed that it was very blue in colour, the barons being both of noble blood. But in spite of their wounds they swore they wouldn't give in, and up sprang Lord Dendraith on to his horse, and up sprang Lord Burleigh on to his, and the clang of their armour when the lances came down upon it could be heard within a radius of fifteen miles. The people at that distance took it for the sound of threshing-flails in the vicinity, and were not interested.'

'And then?' said Viola.

'Then,' continued Philip, 'the battle raged so fiercely that even the fierce members of the Dendraith family were seen to tremble; the plumes of their helmets actually quivered, and a murmur of rustling feathers ran round the crowded ring, when for a second, there was a pause in the combat. The blows were falling so fast now that there was nothing to be seen but a sort of blur in the air in the path of the flashing lances.'

'Oh!' exclaimed Viola, horror-stricken.

'"By Heaven! I swear I will fight thee to the death!" roared Lord Burleigh.

'"The devil be my witness, I will follow thee to hell!" bellowed Lord Dendraith.

'And so they fell to with fresh vigour. The two men were very equally matched, and when one inflicted a wound, the other retaliated with an exactly corresponding injury; when one chopped off a particular portion of his enemy, the other chose the same portion and lopped it off likewise; so that they worked each other gradually down, and it seemed as if they were going to finish the fight with the mere fragmentary remains of what were once exceedingly fine men.

'When at last each had driven his lance into the other's right lung and unhorsed him, the bystanders interfered, and suggested that the noble barons having already lost several limbs, besides cracking their skulls, and mutually causing their teeth (with a few not-worth-mentioning exceptions) to strew the ground, they might consider their honour satisfied; especially as their present plight rendered further fighting highly unsuitable.

'But the furious barons would not hear of it; they declared they had never felt better in their lives, and with a violent effort they dragged themselves to their feet (they had now only two between them), and each with his dying breath dealt the other a death-blow. And that was the famous combat between Lord Dendraith and the Lord of Burleigh,' concluded Philip.

'Is that the end?' asked Viola.

'Yes; though I may mention that the widows shortly afterwards married again.'

Viola remained silent and thoughtful; the tragic finish of the tale weighed upon her.

'One can see where you get your absurd obstinacy from,' said Harry.

'I don't own to being obstinate,' returned Philip 'obstinacy is the dullard's quality. I have tried to avoid it, as I fancy it is in the Dendraith race.'

'Who were anything but dullards,' Caleb threw in.

Philip bowed.

'They improved towards later times,' he said. 'Some foreign blood came into the family, and, rather curiously, it developed on a substratum of the old stubborn, stupid spirit a subtlety almost Italian. Andrew, who repaired part of the castle and built the house, combined these qualities very strikingly. He murdered

his sweetheart, you know, little lady,' Philip went on, seeing that Viola was interested, 'because he found that she liked another man better than she liked him,
and no Dendraith could stand that. He offered her his love, and she coquetted a
little with him for a time, and then' –

'What is coquetted?' asked Viola.

'Well, she wouldn't say plainly whether she liked him or not; but he swore
that she should be his, or no other man should have her. Unluckily, he found she
had a more favoured lover, and then and there, without foresight or consideration, he stabbed her. The other more cunning side of his character showed itself
afterwards in his clever manner of eluding detection for years. The truth never
came out till he told it himself on his deathbed. It is said, of course, that the ghost
of the murdered lady haunts the castle to this day.'

'Is this your castle?' asked Viola, after a long and thoughtful pause.

'No, it is my father's at present; but he is going to give it me as soon as I marry.
It used to be a fine place, and it can be made so again. So you see, Viola, I am
worth making friends with. Perhaps when you grow up, if you are good, I will
marry you! What do you say to that?'

'I don't want to marry you,' said Viola, her old resisting spirit roused again.

What! not after all the nice stories I have told you?'

'No,' said Viola curtly.

'Not to become mistress of the castle, and to have that big house and garden
for your own, and some beautiful diamonds that I would give you?'

She shook her head.

'This is *not* like the sex,' Philip observed, with a laugh. 'Think how nice it
would be to have a big house all to yourself, and diamonds, and a husband who
would tell you stories whenever you asked him! The luxury of that can scarcely
be overrated. You had better think seriously of this matter before you refuse me;
there will be a great many others only too delighted to have a chance of all these
good things.'

'Husbands with a turn for narrative being proverbially popular,' Harry threw in.

'And husbands with a turn for diamonds still more so,' Philip added. 'I am
sure that Viola will see these things more wisely as she grows older. So confident
am I of it, in fact, that I intend to regard her from this time forth as my little
betrothed' –

Philip laughed at the flash that came into the child's eyes. Presently he went
on in a coaxing tone: 'Now, Viola, you are going to be nice and kind, and say you
are fond of me, and give me a kiss, aren't you? Remember, I let you go free when
I might easily have kept you prisoner all this time.'

'I think your arms would have ached by now if you *had*,' observed Caleb,
with a chuckle.

Viola had drawn herself together as if preparing to spring to the ground and escape, but Philip quickly frustrated her design. She was still untrammelled, but a strong arm across the window barred the egress.

She tried to push it away, but she might as well have tried to break down the Norman stonework against which the large well-formed hand was resting. She beat it angrily with her clenched fists.

'Oh! that's naughty !' cried Philip, much amused. 'Supposing you were to hurt me?'

'I want to! 'Viola continued to strike the hand and arm with all her might.

'Now, you know, there is but one cure for this sort of thing,' said Philip, with a brilliant smile.

Relaxing the tension of the obnoxious arm, he placed it round the child, and drew her towards him, saying that he must give her a mixed kiss, combining the ideas of punishment and betrothal.

'Upon my word, you *will* be over that precipice if you don't look out!' warned Harry again.

'Pooh! I'm all right,' said Philip impatiently.

Expecting Viola to struggle away from his clutches, he had adjusted his attitude accordingly, but instead of this she flung herself wildly upon him with rage-begotten strength, and before he could recover from the shock, in his dangerous position, he had completely lost his balance. The whole thing was over in an instant.

'Good God! he's gone!' exclaimed Harry, springing into the embrasure with one bound, followed by Caleb.

The two men looked in each other's white faces for a second of awful silence.

Harry leant back against the stonework with a breathless groan, drawing his hand across his brow.

He was on the very spot where, a second ago, Philip had been lolling in his indolent way, defying the danger that lay within an inch of him, the danger that Harry had warned him against in vain.

The unceasing lapping of the waves on the cliff below made the moment absolutely ghastly. It was like the licking of the lips of some animal that has just devoured his victim.

'What's to be done? He *can't* be killed!' cried Harry at last. It seemed incredible. Caleb laid his arm round the young man's shoulders, and together they peered over the verge. White and pitiless the cliff dropped dizzily to the sea. Philip was an athlete and a splendid climber, but who could keep footing on such a place as this? The only hopeful sign was that they saw nothing of the body. The cliff was not perpendicular; that gave another faint consolation. They had forgotten all about Viola in the horror of the moment, but the sound of low passionate sobbing recalled her presence to their minds.

'I have killed him; I have killed him,' she moaned in accents so utterly heartbroken, that they sent a horrified thrill through the hearts of her companions. There was something so grief-experienced in the despair of the child; almost it seemed as if she were bewailing the inevitable accomplishment of a foreknown doom. She might have been the heroine of some Greek tragedy crying 'αἰ αἴ'[59] at the fulfilment of her fate.

Harry tried to soothe her.

'Oh! find him, find him: he is not killed; he cannot be killed,' she wailed. 'Come and find him; come and find him.'

Feverishly she took Harry's hand to lead him away.

'It was my fault; I have killed him. Come – come!'

In pursuit of a most forlorn hope the three set out together, under Caleb's guidance, he being familiar with the cliffs, and able to lead them by comparatively easy descents to the foot of the rock. Viola was most anxious to go all the way, but Harry told her that she would delay him and Caleb in their search, and this alone induced her to stay and watch from above.

Rough steps had been hewn out of the rock in places, to enable people living in the castle to get down easily to the sea, and these now proved of immense value, though at best it was dangerous work, and very exciting. The slightest slip would have been punished with death. Now and then they had to take little jumps from ledge to ledge, or to crawl on their hands and knees, clinging for dear life. They stood still now and then to rest, and to shout at the top of their voices in case Philip, by some miracle, had been saved and might answer them. But no answer came.

'It does not seem to me quite impossible that he should have broken his fall by means of some of these inequalities in the side of the cliff. The absolute smoothness vanishes on closer acquaintance.'

It was Caleb who spoke.

'And there is an inclined plane here,' Harry observed; 'steep, indeed, but one's momentum would be checked in striking it.'

'Certainly; and Philip is the man to have that good fortune, if any man *could* have it; and to take advantage of it.'

Cheering themselves with these suppositions, they slowly continued their journey. The sun was sinking, and sent a fiery line of gold across the water, dazzling them with its brilliancy, and making their difficult task more difficult still. The gulls were wheeling overhead, congregating and settling on the waters with beautiful airy movements. It made the two men feel giddy to look at them. Glancing towards the fatal window, whither Viola had returned to sit tremulously watching, it struck Harry that if he and Caleb were both to be killed, the child would be without a protector. Standing on a narrow ledge of rock, he shouted up to her, 'Throw down a small stone if you hear me.'

A pebble came straight as a plummet-line from the window, striking the inclined plane, bounding up and taking a curved path thence into the sea, which it entered with a faint little plump.

'If we should not return, go at once to the coastguard station – it's not two hundred yards off; tell them who you are; ask them to take care of you for the night, and send a message to your home that you are safe. Another stone if you hear; two stones if only partly.'

Two stones came down and behaved in the same manner as before. The advice was repeated, and then a single stone fell in token of understanding. With an encouraging wave of the hand, Harry pursued his perilous journey. From above the cliff had appeared smooth and uneventful, but now a thousand secrets betrayed themselves. Caleb was working his way towards a part of the rock that lay at present out of sight below the inclined plane. Struck by the action of the pebble, it had occurred to him that Philip's body might have followed the same route, but being heavier in comparison with its momentum, would not have described a parabola (as the philosopher put it to himself), but would have fallen or slipped to the surface immediately below. If here, by some good luck, there were a resting-place, hope still remained. This idea Caleb communicated to Harry, who checked an impulse to pass on the encouraging view to Viola. It was a pity, he thought, to rouse her hope on such slender grounds. The search had by this time insensibly changed its character in Harry's eyes. He now regarded it partly as it affected the mind of the little girl whose passionate action had caused the mishap. Her remorse and horror had been terrible to witness, and Harry felt that if Philip proved to be really killed the shock to her might prove to be very dangerous indeed. Her conduct that afternoon had showed him of what sort of stuff she was made.

This was a nature, like a deep sea, capable of profound disturbances. At that time Harry had not learnt that the nature with material for such storms has generally within it also a strange cohesion and power of endurance which enable it to stand together through crises that would seem more than enough to shatter the most firmly-knit intellect.

'Look out,' Caleb called back to his companion, as a stone rolled down the slope; 'you are coming to an awkward place now.'

Harry found that he stood on a projecting ledge of rock, where below him for about twenty feet there was no further resting-place; to the left rose a buttress of rock; to the right the ledge shelved away to nothing, the slight foothold dwindling till it disappeared altogether.

'How in the name of wonder did you get past here?' he called to Caleb.

'I climbed up, and got round the projection on the other side; but the bit of stone I got up by gave way under my feet, and I fear you will have to stay where you are for the present.'

As this fact was borne in upon him, Harry cursed his ill luck. The loosened flint that had enabled Caleb to climb the escarpment lay resting on the slope of rock below him twenty feet. The prisoner looked anxiously at the sun. Nothing could be done when the darkness came on, and if it should overtake him he would have to stay here all night, unable to lie down, scarcely able to turn, – it was not a pleasant prospect.

'I can't possibly get out of this position without help,' he called out; 'but how are you getting on?'

'I am working my way to the place I told you of; I shall soon be there. If I find him, I will shout to you; and we can consult as to what is to be done. Perhaps the little girl could find you a rope somewhere about the house. There is one in my kitchen, do what you can as to that; meanwhile I will not forget you. The sun won't be down for another two hours yet.'

With these words Caleb passed entirely out of sight, and Harry was left to solitude and his own reflections.

He shouted up to Viola above, and was answered by a tiny pebble.

'We want a rope,' he called up. 'Will you go to Caleb's house and bring one that you will find there in the kitchen? His house is in the castle keep; it has been repaired and made into a dwelling for him; it stands at the end of the castle, right out to sea – you can't mistake it.'

'I understand,' was signalled back in pebble language.

Harry knew that the child's anxious misery would be relieved by action, and, besides, her help might be very valuable. The thought of her strange and terrible situation at this moment recurred to him with increasing insistence. Philip Dendraith had been to Harry only a newly-made acquaintance and his accident affected him little more than if it had befallen a total stranger. There was no personal grief in his heart, and he was therefore free to speculate on the feelings of one more tragically interested. He was beginning to feel anxious about her, for he doubted if she could be persuaded to leave the spot until Philip had been found, and there was the sun racing towards the horizon, and still Caleb gave no sign.

Everything depended upon him.

Viola found the rope, and as soon as she returned Harry directed her to go to the coastguard station for help. She was to ask to have the news forwarded to the Manor-House and Upton Court, and also to bring some brandy. Pebbles came down in token of understanding, and the little figure disappeared from the window. Harry found himself alone in the hushful twilight.

It seemed as if Nature were doing her utmost to soothe his anxieties and whisper messages of peace in his ears. Long lines of cloud and sea swept serenely from coast to distant coast; the sunset lights were rich and glowing, promising a glorious morrow; while at the cliff's foot the glossy waters lapped with a soft sea-sound that might have lulled the frenzy of a madman's dream.

Harry felt the influences steal into his heart, and as the glow grew fainter in the sky, and the cold evening light – almost electric in its still lustre – crept over the waters, he realised with a start that the last quarter of an hour had been one of the happiest of his life. Full of emotions, of delicious insights and longings, it had brought to him, upon the inflowing tide of heightened consciousness, a thrilling sense of the glory and the sweetness of existence.

Then for the first time he fully realised the tragedy that had occurred that afternoon; a strong fresh life hurried perhaps into dark unconsciousness, with all its infinite possibilities blotted out.

Away 'pale Philosophy,'[60] which would persuade the life-intoxicated soul that death is no calamity! Death is *the* great calamity towards which our sins and our errors are for ever thrusting us. Life – full, rich, wide-spreading life – the one great universal Good, in whose delicious ocean all right and healthy things in heaven and earth are steeped till the sweet waters steal in and fill them through and through. Such was Harry Lancaster's present creed.

A shout broke the stillness.

'I have found him!'

'Alive?'

'Don't know; he does not move; – I am trying experiments.'

It was maddening to be imprisoned here when help was so much needed! Harry, for the hundredth time, tried to persuade himself that he could escape by some deed of daring, but had to own that none but suicidal attempts were possible. He told Caleb that Viola must shortly return with help.

'That's lucky!' shouted the philosopher. 'I believe he is alive, though he has been severely knocked about; he is stunned, but he seems to me to breathe still faintly. It is an absolute miracle! I wish I had some brandy. When the little girl returns with help' –

'Ah! well done, well done ! Here she is! – and the coastguardsman himself to the rescue.'

'Thank Heaven!' exclaimed Caleb. 'Come to me as soon as you can. No time to be lost.'

Harry shouted up to the man to let down the brandy and to attach the rope firmly somewhere above. In a few seconds he had the joy of seeing a quaint-looking flask sliding down the cliff towards him. Quickly detaching the flask, he put it in his pocket, and seizing the rope, swung himself down obliquely, the coast-guardsman moving it from time to time along the castle wall. It was not long before he had scrambled almost to the foot of the cliff, where he found Caleb beside the motionless body of Philip.

Harry sprang to his side and handed him the brandy without a word.

'This may save him,' said Caleb, as he raised the body in his arms and administered the life-draught. 'Now, there is no time to lose; he must be moved to my house at once, while he is unconscious; after he revives the pain would retard us. His left leg is broken, I fear, and I dare say that is not the only injury, poor fellow! You take his feet, I'll take his head, and forward.'

Caleb, giving the word of command, led the way to the beach, the two men carrying the burden for about a quarter of a mile over the shingle, and then up by a rough but moderately easy ascent, at a point where the cliffs were less steep and less lofty. They had perforce to pause for breath now and again, and then the dose of brandy was repeated. At the second pause a faint movement, showing that Philip was still alive, was the signal for moving on at a still more rapid rate.

The distance seemed very great, for Philip was no light burden, and their wishes so far outstripped their powers that progress appeared slow indeed.

'What's that?' said Harry, peering through the dusk. 'I think I see two figures coming towards us.'

He was right. A few minutes brought them face to face with Viola and the good-natured coastguardsman, who had guessed what the others had done, and come on to lend a hand. He turned Harry off altogether, and insisted on taking his place till he had 'got the wind into his sails again,' after which Caleb was subjected to a similar process of nautical recuperation.

Before Viola's white lips had time to frame the question, 'Is he alive?' Harry had communicated the fact of Philip's almost miraculous escape.

The blood ebbed away from her face for a moment, and then came rushing back again in a great tumult. She said not a word, but kept close beside Philip, watching his still face intently.

'Did you get a message sent to your mother?' Harry inquired.

'Yes; I said I was quite safe, and that you had told me what to do, and were taking care of me. Also I asked her to send on the news, as you told me.'

Caleb's hermitage at the far end of the castle was a strange, romantic little dwelling, patched together by his own hands out of the ruined keep; the arrow-holes having been widened into windows, while the old spiral staircase still served the ingenious philosopher as a means of reaching his little bedroom, where every night he was lulled to sleep by the ceaseless music of the waves. From this haven of repose the mattress and blankets were brought down to the kitchen, where a good fire was burning; Philip was laid upon the bed close to the hearth, and then Caleb proceeded to apply all his wide and accurate knowledge to the task before him.

While engaged in arduous efforts to restore the lost animation, he was giving explicit directions to his colleagues to assist him, and to collect various things that he required in order to set the broken leg and bind up the wounds.

'He is badly hurt,' said Caleb; 'but if he lives, he will be none the worse for this, if I am not much mistaken.'

'Oh, he'll live all right,' said the coastguardsman, seeing, with singular quickness, that Viola turned white at the philosopher's '*if*.' 'There! I saw a quiver of the eyelid. You are breathing your own life into him, Mr. Foster; – he *must* come round. Don't you never be afraid, little 'un,' he added, patting Viola on the head; 'the young gentleman'll live to be a sorrow to his parents for many a long day yet! You mark my words.'

The coastguardsman's prophecy proved true. Caleb, with the assistance of his companions, did, after much effort, succeed in fanning the dim little spark of life to a feeble but certain flame.

Philip opened his eyes, gave a sigh, and sank heavily back on the pillows.

'The leg must be set,' said Caleb. 'Happily I know how to do it. Now I want you all to be very intelligent,' he said, as he bent down to perform the operation; 'upon my skill and the general good management of the affair hangs the issue of a life-time. If I do not set it with perfect accuracy one leg will be shorter than the other.'

There was an anxious silence in the little room as the philosopher, with skilful, decided movements set about the momentous task.

Philip was by this time vaguely conscious of his surroundings, but too weak to ask any questions. Perhaps his rapid mind had taken in the facts without assistance. He very much surprised the bystanders by saying in a weak but clear voice, 'Are you going to set my leg, Foster?'

'Yes; we can't wait for a doctor. I have done it before – trust to me.'

Almost as he spoke he wrenched the parts into position, and Philip gave a groan.

'The worst is over,' Caleb said cheerfully; 'brace yourself for another wrench, and then the deed is done.'

This time there was only a laboured drawing of the breath from the patient, and then the limb was bound to a bar of wood by means of bands made, on the spur of the moment, out of cloths and towels, and the patient was told that for the present he would be left in peace.

Very quietly and rapidly Caleb made arrangements for the night. The coastguardsman was thanked for his services and assured that no further help was needed. Caleb and Harry would take turns in the night-watch, while Viola could go to bed in the room sanctified by philosophic slumbers, and dream that she was a mermaid playing with her own tail in the depth of the green ocean.

So said Harry, recovering already from the afternoon's strain of anxiety and fatigue.

Caleb silenced at once Viola's pleading to be allowed to sit up and watch the patient. Not to-night, he said, or she would be another patient on his hands by the morrow, and then how could Philip be properly nursed?

'Say good-night to him, my little friend,' said Caleb kindly, 'and then I'll take you upstairs.'

The child went up to the bed and knelt down by Philip's side. In spite of manful efforts, the tears welled up into her eyes, but she made no sound. She seemed to be struggling with herself; her lips moved. Then suddenly she bent forward, uttering Philip's name, and as she bade him good-night she kissed him on the brow.

'I am so sorry; I am so very sorry!'

Philip, weak as he was, gave a slight laugh. The afternoon's event, nearly fatal though it had been, amused him.

'You almost did for me, little one,' he said, 'but it's all right, and you didn't mean to do it, you know.'

Viola turned abruptly away from the bedside, and Caleb, taking her in his arms, carried her tenderly up the dark winding staircase to the strange little room, through whose lozenge-paned windows a faint moon was tracing diamond patterns on the bare floor.

'You won't be frightened here, will you?' Caleb asked. 'Mr. Lancaster and I are in the room below, and should hear you in a minute if you called.'

'I shall not be frightened,' said Viola.

Yet a thrill of terror went through her when Caleb, having done all he could think of for her comfort, shut the door and left her alone.

The excitement of the day had unstrung her nerves, and the strangeness of the place filled her with alarm.

But it was not this that most disturbed her. All minor fears were lost in the terror of one secret and horrible thought; a memory which had made the very sunshine seem hateful, and now haunted the darkness with faces so hideous in their mockery that the child grew well-nigh distraught.

'*We* see; *we* know,' said the faces, and then they laughed and mocked, till Viola, falling on her knees beside the window, prayed as she had never prayed in her life before. The face of the earth was changed to her since that afternoon; no prayer, no forgiveness, could restore to the sea and sky their friendly benignity. That was all gone, and in its stead were terrible accusations and sinister smiles and laughter. That she herself had altered did not occur to her; she was the same Viola, capable always of the crime that she had this day committed; capable always of – she shrank frantically from the horrible word.

As a man fighting with some wild beast for dear life, this child wrestled, in the loneliness of that little seahaunted chamber, with a demon born within her own consciousness, who assailed her without pause or mercy through all the waking hours of that dreadful night. It seemed as if this Creature – for living form the unspeakable Idea actually took in her distraught imagination – were devouring her inch by inch, her and all that she possessed. Her childhood shrivelled up in the blast of his hot breath; her innocence, her childish dreams, her ignorance of the deepest gulfs of human misery. The gates of the great Darkness were opened to her, and she could already see, stretching far away, the dim, woeful plains and midnight mountains in whose black chasms human souls lay rent and bleeding. The air was heavy with sighing and lamentation.

Upon how many scenes of human agony had those old stones looked down, while the sea sung its eternal requiem to hope and sweet desires? Yet never, perhaps, had they witnessed a struggle more terrible than the succourless soul-travail of this solitary child – a soul battling in the darkness with the image of a great crime, warding off with vain and desperate efforts the memory of a moment's flash of insane fury, – that moment, which had blazed out upon the very sunshine in hues of flame, fierce and crimsoned with the wild image of – *Murder*!

CHAPTER VIII

A SYMPOSIUM

The news of Philip's accident brought, as Harry said, 'a large and fashionable circle' to Caleb's little Hermitage. Mrs. Sedley drove over early in her solemn old carriage to fetch her daughter and inquire for Philip. 'Aunt Augusta' and her husband also trundled across country in their more lively vehicle, but delayed their visit philosophically till the afternoon.

Far from philosophic were the fond parents of Philip, who arrived breathless with a captive doctor at an unearthly hour in the morning, and rushed to their son's bedside with a thousand exclamatory questions.

The examination of the injured leg by the doctor was followed by the cheering announcement that it had been perfectly well set, and that with proper precautions there was no reason to fear any permanent injury.

Viola looked on and listened in the deepest anxiety. She shrank guiltily away from Philip's parents, and answered only by a deep flush when Sir Philip said to her, in rather a severe tone, 'I hope this will be a lesson to you not to give way to temper, my child; if it hadn't been for my son's marvellous strength and presence of mind, he would have certainly been killed.'

'Indeed, yes,' said Lady Dendraith, shaking her head; 'passion is a dreadful thing, and always leads to trouble.'

There was something ludicrous, if Viola could have seen it, in this plump, well-to-do lady moralising about the evil results of passion; but the child was inaccessible to all ideas of the ludicrous just now; indeed at no time was she very keenly alive to the humorous side of things.

Reluctantly she had to leave the Hermitage and go home with her mother, who promised that she should come and see the invalid as often as the doctor would permit.

Mrs. Sedley did not say a word of reproach to her daughter for her disobedience; she felt that the child had been already severely punished, though she little guessed *how* severely.

The next time that Viola saw Philip he was looking as strong as ever, and complaining bitterly of the restraint still imposed upon him.

'The doctor says I shall walk again as well as ever, for which all praise to '*mon cher philosophe*,'[61] and the rest of you. Lancaster here behaved like a Trojan.[62] As to the coastguardsman, he is a true Briton! And Viola – what shall I say of her? Well, she did her very best to make up for pitching me over the cliff in that spirited manner! I can't get over the idea of this mite having actually brought me to death's door! It is really splendid. She will be a fascinating woman when she grows up. It isn't the quiet nondescript women that take one's heart by storm; what we love is life and passion.'

'Yes, in other men's wives,' said Harry. 'In the East, when a woman marries, her father presents her with a sword,[63] which is the symbol of her liberty, and this sword she is expected at once to transfer to the bridegroom, who holds it over her head, making her pass under it as a sign that she promises to be henceforth subject unto him. Whatever is powerful and brilliant we either admire or hate. I leave you to draw your own inferences.'

'Thank you,' said Philip, 'we will.'

'And to assist you in the effort,' Harry added, 'let me repeat a significant remark which I once heard a fellow make about two sisters: the elder, he said, was the girl to fall in love with, the younger the girl to marry. I expect the woman of the nineteenth century is going to make hay of our cherished institutions.'

Philip raised his eyebrows.

'Do you really think that the great, badly-dressed old sheet-anchor: our uninteresting but valuable *bourgeoisie*,[64] is going to stand any nonsense about its institutions? Don't imagine it for a moment. The more musty and fusty they are, the more passionately they will be clung to!'

Harry smiled.

'I suppose if our existence were made a little less dull and uncomfortable, the national Bulwark[65] would think we had come to terms with the Evil One[66] himself! Being tied hand and foot like a Gulliver,[67] and generally ill-treated, gives us a sense of moral safeness, and is wonderfully conducive to the serenity of the average conscience. The 'badly dressed sheet-anchor' (a singular figure, by the way) is a trifle thick-headed; we must calculate on that.'

Of such conversations was Viola now often the puzzled hearer, for where Caleb was, there, to a dead certainty, discussion would be also. Both Harry and Philip expressed unbounded amazement that he had ceased discoursing learnedly during the time of the accident. That he had not then insisted strenuously on the non-calamitous nature of death was regarded by the two young men as an evidence of singular moderation. His way of treating Viola was a source of perpetual amusement to them. Do what he would, poor man! he found it impossible to project himself into the consciousness of a being who did not understand the nature of a syllogism, and (if Harry was to be believed) he always addressed Viola with deep respect in the language of 'pure reason.'[68] That young man used to return to Clevedon after a visit to the Hermitage, and amuse his cousin by describing how Caleb in moments of close-knit argument had turned to Viola with some such remark as, 'To this you will at once reply that Kant[69] regards our religious beliefs as either *statutory*, that is, arbitrarily revealed, or *moral*, that is, connected with the consciousness of their necessity and knowable *a priori* –

This, no doubt, was one of Harry's exaggerations, but the story was not destitute of foundation.

Viola took a keen interest in Kant; why, Harry never could understand. He did not realise the natural avidity with which a starved intelligence absorbs any fresh idea, however unattractive. Mrs. Sedley's careful selection of books for her daughter's reading, had the result of making the child eager for mental food of some other flavour; it mattered little what the food might be, so long only as it was quite unlike the severely wholesome diet on which she had been monotonously reared.

Besides being introduced to Kant, whom she found a pleasant and intelligent person, Viola made the acquaintance of Socrates,[70] or Mr. Socrates, as Philip insisted he must be called, on the ground that 'familiarity breeds contempt.'[71]

Viola was indignant at the injustice of the treatment he received at the hands of his countrymen; she made him into a hero, and regarded all his utterances as inspired. Harry shocked her greatly by saying, 'Well, after all, you know, he is distinctly the greatest bore on record. We should never endure such an old proser now! Think of the way he nagged at those long-suffering people in the Dialogues! I don't wonder that the Athenians resorted in despair to hemlock.[72] As for Xantippe,[73] poor woman! I have always had the deepest sympathy for her. I am certain the man deranged a naturally fine intellect, and destroyed the temper of an angel.'

Poor Viola! she scarcely knew what to believe! The mixture of jest and earnest which ran like tangled threads through the whole conversation was most confusing to her. She was utterly unaccustomed to lights and shades of thought, or to quick changes of mental attitude. The three men into whose society she was now thrown opened up a new world of ideas, delightful but bewildering. Caleb's position in the group did not puzzle her as it would have puzzled an older person, but she was interested to learn that this amazing and indefatigable scholar – battening on the literature of second-hand bookstalls – had been discovered by Harry Lancaster in London in a state of terrible privation; that a friendship had sprung up between the two men, and that, finally, Caleb had been installed by Sir Philip at the ruin, of which he was now custodian, keeping it from falling into utter decay, while he took charge of the stables, outbuildings, and gardens belonging to the empty house.

Sometimes Caleb would propose to make the meeting into a genuine symposium, setting glasses on the table and bringing out a bottle of home-made wine, presented to him, as he informed the company, by his amiable friend Lady Dendraith, and made by her own kind hands.

It was an incongruous group, with an incongruous background, of which Philip, on his couch in Caleb's picturesque kitchen, formed the central figure.

The shadows and sombre colouring threw the four faces into relief. The splendidly handsome features of the invalid formed a fine nucleus to the picture, and Viola's pale questioning face, with its strange melancholy, seemed to correspond to that note of sadness that can be caught in all things human, if we listen for a moment, ever so carelessly.

The eagerness with which she waited on Philip was touching, even to those who did not know her secret; to an onlooker who had guessed that soul-corroding trouble, the whole scene would have seemed no less than tragic. Had her sense of guilt been able to overcome her old dislike to Philip, one source of conflict would have disappeared; but it was not so. After the first rush of pitiful remorse, which had drowned for the time every other sentiment, Viola was again assailed by the old antipathy.

With this she had continually to struggle, and those who have realised the strange intensity of the child's nature will understand what such a struggle implies.

Philip's bantering, familiarly affectionate manner was perpetually stirring up the old angry feelings. A sudden flash of her dark eyes would make him laugh and pretend to cower away as if in fear.

'I'll be good; I'll be good! Don't murder me outright, there's a good child!'

And then the light would die out of her eyes, and she would turn away, perhaps going to the window or to the open door, where she would stand looking out upon the sea.

Mrs. Sedley had permitted, and even encouraged, these visits to the bedside of the invalid, because she regarded them as acts of atonement. The horror of

causing a fellow-creature's death had come so near to the child that she could not
fail to be deeply impressed by it.

Philip's recovery was very rapid. As soon as he was able to be moved, his
mother bore him off in triumph to Upton Court. That broke up 'the symposium,'[74] and finished one of the most exciting chapters in Viola's short life. Her
visits to Philip were still continued, but at longer intervals, and under conditions
entirely changed. She used to bring him flowers as votive offerings; wild flowers
that she had gathered in the woods; and sometimes she would shyly offer him
some worm or beetle which she imagined must be as valuable in his eyes as it
was in hers.

She tried to discover what his soul most yearned for, whether tadpoles or
'purple emperors'[75] or piping bullfinches, or it might be a retriever puppy! Then
she would spend her days trying to gratify his ambition. On one occasion a
round fluffy squeaking object with a damp pink nose was placed in Philip's arms,
with the words: 'You said the other day that you wouldn't care to live without
a retriever puppy; I have brought you one, and you can have four more if you
like.'

Philip kept the puppy, and said that now he was reconciled to life.

To Viola's delight, Bouncer – grown by this time into a charming, pulpy,
blundering creature, with the sweetest disposition – had the honour of being
taken up to Oxford when his master returned thither at the commencement of
the term.

After that things rolled back to their old course; Viola seldom saw the outside of the gates of the Manor, and she had ample opportunity, in the stagnant
solitude of her home, to brood upon the secret that clouded her colourless life.
It helped to exaggerate many qualities in her that were already too pronounced,
while hastening unduly the maturity of her character.

She made no further attempts to wander out of bounds, and Miss Gripper now seldom caught her climbing trees, or engaged in any other unlady-like
occupation. She delivered herself over to the influence of her mother, and about
eighteen months after Philip's accident she passed through a phase of fervent
religious feeling, during which she rivalled in devotion and self-mortification
many a canonised saint. Her mother had some trouble in keeping her from doing
herself bodily harm, for in her new-born zeal she preferred tasks that gave her
pain, and never thought it possible to be well employed unless the occupation
was severely distasteful.

She used now rather to enjoy her father's fits of anger, for they gave her an
opportunity of showing a saint-like meekness under persecution. At this time
her behaviour was a grotesque caricature of her mother's whole life, but Mrs.
Sedley did not recognise the portrait. She rejoiced in her daughter's piety, and
half-believed, perhaps, that in the service of Heaven one might fly in the face of

mere natural laws (against which Mr. Slater preached such severe sermons) with impunity.

Days and weeks passed on; the daily routine was never altered; the only change that marked the course of time at the Manor-House was the presence of a lady who came daily from the village of Upton to carry on Viola's education.

Miss Bowles was a worthy, conscientious, washed-out person, who had long said good-bye to joy, poor woman! and lived her dim, struggling, dreary life with lady-like propriety.

She scarcely seemed a real human being; she was the incarnated emblem of sound religious principles, Arithmetic for schools, French (with Parisian accent), German (Hanoverian), English Grammar, Composition, and History – all these things and, many others Miss Bowles represented; – but try to compound out of them a personality, and miserable was your failure! It lay so deeply buried, so thickly incrusted – like some poor bird's nest petrified in the Derbyshire springs[76] – that you searched for it in vain. Perhaps a genial, sympathetic person might have warmed it into life once more, but Mrs. Sedley was neither genial nor sympathetic.

Viola applied herself conscientiously to the dry tasks which this lady imposed upon her, associating all that was sapless and without colour in these daily tables of facts and figures, with the neat but certainly not gaudy drab bonnet and pinched-looking jacket of her governess.

Viola was growing now into a slim girl, graceful and swift in her movements, with a reserved, melancholy expression and a rich, sweet voice. Philip Dendraith had prophesied that she would turn out a fascinating woman, but, according to her father, she threatened to be a dead failure.

'How are we going to marry a pale-faced frightened creature like that?' he demanded, 'She's only fit for a cloister; and I, for my part, think it's a great pity we haven't got nunneries to send our plain girls to. What's the use of keeping them idling about at home, every one laughing at them because they can't get husbands?'

At such remarks Mrs. Sedley, meek as she was, would wince.

In her simple creed, marriage, no matter under what conditions, was intrinsically sacred, but she would not counsel her daughter to marry for money; that seemed to her very sinful. Yet she knew well that Mr. Sedley would never tolerate for Viola a poor marriage; he had long been resting his hopes of the restitution of the family fortunes upon his daughter; and without reserve he had told his wife what he expected and what she must exert herself to bring about. The anxious woman watched her child's development with dread; for every day that passed was bringing her nearer to the crisis of her life. And what was the mother's part to be in that fateful moment? Her influence over the girl was supreme: upon her action all would depend.

The responsibility seemed unendurable, the problems of conscience pitiless in the terrible alternatives which they offered to the tortured will.

Suffering, which Mrs. Sedley had borne herself without a murmur, made her tremble when it threatened her child. Yet her teaching to that child was perfectly consistent with the whole tenor of her life: 'Endure bravely, and in silence; that is the woman's part, my daughter.'

She was ready, with hands that trembled and quailing heart (but she was ready), to give that nerve-thrilled being to the flames – for Duty's sake – and quickly that insatiate woman's Idol[77] was advancing to demand his victim.

Year by year the state of Mr. Sedley's money-matters grew more hopeless, and a possibility which had long been thought of in secret, was at last acknowledged openly between husband and wife. Mrs. Sedley had never seen her husband so deeply moved as when he confessed that they might have to leave the Manor-House, the home where he had lived as a boy, where his father had lived and died, and his ancestors for many a generation. The man who was devoid of sympathy, coarse, brutal, and narrow-minded, was yet moved almost to tears at the prospect of banishment from the home of his race. Sentiment – like a sudden flame in seemingly dead embers – sprang up on this one subject, though it answered to no other charming.

'If it be in any way possible to avoid it, we will not, we *must* not leave the old place,' said Mrs. Sedley earnestly.

'There is only one way to avoid it,' he replied; 'Viola must make a rich marriage.'

'Yes; if she loves the man,' Mrs. Sedley ventured to suggest. 'Loves – fiddle-de-dee!' cried her husband angrily; 'don't talk schoolgirl twaddle to me, madam. What has a well-brought-up young woman to do with love, I should like to know? I have no patience with this spoony[78] nonsense. I call it downright improper. Let a young woman take what's given her and be thankful. Confound it! it's not every woman that can get a husband at all!'

With these words ringing in her ears, Mrs. Sedley would look with something approaching terror at the sensitive face of her daughter, who, as she grew more womanly in appearance, seemed to become more than ever shrinking and reserved.

Her father shrugged his shoulders angrily.

'Who's going to marry a girl like that?' he would ask contemptuously; 'she looks half-asleep.'

With her customary want of tact in appreciating character, Mrs. Sedley used to confide some of her anxieties to Lady Clevedon, who scoffed long and loudly, not at Mrs. Sedley, but at Viola.

'Dear me; it's very interesting to be so sensitive! quite a fashionable complaint among girls nowadays. Too sensitive to marry, too sensitive to be mothers! Is there anything that they are *not* too sensitive to be?'

'You know that I cannot answer you if you speak in this vein, Augusta; but Viola gives me great anxiety.'

'My dear, something ought to be done; the machinery of the universe must be stopped; it is too coarse and noisy for these highly-strung beings; they can't stand it. Clearly "gravitation ought to cease when they pass by."'[79]

CHAPTER IX

ALTERNATIVES

In silence, day by day and month by month, the clouds swept over the Manor-House, and silently the scroll of the years unfolded, revealing little, but hinting many things. Nine times the leaves had fallen since Philip's accident; and Geoffrey had now shot up into a gawky, good-natured youth, and his parents began to cast about anxiously in their minds to find him a profession. His hearty loathing of the drudgery of office-work made the choice difficult. Geoffrey would have preferred the army, but his father swore a great many oaths, and declared that he was not going to be bled to death by a lot of idle sons who couldn't live upon their pay. He had had enough of *that*. Manitoba[80] was bruited (for no congenial work nearer home could be heard of), and this, as an alternative, in case nothing better offered, Geoffrey had come to regard as his destiny. Meanwhile he remained at home, and was understood to be 'looking out for something.' The intervals between the times of 'looking out' he used to spend in fishing his father's trout-stream, for this was the delight of his soul.

Geoffrey's presence made a great change in Viola's life, and her father began to feel more hopeful about her future achievements, after the boy had driven away the dreary depressed look, and summoned in its place an expression that entirely transfigured the girl's face. Her rich dark skin and black hair, the fine eyes kindling with youthful delights, gave her genuine pretensions to beauty.

It was a sombre beauty; still beauty it was, and of a subtle and haunting kind. During the nine uneventful years which had ushered in her girlhood, Viola had only now and again met either Philip Dendraith or Harry Lancaster. Caleb she occasionally saw. He was still living among his beloved books in the little sea-haunted Hermitage.

Harry had gone to India with his regiment, and Clevedon mourned his exile, and looked forward to his shortly expected return with much joy. Philip was reported to be leading a dissipated life in London, where his good looks, his brilliant prospects, and his undoubted social talents carried all before him. Whenever he was at Upton Court, he made an effort to renew his old acquaintance with Viola, but this was no easy task. Shyness, partly hereditary, partly induced by a solitary life, had become almost a disease with her, and she used to flee from her fellow-creatures whenever they approached.

For the third time during a three weeks' visit, Philip arrived one afternoon at the Manor-House, and asked for Viola, but she was not to be found. She had seen the visitor arrive, and instantly set off at her utmost speed to the farthest confines of the park, where, shivering with excitement, she lingered for hours and hours, not venturing to go back to the house, in case Philip should still be there. Unfortunately for her, her father happened to be in, and he was so angry when, at last, she did cautiously return, that she thought he would have struck her. She had never seen him so enraged, although outbursts of this sort, after his drinking-bouts, were not uncommon. Fury carried the man out of himself, and he said things which even he afterwards owned were 'rather strong.' Viola listened in silence. She was learning lessons never to be forgotten to her dying day, lessons which perhaps every woman has to learn in some form or another, but which few are fated to be taught in so many words by their own fathers.

In the name of Heaven and common-sense, how did she expect to get a husband if she behaved in this crazy, addle-headed manner? Half the women in London were ready to throw themselves into Philip Dendraith's arms, and yet Viola would not condescend to the common politeness of coming to see him when he called! She had run away on purpose, of course; it was an old trick of hers, very girl-like and engaging no doubt, but might one make a polite request that these graceful exhibitions of coyness might not occur again? Coyness was all very well when a man had expressed himself distinctly, but really, before he had made any advances at all, it was what one might call premature.

'You are not a queen of beauty, let me tell you, that you can afford to indulge in these womanish devices. My doors are not besieged with suitors for your hand.'

'Not want to marry? Not want to marry?' Mr. Sedley yelled, with a burst of fury. 'You – you – miserable little fool! Do you know what you are saying? Can't you speak? Can't you say something instead of standing there before me like a block of wood? Not want to marry indeed! And pray, what do you think would be the use of you if you didn't marry? What can you do but loaf dismally about the place and serve as a wet blanket to every one's enjoyment? What's the good of a woman but to marry and look after her husband and children? What can she do else? Tell me that, if you please. Do you hear me, Viola?'

'I would try and earn my own living,' said Viola at last in a low, trembling voice.

'*Earn your own living!*' echoed her father, with a shout of laughter. 'Well, that *is* good, upon my word! *You* earn your own living! And pray, in what profession would you propose to become a shining light? The army, the navy, the Church, or the law? Or would you perhaps enter upon the field of politics? Everything is open to you; you have only to choose. And you know so much, don't you? You are so learned and capable, so well able to force your way in the world. Oh! pray don't think of marrying; a far more brilliant and congenial career lies before you.'

Viola answered nothing; she was suffering too keenly, realising miserably that in her father's mockery lay a deadly truth; that she had, in fact, nothing to reply but, 'Thou hast said it.'

What was she? What did she know? What had she seen? What could she do? To all this there was only one answer: Nothing. Books had been forbidden her; human society had been cut off from her; scarcely had she been beyond the gates of her home, except once or twice when she had gone for change of air to Wales or Yorkshire, or for a day now and then to London to see 'the sights'!

'O mother, it was cruel!' From the depths of her heart that bitter cry went up, the first word or thought of reproach that had ever arisen there for that much-adored and devoted mother. And this was the result of those anxious days, those fervent prayers, that ceaseless self-denial! By her own father, this carefully, anxiously tended child was taunted with her helplessness, and reminded not only that the sole career open to her was marriage, but that she must make deliberate efforts to secure it for herself, or to aid and abet in schemes which others undertook on her behalf. She must bestir herself in the matter, for it was her appointed business.

In after-life Viola learnt about the outcast of her sex facts which at this time were unknown to her; but that revelation was not more painful, nor did it even strike her as very different from what she had learnt to-day about the lot of women who were *not* outcast, but who took upon themselves to cast out others.

The girl's stunned silence irritated her father beyond endurance.

'In the name of Heaven, why can't you speak?' he thundered, 'it's your confounded obstinacy; and you get it from your mother. But we have to see yet who is master. Understand that I mean to endure no more of this nonsense, and the next time you are asked to appear in the drawing-room, you will please to do so, and to make yourself pleasant to the visitor into the bargain. Too much of this accursed nonsense would land you high and dry, a burden to me for life.'

Viola drew a quick breath.

'Yes, a burden, a dead weight, hanging like a millstone round my neck. Do you know what a woman is who does not marry? I will tell you: she is a cumberer of the ground,[81] a devourer of others' substance, a failure, a wheel that won't turn; she has no meaning; she is in the way; she ought never to have been born. She is neglected, despised, left out; and who cares whether she lives or dies? She is alone, scorned and derided, without office, without object, without the right to exist, all doors are closed to her and all firesides forbidden. If you are minded to choose such a lot, at least you shall do it with your eyes open. I tell you a woman is worse than nothing on the face of the earth who is not performing her natural duties, serving her husband and her children. That's what she's made for, and if she doesn't do it she's an absurdity, – a – an anomaly, a ramrod without a gun, a key without a lock, – a – a ship without a sail – she's – she's a DAMNED NUISANCE!' roared Mr. Sedley, with a final burst of fury, as he turned on his heel and stamped out of the room, banging the door so ferociously that it shook the old house from cellar to roof.

'The master's been drinking again,' announced the butler to the inmates of the servants' hall.

It was in the drawing-room that this stormy interview took place; the chill, ghostly old room where the lost souls dwelt and the Spirit of Music held her court. It was a dreary day; Philip had chosen it for his call, thinking that Viola was likely to be home. Outside, old William was weeding the gravel in his usual steady, patient way; the ceaseless chip-chop of his hoe, regular as the dropping of water, sounded forlorn in the silence.

Viola stood for full five minutes exactly where her father left her, with her eyes fixed upon the dull forms of the mist-dimmed trees, upon the melancholy avenue whose few remaining leaves awaited the first breath of wind, to fall shivering to the sodden ground. Then with a low sob she flung herself into the nearest chair and buried her face in the cushions. She was shaken from head to foot, but not a sound escaped her. Grief which finds its easiest expression in tears was reserved for souls less passionate.

There was something frantic in her present distress; she was like a hunted creature at bay. Her position, as represented by her father's words, seemed utterly unbearable, utterly humiliating.

Why had her parents forced existence upon her if it was to be one long degradation? Better indeed that she had never been born! 'Better, ah! better a thousand times,' old William's patient hoe seemed to say, as it beat its rhythm on the gravel without; 'better, a thousand times, a thousand times!'

With a strange desperate pleasure in self-torture, the girl placed the whole picture clearly before her mind; showing herself exactly how she stood, how helpless she was, how closely the two alternatives of the woman's lot encompassed her. The next time that Philip called, it would beseem her to put on her best frock and her best smile, and try all she knew to charm him. Were not her future prospects dependent on his (or on some man's) favour? Had she not been informed (and in most explicit terms) that her father had no mind to keep her always in his house, and that he expected her to betake herself without delay to her 'natural duties?'

The chip-chopping of the hoe had ceased now, but only to be succeeded by the swish-swish of the broom sweeping away the withered leaves.

'I could sweep away withered leaves, or hoe out weeds; I could dust or cook, or wash, or – or anything that requires only health and strength. I might even be like Miss Bowles and teach, but it would have to be very young children, – I know so little, so little!'

She gave a shiver.

'Until to-day, – O mother, dear mother, I did not even know what it meant to be a girl!'

As a pulse, the broom went beating on the gravel outside, and upon the window-panes struck the first drops of coming rain. A sound of wind among the trees heralded its approach, and presently it arrived; a gush of tears from the sorrow-laden heavens. Old William worked on as if he did not notice it, patiently bending his head to windward, without so much as looking up to see where the rain came from. Viola could bear the sight no longer. She rose, drew up the heavy ill-fitting window, and stood with the rain drifting in upon her face and hair.

'William,' she said, 'why do you go on working? You will get cold; you will get rheumatism; it is so bad for you. Why don't you go in?'

Old William paused for a moment, and raised himself slightly (only slightly) from his bent attitude, leaning on the handle of his broom.

'The rain don't do me no harm, Miss,' he said, with a slight smile; 'I'm used to it. Thomas says I'm to get this gravel done to-night, and Mr. Sedley he wants to see it done; and I'm just a-doin' of it.'

'Oh, what does it matter?' cried Viola. 'Rheumatism must be so hard to bear.'

William gave a sadly knowing shake of the head.

'Ay, that it be, Miss,' he said. 'I has it so bad at times as I can't scarcely move – the rheumatis' is very bad, very bad indeed. My father, 'e 'ad it dreadful, 'e did; his joints was all gone stiff, and his fingers was all crumpled up like.'

'Then it is madness for you to stay out in the rain,' urged Viola.

But the old man had not arrived at that highly advanced stage of mental development when things immediate can be balanced against things future. As he had done for years, he went on working in the rain, and endured his rheumatism when it arrived with his usual patience. The act of mind and will necessary to alter his habitual conduct in deference to experience, was beyond him.

All he would do, was to put on his coat, at Viola's urgent entreaty.

There was something in the dim, forlorn lot of this old man that had always filled Viola with sadness; but to-day she could have taken his hard old hand and kissed it and wept over it in an ecstasy of pity and fellow-feeling.

Had she spoken aloud the words that came welling up into her heart, she would have made old William open his eyes as he had never opened them in his life before.

'Let me come to you and comfort you; let me be a daughter to you; let me work for you and for myself; and then perhaps your lot might be brighter, and then I should not need to seek the favour of any man for the sake of house and home, or to avoid remaining here to be a burden to my father and the world!'

Seldom do civilised men and women speak according to their impulses. They are too well drilled, too discreet; their lives are guided by anything and everything except their own deepest longings and their own soundest reason. Reason may be consulted, but it does not turn the scale. The caprice of others is the most frequent civilised motive, while often mere force of habit will hold people in an old and painful groove for long pathetic years, because they consistently subordinate the great to the little, matters of life and death to some present, importunate, but perfectly trivial claim. Broken hearts, oftener than we think, are the handiwork of feeble heads. As Harry Lancaster had once said, with his usual extravagance, 'Give me the making of the people's intellect, and let who will make their morals!'

When the rain and wind became so violent that old William could not continue his work, he yielded to the logic of events and took shelter in the potting-shed.

The rain was driving in great hissing sheets across the country; the windows streamed, and shook with angry clamour.

Throwing on a cloak and drawing the hood over her head, Viola went out into the storm. She could scarcely make way against it, the wind and rain beat so furiously against her. But she pressed on, seeming to find relief from the tempest of her own feeling in the tumult of the elements. One of the most painful features in her trouble was, that there was no one to be angry with; her whole nature rose in fury against what she felt to be the alternative indignities forced upon her, and yet her anger could not pour itself upon any individual; she could not fling back the insult in his face and be free of it.

It clung to her defilingly, as some slimy sea-weed clings when it loses the sustaining of the water. The consciousness of it was fast saturating her whole being, so that the very texture of her soul was changed.

Struggling blindly on, harbouring a thousand wild thoughts, her attention was arrested by a low whine, and turning, she saw coming towards her the faithful Bill Dawkins, – a decrepid old dog now, so sadly different from the sprightly poodle of bygone days, 'who looked as if the speed of thought were in his limbs!'[82] Quietly and with how sedate a mien Bill Dawkins dragged his slow limbs across the lawn, his ears adroop, his tail no longer quivering (as a compass-needle) with electrical intelligence!

He and old William might have mingled their tears over their rheumatism, for poor Bill also suffered from this cruel malady; and had he been capable of mounting the hill of human thought and overlooking thence the plain of universal destiny, he might, in his pain and discouragement, have made an adaptation of the Japanese proverb[83] and cried gloomily, 'If you hate a dog, let him live.'

Viola went to meet the limping creature with sorrowful heart.

Such was the end of life, and the beginning – ? the rosy, riotous beginning? Of that was Viola herself a shining example!

'Are you coming with me in all this rain?' she asked, as she stooped to stroke the dog, who sat down at her feet and raised his expressive brown eyes to her face.

He looked up at her pleadingly, wistfully, as if he were trying with all his might to speak.

'What is it? What is it?' she asked pitifully. 'Are you in pain? Are you miserable and lonely? Are you a burden to the world, – a wheel that won't turn? Does no one care whether you are alive or dead? But, indeed, *one* person does care, and *one* heart sickens at these dumb tragedies that nobody heeds.'

She bent down and took him tenderly in her arms – great creature as he was – and carried him into one of the many tumble-down old outhouses where the apples and pears, and the watering-machines and rollers, and a thousand and one odds and ends were stowed away.

The place had a fresh earthy scent, redolent to Viola of subtle memories of childhood, bringing back in sweet overpowering rushes feelings of the bygone days. How many a joyous hour had she and Geoffrey and Bill Dawkins spent in this old shed, potting cuttings, trying experiments (and such experiments!) with the watering-machine – growing instantaneous mustard and cress, eating apples, and indulging in a thousand other pastimes, in all of which the poodle had more or less taken part! There was some straw and a piece of old sacking on the floor, and upon this Viola laid him, covering him up as much as he would allow her, for he was shivering all over and looked most wretched. He seemed very weak, but he wagged his tail now and again, and he had a heart-breaking way of offering to shake hands at intervals in a feeble, affectionate fashion. There was something in his demeanour besides gratitude; he seemed to have divined that his mistress was in trouble, and was doing his best to comfort her.

Love is one of those lawless emotions that cares nothing for what is 'natural' or expected; and Viola's love for this faithful creature did not pause to moderate itself on the reflection that to expend so much time and devotion upon an animal argued an ill-regulated mind.

The good poodle had a personality as distinct as that of any human being, and a more lovable one, human being never had!

Viola was down on her knees beside him, caressing, soothing, speaking loving words, with a desperate feeling in her heart, all the time, that the poor creature was dying.

'It would not be kind to keep you if I could,' she said; 'but oh! how sad, how sad I shall be without you!'

Almost as if he understood, the dog half-turned and laid his paw, in the old pleading, caressing way, upon her arm. The next moment he sank down again panting; his body gave a spasmodic twitch, and then lay very still. With a low cry, Viola flung her arms round him passionately, and kissed his shaggy head again and again.

'Good-bye, good-bye; my noblest, kindest, faithfullest friend! Good-bye for ever! and oh that I could tell how I have loved you!'

The dim, beautiful eyes opened slowly; the dying creature looked up with an almost human expression of love and gratitude; then he feebly licked Viola's hand for the last time, and died.

Viola, lying down beside him on the rough straw, sobbed her heart out.

CHAPTER X

ADRIENNE

Not many days after Bill Dawkins' death Harry Lancaster arrived in England. His home-coming was a great joy to his mother and sister, who lived at Upton, in a tiny house belonging to Lord Clevedon, about a mile from the home where they had passed their prosperous days before Mr. Lancaster's death. Mrs. Dixie – who had married a second time, and lost her second husband almost immediately afterwards, – had a bland expansiveness about her manner which referred directly to her former glories, just as her old lace and miniatures, and sundry valuable pieces of plate, made eloquent allusion to that past which threw so much effulgence upon her and her only daughter, Adrienne. Adrienne, however, was a cultivated, keen-witted young woman, dainty in ideas as in her person, and she made her allusions to the past with delicacy, and indeed very seldom made them at all. She did not follow her mother's example of wearing unremittingly at her throat, a gigantic ancestor,[84] with pink cheeks and a light blue coat. Harry used to say of Mrs. Dixie that she was like a gorgeous sunset after a hot midsummer day; the sun and its glories had gone down, but the glow still remained.

'Well, mother, still the lady of the Castle!' he said, not many days after his return. 'I declare you wear your vanished crown more royally than ever you did its antitype. It makes me feel like an involuntary Prince of Wales merely to look at you!'

As Mrs. Dixie liked to think that she possessed the 'grand air,' and as her sense of the ridiculous had its own very exclusive walks in life, she was able to draw up her portly figure with a peculiar wave of the spine presumably characteristic of royalty, while she smiled graciously, down her not perfectly straight nose, remarking, with a sway of the head like that of a poplar in the wind –

'My dear boy, I trust that I am as well able to fill a humble position with dignity as one more elevated. It is not wealth and prosperity that make the lady' (this with an air that beggars description).

Harry gave a queer smile, expressive of so many things that it would be hard to name them all, without making an exhaustive analysis of his character, and that would be a hard task indeed. A few characteristics may, however, be given. He was contemplative, critical, with an abiding enjoyment of the comedy of life, and a continual consciousness of the great deeps that lay beneath the feet of the players.

It was this eternal mystery of life that gave such a wild zest to the never-ending game, such a ring to the laughter echoing dimly through those dark gulfs, – such wings to the jest and the fancy!

Harry was regarded at the Cottage as a joke personified; his mother used to treasure up his sayings, and repeat them afterwards, minus the point, to her friends, with great pride and pomp.

It was almost impossible to annoy Harry Lancaster, although he was capable on rare occasions of furious anger. The little mortifications that irritate most people, served only as a fresh subject for some ridiculous pseudo-philosophy, on his part; so that in truth he was a very pleasant inmate of any house, for he had an alchemist's gift of turning base little troubles into golden opportunities for laughter. His sister Adrienne, who bore the whole burden of the household and family affairs upon her wise shoulders, used to declare that Harry's presence acted upon her health as a change to the seaside, and that he was the only infallible cure she knew of for headaches.

For the rest, he was more or less of a mystery; no one seemed to know what he thought in his serious moments, or if he had any serious moments at all.

His manner was genial, even gaily affectionate; but the light, nonsensical vein always ran through everything that he said, cropping out unexpectedly in his gravest moments, and constituting a wall of reserve far more impenetrable than mere silence. His air of perfect frankness was most misleading. Brother and sister had been confidants as boy and girl in the early days at 'the Palace' before the 'Sunset,' as Harry called respectively their old home and their change of fortune. Together, in the dusk, they used to talk of the mysteries of life and death, of immortality, of free-will, of good and evil, of the formation of character, and the service of God. Adrienne used often to wonder what her brother thought of these things now, after his man's experience of life. She herself had adopted a more or less conventional view of things in an unconventional way.

She was too clever to be a mere passive echo: thinking for herself within adamantine boundaries, she had now become a refined, elevated, intelligent expositor of current views.

She leant towards ideas of great moral elevation, while in the regions of the intellect her admiration and capabilities ran towards a certain French *finesse*[85] and sparkle, these qualities being shadowed forth in the daintiness of her dress and the delicate *nuances* of her manner.

Without being pretty, Adrienne was attractive in appearance; she was one of those people whose person cannot be separated in thought from their personality and judged apart. Every movement, every gesture had a certain finish, just as every detail of Adrienne's dress had a definite effect calculated with reference to the whole. The swift pliancy of fancy which was one of Harry's most attractive peculiarities Adrienne shared with him, but there was a singular difference in the manifestation of the same quality in the two characters.

In Harry it suggested a certain largeness and freedom of nature; while in the sister, it expressed fineness, brilliancy, cultivation; but so far from giving the idea of liberty, it implied that of strict limitation. It suggested a nature close-set, concise, with crisp outlines, guiltless of expansive wandering into the untried. Adrienne Lancaster never wandered carelessly into any region. She must be quite sure if she approved of a region before she entered it. There was no reckless touch in her disposition, and under no conditions could one imagine the quality developing in her. Harry, on the other hand, had it to a dangerous extent; though, so far, it had shown itself in a mere riot of fancy and humour. So alien to Adrienne's consciousness was the attribute, that she even failed to notice it in her brother, closely as she studied him.

It may be supposed that a good-looking young officer, of genial temperament and pleasant manners, became very dear to the village of Upton; and 'society' claimed him passionately for its own. The vicar's family was inordinately large, and the prevailing impression left upon the mind after an introduction was of the 'eternally feminine,' a circumstance which the village thought most unfortunate, for how were all those girls to get married?

How indeed? for though Harry might do his duty as England expected of him, he could not marry the whole contingent of amiable sisters. England would have shown herself ungrateful if he had!

And then, was he in a position to marry even *one* of them? The village feared not, much as it desired to see a break made in the firm ranks of the vicar's charming family. Dick Evans, the eldest son, a pleasant, clever young fellow, now became Harry's frequent companion, though he was scarcely a greater friend to him than Dorothy, the youngest sister, still little more than a child, a fresh, robust, joyous creature, with bright cheeks and untidy auburn hair, and an incurable love for climbing trees and other unladylike pastimes, in which Harry wickedly encouraged her. She was an amusing proof of the inadequateness of commonsense for achieving reasonable views of life; for Dorothy had, as Harry said, enough of this quality to supply the deficiency of the House of Commons (and he could not say more), yet her ideas on men, women, and things were the most laughter-moving that it had ever been his fortune to encounter.

She was one of those rare beings who are predestined to be happy, to whom 'whatever is, is right,'[86] in the social world as in nature.

Upton was twelve miles from the Manor, so that Viola, unfortunately, could not enjoy the enormous advantage of knowing intimately a girl so different from herself as Dorothy Evans. Once Viola had been to Upton, and remembered it as a little cluster of thatched cottages with pretty gardens, and one or two old-fashioned houses, which looked so calm and beautiful that it seemed as if the current of life must have been arrested, as if some satisfied Faust had at last said to the passing moment, 'Stay; thou art so fair,'[87] and the command had been obeyed by Destiny.

It was on a balmy summer's day, that Viola first saw the place, and the picture remained very vividly in her memory. She wondered afterwards if some premonition of what was to come had made her regard it with special interest.

Do not all sensitive men and women feel driven at times to believe that certain places, just as certain people, are fateful for them? – that there is some subtle link which cannot be broken if they would?

Beautiful as it was, Viola had a faint, unaccountable dislike to the village; it seemed like a lovely grave, it was so 'hideously serene.'[88]

> 'No swellings tell that winds may be
> Upon some far-off, happier sea,'[89]

though the sea lay so near, out of sight beyond the undulating downs.

The second time that she saw this place was on the rare occasion of a two days' visit to her aunt at Clevedon. By this time the 'demon boy,' as Harry called the hopeful heir, had grown up and gone to Oxford, while the girl, who was some years older than Viola, had married, and lived in town – 'prosperous and miserable,' according to the same authority.

For a wonder, 'Aunt Augusta' had just now only one friend staying with her, a supernaturally stylish lady called Mrs. Russell Courtenay, who had so much 'manner' that Viola was alarmed and overwhelmed – little guessing that this small-waisted being, with her vast assortment of turns and twists and wriggles, her bewildering pranks and gestures, was in reality a prey to shyness, greater if possible than Viola's own.

Lady Clevedon drove her two guests over to call on Mrs. Dixie and Adrienne.

'I hope that Harry will be in, but I don't think it's likely,' she said;' he is the most erratic person I know; and I fear he is either walking poor old Mr. Pellett off his legs, undoing Dorothy Evans' careful education, or talking nonsense to that ridiculous creature who poses as a philosopher, Caleb – Caleb what's-his-name?'

'Williams,'[90] suggested Mrs. Russell Courtenay, who knew something about literature, but whose memory her unfortunate shyness sometimes confused.

Lady Clevedon treated her suggestion with friendly derision, and Mrs. Courtenay suffered as keenly as if she had had on a shabby dress, or there had been a want of style about her bonnet. Effect was the idol of her soul. She posed, even to herself.

The neat little cottage, covered with wisteria in full bloom, looked radiant this afternoon.

Adrienne, in a dainty but serviceable holland apron, was gardening when the visitors drove up.

Poor Viola! this young woman, too, had 'manner,' though it was less artificial than Mrs. Courtenay's, and therefore less alarming.

'O Augusta! I am so glad! And Mrs. Courtenay too!' she cried, running to the gate to let them in. 'This is heaping coals of fire upon my head; for I ought to have called on you long ago. You must forgive a busy person who has cares of state upon her shoulders. Do come in; my mother will be delighted.'

'Adrienne,' said Lady Clevedon, 'this is my niece, Viola, whose acquaintance you ought to have made long ago. However, better late than never!'

'Better, indeed,' said Miss Lancaster, with a pleasant smile. 'I scarcely feel like a stranger to you, Miss Sedley, for your name has so long been familiar to me. Alas! those horrid twelve miles between Upton and your place have much to answer for, have they not?'

'A punishment for flying in the face of Providence and living in the country,' observed Mrs. Courtenay, with a stylish undulation.

This proposition led to a gay dispute, during which Adrienne conducted the visitors indoors, where they found Mrs. Dixie indulging (if the truth may be told) in a regal nap, from which, however, she woke with creditable rapidity, and received her guests in what Harry called her best 'sunset' manner.

He came in, in the midst of the interview, looking very warm and travel-stained. Adrienne said that a clever geologist might tell exactly where he had been walking by a study of his garments.

'I have been exploring the cliffs with Dick Evans,' said Harry.

'Would he not come back with you to tea as usual?' asked Mrs. Dixie.

Harry smiled.

'No; he preferred returning to the Rectory by the back entrance, "for reasons" (as Mrs. Carlyle says) "which it may be interesting not to state."'[91]

Being pressed for explanations, Harry said that Dick had unhappily rolled down a soft chalky incline, and that the general tone of his colouring had been so materially altered thereby, as to make him feel a delicacy about appearing in refined society.

Dorothy had met him in the back avenue, and had been driven, for the expression of her feelings, to roll over and over on the lawn, regardless of the fact that her mother had never encouraged her in such emotional excesses.

After a burst of laughter, which the mere name of Dorothy was usually enough to call forth at the Cottage, Lady Clevedon laid her hand on Viola's arm.

'Now, Harry,' she said, 'tell me if you know who this is?'

Harry roused himself, uncrossed his arms, and looked inquiringly from his cousin to Viola. She blushed and smiled a little, and as she smiled, a faint memory of a memory, like a whiff of scent, came to him, and faded away again. He struggled to recall it in vain, and then a thought seemed to strike him.

'Not Miss Sedley?'

He rose with a pleased smile and went over to her.

'I am very glad I came in this afternoon,' he said, 'for I am most interested to renew our old acquaintance. I have often laughed over that day at the ruin when you were so angry with Philip Dendraith; do you remember? It was splendid the way you fought him. Do you know, I can still see a resemblance to what you were at that time ; though you don't look quite so like fighting as you did then,' he added, with a smile.

'Oh, I hope I am not so bad-tempered now,' she said, blushing. 'I was always very angry if any one behaved unkindly to my dog, and you know Mr. Dendraith *was* unkind to him.'

There was a faint, very faint gleam in her eyes even now as she thought of it.

'The old spirit has not died out,' Harry said to himself, with a smile; 'she thinks it is dead and gone, but some day, when least expected, it will break out again, and in the woman it will mean a good deal more than in the child.'

'I suppose you sometimes see your old enemy, now that he is at Upton Court?' Harry continued. 'Being a rider, he could get over to you without much trouble, across country.'

Harry wondered why Viola blushed again so deeply and so painfully. He was not foolish enough to jump to the usual conclusion in such cases, but he did nevertheless think it possible that the girl had followed in the footsteps of so many of her sex, and lost her heart to Philip Dendraith. In making up their old quarrel, it would be so easy to overdo it. A mere hair's-breadth would take them across the line of mere reconciliation, and Philip was 'fearfully and wonderfully'[92] handsome.

Harry felt regretful, almost indignant, at the notion of this possibility. From a worldly point of view Philip would, of course, be a brilliant match ; but he was cold, self-indulgent, cynical, with the same unbending will that he had shown when a mere youth, further strengthened by the easy conquests which it had since brought him. Besides, Harry knew that Philip had lived a life of low and selfish pleasure, only a little more prudently than others, so that, while many of his companions had gone to wreck and ruin altogether, he was still prospering.

But this cold prudence which had saved him, was no ornament to his character in his critic's eyes. Viola married to such a man was almost unthinkable, and yet (Harry said to himself) Society is every day bringing about these inconceivable things. The woman marries and gives no sign; no one knows how the unthinkable is worked out in daily detail.

He studied the face beside him with interest. It attracted him far more than many a girlish face which he would have called pretty, and have forgotten again the next minute. Was Viola pretty? He did not quite know. The appeal that her face made was new in kind, and had to be considered. She had a very dark skin, and her colouring when she blushed was rich and fine. The face gained upon one rapidly; it was a haunting face – yes, certainly it was pretty; – very pretty. What had come to him? It was *beautiful*!

Harry drew his hand across his eyes, as if he thought they had deceived him, but no; in a little over twenty minutes, during which the conversation had been upon quite trivial topics, these changes of impression had taken place in him, and the face which he had hesitated at first to call pretty had acquired in his eyes an unaccountable charm.

'I suppose not very much has happened at your home since I left,' he said, musingly. 'It is just the same here. I go away, for years; a thousand things happen to me; I see hundreds of new faces, new scenes: I have many experiences great and small, – and I come back to find precisely the same life going on as when I went away. I ask what has happened; and I am told that old Sally is dead, and so-and-so is married; that a new window has been put in the church, and that Lady Clevedon has built a wing to the schoolhouse! But I suppose these are very important matters after all,' Harry added, remembering that such interests were all that Viola possessed.

'I know very little of what goes on outside my own home,' she said. 'I go to visit the people in our village with my mother sometimes, but I don't like it; – I never know what to say, and I feel intrusive and uncomfortable. The people always talk to mother about their Heavenly Father' – Viola hesitated a little, for a sudden suppressed smile had flitted across Harry's face, a smile not to be hidden by the moustache which Adrienne used to say endeared him to his fellow-creatures so inexpressibly.

He looked very grave the next minute, and expressed great interest in Viola's account of her district-visiting.

' My mother gives the cottagers soup and blankets, and she reads the Bible to them,' Viola continued, drawn out of her reserve by something simple and genial in Harry's manner which no one had yet been able to resist. His dramatic faculty of entering into all varieties of human feeling gave him a power over his fellows, different from, but perhaps not less remarkable than Philip Dendraith's. It was irksome to him to have to retire into the limits of his own personality; he preferred to explore that of others. The simple, firm outlines of Viola's character, and its intense concentration, formed an attractive study to a mind so entirely opposite in type.

'And do you think the villagers like to have the Bible read to them?' he inquired gravely.

'Of course,' said Lady Clevedon, overhearing the question; 'there has been established an intimate relation, of the nature of cause and effect, between the Bible and port wine, which is very favourable to the propagation of the Gospel among the labouring classes in this country.'

'Augusta, you are really very naughty!' cried Mrs. Russell Courtenay, with one of her favourite wriggles. 'This fresh innocent mind will lose its bloom if the young ears are assailed with such ideas.'

'Oh! she had much better listen to me than to Harry,' said Lady Clevedon; 'I think he really must be 'The Ambassador Extraordinary'[93] (you know the book?) – (Mrs. Courtenay murmured, 'Oh yes.') – 'He has all the plausible exterior of that emissary, and I can vouch for the Satanic character of his sentiments. I thought India would have cooled him down' – ('Not a usual result of the climate,' threw in Adrienne) – 'but instead of that he is worse than ever!'

'*You* seem to have been able to draw him out,' said Mrs. Dixie, a little annoyed; 'he never tells us what he thinks. I suppose he doesn't consider us capable of understanding him.'

'Oh! nonsense,' cried Lady Clevedon; 'he wisely shrinks from your criticism.'

'This is crushing,' said Harry, lazily. 'I wonder why it is that a peaceable fellow like me should always be attacked. "Can you fight?" "No." "Then come on." That is how the world treats me! And yet I smile forgivingly upon it.

> 'She was more than usual calm;
> She did not give a single damn,'[94]

he murmured, softly quoting.

'Mr. Lancaster, Mr. Lancaster!' cried Mrs. Courtenay, '*respectez l'innocence*.'[95]

'I beg your pardon?' said Harry, bending towards her in courteous inquiry.

'*Respectez l'innocence*' repeated the lady, with increased emphasis.

'Might I ask you to repeat the phrase once more?'

Mrs. Courtenay lost her presence of mind.

'I said you should respect innocence, Mr. Lancaster.'

'Oh! I always do,' said Harry, with an air a little shocked that the lady should have thought it necessary to recommend so obvious a duty. 'Lives there a soul so black'[96] –

'Now, Harry, no more of your nonsense,' said his cousin; 'Mrs. Courtenay isn't used to you yet, and she must not be badgered. When are you coming over to see us? And you, Adrienne? Now don't say you are busy; people needn't be busy unless they like. Business is the mark of a feeble mind. Come over soon, while Viola is with me; you must get to know each other. I am going to make her stay longer. – No, my dear, you needn't talk about your mamma, – your mamma will have to do as she is told. I explain to her that it's exceedingly bad for a girl to be shut up and never see a living creature. Harry, I give you *carte blanche*[97] to badger *her* as much as you like; it is just what she wants. Viola, then, will stay with me for the next week – (be quiet, my dear!) – and you will all come over and have some tennis, or anything you like – let me see – (the Featherstones are coming to-morrow) – say on Wednesday, then. So that's settled. No, Adrienne, excuse me, you have nothing whatever to do. Australian letters?'

'Nonsense. Haven't got a dress? Borrow one of your mother's.'

'Or,' suggested Harry, ' adopt the idea of the poor woman whom a narrow-minded world condemned to a madhouse because she insisted on wearing costumes made out of advertisement sheets of the *Times* on week-days, and brown-paper on Sundays.'

'If they were well made, I am sure they would look very effective,' said Mrs. Courtenay.

'But, alas! they would have a fault quite fatal in this age of the Worship of the Golden Calf,'[98] said Adrienne in a tone which only to Harry betrayed its latent bitterness. 'No one could stand before them and exclaim – like Mrs. Carlyle's maid[99] before the pictures at the National Gallery – 'How expensive!''

CHAPTER XI

THE SPIDER AND THE FLY

When brother and sister arrived at Clevedon on the Wednesday as arranged, Harry felt a pang of disappointment at seeing his cousin only, and Mrs. Russell Courtenay, on the tennis-ground.

'Your niece is gone, after all?' he asked.

'Oh no, she is coming presently; she is so absurdly shy that I could not persuade her to be here when people arrived. Most ridiculous! She is going to slip in presently, when you are all engaged in tennis, and thus escape observation.'

Harry opened his eyes.

'How very painful it must be to be so shy!' said Adrienne, who was standing near.

'Oh! it's absurd,' cried Lady Clevedon impatiently. 'Poor child!' she added, laughing, 'her misery every evening when she has to talk to my husband is something quite pitiful! You know he is a little stiff and formal, and this frightens her beyond description. It's the most diverting thing in the world to see him at dinner, with Mrs. Courtenay sparkling and undulating on one side of him, and Viola blushing on the other; Arabella trying with all her might to be fascinating, Viola trying as hard to sink into the earth!'

'Poor girl!' exclaimed Harry, laughing. 'She didn't strike me as so very shy as all that, the other day when she called.'

'Oh! well, you and my husband are not exactly the same people; nobody ever is shy with an absurd, lounging, easygoing creature like you.'

'Thanks,' said Harry.

'I half-expect Dick Evans and Dorothy this afternoon, and perhaps Philip Dendraith. *Entre nous*,[100] I fancy he rather admires Viola; so I thought they might as well have an opportunity of meeting.'

'Augusta!' cried Adrienne. '*You* condescending to the *rôle* of matchmaker.'

'Nonsense; I am doing nothing of the kind; but Viola really needs to be drawn out of herself, and I think Philip is a very good person to do it. If he admires her, he will probably succeed better than most people. Viola is a girl who couldn't flirt if she tried, so I am not afraid of starting any silly affair of that sort. I simply want to give her a little experience and *savoir-faire*,[101] and a polished man of the world like Philip Dendraith is exactly the instrument for my purpose; don't you think so?'

'I have no doubt you are right,' said Harry slowly; 'he is certain to teach her *something*, at any rate, but what that will be is another matter. Do you think his admiration is at all serious?'

Lady Clevedon shrugged her shoulders. 'How can one possibly know that about a man like Philip? His heart must be pretty well seasoned after all his experience, and he's not likely to lose it in a hurry to any woman – to Viola least of all. What do you think of her, by the way?'

Harry hesitated.

'Just so,' said Lady Clevedon. 'But she will improve. Her bringing up has been so much against her. Her devoted mother has been the ruin of all that family. Poor Marion! what a life she has had of it! More than half her own fault too. She is really never content unless she is in trouble. I assure you it's a fact. Now it's money-matters, now it's household tragedies, now it's her husband's health, now it's those graceless sons. At present Viola is the source of woe.'

'What does she do to cause anxiety?'

'My dear Harry, she lives; that is enough for Marion. Of course the results of the girl's training are beginning to show, and her mother is quite surprised! Really, the foolishness of women is something quite amazing! Talk about female suffrage[102] indeed! I'd rather enfranchise the madhouses and the asylums; yes, and the clerical profession!' added Lady Clevedon, with a laugh.

'Does Mrs. Sedley regret her daughter's painful shyness?' inquired Adrienne.

'She sees that she is too 'sensitive', as she calls it, and too quiet for a healthy girl of her age. Viola shows a singular preference for her own society, which I should say was anything but entertaining. Her mother declares that she *thinks* –' Lady Clevedon laughed. 'The motherly ingenuity of the idea is quite charming! When I am not angry with Marion she delights me. Poor woman! She came to me almost in tears the other day, because she said Viola had got it into her head that she wanted to earn her own living! It was really too funny! I sat and laughed till I could laugh no longer, and poor Marion looked on; without a smile; and when I had finished she repeated the thing over again, in exactly the same tone of extreme concern; and if Arabella hadn't come meandering in at the moment, I don't know what would have happened.'

'Why does Viola want to earn her own living?' asked Adrienne.

Lady Clevedon shrugged her shoulders.

'My dear, why does she blush if you speak to her suddenly? Why does she allow her mother to dress her in pale lavender sprigs on a white ground?'[103]

'She ought to make a stand for brown paper,' said Harry.

'Infinitely preferable!' cried his cousin. – 'Well, Dorothy, so you have managed to come. That's right. Who are you going to annihilate this time, with that vindictive-looking racket of yours?'

A tennis-set having been arranged between Dorothy and Harry Lancaster on the one side, Dick Evans and Adrienne on the other, the players took their places, Dorothy panting for the fray. Dick was a stoutly-made, reddish-haired young fellow, with a decided, intelligent manner, and a pleasant smile. His capacious head, with square, scientific brow, indicated the direction of his powers. He had that 'sublimated common-sense,' that power of drawing accurate deductions from closely observed data, which, when highly cultivated, marks, according to Professor Huxley,[104] the scientific intellect. His tennis-playing was eminently scientific, 'screws'[105] being very plentiful in his 'service,'[106] as was evident from Dorothy's frequent use of the 'language of imprecation.'[107]

During the game Philip Dendraith arrived in tennis-costume, and joined Lady Clevedon and Mrs. Courtenay in the shade of a beech-tree, where they were sitting, watching the battle.

He was even handsomer than in the old days when Viola first knew him. His figure had filled out, giving him a more manly look; his manner, always polished, was now as perfect as any manner can be that does not take its rise in warmth of heart and wealth of sympathy. He was a man whom Sir Roger de Coverley[108] would have censured very severely, for preferring the reputation of 'wit and sense' to that of 'honesty and virtue.' He would have counted among those who, according to that moralist, deserve hanging: those men who are continually 'offending against such quick admonitions as their own souls give them, and blunting the fine edge of their minds, in such a manner that they are no more shocked at vice and folly than men of slower capacities.'[109]

Philip Dendraith had certainly never been shocked at vice in his life, and at folly he laughed. He could listen to a tale of cruelty without the slightest thrill of anger against the perpetrator of the deed, or of pity for the sufferer. It never seemed to strike him to imagine himself in the place of the victim; he took his stand among the powerful, and had no fellow-feeling for the weak, whether weak through circumstance or by nature.

'Allow me to congratulate you on your picturesque appearance,' he said, as he raised his cap to the two ladies; 'I feel as if I were about to take an unworthy part in a 'Watteau.'[110] The blue-green foliage behind you makes a most characteristic background.'

'Oh! it's only the *background*,' cried Mrs. Courtenay, gaily aggrieved; 'we were flattering ourselves that w*e* formed the attraction of the picture.'

'Nor were you deceived,' said Philip; 'there could be no doubt of *your* efficiency, but the background *might* have failed; therefore I mentioned it.'

'Mr. Dendraith always manages to wriggle out of a difficulty somehow,' said Mrs. Courtenay, laughing.

'He more generally *walks* out of it, I think, Arabella. – Well played, Dorothy! Adrienne, you must bestir yourself! Did you ever see anything like the energy of that child? Her whole soul is in the game!'

Dorothy certainly was worth watching, as she sprang now to this side, now to that, her auburn hair flying behind her, her cheeks flushed, her blue eyes sparkling. Her excited exhortations to her partner, her angry self-reproach if she missed a ball herself, her despair at Dick's impossible 'service,' were all noted with amusement by the onlookers.

'I wish I could see Viola losing herself like that in a game,' cried Lady Clevedon.

'I thought your niece was to be here to-day,' said Philip.

'So she is. I don't know why she doesn't come out.'

'I will go and lead the lamb to the slaughter,'[111] said Mrs. Courtenay.

'Only once have I seen Miss Sedley since I have been at Upton,' Philip observed, when Mrs. Courtenay was gone. 'I have called three or four times at the Manor-House, but till Saturday last she never appeared, and when she did, 'I could only get a few monosyllables out of her.'

'You must remember that she has scarcely been outside the gates of her home all her life, poor child!'

'She has the makings of a charming woman,' said Philip; 'there is a peculiar quality about her, not easy to describe, but it is very powerful. There is something about that particular kind of coldness that suggests hidden fire, and women of that type are always attractive. I want to make way in your niece's good graces, Lady Clevedon. She quite takes my fancy, upon my word.'

Something in Lady Clevedon's movement of the eyebrows made Philip hasten to add, 'Not that there's anything astonishing in that; I have no doubt Miss Sedley is universally admired.'

The lady's half-satirical bow was followed by an amused exclamation; for, crossing the lawn, came arm-in-arm, as if on the closest terms of confidence, Mrs. Russell Courtenay and Viola: Mrs. Courtenay chattering vivaciously into her companion's ear, as she leant over her; Viola as straight as a monument; suffering – all unwillingly – the sprightly Arabella to wreathe herself about her, after the fashion of some fantastic climbing plant.

'You have chosen your co-visitors with infinite discretion,' observed Philip, with a thin smile.

'Yes; they are a delicious pair! And, would you believe it, one is almost as shy as the other. Well, Viola, weazled out of your hole at last! You have lost the best half of the afternoon over your headache.'

'Have you a headache?' asked Philip, in a tone of concern. 'I think it is very good of you to give us a glimpse of you at all, in that case.'

He spoke in the low, flattering tones that most women find so fascinating, and of which no one could fail to feel the charm. Viola looked up; it sounded so exactly as if he were sincere.

His dark eyes, fixed admiringly upon her, gave no further clue to his meaning. If ever eyes were given to conceal the thoughts, Philip Dendraith's were bestowed on him for that purpose. The mystery was *piquant*.[112]

'Oh! Mr. Lancaster, what *are* you about?' Dorothy's voice rang out in dismay. 'That ball would have been out a long way if you hadn't taken it!'

'I'm awfully sorry,' said Harry. 'I'm afraid it has lost us the set.'

And it had. The players came up from the tennis ground (Dorothy disconsolate), and joined the 'Watteau' group under the beech-tree.

'You seemed rather to lose your head at the last,' Philip said, addressing Harry, with a rather keen look in those inscrutable eyes of his.

'Impossible!' returned Harry, flinging himself on a scarlet rug at Mrs. Courtenay's feet. 'I haven't such a thing to lose.'

'Our dear Mr. Lancaster, if we are to take his word for it, has run all to heart,' said Arabella.

'He had better look out and not lose that, into the bargain,' observed Dick, 'or he'll have nothing left to guide him.'

'Except the advice of my friends, and that is always plentiful,' said Harry.

'A man minus both head and heart is such a rarity that he might possibly also distinguish himself from the common herd by consenting to take it,' observed Philip.

'Not he,' threw in Harry; 'it requires the full powers of both those organs to persuade a man, that the rest of the world are not all bigger fools than himself.'

'A curious use to put head and heart to,' observed Dick; – 'self-dethronement!'

'The highest human achievement, I assure you,' said Harry, but whether from conviction or, as Philip said, 'out of pure cussedness,' no one could determine.

Adrienne looked at him inquiringly in vain.

'That is the ever-beautiful doctrine of Renunciation in a new form,' she said, seriously.

'Yes,' Mrs. Courtenay chimed in; 'always sacrificing ourselves for others, don't you know? – of course, that is so Christian, isn't it?'

'Well, no, pardon me, I don't think it is,' said Harry. 'I wish that people would give up this inveterate habit of indulging in moral austerities at their neighbours' expense! If they would only be kind enough to leave themselves and their moralities alone, and to take the trouble to acquaint themselves with a few of the simplest facts bearing upon human well-being – were it but the principle of the common pump or of the garden-engine – their friends would have something to thank them for!'

'Oh dear, *do* you think so?' cried Arabella, looking round in a fascinating manner for encouragement. 'Oh! but I think we all ought to try and be unselfish, don't you know?'

'I'm afraid I can't agree with you,' returned Harry, with his usual perverse instinct to exaggerate his own dissent. 'I think we ought all first to try not to be blockheads. I know it's a very hard saying; far harder than 'Renounce' or 'Surrender;' but it rings truer, and stands the test of experience better than all the self-effacing doctrine which condemns the individual (and therefore the race) to the ridiculous position of the egg-and-breadcrumbed whiting,[113] whose energies, arguing in a circle, are employed in industriously devouring his own tail!'

'Listen to him!' cried Arabella.

'Almost thou persuadest me to be a Christian!' murmured Philip, at which there was a chuckle from Harry and a laugh from the others, Viola and Dorothy excepted.

'Now, Mr. Dendraith,' cried Arabella, 'do tell us what you think about it. I confess I belong to the old school in this matter, and prefer the humble office of the whiting (though it *may* be rather foolish) to the enlightened selfishness that Mr. Lancaster so ably advocates.'

Philip shrugged his shoulders.

'I fear I shall shock the company when I say that my idea of life is, to make myself comfortable, and only injure my neighbours as much as is necessary to serve that important end. I may add that I differ from most people in this matter, merely in regard to frankness.'

'I call that quite shocking,' cried Mrs. Courtenay; 'but it's very like a man.'

The last clause was added indulgently, as if it cancelled the first.

'It is,' said Harry, 'the doctrine that most men practise. To oppose it we have, unluckily, no well-grown, robust, unblinking gospel which bids us seek the good, not so much of an abstract humanity, as of individual men and women – we have only a sickly morality addressed to the little personal righteousness, or desire for righteousness, of each candidate for heaven; so that in the midst of a predatory society, where all must suffer more or less, we possess little or nothing to work against this dangerous form of self-seeking but a few of those absurd and heroic whitings painfully eating their own tails! As well try to cure the world's evils with a set of dancing dervishes!'[114]

'I say, Dorothy, what do you think of all this heresy?' asked her brother.

'Oh! Mr. Lancaster is always saying some extraordinary thing that nobody else says. It doesn't matter,' said Dorothy cheerfully, at which there was a universal shout of laughter at Harry's expense.

'I am sure you are quite wrong,' cried Adrienne; 'you are working against the noblest spirit of the age, and plucking the highest motive out of the hearts of our most devoted men and women.'

'I deny it,' said Harry; 'I say to them only: "In the name of humanity, don't mistake mere self-mutilation for the service of man; don't devour yourselves from overmuch righteousness; the chain is only as strong as its weakest link. You are a link in the chain of the general life, and your first business is to see that it is a good one. In the name of Heaven, not the whiting-trick!"'

Adrienne shook her head.

'A dangerous doctrine,' she said; 'too flattering to our innate self love.'

'That is a personal view of the matter,' returned Harry, obstinately, 'and shows the flaw in your doctrine. You care, after all, more for your own virtue than for the good of others, which claims to be the whole object of renunciation. This is irrational, self-contradictory. A personal righteousness that does not conduce to your own and others' greatest welfare is, to my mind, a mere toy, a doll stuffed with sawdust which you hug to your mistaken bosom. We shall have to throw away our dolls, for they are all fetishes;[115] yes, even our new, ingenious, flaxen-haired, blue-eyed doll with the sweet expression, who says, "Papa, mamma, no jam for me; jam for Tommy!"'

The idea of this ingenious creature amused Dorothy, and her comments on the subject shortly reduced the assembly to a frame of mind entirely unsuited to the discussion of ethical questions.

Their thoughts returned to tennis, and several sets were arranged, in one of which Viola was induced to play, with Philip for her partner.

After it was over he suggested a stroll round the garden, and Viola, too shy to dissent, made a sign of acquiescence.

Every detail of that miserable interview with her father returned to her memory as Philip, with flattering deference, led her round the beautiful old gardens, where the sun was drawing the rich scent from the roses and filling the air with a glory that can only be compared to that happiness which is said to visit none but the loftiest souls, and these only brushes lightly with its wings, as if an angel were passing on his heavenward way.

'I ought to smile and flatter and try to charm this man,' the girl was saying bitterly to herself; 'that is my business as a woman, – otherwise' –

But Viola did not smile, except undesignedly sometimes when Philip's amusing talk entertained her against her will. She maintained a politely cold demeanour, appearing a little to lose her shyness in the yet stronger feeling of womanly pride.

The old childish dislike to this man had of course lost its venom, but the memory of it was not without its influence on her present feelings, and these were further complicated by the knowledge of the momentary murderous impulse which had so nearly caused her enemy's death. The desire of atonement was still present.

Philip, who, according to his habit, led the way and decided details, discovered a pleasant sequestered spot among the windings of the shrubberies, where there was a seat, and here he suggested that they should rest and meditate.

The spot seemed consecrated to the Goddess of Indolence, so warm and still and lazy was the air, so sleepy were the sounds of the humming bees and droning insects. Viola sat down, while Philip, finding the seat too cramping, asked permission to lie upon the grass at her feet.

'Now this is what I call true philosophy,' he said lazily; 'the man that knows not how to be idle knows not how to live.'

'Most people know how to be idle, I think,' said Viola.

'Pardon me, but I believe there are very few. Italians understand the art, but the Teutonic races[116] are burnt up with a fire of action that makes our country the most glorious and the most uncomfortable in Europe.'

'Only just now Mr. Lancaster was saying that ours is the only language which has the word *comfort* in it at all,' said Viola, falling into the trap that her companion had set for her.

'Yes; we have comfort in our chairs and tables, perhaps,' he said, 'and that is no small matter; still it is not everything: We eat well and sleep softly, but how dearly we pay for these things! Is there not something a little incongruous in the idea of a man toiling hard all his life to enable him at last to buy an easy-chair?'

Viola smiled, and Philip smiled too, but in quite a different fashion. He saw clearly enough that the girl had no intention of paying the usual tribute to his good-looks and brilliant prospects, but the omission only attracted him. He was tired of girls who could be had for the asking, and less.

It would be a delightful task to kindle those beautiful eyes with an unknown emotion, and to make the proud heart beat more quickly in its owner's despite. That would be a victory worth having; an intoxicating tribute to his power and skill and fascination.

Philip had scarcely believed in the existence of a girl totally uninfluenced by worldly considerations, but he was half-disposed to forswear his customary cynicism in Viola's favour. He was too keen to be uncompromisingly cynical. He saw, too, that in order to arouse in her the feelings he desired to arouse, her ideas must first be led to impersonal subjects, so that her present hostility might be lulled.

His studies of human nature made him calculate that hostility was a better ground to work upon than indifference. Hostility implied feeling, and feeling was always fruitful. Again, women's hostility was of a passionate, unfounded order, that might just as reasonably be amity; therefore it was capable of transformation.

Philip did not think all this out in so many words; the ideas floated through his mind, as idly as the flies drifted through the atmosphere, while all the time he went on talking, waiting at intervals for Viola's answers, and treating them, when they half-unwillingly came, with a deference that was very flattering, in a man of his experience and acknowledged power.

Her expression had begun to change already; she was forgetting herself in what he was saying, and Philip now found a new and *piquant* charm in the face; so much so that he began to wonder if he should be able to keep up the judicial spirit of the experimenter, while he sought to summon expressions yet more beautiful into the deep eyes and the proud, sweet lips. The doubt did not at all detract from the interest of the pastime.

After a time, he ventured to leave the impersonal topics which had served their purpose so well, and to broach the subject of the past and its memories.

'How you used to hate me in those days!' he said, with a sigh. 'It was really rather strange, I think, for I used to be quite fond of you, and one imagines that love begets love, does one not?'

'I have never forgiven myself for what I did,' said Viola, 'and the memory of it haunts me to this day.'

'My dear Miss Sedley, you distress me!' cried Philip, raising himself on one elbow; 'I had no idea you took the matter so seriously.'

'I have reason to,' she said, shaking her head.

'But nothing happened,' he argued. 'Here I am, all safe and sound, and uncommonly jolly (especially at this moment) into the bargain.'

'No thanks to me,' said Viola.

'Yes; for present mercies, thanks to you particularly,' he returned.

She looked at him with a puzzled air. Could he really care, however slightly, for her society, he who had travelled all over the world and mingled with the brilliant and the beautiful of all countries? She gave a faint movement of the shoulders, as if she abandoned the problem in despair. But the conversation, the mere presence of an intelligent human being to one in her monotonous circumstances, was sufficiently intoxicating, without the aid of flattery.

'If you still reproach yourself for that old offence,' Philip continued, 'I think it is high time that it should be expunged from the list of your sins. I will forgive you – there's my hand on it – and now you have no excuse for thinking of it any more.'

'Oh! but you don't know, you don't know!' cried Viola, drawing away the hand he had endeavoured to take. 'I can't let you forgive me in ignorance of my offence.'

Philip looked astonished.

'Do tell me what you mean,' he pleaded; 'I thought I did know your offence, such as it was. I suppose you didn't attempt to put prussic acid in my medicine, or resort to perfume-poisons, after the manner of the Borgias?[117] If you did, upon my honour, you would be an entrancingly interesting person!'

'Interesting because I was criminal!' cried Viola.

'In this age of mediocrity even crime becomes interesting, not because it is crime, but because it is dramatic. There is a craving for the dramatic in these days, for the all-sufficient reason that we are doomed to lives of such monotonous respectability. The Philistines seem determined to make things so deadly dull that they drive us into extravagant excesses, for the mere sake of relief. The poor man takes to drinking because his home is detestable; the rich man plunges into dissipation because irritating social laws make respectability unbearable. I fear I startle you, Miss Sedley; but if you think over what I have said, I believe you will come some day to admit that there is truth in this view.'

He certainly *had* startled her! – *Respectability unbearable*! Had she heard aright? The world was seized with an attack of vertigo; Good had flung its arm round the waist of Evil, and the two were waltzing together as if they had been partners in the dance from time immemorial.

She scarcely understood what Philip meant by social laws; she 'could not see the town for houses.'[118] She had passed her whole life under the shadow of these laws, and was unable to conceive a state of things where they were absent or different. In any case, she felt it her duty to struggle against the thought that Philip had suggested.

She did not believe that he was a good man, and therefore it was necessary to be on her guard against his cleverness.

'But a truce to these heresies,' said Philip, with a smile, guessing her state of mind; 'I want to hear your confession. I assure you of my forgiveness beforehand, if that is of any value in your eyes. Now tell me; what was the secret enormity of which you were guilty at the time of my accident?'

'You talk lightly of the matter, because you don't believe I could be guilty of' –

She hesitated and coloured painfully.

'Let me help you,' said Philip, more and more interested. 'You really *did* put poison in my medicine? – is that it?'

'Oh! no, no, not so deliberate as that,' said the girl, thrusting away the idea as if it were something tangible; 'but when you were sitting at the edge of that window in the ruin, you remember, and you made me so angry; – well, for a moment, as I flung myself upon you, I – I actually meant to – push you over if I could. It was a moment of insanity, but a thousand lifetimes could not blot it out; it is there now and for all eternity!'

Philip looked up at her, deeply pondering.

By some instinct that comes at the right moment to born rulers of men, he felt that he ought not to make too light of this matter. Viola's sense of guilt gave him a valuable handle by which he could work upon her feelings. He looked away without speaking, and allowed the silence to prolong itself painfully.

'You don't think me 'interesting' for committing a crime when it comes to the point,' said Viola at length, fixing her eyes straight before her.

Philip heaved a long sigh.

'Believe me, I admire the force of character that prompts to vigorous actions, but – I confess I am sorry and surprised to learn this of you.'

Smarting under the implied reproach, Viola was yet almost relieved to find that he did not really take a light view of the matter. Philip's instinct had been faultless.

'At the same time you must not forget that you were a mere child at the time, and therefore not responsible. Such an impulse would be impossible to you now.'

'Oh! yes, yes, I hope so; but that memory makes me frightened of myself. I don't know what may be in me.'

'It will be interesting to find out,' muttered Philip, more to himself than to her.

As he spoke the sound of footsteps disturbed the serenity of the scene, and Philip made an impatient gesture.

'Hang it! there are the others.'

But it was only Mrs. Russell Courtenay and Harry, who were taking a stroll round the garden together.

'Oh! here you are!' cried the lady. 'How comfortable you look! Mr. Dendraith, I do think you are the laziest person I ever met.'

'Do you not know the wisdom of the Persians, Mrs. Courtenay, who say that you should never walk if you can ride, never ride if you can sit, and never sit if you can lie?'[119]

'And never live if you can die, they ought to add,' said Harry, 'if they wish to be consistent.'

'I expect they don't though,' returned Philip. 'Miss Sedley and I have been talking over old times,' he went on, 'and we have come to the conclusion that the past is a mistake, and that there is no time like the present.'

As this was a sheer invention on the spur of the moment, Viola looked at him in astonishment.

'Miss Sedley, you really make a very bad conspirator,' he said, laughing. 'You don't enter into the spirit of the creative genius at all; you should never stare in a thunderstruck manner at such a simple *jeu d'esprit*.[120] I assure you it is disconcerting in the highest degree.'

'Don't spoil that beautiful innocence!' cried Mrs. Courtenay. 'Mr. Lancaster, I think our motto is '*excelsior*,'[121] is it not?'

'That motto is my aversion,' said Philip.

'Well, good-bye, and I do hope you won't propound any more heresies to Miss Sedley. I don't know what her mamma would say.'

'Wouldn't it be pleasant to go for a stroll too?' Viola suggested. 'The great heat is over now.'

'What, you too tormented with this disease of energy!' cried Philip. 'So be it, then; let us away. Your will, of course, is my law.'

CHAPTER XII

A WORKING HYPOTHESIS

Philip Dendraith had never been troubled with shyness. He did not hesitate to present himself every day at Clevedon, openly telling his hostess that her house had so many attractions to offer an idle man that she must take the consequences. He made no secret of his desire for Viola's society, singling her out with flattering persistence, and putting forth all his powers of fascination. She had begun to exert a very potent spell over him, rather to his own dismay. As for Viola, her manner was already improving under the influence of the new experience. The first coat of paint had been laid on, as her aunt said.

When Harry called one afternoon, he found, to his annoyance, that Philip was, as usual, among the group under the beech-tree on the tennis-ground.

He and Viola were standing a little apart, Viola playing nervously with a bunch of June roses.

'Do you remember,' Harry heard him say to her – 'do you remember, yesterday afternoon, that you dropped a rose you were wearing, and you walked back along the way you had come in hopes of finding it?

Viola gave a gesture of assent.

'I had not the courage then to confess my sin (let us repeat our stroll of yesterday, by the by), but it lies heavy on my conscience, and I am come to-day to ask absolution. Here is the lost treasure.'

Harry saw him bring out of his breast-pocket a withered rose, just as the two figures turned a corner and disappeared into the shrubberies.

He would have given worlds to hear what followed.

When they presently returned, the rose was still in Philip's hand. What did that mean? Had he obtained absolution and leave to keep the rose as his own? or had she treated the whole incident as too trivial to notice? For the first supposition Viola seemed too repellant; for the second, too shy. As often happens in life, circumstances must have obliged her to do violence to one side or other of her nature.

Harry pondered deeply upon the state of affairs: he half-suspected that Lady Clevedon had been urged by her brother to bring about a marriage between Viola and the heir of Upton Court. For Viola it would surely prove most disastrous. She was as a bird in the hands of the fowler. Philip's power was of a cold and watchful order, not to be gainsaid. Perhaps in the long-run her force of character might be no less than his, but it was of a different kind. She was open to pain, while he was almost insensible. He was a man, she was a woman; – he a man more than usually callous; more than usually overbearing; she a woman more than usually sensitive, more than usually disposed to prefer the claims of others to her own.

Would nobody play the part of Perseus to this Andromeda?[122] Ah! how powerless a man is to help a woman, however much he may wish to do so! – especially if – Harry pulled himself up abruptly.

'This comes of idleness,' he said to himself impatiently; 'the sooner you return to you duties the better, my friend. Have you steered your course so far prosperously, with philosophy for your compass and hope for your pole-star, only to fall into this pitfall after all? It won't do; it is folly, accursed folly, and will only lead to heartache. You can't do things by halves, so if you are wise you will escape while there is yet time. But *is* there yet time?'

'Don't ask yourself that question, you fool, or you are lost!' he exclaimed. 'And don't flatter yourself you can do anything to help her. As for that appealing look that you see in her eyes, that is simply the effect of your own imagination, the result of "expectant attention," as Dick Evans would say. Philip is too much for her powers of resistance. Her will flutters helplessly at the call of his; she is like a terrified, half-bewitched bird when it hears the cry of the hawk. It is an iniquitous piece of work altogether!'

The next time that Harry went to Clevedon, Mr. Sedley was there, making himself agreeable to Arabella, and behaving altogether in his best and sweetest manner. This was an evil portent! He had proposed a walk to the sea, and Harry was asked to join the expedition.

As Viola and Philip were of the party, he assented, and he had the pleasure of listening for two long miles to the not very interesting conversation of Mr. Sedley while the other couple walked on ahead. Mr. Sedley was inclined to hang back to examine the crops, about which he had much to say. These were now in their freshest and greenest stage, gleaming and glistening under the blandishments of the sun, which seemed to be enticing the young life to new, and ever-new development, to end, as Harry moodily thought, in the final massacre of harvest.

The parable was painfully obvious. Seldom had he felt more sad and depressed than he did to-day amid these sunny lands, where peace and plenty beamed, with rosy midsummer faces, while the sea sang its eternal slumber-song a few hundred feet below. In another month or less these scenes and people would have vanished; he must take his part in a new drama, and, alas! in that new drama he felt not the faintest interest!

Life seemed to him a miserable, tantalising, disappointing failure, full of heartache and tragedy; the sunniest temperament in the world could not save one from the universal doom!

So little would suffice for happiness: freedom, work, leisure, music, friendship, and – love. He did not demand fame or fortune, luxury or power; only those essentially human requirements without which no life is complete.

In consequence of Mr. Sedley's delays the other two had now gone a long way ahead, and Harry watched them nearing the cliff's edge and the point where the pathway of descent began. A superstitious feeling possessed him that if they went down that descent together Viola's fate was sealed. It would symbolise the future. He tried to urge his companion forward, but Mr. Sedley was relating an anecdote, and would not be hurried. He even found it necessary to pause now and then for greater emphasis.

Muttering an unintelligible apology, Harry broke away and set off at a run for the cliff-side. But he was too late. He saw Philip hold out his hand, and then the two went down together to the deeps.

Harry felt as if something were tightening about his heart, as he stood there facing the breezes that came freshly up from the sea. The sunshine was beating upon the sweet grass and flowers just as before, and the sea murmured mournfully in the bright loneliness of the scene: 'the gladness is taken away and the joy out of the plentiful field.'[123] Oh! the folly and madness of staking one's whole life upon one human being among the millions, so that the very heavens and earth might be blotted out, or left dark and ruined in their places!

The folly and the inevitableness of it!

* * * * *

'I wonder what is the matter with Harry,' Adrienne said to Dick Evans, whose friendship for her brother made him a suitable confidant on this topic; 'I never saw him so moody and distracted; I can't think what's come to him.'

'I suppose he hasn't got a rash anywhere?' inquired the scientific Dick thoughtfully, but Adrienne laughed at this supposition.

'Liver may be out of order,' said Dick. 'Does he eat well?

'Like a cormorant.[124] No, it isn't his liver. I think (if he *is* to be out of sorts, poor boy!) it would be more convenient if it *were* – from a housekeeper's point of view.'

'He must be in love,' said Dick, stooping at last from the pinnacle of science.

'Nonsense!' said Adrienne, startled. 'Oh dear, I hope not; it, would be such a serious matter with him, and I don't see how it could be otherwise than unfortunate. You know he has only a couple of hundreds a year[125] besides his pay.'

'Don't distress yourself in this anticipatory manner, Adrienne,' advised Dick;' I put forth the suggestion merely as a working hypothesis.'

That 'working hypothesis' haunted Adrienne all night. She longed to speak to her brother, and to comfort him if she could, for her nature was essentially sympathetic; but Harry made some nonsensical reply to every tentative remark, and she had, as usual, to give in.

Mrs. Dixie, unaccustomed to her son's new mood, laughed inappropriately when he was remarking to the effect that all is vanity; and when she discovered that Harry actually meant that all was vanity, she had a whispered consultation with Adrienne about camomile pills,[126] and wondered if Harry would be very angry if she sent for the doctor.

In spite of his wise reflections the young man went next day to Clevedon. Apparently some arrangement for prolonging Viola's visit had been come to, – perhaps on the occasion of Mr. Sedley's call – for Harry found, with distress, that she was not to leave at the end of the week, according to the first intention. This looked very like a conspiracy between brother and sister, of which the girl was to be the victim. Sadly she needed a champion, but who was to take that difficult post? Harry did what he could: he tried to prevent too many *tête-à-têtes*[127] with Philip, regardless of the latter's frowns; and he endeavoured to turn Viola's attention from her admirer, and to rivet it – if that were possible – upon himself. There was very little to be done, and Harry feared that Lady Clevedon would be annoyed at his interference, carefully as he tried to veil it.

Philip at this period was in his happiest mood – not at all a good sign, Harry thought, especially as he seldom mentioned Viola's name. He was loud in his praises of Lady Clevedon, who was one of the most agreeable women Philip had ever met, and, 'ye gods, wasn't she sharp!'

If Harry seemed moody and out of sorts in the bosom of his family, he took care not to let that accusation be made against him at. Clevedon. Philip, above all, must not suspect his secret.

'I will say this for our hostess,' said Philip expansively, 'she knows how to make her house attractive. And what women she picks up! Arabella is simply bewildering!'

'So her host seems to think – a man who would 'rather face a crocodile than meet a ladies' school.'[128] I believe, when all secrets are made known, that that poor fellow will be found to have undergone excruciating agony on account of Arabella.'

'Hail, Arabella!' exclaimed Philip, raising an imaginary goblet to his lips; 'tricksey-wicksey Arabella, sweet and stylish Arabella, who would not love thee, Arabella?'

'Poor woman! I am sure she does her little best to please you, you ungrateful fellow!'

'I am tired of women who try to please me,' said Philip, stretching himself lazily. 'It is quite extraordinary how they will run after a man in these days of universal competition! The marriage-market is overstocked; a woman has to get married at all hazards, and she will stick at nothing in the way of business. A man must be circumspect indeed to escape the dangers that beset him in the highways of society. "He that fleeth from the fear shall fall into the pit; and he that getteth up out of the pit shall be taken in the snare."'[129]

'Well done!' exclaimed Harry. 'I didn't know you could quote Scripture.'

'My dear fellow, I was brought up on it; perhaps that may account for my cynicism regarding the adorable sex. However, I need no excuse, if you had run the gauntlet with as many mothers of daughters as I have, you would be a blasphemer too. They are simply pirates, neither more nor less!'

'It must be hard lines on a girl who doesn't want to be flung at a man's head, to have a predatory mother.'

'Show me that girl, and I will wear her in my heart of hearts!'

'Well, without aspiring to that honourable post for my sister, I may point to her, – and then there is Miss Sedley.'

Philip smiled.

'She is inexperienced, and she has been seriously brought up.'

'I doubt if all the mothers in Christendom would have made her into a fisher of men.'

Philip shook his head.

'Lives there a woman who is not Fortune's slave? Upon my soul, I believe (with the exception of one or two who don't know anything about life) that such a being does not exist!'

'She must be a considerable heroine, I admit,' said Harry, 'for Fortune is hard upon women who refuse her obedience, and, in point of fact, I suppose even a woman must live. My sister at least goes so far as to hint it.'

'Well, I suppose she must, in spite of Talleyrand,'[130] said Philip, with a shrug of the shoulders. 'Henry VIII, when he cleared away the monasteries, might have left the convents, I think.'

'Do you? Ask my sister, and Mrs. Lincoln for *their* opinion on that point.'

'Oh! Mrs. Lincoln's eccentricities put her out of court,' said Philip.

The appearance of Viola at this juncture interrupted the colloquy. Philip sprang up and waved her to his place on the seat, and Harry rose also.

'Please don't move; my mother is here; she came about two hours ago; and Aunt Augusta says, will you come in and see her, Mr. Dendraith?'

'With the greatest pleasure; but how cruel of her to send such a messenger,' cried Philip, allowing his meaning to be guessed by the ingenious. 'Lancaster, try and be entertaining enough to keep Miss Sedley till I return,' and he strolled off with his easy, swinging walk across the grass.

'Philip has set me a task that I don't feel at all equal to,' said Harry, piercing a plantain with his stick.

'Oh! Please don't trouble – I don't want you to be entertaining – though you always are so.'

'A man can take no heavier burden upon himself than the reputation of a buffoon,' said Harry. 'Nevermore – though the role of chief mourner would better become him – may he lay it down.'

'Are you – a chief mourner?' asked Viola, her voice softening at the call for sympathy.

'I am indeed,' said Harry; 'and sole mourner too, if that is not paradoxical.'

There was a pause; then the very atmosphere around seemed to throb, as Harry heard his own words escape him: 'My trouble is on your account.'

'*On my account!*'

Her surprise made him add hastily, 'I ought not to have said this much, as I can't say all I should like to say; – in fact, I fear I am very impertinent to speak at all; it was not premeditated.'

She looked fairly bewildered.

'I wish you would tell me frankly what you mean,' she said; 'you don't know of any pending misfortune for me or mine, do you? But if you did, you could scarcely take it so much to heart.'

'There you mistake,' said Harry; 'but' – he pressed his hands to his head – 'I ought really not to have spoken in this way. Forget and forgive it.'

It was impossible to speak out! it seemed so underhand, so mean, especially since he had a new and selfish motive to prevent the marriage. If Philip had won the girl's heart, and was trying to win her hand, what right had any one to interfere? It was not as if she were being actually forced into the marriage. Yet could this inexperienced creature; brought up to submit her own will in all things, be regarded as a free agent, when people like Lady Clevedon, Philip Dendraith, Mr. Sedley, and even Arabella were conspiring against her?

'If you can warn me about something, and will not, Mr. Lancaster, I think you are unkind,' said Viola reproachfully.

'Oh! don't say that; if you knew how it hurts me to hear it !' he exclaimed. 'What can I do?'

He paused in deep and painful thought.

'This much I think I may say, and I must trust to you to take it in good part. It is my earnest advice to you to leave this place as soon as you can, no matter on what pretext, and if possible to leave the neighbourhood; at any rate, refuse to see, or avoid seeing, all callers. I know it sounds ridiculously like an advertisement in the Agony Column,[131] but I can't help that. If you would only take what I say on trust, and not demand further explanation, you would do me a very great favour. My desire to serve you is most heartfelt, believe me.'

His manner and the thrill in his voice amply confirmed his words.

Viola's reply was cut short by the arrival of Philip and Arabella, and Harry had no means of finding out for the rest of that day how she had taken his strange advice, or whether she intended to act on it.

With increased seriousness Mrs. Dixie, on his return to the Cottage, began to talk of sending for the doctor, and Adrienne to ponder over Dick Evans' 'working hypothesis.'

CHAPTER XIII

A CRISIS

'Well, Marion, what now? Has Richard been forgetting he is a gentleman again? Drinking, swearing, or both?'

In his sister Mr. Sedley always found one of his severest critics.

'I did not come here to complain of my husband, Augusta.'

'I wish to Heaven you had! You really ought not to allow him to trample on you as he does. Remember, a man will always be as much of a fiend as you will let him.'

Mrs. Sedley was silent.

'Well, Marion, what is the trouble?'

'It is about my poor daughter,' replied Mrs. Sedley; 'her father has been speaking to me very peremptorily on the subject of her marriage.'

'He spoke to me about it too,' said Lady Clevedon; '*not* peremptorily,' she added, with a laugh.

'He has so much respect for your judgment.'

'He has such a wholesome dread of my agile tongue,' said Lady Clevedon. 'Well, Marion?'

'Mr. Dendraith has spoken to Richard on the subject, and asked his consent to an engagement between him and Viola, but he has not yet spoken definitely to Viola herself.'

'I thought it was coming to that,' said Lady Clevedon, 'and I think it is a matter for rejoicing. The girl could not make a better marriage, and I need not remind you of the important bearing that it will have upon the affairs of the family in general – the boys and so on.'

Mrs. Sedley sighed. 'Yes; I do not overlook all that; but – will it be for Viola's happiness? I fear greatly that Mr. Dendraith is a man of no religious principle.'

'Perhaps he may have what is better,' said Lady Clevedon, with pagan calmness: 'moral principle.'

'I fear he is not even all one might wish as to that, if one is to believe rumours.'

'He has his enemies, and I dare say he is not immaculate, but I think he is just the man for Viola; he is born to rule and has the devil's own temper. Women are all the better for a little frightening.'

It had, however, never occurred to Lady Clevedon to look out for the terrific creature who could frighten *her.*

'Before Viola came to stay with you,' continued Mrs. Sedley, 'she made her father very angry by avoiding Mr. Dendraith when he called. Richard spoke to me about it, and insisted on my using my influence to bring her to a different frame of mind. It was very painful to me, for the poor child took it so much to heart, and cried out that even I had forsaken her.'

'So you told me at the time,' said Lady Clevedon, 'and very miserable you were about it.'

'Now, however, by all accounts,' Mrs. Sedley went on, 'she seems to be changing in her feelings towards Mr. Dendraith. Is that really the case?'

'He has certainly made an impression.'

'Ah! that troubles me!' cried Mrs. Sedley; 'that troubles me greatly!'

'Oh! was there ever such a determined miserable!' exclaimed Lady Clevedon. 'To-day she comes to me like Niobe,[132] all tears, because her daughter objects to the marriage proposed for her by her parents; to-morrow she comes to me once more – the identical drops still wet upon her cheeks, ready to do duty over again; but this time because the daughter is *favourable* to the marriage! My dear Marion, what would you have?'

'I would have my child both good and happy, and I am sadly afraid that no woman can hope for such a combination in this world.'

'Depends on what you mean by good and what you mean by happy,' said Lady Clevedon.

'My position,' continued Mrs. Sedley, 'is the more trying because dear Viola would do anything that I asked her to do. She makes me her guide and her conscience. How can I persuade her into a marriage which, I fear, may not be for her happiness? And how, on the other hand, can I conscientiously urge her to oppose her father's will? Can the blessing of Heaven descend upon the rebellious child, or upon the mother who encourages her rebellion?'

'If the woman hasn't ingeniously got herself impaled upon *another* two-legged dilemma!' exclaimed Lady Clevedon. 'Marion, how do you manage to fall in with these monstrosities? You can't be content with a sound, able-bodied trouble, like any other Christian; you must needs pick up creatures with more heads and limbs than they ought to have – a sort of Briarean woe[133] dreadful to contemplate. If you had been a general, Marion, the Caudine Forks[134] is the battle that you would have fought, and straightway you would have gone and got yourself ingeniously wedged between the prongs!'

'I think life is made up of these many-sided difficulties,' said Mrs. Sedley sadly. 'Augusta,' she went on, laying her hand on her sister-in-law's arm, 'you have influence with Richard; should the poor child really show a repugance to the marriage, you will not refuse to use it on her side.'

Lady Clevedon shook her head.

'I can't promise anything. The marriage seems to me so rational that I hope Viola will be wiser than to show any repugnance to it. I don't think, mind you, that a girl should marry a rich man when she dislikes him, but there is no reason to dislike a man simply because he is rich and well-born. Many romantic girls make a point of doing that as in duty bound.'

No help was to be had from her sister-in-law in this matter, and Mrs. Sedley had then to come to the second object of her visit, namely, to take Viola back to the Manor-House. Lady Clevedon scoffed and scorned, and insisted that her niece must stay, but Mrs. Sedley was quietly determined. She did not tell her sister-in-law that the girl had herself written, earnestly entreating her mother to recall her.

Strangely still and lifeless seemed the old home when Viola saw it again after her ten days' absence. With all its familiarity, it was to her as if she had never seen the place before. And the routine of the days! without change, without movement; they were like a stagnant, over-shadowed pool, where there was never a glimpse of the blue heaven, never a ripple or a sparkle from dawn to dark. Viola thought the life of Clevedon empty and flippant, but at least it had some flash and brilliance.

She felt restless and unhappy: She could not settle to her old life; memories of the past ten days haunted her, and filled her with a vague longing for excitement.

Some new chord in her being had been touched; she was angry with herself; angry with her surroundings; ashamed at her own inability to resume her former simple life. She felt she had lost ground; new feelings made havoc with her self-control; she was like a rudderless ship at the mercy of contrary winds. Gardening was the best sedative for this restlessness, though that occupation had the disadvantage of allowing her thoughts to work as well as her hands.

Contrary to Mr. Sedley's hopes, Philip Dendraith did not at once follow up his preliminary overtures. He was reported to have gone up to town, a proceeding which caused much suffering to the family of the Lord of the Manor. Mr. Sedley suspected that Viola had rebuffed her lover, and she had to listen to some parental plain-speaking on the subject.

'If it were not for my mother, I would not remain here another moment!' Viola had once cried out passionately, bringing down upon her head such a torrent of rage and scorn that she actually left her father fully meaning to do even as she had said. Such taunts were more than she could endure. But at the sight of her mother her resolution broke down; she could not make yet sadder that sad, pale face, and bring tears to the eyes that had shed so many bitter ones already.

On one balmy afternoon Viola betook herself to the rose-garden, a narrow grass-plot beside the Lovers' Walk, the dark foliage of whose yew-trees formed an almost tragic background to the beds of roses and summer flowers among which Viola was moving, busy with her scissors and her hoe.

She was dressed in white; her sunlit figure stood out in strong contrast to the dark masses behind her. A fanciful person might have seen symbols in the picture.

A tame jackdaw, Bill Dawkins' successor but not supplanter in her affections, hopped amiably around, amusing himself with pecking at pieces of stick, hauling weeds out of Viola's basket on the sly, and other mischievous actions which he knew he might venture on with impunity.

'Charming!' cried a voice, breaking the sunny silence. 'Would that I were an artist!'

Viola turned, and the admired picture was by no means marred by the addition of Philip Dendraith's handsome figure as he raised his hat and strode across the grass-plot.

She coloured and smiled in a manner that pleased him well.

'So it is to you that the Manor-House owes its wonderful roses! *L'art être belle!*[135] What better teacher could they have?'

Viola sighed. She wished that she could understand this man, but not being able to, she resigned herself to her ignorance.

'I find they learn best how to be beautiful by being happy,' she said, 'so I try to make them so.'

She was going on with her hoeing now in a desultory way.

'And you make then happy by bestowing on them the light of your presence,' said Philip in a low voice.

'And by introducing them to my most agreeable friends,' added Viola, with a quick glance.

Philip almost started; the speech was so unlike one of Viola's. He had expected blushes and downcast looks, and he encountered instead something distantly approaching mockery. It was one of those excursions from her normal self which had now and then, of late, caused her to wonder at herself. She had caught unconsciously the trick of phrase characteristic of Clevedon and its guests; and this, still echoing in her memory, was given forth, here and there, almost mechanically, as we hum some haunting refrain. But the change of tone passed away as suddenly as it had come, and she blushed at her own masquerading.

'My dear Miss Sedley, I think you have worked long enough,' said Philip, taking the hoe from her with gentle insistence. 'Your roses have had you all to themselves too long; it is my turn now to be made happy' –

'And beautiful,' added Viola. 'I make my roses happy by watering them' –

'Miss Sedley!' exclaimed Philip, looking round at her, 'I am afraid you have become rather flippant since I had the pleasure of seeing you.'

'I fear I have,' said Viola, with a sigh.

'Don't sigh; it is quite charming, I assure you, and becomes you mightily. Only please don't be too hard upon *me*.'

Without reply she allowed herself to be led to the rustic seat opposite the sun-dial, whereon the jackdaw sat, alternately pruning his feathers and pecking at the shadow with his beak.

The bird seemed agitated when Philip took his place beside Viola.

'Your jackdaw is apparently jealous,' he said. 'I suppose you are very fond of him. I should imagine you had a large power of loving.'

'And of hating,' added the girl.

'Yes; *I* can answer for that!' exclaimed Philip, with a laugh. 'Don't you think, now, that you owe me some reparation for having hated me so fiercely in the past?'

She looked troubled.

'Don't you think,' Philip went on, drawing nearer to her, 'that if the possession of your love had become the supreme desire and object of my life, you ought at least to try to give it to me?'

She breathed quickly, but answered nothing.

'You must know, dear Viola, that such *is* my supreme desire; that you have entered and possessed my heart as I thought no woman ever could have possessed it; you have enslaved my thoughts, my dreams, my very will! This last week has been a blank to me because you were absent. I am telling you the absolute truth – I have never felt before what I feel now; I shall never be happy till you promise to love me and be my wife.'

He was so much in earnest that he had thrown off his usual calm manner; his measured periods had given place to the rough, quick utterance of strong emotion.

There is something peculiarly moving in the emotion of a person generally very self-possessed, the more so if the person is of Philip Dendraith's type.

'Viola, don't turn away from me; tell me, do you not love me?'

'Kiaw!' said the inconvenient jackdaw, in a loud voice. This was merely a displeased comment upon the arrival of Thomas with a watering-pot, Thomas not being in the habit of showing that deference towards Jack which Jack thought was his due.

'Ill-omened old man!' exclaimed Philip; 'and you, most obstructive fowl, well is it for you that you enjoy the protection of a lady's presence! Who was it that said that a woman can forgive anything in her lover, except that he should appear ridiculous? Have I committed the unpardonable offence?'

'Oh! don't talk to me like this!' cried Viola, with a desperate gesture. 'I am not a clever lady of society who can understand and answer you.'

She looked round in search of Thomas, but that discreet person, having (after a certain lapse of time) seen what was going on, took up his watering-pot and trudged off to 'pastures new,' with an expression about his left eye absolutely beyond human power to describe.

Geoffrey finding him in this sublimated state of knowingness, and receiving from him sundry oracular hints, was 'prepared for the worst,' as he said, more especially as he found his father in a seraphic temper pacing the terrace with Mrs. Sedley, and calling her attention to the exceeding fineness of the 'immemorial elms.' Those elms were in process of being secured to the family, perhaps for centuries.

'I fear you think that because I am sometimes flippant I can never be serious,' said Philip earnestly, 'but you never were more mistaken in your life. I own that I think very few things of much consequence, but for that very reason I have the more ardour to throw into those that I *do* care about. Ah! Viola, don't tell me that I have set my heart on the unattainable!'

The conflict that was going on in her mind at this moment was entirely unsuspected by Philip; he supposed that her efforts to silence him proceeded from mere girlish bashfulness, and that he had only to persevere in order to complete his triumph.

He leant forward and took her hand.

'Dearest,' he began – and then stopped abruptly, for at his touch Viola had drawn her hand away with a sharp movement anything but suggestive of a coming triumph for him.

'I wish you would not speak like this; you distress me,' she said, in a strange, bewildered way.

'Viola, I think you are really very unkind,' cried Philip, 'when you know how devoted I am to you!'

'I am very sorry,' was all that she would say in reply to this and to other pleading of the same kind.

Philip was astonished, piqued, but all the more determined to achieve his object. He knew that practically it was achieved already, for he had her father on his side, and through him Mrs. Sedley also; that was enough; only he longed to make the girl come to him willingly and gladly. As a last resource alone would he employ the parental influence, but he had no intention of surrendering his purpose, let come what would. Did he not love her as he had never loved before, and was he not ready to lavish upon her every indulgence that money and influence could command? If an unwilling bride, she should become a loving and a happy wife, and what more could the heart of woman desire? Besides, a woman of this type was the slave of her conscience. Marriage changed the colour of things to the feminine mind; what once was black became suddenly white, and *vice versâ*. Duty, religion, convenience, all came trooping to the front after the wedding-ring was fairly on; a man ran no risk in marrying a woman of the dutiful kind, though she had to be dragged to the altar by wild horses. So spoke unequivocally the voice of experience.

'Viola, am I, then, entirely indifferent to you? Would you not care if I were to go away and never come and see you any more?'

Viola's truthfulness obliged her to confess that she *would* care, and Philip, pressing his advantage, made her own that he fascinated her.

'Then why do you repel me as you do? Why will you not accept my love?'

'Oh! don't ask me; – for pity's sake, don't speak of this any more!'

Philip was fairly puzzled, and not a little annoyed. He was silent for a moment, and then said, with an abrupt energy, startlingly different from his ordinary manner, 'You are not engaged secretly to some one else?'

'Oh! no, oh! no,' she said quickly.

The expression of relief that came into his face was as striking as the anxiety that preceded it.

'And your affections are not engaged elsewhere?'

'No.'

'Then I shall prevail! Think of your parents, Viola, if you will not think of me; consider how happy you would make them. I have already spoken to your father, and he gives his consent freely.'

'I do not doubt it,' she said, with bitterness.

A smile flitted across Philip's face.

'And your good mother; she too has set her heart upon our marriage, though she may not tell you so, because she wishes your own heart to decide the question!'

'*My mother!*' exclaimed Viola; 'does *she* wish it?'

'She wishes it, undoubtedly. Why not talk the matter over with her? I do not want to hurry you for an answer, impatient as I am to know my fate. Will you do that? I will come to-morrow, not for my answer, unless you like, but merely to see you again. Do try and think of me as kindly as you can. Ah! dearest, it is hard to leave you in this state of suspense. *Au revoir*,[136] and be merciful. My happiness is in your hands. Good-bye till to-morrow.'

'Kiaw!' said the jackdaw derisively.

CHAPTER XIV

DECIDED

Mrs. Sedley was discovered in the cold shadows of the morning-room which she had chosen for her special domain. It faced north, was severely furnished, and colour apparently had not been invented at the time of its upholstering. She was dressed in black, with dead white folds of muslin at the throat and wrists. Once she had been persuaded to order a gown of stone-colour, which she scarcely ever wore, on the ground that it was too gay for her.

When Viola entered, her mother was sitting working in a low chair; a quiet, grave figure, with smooth, shining hair severely brushed down over the temples, the busy fingers alone giving sign of animation.

She looked up and greeted her daughter with a sad, loving smile.

'What is it, dearest?' she asked, laying her thin hand on the table.

Viola struggled with her habitual reserve for a moment; then she said, 'Mother, Mr. Dendraith has just left me; – and – I want to speak to you.'

Mrs. Sedley dropped her work; her hands trembled. Viola had placed herself beside her mother, with her back to the light. She leant her head on her hand, and spoke in a quick, low tone.

'Mr. Dendraith wants me to marry him; he says he will never be happy until I consent. He says that my father wishes it (which I knew) and that *you* wish it. Is that the case?'

Mrs. Sedley took her daughter's hand in hers, and silently caressed it for a few seconds. Then she bent her head and laid the little hand upon her brow, with a movement more emotional than Viola had ever seen in her before.

'I will tell you all that father and I have been thinking about the matter, dearest. You know that of late there have been many business difficulties, so great that we shall not be able to live here much longer unless some relief comes. In proposing for you, Mr. Dendraith made most generous offers to your father, and as Mr. Dendraith is a man of good family and fortune, handsome, clever, and of agreeable manner, your father thinks that you can have no possible objection to such a marriage. He is naturally anxious for it, as you may suppose, and he cannot understand that you may not care for Mr. Dendraith enough to marry him. Seeing your father so bent upon it, I entreated him to let you have ample opportunity to judge for yourself. I trust your visit to your aunt has given you some insight into Mr. Dendraith's character and your own feelings towards him. Your aunt seemed to think that you were beginning to care for him.'

Viola looked startled.

'Question your own heart searchingly, dear child and consider, too, what is your duty in this matter. Pray for guidance where alone you can obtain it. I have thought and thought till my head and heart ache, and I have prayed, and I fear that I can see only one path of duty for you, my child. Earnestly do I trust that you may be given strength to tread it.'

'Then you *do* desire this marriage?' said Viola.

'I desire only that my child should do what is right and dutiful, leaving the rest to God. Her father, her brothers, all are depending on her decision' –

'And her mother!' cried Viola.

'Oh! do not think of *her*, dearest! She suffers only through the sufferings of her beloved ones. But your father's state of health gives me great anxiety, and if we should have to leave the Manor-House' –

'It might kill him,' said Viola, 'and you too!' – Was it the cold light of the room that made her look so pale?

'On the other hand,' said Mrs. Sedley, 'I do not wish you to enter upon this marriage if it is really repugnant to your feelings. That I cannot countenance. Consider the question from every side, and do not forget that this opportunity may have been given you for the saving of this young man's soul!'

'O mother! it is no more possible to talk to Mr. Dendraith about these matters than to Aunt Augusta. And who am I, of little faith, to move such a man?'

'We know not what instruments it may please the Lord to use,' said Mrs. Sedley.

* * * * *

'Well, Viola, your mother tells me that you have been speaking to her about Philip Dendraith's proposal. I hope you appreciate your wonderful good fortune.'

She was silent.

'The affair had better be brought to a crisis at once; I can't understand why you did not accept him on the spot without this silly girlish shilly-shallying. I am going over now to Upton Court,' and will take your answer and settle the matter out of hand!'

A moment of terrible inward conflict; Viola stood with bowed head and clasped hands, her mother's words burning into her brain: 'duty, right – the rest to God – your father and your brothers – to leave the Manor-House might kill him,' – and above all rose the thought of that mother herself, racked and tortured in the impending misfortune of her family, the real weight of which would fall upon her shoulders.

Viola raised her head. The garden seemed to spin round her; the air became thick and black.

'I'll tell him you say 'yes,' of course,' said her father.

'Tell him I say "yes,"' repeated Viola.

END OF VOLUME I.

THE WING OF AZRAEL

by
Mona Caird

Yesterday, this Day's madness did prepare
To-morrow's Silence, Triumph or Despair.

In THREE VOLUMES.

VOL. II

LONDON:
TRÜBNER & CO., LUDGATE HILL.
1889.

CHAPTER XV

BETROTHED

Sir Philip, noted throughout the county for his dashing equipages, drove over to the Manor-House in the very sprightliest vehicle which it could enter the heart of man to conceive. A brilliant pair of high-stepping, spirited chestnut horses, always stylishly on the point of running away, came spanking down the avenue, 'Youth at the helm' and Lady Dendraith at the prow. Nothing would persuade the old lady to take the box-seat on her husband's many chariots; it made her nervous; so she always took the post of 'Pleasure' in Etty's famous picture.[1] Philip, on the wings of love – as Mr. Sedley jocularly put it – had already arrived, and he and Viola, with the radiant proprietor and his wife, were assembled on the doorstep to welcome the visitors. Sir Philip, waving his whip in gala fashion, drew up the prancing chestnuts, sprang down, helped 'the old lady'[2] to alight, and broke forth into loud expressions of satisfaction at the news.

The two fathers shook hands with the utmost effusion, exchanging boisterous jocularities, and between them making so much noise that the dashing steeds very nearly took fright and ran away down the avenue. Only Philip's dexterity prevented the calamity.

'Well, my dear, I suppose you won't refuse to kiss me *now*,' said Sir Philip, patting Viola on the back.

She made no resistance to the sounding salute of her father-in-law elect, but she did not receive it over-graciously.

She was quiet and cold, and treated Philip with extreme politeness in return for his graceful and flattering homage.

However, the others were too preoccupied to notice this, especially as Viola received Lady Dendraith's hearty expressions of pleasure with answering warmth.

'My dear, there is no one I would rather have for a daughter-in-law than yourself, and I assure you this is to me the best news I have heard for many a long day!'

The Dendraiths stayed to lunch, and heartily enjoyed themselves, Sir Philip undertaking to 'chaff'[3] the betrothed couple in his usual graceful fashion, to Viola's utter bewilderment and dismay.

Philip took it coolly; he owned to having risen an hour earlier than usual that morning; in order to arrive in time for breakfast at the Manor-House; admitted, with a 'What would you?' and a shrug of the shoulders, that he had stolen Viola's portrait from her aunt with all the audacity of a thoroughgoing housebreaker, and generally disarmed his adversaries, by making more severe jests against himself than any one else was able to make against him.

He ate a most hearty luncheon, and drank largely of the champagne that Mr. Sedley brought out in honour of the occasion. He made no secret of his joy, but that was clearly because he chose to take the company into his confidence. He even paraded it in a half-serious, half-jocular manner. It did not beam out of his eyes and suffuse his whole being, as it might have done in a man simpler, and less skilful in self-management.

Fortunately for Viola, even after the departure of the radiant parents, she managed to avoid a *tête-à-tête* with her betrothed. Her bewildered, unwilling, almost somnambulistic repetition of her father's words on the night before, had suddenly – as a whisper may start an avalanche – brought down upon her head a series of consequences for which she was totally unprepared, and which she had not even realised.

The congratulatory visit of Philip's father and mother had startled her into the consciousness that a great step had been taken, never to be retraced.

The position threatened to become very difficult, especially as Philip was far from pliable, and as Viola felt a certain undefined awe and even fear of him, partly on account of her sense that she did not understand him, partly because she felt the merciless grip of his powerful nature underneath the smoothness of his manner. In dancing, the most perfect lightness and grace is the outcome of strength, and this was what Philip's suavity suggested.

He, on his part, had not found the day unsatisfactory, in spite of Viola's rather repellant manner. After all, shrewd as he was, he failed – where so many shrewd men fail – in the interpretation of female character. He thought Viola was simply a little shy. Perhaps a man's views about women are the crucial test of his own character: if there is in him the slightest taint of vulgarity, *there* will it inevitably betray itself.

Whether through the education of his sister's influence, or by the help of some innate sense denied to average men, Harry Lancaster had managed to steer clear of the shallow but popular dogmas which are so often repeated, and with so much *aplomb* that they come to be recognized in literature and life almost as axioms. Many men, he said, while rejecting the worn-out superstitions of dogmatic religion, still cling to the superstitions of society with the simple faith of little children. He had often laughed at Philip's cynicism, on the ground not that it *was* cynicism, but that it was merely the echo of other men's echoed ideas.

Philip denied this. If ever a man was justified in being a cynic – especially about women – he was that man.

He admired Viola Sedley (as he frankly admitted) because she was so entirely unlike the women of society, who had imbued him with a rooted contempt for the sex.

'In proportion as they are clever they are bad,' he said. 'Safety lies in dulness. Talent is agreeable to amuse one's self with, but stupidity is the thing to marry. That is the conclusion that my experience has led me to, though one does not always put one's theories into practice, mind you. Come now, you agree with me at heart, though that sister of yours won't allow you to say so. If you had a few thousands a year, my dear fellow, your ideas of human nature would panorami-cally alter, sister or no sister; a most stupendous piece of scene-shifting! By the bye, I have news for you – no, not about myself just at present – there is a chance of a friend of yours coming to settle in this neighbourhood. Can you guess who it is?'

'Mrs. Lincoln?'

'Right! – the divine Sibella! I wonder how you guessed. You know my father has a small house not far from Upton, and he has offered it to Mrs. Lincoln at a low rent, being glad to get it kept in repair. The mother is opposed to the arrangement; she doesn't think the 'Divinia Commedia,'[4] as I call her, a proper person. I tolerantly represent to my parent that the separation was *his* fault, but, of course, without effect. My father is dazzled with the 'Commedia's' *beaux yeux*[5] (though he denies it), and declares that she is an injured and immaculate crea-ture, deserving all sympathy. You know there was some scandal about a fellow, – I don't remember his name' –

'Mrs. Lincoln shrugs her shoulders at the scandal,' said Harry.

'But my mother shakes her head. You seem ready to be her champion, as of old. Well, she wants backing. Upton will not have her at any price.'

'*Tant pis pour Upton.*'[6]

Philip laughed.

'How do you suppose Lady Clevedon will act in the matter?'

'I doubt if she will call,' said Harry. 'Mrs. Sedley herself is not more strict in her notions of conventional propriety. My cousin always speaks of Mrs. Lincoln as 'that woman,' which does not look encouraging.'

'The feminine anathema!' exclaimed Philip, laughing. 'How hard women are on one another!'

'Who is it says that a woman in the pillory restores the original bark to man-kind?'[7]

'Good!' cried Philip; 'and the feminine "yap, yap," how sweet it must sound in the ears of the condemned!'

'Mrs. Lincoln once said to me that where a woman blames, a man simply laughs disrespectfully, and gets credit for more tolerance while committing the greater cruelty.'

'She is very keen,' observed Philip.

'She also says that, take it altogether, there is nothing a proud woman has more to dread than the approval of society.'

'One of her many paradoxes. The divine one is clever, but unbalanced. If she had played her cards well, she might at this moment be held up as a model of all the virtues.'

'Yes; but she does not value such bubble reputation,'[8] said Harry. 'Upton need not imagine that she is waiting in her best frock, with beating heart, for it to call upon her. Ten to one, she won't notice whether she is called upon or not. She comes here to be quiet, not to be called upon.'

'To "wait till the clouds roll by,"'[9] said Philip. 'Well, that's piece of news number one; now for piece of news number two. Can you guess it also?'

Harry gave a visible start. 'Anything important?' he asked.

'Not, perhaps, as regards universal history, but as regards local celebrities, – very much so.'

'Local celebrities? – Mrs. Pellett has dismissed the pupil-teacher for wearing pink ribbons on Sunday.'

'No; try again?'

'Something very surprising?'

'Nothing ever surprised me more, I can assure you,' said Philip, with a laugh.

'Mrs. Pellett has been wearing pink ribbons herself.'

'No; something more astonishing than that.'

'Mr. Pellett recognised her when he met her unexpectedly out walking?'

'No – worse than that.'

'Arabella has joined the Salvation Army?'[10]

'Good Heavens, no! What next?'

'I am exhausted. Caleb Foster has ceased to allude to Kant, and has nothing to say about Socrates; Mrs. Pellett has attempted the life of the Queen,[11] and has been discovered with an infernal machine[12] concealed about her person; Mr. Evans has given up trying to get subscriptions for a new spread-eagle lectern (that 'abominable idol'[13] condemned by our ancestors); and Mrs. Evans ceases to take interest in the school-children's plain needlework. Now, I will guess no more; human ingenuity can go no further.'

'This is embarrassing,' said Philip. 'I hoped you would have relieved me of the duty of making announcement of my own engagement.'

'*Engagement*! You, the despiser of women, the 'old bird' not to be caught with chaff,[14] – you who have kept a firm front against battalions of seasoned veterans! Philip Dendraith, I blush for you!'

'I rather blush for myself,' said Philip, with a shrug; '"He that getteth up out of the pit shall be taken in the snare,"[15] you know. Well, it can't be helped; a man in my position has to marry some day, and I don't think Viola will make the bondage unbearable – nice disposition, you know.'

'Very,' said Harry dryly. 'Accept my congratulations. Is the engagement' – he stopped abruptly and cleared his throat – 'is the engagement publicly announced yet?'

'Scarcely. We do not consider anything public till Mrs. Pellett has been confided in, under pledge of secrecy. The matter was only settled last night; this morning the four parents have been passionately congratulating one another, and I imagine by to-morrow "society" will be in possession of the facts.'

'To-morrow "society" will enjoy itself,' said Harry.

When he returned to the Cottage, Mrs. Dixie, who had been holding a *levée*[16] during the afternoon, showed traces of her royalty still clinging to her. Her ancestor with pink cheeks and a blue coat, reposed majestically among family lace at her throat.

'Well, mother,' he said, kissing her, 'tired out with the pomps and ceremonies? "Uneasy is the head that wears a crown."'[17]

'My son,' said Mrs. Dixie (who might have made her mark in provincial melodrama had she not been called to higher things) – 'My son, your mother wears no crown but that of sorrow.'

'Poor mother!' he said, stroking the white hair affectionately; 'there are many kings and queens so crowned.'

Mrs. Dixie did not appear quite to relish the idea of a multiplicity of rival sovereigns.

'Not many have been tried as I have been tried; every luxury, and a private chaplain – and oh! what a man your father was, Harry!' exclaimed the widow ecstatically.

'Quite a luxury, I am sure,' said her son.

'Upright and honourable as the day, respected wherever he went, – and *such* religious principle! The good he did among the poor too, and the dreadful places he used to go into – to get his rent – and always cheerful and contented. Your dear father was thankful to Heaven, Harry, whatever befell him!'

'About the luxury, of course,' said Harry; 'but was he also thankful about the "sunset?"'

'It was a great blow to him, of course,' said Mrs. Dixie; 'but, as every one remarked, he seemed even more of a gentleman in his downfall, than he had been in the time of his prosperity.'

'They always are,' said Harry, 'and, of course, nothing but death could sever the Riversdale-Clevedon connexion.'

'Nothing but death,' repeated Mrs. Dixie, with solemnity.

Adrienne, coming into the room at the moment, smiled and nodded to Harry as she took up her work, quietly listening and observing, according to her custom.

'We were talking about Death, Adrienne,' said Harry; 'no, not at all in a depressed manner; were we, mother?'

'Quite the contrary.'

Adrienne looked up keenly.

'Were you singing his praises?' she asked. 'You remember the fable of the man who invoked Death,[18] and when he came did not receive him cordially?'

'No one ought to call upon a man in his bare bones,' said Harry; 'it's not decent. The proprieties of life should be observed in all circumstances.'

'Ah! your father used to be so particular about that,' Mrs. Dixie put in piously; 'he always said that if a man couldn't take the trouble to dress himself carefully when he came to see his friends, he had better stay away.'

'That's exactly what I imagine the man said to Death when he arrived with the wind whistling through his ribs and half his teeth out,' observed Harry.

'I never saw your father with his teeth out in my life,' said Mrs. Dixie, 'nor with his ribs anything but properly covered. He was an example to us all, was your poor father.'

'So you often used to say to our poor stepfather in the old times, mother,' said Harry, with a laugh, and an affectionate touch as he rose and left the room.

Adrienne watched him narrowly, and after he was gone she answered her talkative mother entirely at random.

When the little party of three assembled for the evening meal, Adrienne thought that her brother was looking ill, and he seemed more absent-minded than usual, though talking spasmodically in his accustomed vein.

'Harry, you are not well,' she said when they were alone together in the garden, Mrs. Dixie being left to her evening nap in the little parlour.

'Am I not? What makes you think so?'

'Your appearance – your manner' –

'Oh, this accursed reputation for buffoonery!' he exclaimed impatiently. 'If one is not perpetually standing on one's head and stealing strings of sausages, *à la*[19] pantomime clown, one must be ill or depressed. Is there any more awful fate imaginable than that of the man who must be always in good spirits?'

'My dear boy, I don't want to bother you, but it distresses me to see you look as you do.'

'Oh, the ease and joy of the mourner with the broad hat-band!' exclaimed Harry.

'If you are miserable, dear Harry, can no one help you?'

He was silent.

'Can you not confide in me as you used to do in the old childish days? Do I not know how bitter is the sorrow that is borne alone? Harry, there is nothing on earth I would not gladly do for you. Don't you believe it?'

He pressed her hand, but turned away, with a man's dislike to the exhibition of feeling, especially in the presence of a near relative.

'Nothing more has happened to me than has happened to hundreds of better fellows than I am,' he said at last, after a long pause.

A thrush was warbling from an old elm-tree behind the garden; a song sweet, clear, and plaintive, bringing the tears into Adrienne's eyes as she watched the set face of her brother. His profile was towards her, and he leant upon the little gate leading from the garden into the meadow, where a cow was still contentedly grazing in the twilight.

'I am afraid the grief of other 'better fellows' does not make yours easier to bear,' said Adrienne in a low voice.

'You don't think the eels get accustomed to skinning?'[20] said Harry.

'No, I don't, dear.'

'You show real intellectual acumen,' he returned fantastically. 'Very few people understand that grief can be neither more nor less than one person is able to endure; that twenty sorrowing people represent really no more sorrow than is contained by the one greatest sorrower.'

'O Harry, you are talking at random!'

'No; I am quite serious. I have been thinking this out to-day. You cannot add pain to pain, your pain to my pain, and ours to the pain of Mrs. Pellett, for every organism is a world in itself, and its events cannot be mingled with the events of other microcosms, as if they were continuous. This truth carries with it many issues quite contrary to our ordinary ways of thinking, as a little reflection will show.'

Adrienne looked at him, as he leant calmly on the gate, and sighed. She wished that he would confess and bewail his fate, instead of philosophising about microcosms and 'continuous sorrow.' Did ever any human soul get real consolation out of philosophy when the hour of sorrow struck? Adrienne thought not. On the contrary, this keen, clear habit of mind must heighten the pain and enlarge its horizon. It was a misfortune to see too clearly and too far.

If only Harry would be less reserved! But the custom of treating everything in a light, half-humorous spirit had become so ingrained that he was unable to throw it off. Few things in life are more tyrannous than the *rôle* that gradually comes to be attached to us. Only among absolute strangers can we at last fling off its weary weight and move our limbs in freedom.

CHAPTER XVI

WITHOUT MERCY

No sleep did Viola have on that first night of her engagement. Her dismay at the thought of it increased with every black lingering hour as she lay tossing on her pillow, wondering at times if she were under the thrall of a terrible dream. It was all impossible; she could not go on with the engagement; surely Philip himself could not be in earnest about anything so preposterous. He had said that he would ride over in the morning, about ten o'clock, and when the time drew near Viola was seized with a panic, and flinging on her hat and cloak she rushed into the park, and plunged into the deepest recesses of the underwood in order to escape detection in case of pursuit. She began to feel an actual terror of the man to whom she was betrothed. As she drew near to the park boundary, not far from the unused grass avenue – the great elm avenue which had never lost its fascination for her – she heard angry voices in the wood outside, one of them unmistakably Philip's.

Through an opening in the trees, she presently saw him standing, with his left hand on the bridle of his horse, while with his right he thrashed the animal with all his enormous strength. The creature was flinching, and tried to escape from the heavy blows; his glossy sides were bleeding and foam-flecked, and with every savage stroke of the whip he gave a desperate plunge.

Harry Lancaster, who had just come up, was angrily remonstrating.

'How much longer are you going to keep this up?' he asked. 'Can't you see the creature is half-dead with pain?'

'One would think the beast was yours from the interest you take in his welfare,' said Philip, with a sneer, and using with renewed violence the cruel whip.

'Are you a man or a fiend?' exclaimed Harry. 'I will look on at this devilry no longer – you are literally slicing the miserable beast with that whip of yours? Will you leave off, or must I interfere?'

'Interfere at your peril.'

Harry's answer was to lay hold of the handle of the whip, and to try to wrench it from the other's grasp.

Philip was forced to let go the bridle, and the horse started off at a gallop down the road, followed by a curse from his master.

'Meddlesome fool!' Philip muttered as the two struggled by the roadside for several minutes, silent for very fury.

Viola looked on in terror. *This* was the man whose honeyed phrases had been whispered so softly in her ear! This was her future husband! Well had that instinctive fear been justified! And yet with its justification, it seemed to vanish. Viola could not feel frightened of a man who might be capable of physical violence towards her. That thought roused all her own latent fierceness and her instincts of revenge; her timidity was exorcised. It was the cool, suppressed, self-mastering power which had awed her in Philip Dendraith. Now she actually longed to do battle with him herself, on behalf of the ill-used animal: intense indignation deprived her of all fear.

Thrusting aside the boughs of the trees, she forced her way through a gap in the oak paling and stood with glowing cheeks before the two struggling men.

'Mr. Dendraith,' she gasped, 'you are a cruel, wicked man. I knew you were cruel; I felt it; and now I know it beyond all doubt, and I won't marry you, I *won't* marry you; – and I hope I shall never see your face again as long as I live!'

She was trembling with passion, and her voice shook and gave way at the last word, as if she were going to burst into tears. But her eyes were quite dry, and were flaming with anger.

Even Philip had been a little disturbed by this sudden apparition and outburst. But he quickly recovered his self-possession, and adroitly managed to put Harry in the wrong, as he handed him courteously the disputed riding whip.

'Allow me to confess myself vanquished – by the presence of a lady. The whip is yours.'

Harry laid it across his knee and snapped it viciously in two. The pieces he threw over the hedge into a turnip-field. Philip laughed.

'Although the whip was a favourite one,' he said, 'I don't grudge it, seeing the intense enjoyment you appear to derive from its destruction.'

'The next time you wish to chastise your horse, you can procure a more effective instrument. The Russian knout,[21] for instance, does double the work with half the effort; however, I wrong you in supposing for a moment that you grudge any trouble in the good cause.'

'Surely this is sarcasm, or very like it,' cried Philip, 'Rather good in its way too – irony all through; quite a Russian knout sort of business; good deal of *lead* in it, don't you know.'

'I thought something heavy was suitable in the circumstances,' Harry retorted.

'Good again! But, alas! while I linger here, listening to these lightsome sallies, our bone of contention is rapidly emigrating.'

'Perhaps you had better go and gather up his scattered fragments,' said Harry.

'Perhaps I had, and I can explain matters to you, Viola my love, when I return.'

'I don't want any explanation,' she answered; 'everything has explained itself.'

'So much the better; it is a pity to start with a misunderstanding. *Au revoir*.' He smilingly raised his hat, and strode off at a gradually quickening pace down the road.

Harry looked at Viola, and their eyes met.

'I hope you are not angry with me for my part in this affair,' he said at length.

'Angry! I am most grateful.' Her voice was still trembling with excitement, and had an ominous break in it. They turned instinctively and walked on towards the elm avenue, and towards the house. Just as they were entering the avenue, on the summit of the little hill, Viola suddenly stopped. At this point the sea was visible.

'Listen,' she said. 'Do you hear how the waves are breaking to-day? When I was a child I used to fear that sound, for I always fancied it boded some misfortune. Don't you hear how it moans?'

There was a startled look in her eyes, and as she spoke she stretched out her arm seawards, and then raised it above her head, standing so, like a prophetess gazing upon coming woe.

'The waves bear you no ill-will, I am sure,' said Harry, in a tone that he used only to Viola, 'you who are almost a daughter of the sea.'

'Yes,' she said, still with a deep excitement in her voice; 'from my childhood it has sung to me its slumber-song and drawn me towards it, so that the longing for it became a pain. I was forbidden to go to it, and that made the longing worse.'

'Poor child!'

Day and night, summer and winter, I have heard it; sometimes sighing very softly, and sometimes full of lamentation; – I think its great sweetness comes from its great strength. But oh! when it is stirred to its depths, its song is full of misery so profound, so awful, that no words can possibly tell of it, – no words that ever human being spoke.'

Harry looked at her in amazement. What did this girl know of such misery? She must have terrible capacity for suffering, or she could not interpret the voices of nature after so mournful a fashion. And this was the promised wife of Philip Dendraith, a man who knew not what the word 'pain' meant, who was capable of no feeling much keener than discomfort or chagrin, except the feeling which prompted in him such actions as had led to the quarrel of the morning.

It was cruel, shameful! – the iniquitous work of a dissipated old spendthrift who wanted to save himself from the consequences of his own sins, and of a pious, narrow-minded woman, ready – for all her maternal professions – to wreck her daughter's whole life on behalf of her own miserable piety! Harry had fancied, before to-day, that Viola was at least a willing victim, but the scene of the morning dissipated that idea and excited in him all sorts of wild fancies. Fate seemed to thrust him into the position of champion to this friendless girl – worse than friendless, indeed, for who is so lost and alone as a woman under the protection of those who betray her trust, and take advantage of her obedience?

'Poor child, with the mournful prophetic eyes, what can I do to save you? – I who cannot face the thought of the future without you' –

'I am afraid you have been unhappy,' he said aloud, referring to her last strange words about the sea; 'perfectly happy people do not hear such things in the sound of the waves.'

She was silent.

'I fear,' he went on presently, 'that you did not take the somewhat oracular advice which I gave you at Clevedon the other day.'

'Would to Heaven I had!' she exclaimed. 'I tried but what could I do? And besides' –

That *besides* meant more than Harry could fathom, or than she would explain.

'If there is anything that I can do to help you, you will tell me,' he said earnestly. 'If I may presume to speak on the matter of your engagement, I must tell you that I think you have a perfect right to break it off after what you saw this morning. Such an exhibition of temper is unpardonable.'

'Oh! I can't marry him; I can't; I can't!'

'Then for Heaven's sake don't!' he exclaimed, 'It's terrible to think of!'

'Oh! if you knew how I am placed!'

'I do know – forgive me – and that is what emboldens me to speak. However important may be the considerations which urge you to this marriage, they sink into nothing in comparison with the – awfulness of marrying with such feelings as you have towards your betrothed. You don't know what you are doing! Your whole life is at stake, and my whole happiness! Forgive me, – what can I do?'

'Have it boiled for supper with parsley sauce,' rang a voice through the trees, and at the same instant appeared the stalwart form of Geoffrey with his fishing-rod over his shoulder, shouting directions to the gamekeeper to take to the cook, on the subject of a trout that he had caught weighing twelve pounds.

'Boiled happiness with parsley sauce!' echoed Harry, with a rueful laugh.

'Holloa, you there!' Geoffrey called out. 'Bet you haven't had as good sport as I have this morning! Look here!' and he swung his bag round and displayed the spoil.

'That fellow with the knowing eye gave me a lot of trouble; artful old dodger; but I hooked him at last, – my twelve-pounder I have sent in to be cooked for dinner. Holloa, Viola!' exclaimed Geoffrey, suddenly looking from her to Harry; 'why, you have got the wrong man!'

His look of bewilderment was so comic that Harry heavy-hearted as he was, burst into a shout of laughter.

'But why is this?' persisted Geoffrey.

'"Cos t'other man's sick,"[22] growled Harry.

'Well, to tell you the honest truth,' said the tactless youth, 'I wish you *were* the man.'

Harry coloured.

'No such luck,' he said jestingly.

'If t'other man, being sick, were to die,' suggested Geoffrey, regardless of the feelings of his companions, 'why, then you might step into his place. I'd give my consent and my blessing, – and I'd ring the wedding-bells. Ha! hist! the enemy approaches!'

Philip was coming down the avenue towards them at full speed.

'I've captured my Bellerophon,[23] and taken him to the stables, where he is now enjoying a wash-down and a feed of corn. His frame of mind is enviable, I assure you.'

With the want of insight of even the keenest men where a woman is concerned, Philip treated Viola as if nothing had happened, and as she behaved, as far as he could see, much as usual, he thought her anger had blown over.

Harry and Geoffrey had to walk on ahead and leave the other two to follow; for Philip managed in such a way as to give them no choice.

'At last we are alone, dearest,' he said, stopping and facing his companion, 'and before we go a step further we must ratify our betrothal in due form.'

He put his arm round her, but she sprang back.

'What! still angry about that affair of the horse? What can I do to earn forgiveness? How shall I sue for my dear lady's pardon? I am all submission and repentance. Surely she will not refuse me one little kiss if I ask for it very humbly.'

'Mr. Dendraith, I want you to release me from my engagement.'

'*Viola!*' His check flushed, and his lips set themselves in a thin hard line. 'Do you know what you are saying?'

'Only too well!'

'This is a blow for which I was totally unprepared,' said Philip. 'I hoped that you returned in some measure my boundless love for you, – but if so small a thing can turn you – O Viola, this is bitter! Can I not win your love by any means? It looks as if – if I thought that fellow Lancaster had succeeded where I have failed' –

A certain expressive tightening of the lips indicated his meaning.

'You are mine,' he said, taking her hands in his firmly 'you have no right to withdraw from our engagement.'

'You would not have an unwilling bride!' she exclaimed.

'I would have *you*, Viola.'

She tried to loosen the grasp of his hands, but in vain.

'You have given me the power; you cannot take it back.'

'I entreat, I implore you,' she cried passionately.

He flung away her hands.

'Plead so for any other thing in the world, and see how I will respond, – but this – Viola, you try me too much.'

'Put yourself in my place – but, ah! you cannot.'

'Do you so hate me, then?' he asked bitterly.

'Yes; at times.'

He winced. 'Blow after blow you inflict without mercy!'

'I had a lesson in that this morning,' she said.

'That accursed horse again! O Viola! my love, be merciful and be just. At present you are neither. You fling me away, for one fault, accepting no apology.' He stood looking at her for some seconds gloomily. Then a light came into his eyes and a fixed look about the mouth.

'Why do I woo my betrothed? She is mine, and she shall not escape me. Some day you will thank me for it, Viola; you shall be the happiest woman in England against your will.'

'And if I did become so, you would remain unjustified,' she said.

'But not unrewarded,' he returned, with a smile that haunted her long afterwards.

CHAPTER XVII

ADRIFT

When Viola, trembling and excited, related the events of the morning, to her mother, Mrs. Sedley appeared much dismayed; not, indeed, at the conduct of her son-in-law elect, but at her daughter's way of looking at it.

'Dearest, you must not judge a man's character by his behaviour towards animals; the most tender-hearted of men, after all, find their greatest pleasure in slaying the dumb creatures over whom God has given us dominion. Men are all like that, and though I agree with you that Mr. Dendraith was wrong to lose his temper as he did, I cannot think that it would justify you in withdrawing from your engagement. The family would regard it as a mere pretext or a deliberate slight; and think of your poor father!'

Viola turned very pale, and sank powerlessly upon a chair.

'The engagement is by this time made public,' Mrs. Sedley continued;' the whole neighbourhood is discussing it; really it is not possible, dearest, to draw back now. If your husband never does anything worse than beat his horse rather over hard, I shall not fear for your happiness. Surely you are not afraid of him?'

'Not *now*!' said Viola, with a gleam in her eyes.

'You can use your influence to induce him to treat his animals more humanely; he is devoted to you, and I have no doubt he will do that for your sake. Gentleness, patience, and obedience in a wife can work wonders.'

Oh! marvellous faith that remains unshaken after a lifetime spent in proving its futility!

Philip did not leave Viola much time for considering matters or for maturing her opposition. Although much piqued by her conduct, he put it down to mere girlish caprice. At the idea of giving her up he laughed. When had he ever given up anything on which he had set his heart and his will? He had yet to learn that he could be beaten by a timid, ignorant, parent-ridden girl!

He came again to the Manor-House next morning, and behaved as if nothing had happened. Viola seemed tongue-tied. She treated Philip with a cold ceremony which not even Mr. Sedley could mistake for a satisfactory bashfulness. When Sir Philip patted her on the cheek and attributed her demeanour to this cause, she looked at him with steady wide-opened eyes, and then gave a sad little flickering smile. She made no attempt to repudiate the accusation. Old men had their own hereditary notions about girls and their ways, and it would take an enterprising girl indeed who should undertake to upset them!

Lady Clevedon's quick eye saw that something was wrong.

'Harry,' she said,' what's the matter here? Is there a lovers' quarrel going on, or what?'

'Do you want to know what is going on?' said Harry.' I will tell you. Andromeda has been chained to the rock, for the gods are angry, and must be appeased by sacrifice. And the monster is about to devour her, so that Andromeda is having a rather bad time of it just now – that's all.'

'My dear boy, she's in love with Philip; you are talking nonsense.'

'She may have been so at one time, but she does not wish to marry him now. Some one ought to interfere. A man has no right to marry a woman against her will; it is monstrous!'

'Pooh! What's a woman's will?' asked Lady Clevedon.'

'That *you* ought to know.'

'Oh, I was meant to be a man.'

'You are all making a great mistake about your niece,' said Harry, with renewed energy; 'every fresh event will strike the hidden springs of her character, and I am convinced she will develop into something that her family will not like, if this moral coercion is persisted in. For my part, I hope she will. She tries to tread in her mother's footsteps, but her nature is too passionate; she cannot do it, for which Heaven be praised! Once she is fully roused, the artificial, imitative self which she shows at present, will burn away like so much tinder.'

'You are either very imaginative or very penetrating,' said Lady Clevedon.

'Time alone will show which,' he returned.

Perhaps it was the strange look in Viola's eyes which had suggested the prediction. The weather being stormy, the sound of the waves was more than usually distinct, and she seemed to be listening restlessly to that ominous moan which had haunted her childhood with presage of misfortune.

Having promised to go with his mother on a round of calls, Harry had to return to Upton early, and Philip followed his example. He found Viola very unresponsive, and thought it prudent not to force his society upon her till her fit of ill-temper (as he called it) had passed off.

In the late afternoon, when his servitude was over, Harry announced that he was going for a walk, and did not know when he might be back. He said that he panted for a sight of the sea.

Very fresh and delicious the sea-breath was when he reached the shore, and stood watching the waves rolling in, and the foam sweeping to his feet. He drew a deep sigh. The freedom of the place and the wonderful sea-freshness gave new audacity to his impulses. Hesitations were overwhelmed, as children's sand-castles by the sweeping of a wave.

It was scarcely a surprise, only a great joy, on looking round at some instinctive suggestion, to discern the white fluttering garments of a figure which he could not mistake, even at this distance. It was Viola talking to Caleb Foster, and pointing to a boat that lay on the beach. So intent and eager was she, that Harry's approach remained unnoticed till he stood beside her. Then she started and coloured vividly.

'Ah! you are much wanted here, my friend,' said Caleb.' I have been explaining to this young lady that she can't manage a craft of that size (with a will of her own too) on such a day. The waves are strong, and it may come on to blow harder any minute.'

'I have often been out with Geoffrey, and understand all about it,' Viola said hastily, and colouring once more.

'Were you really going to attempt it alone?' cried Harry in dismay. 'What madness! Presentiments do come true sometimes. I felt I should be wanted here to-night. Let me come with you, if you wish to go; soldier as I am, I consider myself no bad seaman.'

He held out his hand, and Viola, seemingly half-stunned by the frustration of her own design, allowed herself to be led into the boat.

'The centre of gravity is improperly adjusted,' said Caleb; 'a little to the right, Miss Sedley, if you please. You will find the *Viola* (as I call her in compliment to yourself) a brave little craft, but she wants humouring, like the rest of her sex.'

'Like them, she answers to the touch of intelligence, and rebels against coercion; isn't that it, Miss Sedley?' asked Harry, with a smile.

She shook her head. 'I don't know,' she answered. 'I don't know anything.'

'Give a shove, Foster,' said the young man. Together they laid their weight against the boat and launched her, and as she grated off the beach Harry sprang in, and the *Viola* darted eagerly forward through the surf into deep water. Harry gave an exulting wave of the hand towards the shore.

'Good-bye, old shore!' he cried. 'Good-bye to etiquette and formality, and all the gags and muzzles of our crazy life, – good-bye to everything but the winds and the deep sea! There's an exordium[24] for you!' he added, with a smile, as he sat down and took the sculls.

'I won't ask where we shall go to,' he went on; 'I will just go on at haphazard. This movement is glorious, isn't it? Look at those waves! How they curl, and how they are green! as the French would say. Now I am going to forget that you are Miss Sedley, and think of you as some sea-spirit – consolidated like a nebulous young world – out of sea-spray and ocean-winds. Then I may say what I please to you, may I not?'

Viola smiled. She did not seem surprised at his buoyant, fantastic talk; the poetry of the scene had attuned her mind to his. Her pulses, too, beat fast as the boat swung out to sea; she, too, thrilled at the sight of the heaving miles of green water. She leant over the boat-side to watch the sculls dipping with even recurrence into the deep, and her face seemed to grow every moment more beautiful as the old bondage was loosened, and the half-freed spirit fluttered out, – as a panting bird from its cage, into the sweet bewilderment of sudden freedom.

Her hat, which threatened to be blown off, had been discarded, and she had no covering for her head but her own thick hair, which was fluttering in the wind.

'I need no help now to believe you are the spirit of the sea!' exclaimed Harry. 'You only want a crown of sea-weed to make the resemblance perfect.'

He caught a spray as it floated by and handed it to her; and she smiled and blushed and laid it dripping among the coils of her hair.

A wild, poetic beauty was in her face; all trace of the 'young lady' had disappeared; her womanhood was uppermost now.

She was like some dark-eyed sea-queen, daughter of the Twilight; some mystic, imaginary figure, with all the loveliness of ocean and of evening in her eyes.

Once past the current that swept round the distant headland on which stood the lonely ruins of Upton Castle, Harry slackened speed, and, after a time, he let the boat drift out to sea with the wind, which was blowing off shore.

He felt that this would be one of the memorable days of his life, one of the few moments of almost unearthly joy that come now and again as pledges of a possible Paradise, realisable even in this bewildered world – according to his creed – when self-tormenting mortals shall at last have groped their way thither through the error and the suffering and the wrongs of weary ages.

'I said that I was going to speak openly to you to-day,' Harry began, 'and I feel that anything else would be ludicrous and even unfair to you and to myself. This is no time for hesitation. Our whole lives are at stake, and I *must* speak out.'

Viola did not look startled; nothing would have startled her to-night; she was in a waking dream.

'When you came down to the beach this evening I know that you were very miserable; it was a desperate impulse that made you long to be afloat on the waters, and with it was a secret hope – secret from yourself – that they would swallow you and your troubles for ever.'

She flinched from his earnest gaze, and coloured, while a look of pain came into her face.

'I do not say this in detection or reproach, but in sympathy,' Harry went on hastily. 'I know that you are being driven to despair, and it is no wonder such thoughts overcome you.'

'I know it is very wrong' – Viola began.

'For Heaven's sake, talk no more about "right and wrong,"' he exclaimed; 'those words have been used against you too long and too successfully. You must assert yourself and resist.'

'It is too late; and besides' –

'It is not too late, and there is no 'besides,"' cried Harry.

'My father, my mother' –

He gave a fierce gesture and exclamation.

'Do they not know that the slave-trade is illegal in England?'

'I do not understand – I' –

'No; you are brought up not to understand; the thing couldn't be done otherwise. O Viola! let me save you; there is nothing I would shrink from doing; there is nothing that *you* should shrink from doing. You do not realise your own position.'

'But how can I escape?'

'Ask him to release you.'

'I have done so.'

'And he refuses.'

'Yes.'

Harry was silent for a moment.

'You have not the courage to go to your father and say that you will not be forced into this marriage?'

'I could face my father, but not the consequences for my mother. He punishes *her* for my misdeeds.'

Harry set his lips. 'How securely they bind you through your own pity and compunction! It is quite masterly. Loyola[25] himself had not a more subtle method of playing the potter with human nature.'

'My mother thinks it impossible for me to draw back now,' said Viola. 'I told her about the beating of the horse.'

'Strange beings that good women are!' he exclaimed. 'O Viola, it is unendurable! I who love you so, that literally my whole soul is bound up in you, – not simply my happiness, but my whole self and being, – I would rather that you should die and be lost to me for ever, than that you should continue to live in the same world with me at such a cost! I know the man!'

Even this absolutely unexpected outburst, made as it was with startling passion, did not appear very greatly to surprise Viola. Perhaps in her distraught state, exhausted physically and mentally by the emotions she had gone through, she scarcely knew what was happening, or, if she did, was unable to grasp its relations to the facts of her previous life, whose thread seemed to have slipped from her fingers when she left the land behind her.

'I have told you that I am ready to do anything in my power to save you, but without your assistance I am helpless. Will you come with me now, or perhaps to-morrow, to my friend, Mrs. Lincoln?' – Viola started. – 'Ah! you have been prejudiced against her, I see, but I know she could advise and help us both as no one else could. She will sympathise deeply with you; her marriage was arranged very much as yours has been arranged; her inexperience and conscientiousness, and fear of giving pain, were played upon as yours are being played upon. I cannot tell you how lovable she is, – that I should like you to find out for yourself. Dear Viola! will you let me take you to her?'

'Oh! no, no,' she said, in a dreamy tone, almost as if the answer were automatic; 'my mother and my aunt tell me that one must not know her.'

Harry sighed. 'But won't you judge for yourself for once?' he urged. 'Mrs. Lincoln has done what most people think wrong, no doubt, but most people are doing with the utmost self-congratulation what Mrs. Lincoln, on her side, thinks degrading. There are different ideas of right and wrong in the world, you must remember.'

'There can surely be only one right and one wrong,' said Viola.

Her mother's teaching was doing its work thoroughly at the critical moment.

'If you won't go to her, then, will you let her come to you? – not to your home, of course, but to some appointed place outside?'

'That would be deceiving my parents,' said Viola; 'I cannot do that.'

'And what resource do they leave you but deception?' he asked hotly. 'You and they are not on equal terms; they can coerce you. Their power over you is despotic; and to resist such power all methods are justifiable.'

'Oh! you cannot mean what you say! I have always been taught that the will of parents is sacred, and that no blessing can come to a child who acts in opposition to their wishes.'

'Taught by whom?' Harry inquired; 'by your parents.'

'Every one would say the same,' Viola replied.

'Every one has been taught by parents,' retorted Harry.

'Oh! take me home, take me home!' she cried suddenly. 'It is wicked to listen to such things.'

'Stay with me a little longer,' he pleaded. 'Such moments as this come but once in a lifetime; and besides, even at the risk of your displeasure, I *must* speak plainly on a matter of such deep moment to us both. You seem to forget that I love you, Viola. Have I no hope of winning your love in return?'

She looked disturbed and bewildered, as if her ideas of right and wrong, in spite of her teaching, were becoming confused.

'Anyhow, I mean to try with all my might and main to win it,' Harry continued; 'nothing can daunt me, and I shall never despair. The strength and depth of my own feeling justifies my obstinacy in hoping.'

'Oh! take me home. I will *not* listen.'

'Is that fair to me? Why will you not listen? Because you fear my pleading might move you? O Viola! if that is so, you have no right to forbid it, for your heart is half won!'

'It is not half won; it is *not* half won,' she protested. 'Why are you talking like this and making me feel so wicked? What would my mother say to it? It must be horribly wrong, for I dare not face the thought of what she would say. Mr. Lancaster, please take me home.'

'Only tell me that I have some hope – just a faint gleam.'

'Take me home,' she repeated.

Slowly, regretfully, he turned the boat's head and rowed back towards the shore. He saw that to say more just now would be to injure his cause. Viola was becoming frightened by her own feelings.

The return journey – how different from the exultant half-hour when they were outward bound! – was made almost in silence. As they touched the shore, Viola sprang out so eagerly that she almost fell; Harry's arm was only just in time to save her.

'Let this be symbolical,' he said, retaining the hand which she gave him; 'I have saved you. Farewell, and remember that you can always come to me for help – and never be afraid that I shall misinterpret your appeal if you make it. My advice to you is, to announce firmly and simply that you will not carry out your engagement, since to all intents and purposes it was forced upon you. In any case do let me know how things go on, and remember that I am entirely at your command, always.'

He raised her hand and kissed it and held it between his own.

'You are too good to me,' she said; 'and I am very, very miserable. Thank you, and good-bye.' Her voice broke; she drew her hand from his and hurried away.

He would have followed, but she waved him back, quickening her pace, and presently vanished behind the first small headland.

Harry stood gazing at the spot where she had disappeared till a voice behind him made him start round.

'Love,' said the philosopher, 'is a temporary madness. Under its influence the human being' –

'Oh! what do *you* know about it?' cried Harry ferociously.

'Ah! a bad paroxysm,' remarked Caleb; 'very lowering to the general tone, and apt to disturb the intellectual balance if long persisted in.'

'I abominate intellectual balance,' said Harry irascibly.

'Naturally, naturally,' returned the philosopher. 'My young friend, if energetic movement relieves your feelings, do let me walk rapidly up and down the beach with you; I have time at my disposal.'

'Oh, hang you!' Harry exclaimed; 'can't you leave a fellow alone?'

'*Very* disturbing to the intellectual balance,' murmured Caleb.

'Have *you* never had the heavens falling about your ears, and the sun darkened and the moon put out? Have' –

'On my recovery from a severe illness, on one occasion, I remember that' –

'Oh, this is more than I can bear!' Harry exclaimed; 'I had far better pour out my woes to the stony rocks than to you!'

'I assure you I deeply feel for you,' said Caleb.

'Yes, because of the disturbance to my intellectual balance,' retorted Harry, with a snort. 'Caleb, you are the most ridiculous man I ever met; you know everything and understand nothing; all is revealed to you, and you are blind as a bat. Free as air, you never move beyond the radius of a five-foot tether; and in the midst of life you are in death. Good-bye; and pray fervently for the intellectual balance.' With this parting advice, Harry strode off and left the philosopher chuckling.

CHAPTER XVIII

AN ENCOUNTER

'And so Miss Sedley's wedding is fixed for the 7th,' said Adrienne, cheerfully unconscious that she was inflicting torture upon the being for whom she would willingly have laid down her life. 'I do hope the marriage will turn out happily!'

'That we shall never know,' observed Dick Evans. 'Marriages are always made to look well outside.'

'Yes; unless one of the couple drinks,' said Adrienne; 'and even then it doesn't often come out till they give a garden-party.' (This allusion to a recent scandal was received with smiles). 'For my part,' Adrienne continued, 'I think Philip Dendraith has misconceived his vocation. He ought to have gone on taking ladies in to dinner all his life. I would choose him out of a multitude for that office, but for marrying' –

She shook her dainty little head expressively.

'Young men always settle down after they are married,' said Mrs. Dixie. 'I am sure he is a most agreeable young fellow.'

The agreeable Philip had admired the family plate and talked to Mrs. Dixie about ante-sunset times, thus enrolling her at once among his allies.

'I am glad it's not one of the girls,' Dick Evans said, recklessly disregarding the fact of their large numbers and limited opportunities; 'and I am glad not to have to congratulate *your* sister, Harry.'

'Thank you,' said Harry curtly.

'They seem to be hurrying it on,' Dick continued; 'the 7th – scarcely three weeks from now!'

'I wonder how the trousseau can be got ready,' said Mrs. Dixie. 'I know that mine took six months to prepare; but then, of course, I had four dozen of everything, and the most exquisite work, all real lace – I was one mass of insertion (Valenciennes).[26] My poor mother *would* have everything of the best, and' –

It suddenly struck Mrs. Dixie that she was committing an impropriety in alluding to underclothing in a mixed company, and she relapsed into a decorous but unexplained silence, preluded by a little cough which would have amply atoned for the grossest of improprieties.

Dorothy Evans, Dick's scapegrace sister, also took a hostile view of the marriage.

Philip's good looks and fascinating manner had not succeeded in lulling the girl's instinct for what is straight and genuinely chivalrous in man. 'He's all talk and bows,' said Dorothy, 'and you always feel he is laughing at you to himself, though you would think, to hear him, that you were the loveliest and the most fascinating person that ever lived. He's a nasty man, and I hate his eyes.'

Dorothy had hit upon the one traitorous feature in his face; perhaps no such man ever had eyes entirely trustworthy. Not that Philip's had the proverbial difficulty of looking one in the face; he could stare most people out of countenance. But his native subtlety, and the coldness which lay at the root of his character, gave their expression to the eyes, and won for them Dorothy's dislike.

Harry had received the news without betraying himself, but it was more than he could endure to stay and hear it talked over. The discussion was in full swing when he left the room, quietly whistling an air from a comic opera. He ruefully admired his own acting, although thinking at the same time how very easy it always is to deceive the people who imagine they know one best! He set off at once for the Manor-House, determining, rashly enough, to make an attempt to see Viola. He thought that probably a violent reaction had set in after the heretical teachings of that afternoon on the water; that in the exaltation of repentance and the return to duty, she had cut off her own possible retreat by at once fixing the day of her marriage. It was an act of atonement. Probably, however, a second reaction had taken place since then, and upon this Harry built his hopes. Having searched the gardens in vain, there was nothing for it but to go to the house and ask for Mrs. Sedley in the usual way.

Mrs. Sedley appeared, and entertained her visitor solemnly in the drawing-room, among the 'lost souls' and the grand piano.

Harry had never in his life found conversation so difficult; that was not usually his weak point, but to-day his mind became a blank every time he looked at the dull grey face of his hostess, whose voice alone was sufficient to check the imagination of a Shelley.[27]

'Is your daughter at home?' he asked at length, feeling, if not looking, very guilty.

'Yes; she is at home, but she has a headache. Of course, we are all very busy preparing for the wedding.'

'Naturally – I am sorry she has a headache' –

'Thank you; I have no doubt it will not last very long.'

'I suppose I – may I see her?' asked Harry, with sudden boldness.

Mrs. Sedley looked rather surprised, but she said, 'Certainly,' and led the way to her own sitting-room, where Viola, in the cold northern light, among colourless cushions, was lying upon a severe-looking sofa. She sprang up to greet the visitor, whose presence appeared greatly to astonish her. She appeared pale and ill. The same constrained conversation went on as before, until the advent of tea afforded a merciful relief to the unhappy trio.

Harry was at his wits' end, yet determined to effect his object, though he had to prolong the call till the curfew hour. Some diversion, he hoped, might sooner or later occur, although Mrs. Sedley sat there, with a polite and patient air of waiting till he should go, that was most disconcerting. She looked, as usual, quite uncomplaining, but very suffering. Harry, however, was resolved. He went to the window on pretext of admiring the view, and, to his joy, he saw Geoffrey crossing the lawn. He at once shouted to him.

'Holloa, you here!' said Geoffrey, changing his direction. 'Don't know if the mother will let me in with my dirty boots... Well, Viola, how's the headache? Look here!' and he held up a trout by the tail.

'Eight pounds, – there you are, mother: I lay it at your feet. Look here, Harry, you might take the other ones to your mother, with my compliments.'

'Thanks! She will be delighted.'

Mrs. Sedley brightened a little, as if expecting that he would take the trout and go, but, on the contrary, he established himself in an easy-chair and engaged in a dialogue with Geoffrey upon the subject of fishing, which contained a vital principle so vigorous, as to promise for it little short of immortality. Mrs. Sedley sighed. She had a great deal to do; and very little time to do it in. Harry knew that, and glued himself more firmly to his chair. He had propounded a theory about flies that Geoffrey would not hear of for a moment, and as Harry stuck to it obstinately, a long argument was the result; – as Geoffrey said, it was distressing to see a sensible fellow making a fool of himself.

At last Mrs. Sedley rose. Would Mr. Lancaster kindly excuse her. She had some important letters –

Harry sprang up, polite beyond all expression, – certainly Mrs. Sedley must not for a *moment* think of letting him detain her. In the interests of science he felt it his duty to root out a common error from Geoffrey's usually clear mind, but –

This created a clamour, and in the midst of it Mrs. Sedley retired. After that Geoffrey found his opponent singularly improved in mental grasp. His arguments grew milder, and before long he was brought to confess that he saw and repented his error. Geoffrey then became restless, as he usually did within four walls, and proposed to go out.

But Harry's politeness would not allow him to desert Viola.

'Oh! she won't mind,' said Geoffrey.

But the courteous guest, in spite of her assent, could not bring himself to commit this breach of manners.

'Well, then, you'd better stay and entertain her, while I go and have a wash and brush up. I feel more picturesque than beautiful, more beautiful than clean!' and he went off by the open window.

Harry watched him out of sight, then he turned rapidly, glanced at the door, and went over to where Viola was sitting. He took her hand in his and said quietly, 'Viola, you have finally consented to this marriage in a fit of self-sacrificing ardour, and you are even now frightened of your deed. I have come to tell you again that you are wrong, and that you are doing what you will repent all your life. I have also come to tell you once more that I love you with all my heart and soul, and that I want you to promise to come with me to-morrow to town, not that I may make you my wife, but that I may protect you from being his. If the pressure upon you is as irresistibly strong as it seems to be, will you take my name, – don't start, – take my name, so that you cannot take his? You will return to your home, or do whatever else you please, without feeling that I have in any way, or at any time, a claim on you. I know my proposal would receive hard names from most experienced people, but I regard all things as of less importance than your salvation. Wait one minute – let me speak – we may be interrupted at any moment. I must not disguise from you that there is some risk in this plan. It would create a scandal; your good name would be attacked. But is that worth considering in comparison with – with what is proposed for you?'

She winced and turned away with a gesture of passionate despair.

'I don't know anything; I can't balance things; I am bewildered and terri-fied.'

'Upon my soul, I believe mine is the only way to save you!' he exclaimed. 'I entreat, I beseech you to consent to it.'

'It is impossible – it is so deceitful. And how could I accept such a sacrifice?'

'To have saved you would be my reward. I have thought it all out; this is no hasty idea of mine. Viola, Viola, have pity on yourself and me. If you had con-sented to take refuge with Mrs. Lincoln, it might have been managed without this more serious step from which you shrink, but since you will not' –

'*What's that?*'

Viola gave a little half-suppressed cry, for at the open window, playing with the tassel of the blind, stood Philip Dendraith, blandly smiling. When he smiled so Viola always felt a nameless terror.

'I hope I do not intrude,' he said, advancing into the room with slow, firm foot-steps, as if he were enjoying something leisurely. 'Viola, my love, I am sorry to hear you are not well to-day.' He went up and kissed her with an air of familiarity.

Harry set his lips.

'You must excuse these little demonstrations,' said Philip, with a wave of the hand. 'We haven't met for a whole day, you know.'

'Pray don't apologise to me,' said Harry, keeping guard over his voice; 'any apology you might think necessary would be due to Miss Sedley.'

Philip glanced at the visitor out of the corner of his eyes, and gave a cold smile.

'I do hope I wasn't interrupting something interesting,' he said. 'I know what you can be at your best; quite a Sheridan,[28] upon my honour!'

'Shall I go on for your benefit?' said Harry, looking at his rival with steady eyes.

'Pray do,' urged Philip, while Viola gave a frightened gesture. 'Kindly allow me to find a comfortable chair first, that I may the more enjoy the treat in store for me. So – this is most luxurious. I didn't know your mother would have toler-ated such a lounge in her house, Viola – *une chaise de Sybarite*.'[29]

He leant back luxuriously, moving first a little closer to Viola, so that he could lay his hand on the arm of her chair, or touch hers now and again when it so pleased him.

From such a man it would be impossible now to conceal that something of a secret nature had been taking place when he entered. Viola's cry of dismay had betrayed them. Seeing how matters stood, and knowing what sort of enemy he had to deal with, Harry took a characteristic resolution.

'Your suspicions are correct,' he said calmly; 'you did surprise a conversation between Miss Sedley and myself, which we did not wish to be overheard.'

'*Candide*'[30] murmured Philip, reaching out and taking a very musty and mouldy copy of that work from the long-undisturbed bookshelves. 'There is an interesting proverb of George Herbert's which you may, perhaps, be familiar with: "When the tree is fallen all go with the hatchet."'[31]

'Not yet is the tree fallen,' said Harry; 'but I think it is better that it should fall. You must know that I have become acquainted with all the circumstances of your engagement.'

Philip bowed. 'Your interest in our affairs is most flattering.'

'I will not mince matters,' Harry continued hotly, 'now that Miss Sedley is being forced into the marriage' – (Philip looked round) – that you have taken advantage of her helpless position in the hands of parents who are willing to sell her to you – that is the long and short of it – in order to extricate themselves from their financial difficulties' –

Viola started up.

'I cannot hear such things,' she cried.

'I beg your pardon,' said Harry. 'I was wrong to speak as I did, but I am at liberty to say that Mr. Dendraith is to all intents and purposes intending to marry you against your will, that you have asked him to release you, and that he refuses. I consider myself also at liberty strenuously to advise you to refuse to carry out your engagement, and to dare everything rather than fulfil it.'

'There is an audacity about you,' said Philip, looking up at him from his reclining attitude, 'that really carries one away; a degree less audacity – were it but a hair's-breadth – and one would not tolerate you for a moment. I hope you are going to increase the dramatic effect by telling me that you have been proposing to Miss Sedley to elope with you. Keep it up: By the way, there is another proverb which I might appropriately cite; "Where there is no honour there is no grief."'[32]

Harry flushed deeply. 'As I hold it quite unjustifiable to marry a woman who is not really free to refuse you, I hold it justifiable to rescue her by any means in one's power; she is not to be sacrificed to an artificial code of honour.'

'Rather more ingenuity than honour about that view, methinks,' said Philip. 'Do you know, sir, that some men in my place would treat you in a manner that might be somewhat compromising to your dignity?'

'It matters not to me what some men in your place might attempt,' said Harry. 'I have to deal with *you*, and I am quite prepared to do so, in any manner that may seem necessary.'

'Perhaps we had better continue our little chat outside,' suggested Philip, rising; 'it is useless to trouble Miss Sedley with these trifles.'

'Certainly; but I have very little more to say. It is well, perhaps, that you should know that it is my design to oppose your marriage, and that I consider I have the right to do so by every means in my power.'

'The lady to the victor,' remarked Philip coolly, as he led the way to the garden.

CHAPTER XIX

IN VAIN

To the consternation of every one, and the indignation of Mrs. Sedley, Viola fell ill. She was not seriously ill, but the doctor said that her nerves were unstrung, and she must see nobody who might excite her, for at least a week. He regretted to have to be so barbarous, but Mr. Dendraith most certainly must not be admitted.

Mr. Dendraith consigned the doctor to perdition, and tried to prevail upon Mrs. Sedley to allow him to see Viola, notwithstanding. Little did he know that meek and mild lady. She was immovable. He began to fear that the marriage would be put off, in which case Harry Lancaster might give trouble, though Philip trusted to his own powerful influence and to that of Viola's conscience, to overcome all opposition. The doctor said that the invalid needed only a little treatment, combined with perfect quiet, and there was no reason to postpone the marriage, though a very long and fatiguing wedding-tour could not be advised.

On the whole, perhaps, Viola's illness proved a safeguard for Philip, as Harry was unable to have any communication with her, and the appointed day was drawing always nearer.

The prescribed week of quiet spread into ten days, and then to a fortnight – terrible days both for Viola and for Harry. Nor was Mrs. Sedley much happier. Anxious as she only knew how to be, she spent her strength in praying for an impossible faith, and found her only consolation for its continued absence, in a severe self-blame that she possessed it not without praying for.

As for Viola, she did not know whether to wish those dragging days shorter or longer. At nightfall, relief that the day was over, and terror at the thought that another had passed, fought a pitched battle, till exhaustion drew their victim into a restless sleep. There were times when she was cruelly tempted to write to Harry and tell him she was ready to adopt his plan, but the thought was thrust aside as inconceivably wicked. She was ashamed to tell her mother how terribly hard she found it to do her duty. She would fall on her knees at night before the open window and pray, with all the passion of her soul, for strength and guidance; pray that she might forget the words that Harry had spoken to her out on the sea, words that echoed in her brain and haunted her with their subtle and tempting sophistry.

And now the house began to fill; large numbers of rejoicing aunts and cousins and gleeful old friends came crowding in for the happy event (as they would insist on calling it), and Upton Court opened its disused chambers for the delighted members of the Dendraith connexion, who were so pleased that dear

Philip was going to settle down and become a sedate and respectable married man, after his wild career in early life.

Viola was now convalescent, and very busy helping her mother to entertain their guests. Once Harry had written to her, saying that up to the very last moment he was always there, ready and eager to carry out his proposed plan if she would make an appointment. But Viola replied in a few lines entreating him not to write to her; her mother would wonder about the letters, and it could do no good. She thanked him warmly for his desire to befriend her, and said that she could not cease to remember his kindness. She took this opportunity of sending him all good wishes, and remained his very gratefully, – VIOLA SEDLEY.

He called after this, and found her in the drawing-room among a roomful of people, pouring out tea. He fancied that there was a new dignity in her manner, born, thought the on-lookers, of the honour of coming wifehood, but in reality called forth, as Harry sadly divined, by the stimulus of great suffering.

Once or twice he caught her glance, and made another mute appeal, but she shook her head sadly and turned away, and the miserable game went on.

Two days before the wedding there was a ball at the Manor-House.

Philip expressed a desire that Viola should dance with no one but himself that night, unless she first asked his permission. It seemed to her to be taking airs of possession rather soon, but she said nothing, being too sick at heart, and too accustomed to follow her mother's ideal of womanly submission to offer any resistance. Her recent illness would make a good excuse for refusing.

The drawing-room was roused out of its long doze. The 'lost souls,' to their great amazement, had their glass cases taken off, and candles stuck into them; the silken chairs were revealed in all their faded glory, and placed round the walls of the room to make space for the dancers. The dim old room was scarcely recognisable.

The dancing went merrily, thanks to Mr. Sedley's undeniable social talents and to Sir Philip's energy. Mrs. Sedley was unable to depress her guests, though she did her unconscious best in that direction.

A boisterous country-dance was just over; the couples were hurrying into the hall, leaving only Lady Dendraith in a stiff-backed chair, with her chubby hands crossed on her lap and her head drooping on her breast. According to established habit, the old lady had seized the opportunity for a quiet doze. 'My son' was out of the room, and there was nothing to keep her awake.

Her daughter-in-law elect, who had not been dancing, remained behind when the crowd passed out, hoping for a little rest and quiet. Her white dress, soft and long and flowing, was very becoming to her; Philip had told her so to-night, and several others, not perhaps quite so competent to judge.

She had a bunch of white roses in her hair and at her breast, and on her neck a small diamond crescent sparkled.

Thinking she was alone; except for the sleeping Lady Dendraith, she had leant her tired head upon the red cushions of the sofa, and for a moment closed her eyes.

When she opened them again Harry Lancaster was looking down upon her. She started up.

'Oh! why do you come to me? It is not kind; you weaken me. For pity's sake, go!'

'Do you grudge me these farewell moments – I who love you so?'

'Hush, it is wicked!'

'That I don't for a moment believe. The real wickedness is that' –

'You are mad!' she exclaimed. 'We shall be overheard.'

'Who can overhear?' he asked, lowering his voice. 'Lady Dendraith is asleep.'

'Her son would hear you if he were in the next county.'

'Viola,' said a voice, at which she started and trembled violently, 'I have been looking for you everywhere.'

'Except here, apparently,' said Harry.

Philip looked his enemy up and down, and down and up, and passed him by without comment. The whole thing was done with such quiet and exquisite insolence, that Harry coloured to his temples and Viola breathed quickly.

With a sudden impulse he bent towards her.

'Will you give me this dance?' he asked.

He had chosen his time well. Philip took a step forward. 'Miss Sedley is engaged to me for it.'

'No,' said Viola, with sudden spirit, 'I did not promise it to you.' And she rose and laid her hand on Harry's arm.

Philip's shrugging of the shoulders and smile were not pleasant, as the two went off together. He had hidden his amazement and anger as he hid, or could hide, almost any emotion, however violent.

But not for a moment did he lose sight of the couple as they whirled together among the dancers. He thought that Viola danced with more appearance of pleasure than she had danced before that evening, though previously *he* had been her partner. When had she vouchsafed to him such looks and tones? Her face, to his jealous eyes, seemed softened and glorified. Never before had her imprisoned beauty made so triumphant an escape. Could it be possible that some other man had succeeded in quickening the throbs of that steadily beating heart, when he, Philip, had failed? It seemed incredible; yet Viola's coldness towards himself required some explanation.

When the dance was over, and the couple left the ball-room, Philip rose and followed them at a distance. He was too prudent to openly display his jealousy, too jealous to let them out of his sight.

A crowd in the doorway, however, prevented him from leaving the room for a few seconds, and when he reached the hall the rebellious pair were nowhere to be seen.

They had been tempted by the brilliant starlight to wander out on to the terrace, where the mildest of night-airs was moving now and again a breathless leaf, murmuring here and there among the ivy. The great avenue looked very solemn and dark under the stars, the vast old trees showing against the sky like silent Sphinxes,[33] full of a secret knowledge never to be revealed, deep as life and terrible as Destiny. The human element was utterly excluded, and the heart ached at the penetrating coldness of that awful omniscience, wherein there was no love and no pity.

From the open windows of the ballroom stole presently the sad, sweet notes of a waltz; – *that* was the human note, full of longing, and of melancholy almost rising to despair.

The music poured out flood-like, assailing, as a sea in tumult, the fortress of that all-knowing Silence. It was like the human heart rising in revolt against its narrow destiny, yearning unceasingly towards the larger and the lovelier and the better which haunt it evermore, like the refrain of a sweet song, heard and half-forgotten in the bygone days.

'Heaven help us! I love you and I can't move you!' exclaimed Harry desperately. 'I should like to know what were we sent for into this vast machine of a world that goes spinning on century after century, grinding human nerves and hearts to powder! What fiend was it who invented consciousness, who made torturable nerves, and hearts that are mere insignificant atoms of the universe, and yet capable, each poor atom, of such infinite woe? Surely we must be a mistake, an unlucky accident that occurred during the cosmical experiments of some meddlesome god, which he has not taken the trouble to rectify or expunge.'

'I fear it is very wrong,' said Viola, with a deep sigh; 'but I have wondered myself of late why we were given such power to feel pain, and at the same time placed in a world where duty seems always to lead to it.'

'Yes, and *not-duty* too,' said Harry. 'You can't dodge it, try as you will. I think the world is divided between people who are dull and don't live at all – people who call themselves happy, but don't know what the word means – and people who suffer mortal anguish, but who might know the joys of Paradise; whose life is turned into a fiery torrent which scorches instead of warming and invigorating. That troublesome young god had a magnificent idea when he thought of us, but he failed in the execution; and the result is wreck and ruin as terrific as the Creation might have been splendid. We are brothers of the gods, but we are broken into a thousand fragments.

'Perhaps some day we shall be able to glue ourselves together again,' said Viola, with a sad little smile.

'We want the glue,' he said 'and that glue is happiness and love; the two things that good people and bad alike deny us. The world resists its own salvation.'

Viola was silent.

'Duty is better than happiness,' she said presently, 'and better than love.'

'Yet St. Augustine said, "Love, and do what you will!"[34] And what else have we to save us from the loneliness of life? What else can protect us from its awful coldness and silence?'

He gave a movement towards the dark, still avenue, and the glittering mystery of the heavens.

'The more clearly one realises what man's position in the universe is, the more he feels the need of close fellowship and passionate love, and the more he must cling to the idea of immortality. It is not so much the eternity of the personality as the eternity of love that our hearts imperiously demand. Now you see why I am so persistent, why I allow nothing to overcome me till hope is absolutely lost. Though you fancy that you think and feel very differently from me, though my ideas even shock you, I know that underneath the crust of your acquired sentiments there lies some feeling which responds to mine. We can break the loneliness and the silence for one another; we can piece together some of our broken fragments, and be more clearly whole and sane, more nearly complete beings, together than apart. If the artificial crust has so far prevailed, yet I am sure that if only I had a fair chance to make you understand your own latent self,[35] I should prevail – don't be angry with me, Viola; if I am right, consider what you are doing in turning from me.'

'If my life proves unbearable perhaps I shall die. God can't let me live and suffer always.'

'I don't remember many cases in which God has shown Himself so considerate,' said Harry bitterly.

'Oh! don't say such things, I implore you,' she cried.

'Dear Viola, you are bearing yourself up with false ideas, false hopes, false pieties; – forgive me for saying so – but they *are* false, because they flatly and openly contradict the facts of life as we know them.'

'I can't argue with you; you confuse my ideas. I can only cling to what I have been taught, and try to do my duty accordingly. What else is possible to me? *You* may be able to do right in your own way – I don't know – but how can I?'

It was said pathetically, sadly.

'It wrings my heart to see you fluttering like this in the meshes of a worn-out, lifeless old error. It is as if you were drowning in some deep sea, dragged down and smothered by a mass of tangled weeds which you would not let me pull away. Some day you will see it all yourself; a rough, rude hand, instead of a loving one, will tear it off, and then how bitter will be your regret with no human being to comfort or to help you!'

'Except an insignificant creature called a husband,' observed a cool, polite voice through the darkness. 'He, however, having not yet assumed that extinguishing title, ventures to claim the fulfilment of a promise to dance the next waltz with him, if it is not asking too much. Perhaps the fact of being a husband minus only two days, depreciates him in anticipation.'

Viola laid her hand on his proffered arm, murmuring something about not knowing the dance had begun.

'Pray don't apologise,' said Philip; 'it is for me to apologise for my tactless intrusion.'

They walked up the terrace together in silence.

At the end Philip paused, leaning against one of the stone pillars of the terrace. 'You seem to find Mr. Lancaster's conversation spiritually nourishing,' he remarked.

Viola looked up, but made no reply.

'He is a very interesting young man,' said Philip.

Again no answer, only a steady gaze.

'His only fault is an unfortunate prejudice against myself; and as my own experience somewhat confirms his opinion, I have, of course, few objections to make to it.'

A pause.

'I pride myself upon my tolerance,' Philip continued urbanely; 'I consider it uncouth to be intolerant or even fractious. I don't dissipate my forces in guerilla warfare.[36] You understand.'

In his insolent attitude, with his arm upon the pillar of the parapet, he looked down at his companion steadily, telling off his sentences one by one, and leaving a pause between each, so that they seemed to fall like stones into silent water.

Viola's eyes at last sank before his, and a tremor passed through her.

'You are cold,' said Philip. 'Would you like to go in?'

'I am not cold.'

He bent forward and drew her white shawl closer round her. She shrank under his touch.

'Why, you are shivering!' he cried. 'It is dangerous to stay out here in your thin dress. I don't want to have you laid up again. Delays are dangerous, especially with such a very interesting young man coasting round. Flowing moustachios and blue eyes, even in the absence of regular features, are not to be trusted. Don't imagine for a moment that I bear him any ill-will; on the contrary, I sympathise heartily with his admiration for yourself; but you will allow that I am justified in endeavouring to frustrate his designs if I can.'

He offered her his arm with a bland smile, and led her into the house.

'I think, by the way,' he said as they crossed the hall, 'that I asked you not to dance with anybody but myself to-night. It is perhaps a little freak of mine, but do you mind gratifying it?'

'I am not anxious to dance any more with any one,' said Viola; 'I am too tired.'

Philip laughed. 'You are no diplomatist, my love. You might have pleased yourself and me at the same time there, if you had been less uncompromisingly honest. How do you expect to govern your husband at that rate?'

'I don't expect it; my place is to obey.'

'Yes, ostensibly; but you know there are circuitous routes as well as straight ones to the same spot. A wife can generally attain her object if she knows how to manage cleverly; and I shall be charmed to be managed cleverly, I assure you, and promise to keep one eye permanently shut so that you will have no difficulty in finding my blind side.'

'Thank you,' said Viola,' but I don't wish to find it.'

'On one or two points I admit I am apt to show my teeth, and I am afraid – such is the infirmity of human nature – that Mr. Lancaster might cause me to snarl, if he is not careful. However, I have been weak enough to fall in love, and that makes me very manageable. I am waiting, *pining* to be managed. Two short days more to pass, and then, my love, you will take me under your charming jurisdiction. What prospect could be sweeter?'

How did it happen that, after all this profession of submission on the part of the bridegroom-elect, Viola left him that night with a sense of being absolutely crushed beneath his dominating and resistless will?

CHAPTER XX

A BAD BEGINNING

Great anxiety prevailed at the Manor-House that the wedding-day should prove fine. The bride alone did not share the anxiety, though she said 'I hope so' without flagging, when the guests expressed their feelings with regard to the desirable omen. Lady Clevedon had come over the night before the wedding with the intention of preventing Mrs. Sedley, as much as possible, from dwelling on the sadder aspects of the event. She brought, as aides-de-camp,[37] with Mrs. Sedley's consent, Harry Lancaster and Arabella, whose unremitting sprightliness might be expected to have a cheering effect.

But Arabella was only an accessory; Lady Clevedon discreetly chartered Geoffrey for her enlivening purpose, Geoffrey being the only person who had ever been known to make his mother laugh.

He reminded his aunt that this had been done at an enormous expenditure of vital force, by means of a terribly energetic imitation of an Irish reel, and only in the last wild paroxysm had his mother displayed the slightest amusement. Geoffrey appealed to Lady Clevedon's sense of propriety to convince her that the experiment could not be repeated in the present circumstances.

'My dear boy, be as foolish as you know how; regard the occasion as a sort of carnival, and no one will say you nay.'

'A most cheering invitation,' said Geoffrey; 'but how is one to get up a carnival in a roomful of stuck-up wedding-guests?'

'They are only stuck up because they are not amused; go and amuse them.'

Geoffrey gave a rueful whistle. 'Well, I call this simply cruelty to animals. What would you have me do? Go up to my mother with my hands in my pockets and ask her how she feels to-morrow?'

'Graceless boy! To-morrow your mother will want all the consolation we can offer her.'

'Well, that's the sort of thing I never *can* understand,' said Geoffrey, with a shrug of the shoulders. 'Mothers bring up their daughters on purpose to get married, and then require more pocket-handkerchiefs than can be afforded by any family of moderate means when the happy event comes off.'

'You have much to learn before you understand women and their ways, my dear,' said the lady, with a laugh.

'Oh, I've watched 'em,' observed Geoffrey, 'and it seems to me very much like watching a lot of young tadpoles in a pond. You see them wriggling and scuttling about, but you can't for the life of you make out what they're doing it for, and it's my belief they don't know themselves.'

'Which, tadpoles or women?'

'Both; but, of the two, commend me to the tadpoles for method.'

'You young heretic! Wait till you enter the woman's empire, and then tremble! Luckily we have our revenges. Ah! Viola, my dear, let me look at you. Very nice indeed. I'm glad to see the old lace again, and I hope you will wear it oftener than your mother did; I call it wasting good lace to save it. Ah! and the nice old Dendraith diamonds too. Harry, doesn't our bride look beautiful? It is good for a woman to be admired it makes her admirable. Philip has worked wonders already.'

Viola was trembling and colouring either at the praise or at Lady Clevedon's appeal to her cousin to confirm it.

'And this is the bridegroom's gift, is it not? Very lovely and most becoming. Did I not tell you,' Lady Clevedon added, aside, 'that hers was a face to improve? The change has come about sooner and more startlingly than I expected.'

'I think your niece is very lovely,' said Harry simply. Lady Clevedon went off to the assistance of Mrs. Sedley, to whom social duties were always arduous, and Harry Lancaster approached the bride.

She stood with her hands clasped before her, not looking up. He saw that she was breathing quickly.

'I hope you won't be angry with me if I ask you to accept a small wedding-gift,' he said, in a not very steady voice. 'It is a little antique ornament I found in Italy, of little use, but I thought the chasing finely done. It is said to have belonged to the Calonna[38] family, and to have played a somewhat malign part in more than one duel, but it is now put to the peaceful purposes of a paper-knife or a mere ornament.'

He handed her, as he spoke, a little instrument of finely tempered steel, with an elaborate handle exquisitely chased.

'The blade is rusty; the man in the shop where I bought it, assured me, as a recommendation, that the mark is really an old blood-stain! He looked ready to stick it into me when I laughed.'

'How beautiful! and how good of you!' she said. 'I shall value this very much.'

She hesitated for a moment, and then thrust it through the coils of her hair.

'How perfectly charming!' exclaimed the watchful Arabella, rapturously. 'Really, of all your wedding- presents, I envy you this one most. There is something quite fascinating about it. It looks as if it might have done many a secret deed of darkness before it was promoted to these gayer offices. I am sure it must have some sinister history; it makes you look quite dangerous, Miss Sedley, but *so* interesting! Doesn't it, Mr. Lancaster? Quite a Lucrezia Borgia.[39] We shall be hearing dreadful things of you, I am sure; it will be quite kind of you to give us all a new sensation. Do let it be something striking, won't you? Paper-knife or mere ornament as it is, I must confess I shouldn't like to have it raised against me. But it won't be *me*, I am sure; I never made anybody jealous; much more likely this Mrs. Lincoln who is coming to live here and shock us all. Mr. Lancaster, you don't know what responsibility may rest on your shoulders; it is really a dangerous gift – why, it is enough to make one commit a murder for the mere pleasure of using it.'

'It would be a sin to waste it,' said Geoffrey; 'a flying in the face of Providence, which has provided all things for our use.'

'Now then, Viola, my dear, we must be off,' said her aunt. 'Arabella, Harry, Geoffrey, and I, will go in the next carriage, and the bride and her father will follow in the last.'

In a moment the room was cleared, and the carriage drove off.

'What has become of that girl's shyness?' exclaimed Lady Clevedon, straining her eyes to catch the last glimpse of the still, white figure of the bride, as she stood, bouquet in hand, upon the doorstep.

Harry made no reply, but the thought crossed his mind that great misery and great shyness were perhaps likely to counteract one another.

'I am glad the day is so fine,' said Lady Clevedon presently; 'it will put them all in good spirits.'

'Yes,' Harry answered.

The weather was fine certainly, but it was not one of those languorous days of summer that suggest nothing but rest and peace. The sunshine had indeed a singular brilliancy, but there was a blusterous wind careering over the land, swaying the ripening corn and making the trees rustle and complain of the rough treatment. Overhead, the cloud-masses had been scattered by the wild wind; no form had been left them; they were strewn in ragged streamers across the sky, gleaming with captured light. But there was no suggestion of pain or passion in the aspect of the roughly handled clouds; rather a great joy in the infinite breadth of the heavens and the ecstasy of perfect freedom.

The grey old church, roused out of its habitual calm, was the centre of a scene of subdued excitement. Society in the village was stirred to its depths: only the bedridden remained at home to-day; the tiniest infants were rapt from their cradles and carried by eager mothers to the lych-gate,[40] where one by one the carriages drew up and the wedding-guests alighted, sweeping or tripping or hurrying into the church, according to habit and character.

Lady Clevedon was among those who did her alighting deliberately, giving directions to the coachman in decisive tones, and then walking coolly along the paved pathway between the graves to the grey old doorway in the ivy-covered tower.

This was the last arrival before the centre of all interest: the bride.

The old Manor-House coachman, with a backbone that any steeple might be proud of, whipped up his horses on entering the village, and the carriage dashed up to the lych-gate amidst an amount of dust and flourish and prancing that made one or two of the younger children cry.

Mr. Sedley alighted first, and was greeted with a cheer; then came a cloud of something soft and white, like the foam of the breakers, whose moan, even here, in the moment's excited pause which followed her appearance, the bride could just catch above the rushing of the wind.

There was a shout, and then a shower of roses, honey-suckle, and cottage flowers fell at her feet. Many a 'God bless you!' 'Long life and happiness to you!' followed her as she moved between the tombstones on her father's arm, while suddenly the old tower started into life and sent out a peal of wedding-bells which was heard for miles along the quiet country – those eternal wedding-bells, ushering in the sorrows of the ceaseless generations!

The sunshine was pouring down upon the pathway, but the wind seemed as if it would prevent the bride from entering the church, so angrily did it bluster round her and press against her as she bent forward to resist it. As the wind among sea-foam, that western blast made her garments shiver and flutter together, as if in fear.

'She looks like an angel!' exclaimed an enthusiastic woman among the crowd, holding up her indifferent infant for a last look as the white figure disappeared through the church-door.

'They'll make a lovely pair,' asserted another admirer; 'and don't the old gentleman look proud about it all!

'The poor lady don't seem quite pleased, though; she's that white and thin. I'm thinking the poor thing's got something wrong with her liver. As I was a-sayin' to George only the other day' – and so on; the oracular remark made to George being to the effect that only a box of Parr's Life Pills[41] stood between Mrs. Sedley and the grave.

Several people could recall the wedding of Mr. and Mrs. Sedley at this very church, among them old William, he, however, with patient humility, being ready at once to subordinate his reminiscences to those of any person who might think his own superior. Several did so, and 'Willum' faded quickly into obscurity.

There was a dim, wistful look in his eyes as they followed the young bride up the pathway to the church; only yesterday, it seemed, she had chattered to him in her childish way, taken him into her confidence about her tadpoles and her pets, or entreated him, with tears in her eyes, not to go on working in the rain. The lonely old man loved her faithfully, and his heart ached as he thought of the Manor-House henceforth without her.

Within the church, when the bells ceased, was a solemn hush. The wedding-guests were ranged along the chancel, looking like a set of gaily dressed and very properly-disposed dolls.

At the altar stood the bridegroom.

'How distractingly handsome he looks!' exclaimed Arabella in a whisper to her neighbour. 'If he weren't so nearly a married man, I should really fall in love with him!'

'You have still a few seconds to indulge in a transient passion,' said Lady Clevedon contemptuously.

'Alas! he is already claimed,' cried Arabella, with a sigh. 'Look with what grace he greets the bride; it is charming! And those few sweet words that he whispers in her ear.'

The bride's reply, had it been overheard, would have scandalised the spectators not a little.

'Please do not forget that I come here against my own wish, and can have no response in my heart for such speeches. And one thing more: please do not forget that what I say to-day is said with my lips only.'

There was no time to answer, for the ceremony was about to begin.

Philip had counted on the effect of the solemn service upon one of Viola's scrupulous temperament. He thought that she would feel the sacredness of the oaths she was taking, and that victory for him would be half- won by the strokes of her own vigorous conscience. He was quite unprepared for her repudiation of the whole service, and this continued opposition, meek and quiet as it was, roused the worst side of his character.

His bride, he reflected, had yet to learn the difference between a lover and a husband.

Over the altar was a stained-glass window of mellow tinting, through which the sunshine streamed. Every colour and shade of colour was there, blending, softening, gleaming, growing deeper or paler with the changing light and the occasional shadowing of a tree outside, blown back and forward by the wind. Viola was standing in the line of the sun's rays, and the colours stained her dress, passing across her in a broad band of radiance, and falling on the cold stone floor behind her, and on the half-effaced brasses at her feet. Upon her bosom a deep blood-red stain glowed in fiery brilliance, like the symbol of some master-passion in her heart, or perhaps a death-wound.

She remained perfectly still until the time came when the hands of bride and bridegroom were joined, and then she gave a slight, scarcely perceptible shiver, which, however, was not lost upon Harry or upon Philip.

'Those whom God hath joined together let no man put asunder.'

To the triumphant strains of the wedding-march bride and bridegroom walked back along the aisle to their carriage.

Was it only Viola who heard in that wonderful outburst the ring of something infinitely sad and hopeless?

'You look cold, my love,' said Philip, when he and his bride were on their way back to the Manor-House, the sound of the bells still pursuing them in noisy and rather foolish rejoicing. 'Can I put a shawl round you?'

'Oh, I am not cold, thank you,' said Viola.

'Excitement a little too much for you, perhaps. Well, that will soon be over now. They can't amuse themselves at our expense much longer, let us be thankful. Soon I shall have you all to myself –.'

He put his arm round her, and was about to draw her closer, when his eye caught the glitter of the ornament in her hair.

'What's this?' he asked. 'Another wedding-gift? Uncommonly fine work too, – antique, and of the best Renaissance period. But what a murderous-looking thing to wear in your hair!'

'It is meant for a paper-knife, or merely to be regarded as a curiosity,' said Viola.

'It is a real work of art; there's no doubt of that. Who is the possessor of so much artistic *flair*?'

'Harry Lancaster gave it me.'

Philip looked round. 'Indeed! It is very obliging of Harry Lancaster, but I object to your receiving presents from him, especially of this character. If one believed in omens, it might make one uncomfortable. You'll excuse me, but I must take possession of this sinister-looking hairpin. I can't allow you to keep it.'

Viola flushed up.

'It was given to *me*, not to you,' she said, 'and I cannot surrender it.'

'*Cannot* is scarcely the word to use to me, my dear.'

'*Will* not, then,' she said hastily.

Philip looked at her in astonishment.

'I am unable to congratulate you on your wisdom, Viola. To begin your married life by deliberate opposition and disobedience is not the act of a sensible woman, but of a pettish child.'

'I cannot part with my gift,' Viola persisted.

'My dear, I have told you that I cannot allow you to keep it. What is to happen in such a case? You know quite well that Lancaster has behaved in a way that is unforgivable. I consider that his conduct has been throughout ungentlemanly. We stand to one another in a hostile attitude. He did his utmost to supersede me in your affections; we meet on terms of enmity. Such being the case, I consider it a piece of infernal cheek on his part to give you a present, and I must insist on your returning it at once.'

'No, no, I cannot, I cannot,' she cried, with rising excitement, as Philip leant forward to take the object of dispute from her.

'Now don't be foolish,' he said. 'Can't you understand the situation and be reasonable? It is impossible for my wife, in existing circumstances, to wear the gift of Harry Lancaster.'

'I won't wear it, then,' said Viola; 'only don't take it away from me.'

'You must give it back; there is no alternative; and if *you* won't, I must. Will you give it back?'

'I have already accepted it. I can't give it back.'

'Then you leave me no choice.'

She had the knife clasped in her right hand: Philip began gently enough but resolutely to open the fingers. Striving to close them again, she unclasped from her neck the diamond ornament – Philip's gift – with her free hand.

'Will you give back that dagger?' asked Philip once more.

'I would rather give back these,' she answered, holding out the glittering trinket.

Philip's face darkened.

'Infatuated woman! Do you want to ruin our chance of peace at the very outset?'

'I will obey you in all other things. I accepted this gift, not as your wife, but as *myself.* I was not your wife then. Will you not leave me even a little remnant of individuality? Am I always to be *your wife*, never myself? I have not questioned your authority, but you ask for more than authority. You ask me to surrender my personality. The greatest despot only commands, he does not altogether extinguish his subjects. You go too far even for a husband.'

'You talk too much nonsense even for a wife,' said Philip. 'The world regards and criticises you now as my wife, and nothing else. What else are you? You possess no other standing or acknowledged existence. Therefore naturally I have a deep interest in your conduct. I am sorry to have to begin our married life with a disagreement, but you really must understand from the outset, once for all, what our relations are to be. I desire nothing better than to be a kind and indulgent husband; but on such points as this I can brook no dispute. Now pray let's have no more of it. Give me that bauble without further fuss. We are near home, and must have no scenes.'

But Viola's fingers only tightened their grasp as the carriage approached the avenue of the Manor-House.

'Very well, then, I must use a little muscular persuasion; there is no time to lose.'

As he did so, Viola held the diamonds, which she had in her left hand, out of the window.

'On this one point I too am determined,' she said; 'if you take my gift, I drop the necklace!'

With a muttered oath Philip relaxed his hold.

'Obstinate woman! You don't know when the last payment will be made for this.'

CHAPTER XXI

UPTON CASTLE

'Now, Marion, if you are not content, you ought to be, and I will listen to no plaints. Viola writes regularly and cheerfully (her style is really rather stately and good); her husband appears to be kind to her, and I cannot see what you have left to make yourself miserable about.'

'Oh! I am not miserable, Augusta, only anxious – a little anxious.'

'Now, pray, Marion, what for?' demanded Lady Clevedon brusquely. 'Do you suppose that avalanches are lying in wait for your daughter, and precipices defying the laws of nature at every turn?'

Mrs. Sedley was silent. She did not dare to tell her sister-in-law that it was the very cheerfulness of Viola's letters that caused her anxiety. She could gather nothing from these clear unemotional epistles couched in language which had a certain quiet force, and vaguely suggested that the writer held many unsaid things in reserve.

'I must wait till she comes home,' thought the mother, 'and then I shall easily be able to judge.'

The wedding-tour was now nearly over, and the happy pair were expected to arrive at their home at the end of the week.

Lady Dendraith drove over daily to Upton Castle, endeavouring to brighten up the damp tumble-down old place and give it, as far as possible, a bridal aspect. Her task was indeed a hard one. Of all gloomy old houses that ever a well-intentioned mother attempted to make look bridal, surely Upton Castle was the most hopeless. The poor lady gazed at its gaunt rooms and listened to the ceaseless moaning of the waves below its windows, in despair. Her one idea for effecting a bridal appearance was white satin; but after the introduction of an inordinate number of fire-screens, sofa-cushions, photograph-frames, album-covers, and other ornaments made of this festive material, her sole resource became exhausted, and still the shadows lingered gloomily in the corners, and hung, like a canopy, about the ceilings of the vast old rooms.

Lady Dendraith, sitting gazing at her unsuccessful distribution of white satin in the great drawing-room, – her bonnet, from sheer perturbedness of spirit, edged to one side, – was a sight piteous to behold. The dreariness of the place, now in the throes of a thorough cleaning, was enough to discourage the most hopeful.

It seemed as if the effort to make the long-disused house once more a human habitation had disclosed a host of dismal secrets. After a lapse of nearly a hundred years, daylight streamed into musty rooms and corridors, where ancient spiders had established themselves in forgotten corners, – spiders with long pedigrees, and a goodly array of corpses to attest their title to distinction; and, alas! these respectable creatures now found themselves suddenly swept away by a democratic 'Turk's head,'[42] and wondered irefully what things were coming to.

The caretaker of ten years' standing – a person of such intense and awful respectability that Lady Dendraith felt frightened of her – was tall and strangely thin, with a face tapering at each end to a nice point, a pair of small eyes, and a long pale yellow nose. Smooth iron-grey hair, brushed down over her brow and severely plaited at the back of the head, seemed a rebuke to all forms of frivolous hairdressing.

But if Mrs. Barber's appearance was awe-inspiring, her language was something that might turn one to stone. Poor Lady Dendraith felt like a lisping child in the presence of this living Dictionary.

'Well, Mrs. Barber,' she would say with humility, 'how are you getting on?'

With a stately inclination of the head Mrs. Barber would reply, ' I am gratified to be able to inform your Ladyship that the preparations are progressing with as much celebrity'[43] – (the good woman's copiousness and accuracy were not exactly on a par) – 'as the circumstances will admit.'

'Oh, I am glad of that; the time is getting short, you know, and we seem rather behind-hand. You see, my son will bring his wife home on Tuesday, and I am anxious to have everything looking nice and bright for their return.'

'I can enter into your Ladyship's sentiments,' replied the august one, with a stately bend of the head; 'but as to the place looking *bright*, *I* don't anticipate that it is ever likely to do that. I have resided here for ten years, and I cannot remember that I ever saw it look, as we might say, cheerful. Them waves' – (Mrs. Barber did relax a little from the austerity of her language under stress of emotion) – 'them waves are that mournful, beating day in, day out, against the cliff-side, that at times, I do assure your Ladyship, I have felt as if I must give a month's notice and go on the spot. At night, when the place is shut up, it's as still as a churchyard, barring the rats in the garret, which worrits about among the lumber like creatures taken leave of their senses. And the size of 'em! Your Ladyship wouldn't believe it,' said Mrs. Barber with much feeling, 'but the tramp and scamper of them nasty beasts over my head is more like a man's footsteps than a vermin's.'

'Dear me! Why don't you let the cat into the garret, Mrs. Barber?'

The bony form of the housekeeper turned straight round and faced her alarmed employer.

'Did I understand your Ladyship aright? Give my poor Maria to be worried by them great animals!'

'Oh, very well, Mrs. Barber,' said Lady Dendraith meekly, 'if your Maria is afraid of the rats' –

'What cat can do, Maria for many years 'as done,' said Mrs. Barber; 'and for no other family would she have done as much. I say it with respect.' Giving a slight sniff as a delicate finish to her remarks, the housekeeper turned again and led the way to the dining-room.

'Oh, this seems more forward,' said Lady Dendraith. 'But those old portraits look sadly gloomy, and I should much like to give them a little cleaning up; but Mr. Philip laughs at me. Still, for a young bride one feels that everything ought to be as cheering as possible.'

When Lady Dendraith visited the drawing-room her heart sank. It was enormously large and lofty, the light from the windows, which faced the sea and seemed almost to overhang it, was powerless to drive the shadows from the farther end of the room or to rise to the high ceiling. The furniture, of a stately character, stood in severe symmetry along the walls; not a footstool remained unbalanced by a brother footstool, staring at it from the opposite side of the vast fireplace, or from a corresponding sofa. It was difficult to imagine this gloomy room the kingdom of a young bride.

'Poor young thing! I wish the place had been a little less lonesome for her. I dare say she will be able to make a snug corner for herself out of the ante-drawing room, though, do what I will, it looks unhomelike. I *did* think the red carpet and blue curtains would have cheered it up!'

In a somewhat depressed mood Lady Dendraith returned to her own cosy home, leaving the housekeeper to her Maria and the redoubtable rats.

The eventful day proved wet. Before sunrise a mist lay across the sea, and crept inland, spreading over hill and valley, and soon obliterating every object of the landscape. It was to a world without form and void,[44] a blank, expressionless world, that the young wife was to be welcomed. Five months had passed since she had left her home on that brilliant July morning, and the summer meantime had given place to the dreariness of a spiritless November.

As the sound of carriage-wheels at length announced the arrival of the expected travellers, the hall-door was thrown open and Mrs. Sedley stood revealed on the doorstep, her figure defined against the fire-glow of the great hall behind. A little in her rear was Mrs. Barber and the portly butler, while on the stone ledge which flanked the flight of cold grey steps stood Maria, with tail erect and glistening eyes, in an attitude of excited expectancy.

The next moment the occupants of the carriage had mounted the steps and the bride was folded in her mother's arms.

The embrace was long and silent.

Philip then shook hands with Mrs. Sedley cordially, inquiring for her health and thanking her for having come to welcome them.

'You see I have brought back your daughter safe and sound,' he said cheerfully. 'She is rather pale to-night, after all our journeyings, but I hope the rest will soon make her look like herself again. What a magnificent fire! None of *your* ordering, Mrs. Barber, I am sure. You know what sworn enemies you and I used to be in old times about your fires. (It's my belief the respectable person's chilling appearance put them out),' he added aside, with a laugh.

'Upon my word,' he went on, looking round the shadowy hall, now filled with the fitful light of blazing logs, 'the place looks really comfortable. What do you say, Viola?'

'Most comfortable,' she assented.

Mrs. Sedley had led her to a large chair, by the fireplace, removed her wraps, and made her warm her cold feet and hands before the blaze.

Maria, all curiosity, was circling round mother and daughter with curving back and agitated tail. Finally she rubbed herself against Viola's knee, and then jumped on to her lap.

'*Well!*' exclaimed the astonished Mrs. Barber, in amazement; 'I never saw Maria do such a thing in her life before. I wouldn't have believed it!'

With a gesture that was almost passionate Viola had welcomed the animal and folded it in her arms. Her head was bent down for the instant, and when she raised her face again, it was very white.

Mrs. Sedley looked anxiously at her.

What was the indefinable change that she saw in her daughter's manner and expression? – a change too subtle to be described, yet distinct enough to make Mrs. Sedley feel more than doubtful whether she could now discover her daughter's frame of mind. Viola seemed to have wandered away to a great distance. There was something a little careless, a little indifferent, in the carriage of the head, in the voice and gestures, and it struck Mrs. Sedley that she took but slight interest in her new home.

Mrs. Barber, who had secretly resented the idea of a mistress, came to the conclusion that she and the lady might get on well enough together if the lady were careful.

Mrs. Sedley, Mrs. Barber, and Maria presently conducted the new-comer to her bedroom, a vast, dim space over the drawing-room, with the same large, unsuccessful windows and the same symmetrical arrangement of Brobdignag[45] furniture.

Below, a repast awaited the travellers, and Viola was exhorted to come down as soon as possible, as she looked worn out and must be hungry.

'Yes, hungry I am,' said she; 'I feel at present as if food and rest ought to content any human being, and yet curiosity is not quite chased away.' She drew aside the curtains as she spoke and peered out into the night. 'Pitch darkness,' she said, with rather a singular intonation.

'The window looks out to the sea,' remarked Mrs. Sedley. 'But come, dearest; that you can admire at your leisure to-morrow.'

An involuntary sigh escaped the young mistress of the house at the word 'to-morrow,' but it was checked midway, as she added with a smile, 'Absurd curiosity indeed, since I shall have a whole lifetime in which to indulge it.'

Mother and daughter descended the stairs together, followed in a zigzag course by the singular and devoted cat. Viola took her up and placed her on her shoulder, entering the dining-room with the creature curling affectionately about her neck and face.

'I wish I were an artist,' exclaimed Philip, rising and coming over to his wife, 'You have no idea what a charming picture you and Maria make.'

An indefinable change of expression passed across her face as she altered the admired attitude, taking the cat in her arms and folding her close against her breast.

'The credit of it rests with Maria,' she said, moving away towards the fireplace. The butler, a portly person, like an overgrown Cupid,[46] presently announced that the meal was on the table, and the three forthwith sat down, in a rather constrained and uncomfortable manner, to the repast. Their voices wakened a thousand hollow whispers in the vast room, and had a strange ominous sound mingling with the eternal boom of the waves.

To Viola it seemed as if each of the portraits was gazing at her, in the cold omniscient manner peculiar to those works of art. Everything about the place was weird and hushed and mysterious; there was something blood-chilling at times even about Maria, who had a way of appearing suddenly in unexpected places, or springing without warning on to the back of one's chair.

'It's my belief that cat's bewitched,' Philip said; 'see the way she glares at me with her green eyes!'

'I read somewhere that green eyes are the truest of all eyes,' said Viola.

'Perhaps that's why they are so rare,' Philip observed. 'Get away, you green-eyed monster; I know I shall dream of you to-night, and that'll not be a nightmare exactly, but something worse.'

'Well,' said Mrs. Sedley, after some time had passed in desultory talk, 'I think the best thing this tired child can do is to go to bed, and put off seeing her new domain till morning, when I hope the weather will have changed and everything be at its brightest and best. Then she will have to install herself as mistress of the house, and make Mrs. Barber understand that she no longer has supreme authority.'

Philip laughed.

'I expect the good Barber will grievously resent her dethronement, and we shall have some majestic English on the head of it. I hope she won't take umbrage and go. She is honest as the day, and devoted to the family.'

'She shall not go because of me, I promise you,' said Viola, with something in her manner that was new to it. 'It would be better I should go myself. I can perhaps equal her in honesty, but I cannot claim to have served the family for so many devoted years.'

She spoke half jestingly, and Philip laughed a little, but he glanced at her in a manner not exactly amused.

'Dearest,' said Mrs. Sedley again, 'you must really go to bed now, you are looking so tired.'

Viola rose, and mother and daughter left the room together, Philip springing up to open the door for them. He returned to his place by the fire with a changed expression. The polite cheerfulness and even gaiety of his demeanour during the evening suddenly fell from him like a mask; his brow clouded, and his thin lips set themselves in a hard, disagreeable line. Much to her chagrin, Maria had been left behind in the dining-room, alone with her master. A faint '*maiaw*' disturbed his sinister meditations. He looked up with a frown, saw the cat, and following a savage impulse, he put out his foot and kicked her to the other side of the room, hearing, not without satisfaction, a dull thud as the creature struck against the panelling. Philip rose, lifted the cat in his arms, and walking across the room, quietly put her outside the door. There, on the hard floor, with her leg broken, the creature passed the night, and there she was found by her distracted mistress next morning, the animal trying, in her joy, to limp towards her as she heard the familiar footsteps.

CHAPTER XXII

EXILED

Maria's broken leg was at once bound up, and she found herself in a position of even greater importance than usual.

Viola begged to have the wounded creature beside her, in her own sitting room, where she could tend her and give her food. This, and her evident concern for the animal, won the housekeeper's heart. No war was declared between the new mistress and her commander-in-chief. Mrs. Barber was even ready to indulge her well-conducted lady with a semblance of authority.

'If there is anything that you would like altered, ma'am,' said the housekeeper graciously, 'I hope you won't hesitate to say so. Her Ladyship arranged the furniture as she thought best, but of course you are quite at liberty to make any little change as you might prefer. Everybody has their own taste, which, of course, it's no blame to them but only what is natural.'

'I think I have no taste of my own,' said Viola. 'It seems to me impossible that any of the furniture could stand in any other position. I do not wish it altered.'

And from that moment it seemed as if a spell had been cast over the place, as over the palace of the Sleeping Beauty; not a chair or a table, or so much as a footstool, budged by a hair's-breadth from its accustomed spot.

Viola's decree had petrified the house in its present form, and there it remained, solemn, solid, and eternal. It seemed as if its dignity must confound even the thunders of the Day of Doom, and might be expected to live through even that crisis, calm and undisturbed.

Mrs. Barber never ceased to marvel at Maria's strange accident.

'I left her with you and Mr. Philip in the dining-room as safe and sound as she could be, and in the morning – ! She must have left the dining-room with you and your mamma,' the housekeeper suggested.

Viola was never very explicit on this point. She could not, or would not, state whether the cat came out of the room or remained behind with Philip; and as Mrs. Barber had a wholesome dread of that polite gentleman, she dared not question him as she longed to do. So the affair remained a mystery.

Mrs. Sedley had to leave on the following morning, as Mr. Sedley was not very well, but it had been arranged that Viola was to drive with her to the Manor-House for lunch, returning home for dinner in the evening.

'It appears to me, ma'am, that Mrs. Sedley's own indisposition is not what it should be,' said the housekeeper; 'I never saw any one look so like death – never!'

The speech, which was intended in the most friendly and complimentary spirit, made Viola turn pale. Her eyes wandered mournfully out to the sea, whose grey waters could this morning be dimly discerned through sheets of driving rain.

Mrs. Sedley's white face and the deep dark circles under the eyes told a tale she would fain have concealed. Last night, when for a short half-hour mother and daughter had been alone together, Viola had entreated to be allowed to return home for a little while, to look after the invalid and take some of her old duties again; but Mrs. Sedley, with tears in her eyes, had firmly refused. 'Your duty now is to your husband,' she said, 'and I will never let you neglect that for my sake.'

When the housekeeper left her, Viola remained in precisely the same attitude, gazing out to sea. The waves were tossing restlessly, forming for ever in new vigour, like endless generations, to culminate and then roll over and lose their individuality in the waste of waters. How fresh and eager they looked as they climbed up to the breaking-point, wearing their crown of surf for a moment, and then with what a peaceful sweep they sank to the level of the dead waves, broken and gone, losing the fever of their short lives in a gentle annihilation! Viola's thoughts were breaking the bounds of her teaching. She rose, shook her head angrily, trying to banish them, but they streamed out triumphantly beyond all the limits that she set to their flowing. What had come to her? She remembered with a sense of relief that the rest of the day would be passed in her mother's society and in the old scenes of her childhood. Surely these evil spirits would be exorcised *there*! Philip was to be out all day; he had business to attend to; not till evening would he return, and then husband and wife were to have their first *tête à tête* meal in their new home. If only she could ask Mrs. Barber to come in and take it with them!

With this unholy aspiration in her heart, Viola set out through the driving rain for the Manor-House. The anxious questions which she asked about her mother's health were put aside by Mrs. Sedley; she had never been quite well for the last thirty years, never since the birth of her first child, but she was no worse than usual. Perhaps to-day and yesterday her head had ached a good deal, but she had nothing to complain of. On the rack, Viola wondered, would she find anything to complain of?

Through the rain the familiar outlines of the Manor-House loomed into sight. As she alighted at the hall-door, Viola thought that she could realise what a spirit must feel who revisited the scenes of its earthly life after passing into the next phase of existence beyond the grave.

After the midday meal, at which were assembled the same group as of yore: father, mother, Geoffrey, and Viola, the rain cleared, and Geoffrey not wishing to allow brotherly affection to clash with his hatred of being indoors, proposed that the assembly should adjourn to the garden.

Here Viola was greeted by a rapturous company of dogs, and behind them came hopping and flapping excitedly her jackdaw, whose evident delight to see her again was more eloquently expressed, as Viola said, than that of her relations.

'Well, I *do* call that ungrateful,' cried Geoffrey, 'after all my fortnight's practice of the enthusiastic fraternal welcome!'

His embrace had been of the vigorous serio-comic order, by which alone he permitted his British emotions to find expression.

'I say, Ila, I wish you hadn't gone and got married,' he confided to her when they were marching arm-in- arm along one of the straight walks of the old fruit-garden. 'Life won't be worth living here all by oneself.'

'I am sorry to leave you – but you can come over and see me, of course, whenever you like. And then you will be very soon leaving home. When do you expect to get your appointment?'

'Oh, Sir Philip is seeing about that for me,' said Geoffrey. 'Your marriage has its conveniences, Ila.'

She winced.

'I say, what do you think of your husband after five months of his society?' the boy asked, so naively that even Viola, whose sense of humour was certainly not keener than the average, burst out laughing.

'Well, but what *do* you think of him?' persisted Geoffrey.

'I think him very clever, for one thing,' she answered. 'And what else?'

'Very determined.'

'And – ?'

'Very handsome.'

'Then I suppose you are awfully fond of him.'

'One is often fond of people possessing not one of these qualities,' returned Viola. 'I dare say, in course of time, some foolish person may become fond even of you, for instance – that is, if you cure yourself of the habit of asking questions.'

Geoffrey made a grimace. 'But, my dear, the subject, to a brotherly heart, is so interesting.'

She smiled sadly. How this old familiar boyish nonsense made her heart ache! Ah! if only she could wipe out the memory of those awful five months, and take up the thread of her life at the point where she had left it. Even her mother could no longer protect her against the promptings of her evil nature. In Philip's presence all that was hard and bold and reckless came to the surface; she could not believe as she ought to believe, she could not feel as she ought to feel, she could not even *pray* as she used to pray. Her life was like some awful dream, and her husband the presence from which her whole being sought to escape in the frantic horror- stricken helplessness of a nightmare.

Never had she felt this helplessness more terrible than she felt it to-day amid the scenes of her former life, in the old home, whence a decree of eternal banishment had been spoken. '*Your duty now is with your husband, and I will never let you neglect that for my sake.*'

The old talismans were useless; their virtue had gone out of them. The future must be faced alone and unbefriended.

CHAPTER XXIII

A SELECT CIRCLE

Unhappily for herself, Viola was not a person to whom one could remain indifferent. Philip, in spite of his exasperation, was still in love with his wife, after his own fashion. It was impossible for him to acquiesce in the cold and distant relations that she wished to establish between them; her conduct amazed and maddened him. In all his wide experience of life he had never heard or dreamt of such a woman. Her character was to him incomprehensible. He could neither frighten her nor soften her; threats, insults, sneers (and he was not sparing of all these) left her as meek and as cold as before.

If she had been a haughty, rebellious woman, giving him insult for insult, sneer for sneer, he might have understood it; but she professed the most complete wifely submission, obeyed him in every detail, and when he reviled her she answered not again; yet behind all this apparent yielding he knew that thence was something he could not touch – the real woman who withdrew herself from him inexorably and for ever. A stupider man might have been content, when he had so far succeeded in his object as to make her his wife, but Philip knew that this seeming success was, after all, a humiliating failure. That she had evaded *him* of all men in the world, despite his utmost efforts! – that was what galled him.

It was this exasperating conviction that made his manner towards his wife, in spite of its polish, at times absolutely intolerable. Her invariable meekness under extreme provocation served rather to incense than to appease him. It left him nothing to attack; he had no handle even for complaint. The average man thinks himself ridiculous and injured if his wife succeeds in maintaining an attitude independent of him and his commands – or wishes, as he euphoniously expresses it. His power is called in question if she is not at once absorbed into his existence, revolving round him as a satellite, accepting him as her standard and the arbiter of her fate. Any reserve, any withdrawal on her part is an injury which he bitterly resents, because in his own eyes, and in those of others, it stamps him as a man who fails to exact the privileges of his position. Unable to make his partner pass under the yoke after the usual fashion, he loses prestige and sinks in his own esteem.

Philip, accustomed for so long to absolute dominion, was driven almost to frenzy by the consciousness of being quietly held at bay by one of the gentlest and most submissive beings he had ever met. She had none of the usual little ways of women; one could manage a woman who had 'little ways' – little fits of temper, and little fits of repentance; a woman who coaxed and protested alternately, who was sometimes jealous, sometimes angry, about her husband's admiration of other women. There was something to work upon in all this. But Viola! When did she lose her temper, or repent, or weep, or ask to be forgiven? When did she plead for a new gown or coax him for a new bonnet? When did she condescend to be jealous? Had he not pursued Arabella with attentions and compliments till he was sick of the sight of her and her wrigglings, and what notice had Viola taken of his conduct, what remonstrance had she offered? None; literally none. His doings seemed to be perfectly indifferent to her, so long as he kept out of her sight.

It was a scarcely credible situation!

The first few weeks after the return home were very troubled and wretched. Philip seemed to take a delight in humbling and humiliating his wife by every means in his power, and his power in that direction was unlimited.

Though it was all done in his most polished manner, though he never forgot that he was what he called a '*gentleman*,' his conduct towards her was of a kind that no woman of her type could forgive, even if she tried. She knew now the reason of Harry Lancaster's passionate warnings; she knew now why he had said that he would rather see her lying dead before him than married to Philip Dendraith.

He was right! 'Ah! mother, you will never know what I suffer for you; you never *shall* know, for it would break your heart, as it has broken mine!'

The sense of duty, desperately as it had been assailed in this hurricane of horror and disaster, still held firm, and still the poor mummied[47] religion which had been offered to this passionate heart for a guide, held up a withered finger of exhortation. With these motives and these faiths Viola struggled on, fighting that desperate fight against herself and her own nature which fills the lives of so many women with inward storm and wreckage. Her faith now was her sole anchor. Without the belief that it was *right* to endure all that she endured, it would have been literally impossible for her to live her life for another day. That gave it – even *it!* – a sort of consecration.

Not long after the return of the bride and bridegroom to their home the neighbours began to call upon them. They came to criticise, to indulge their curiosity and to perform their social duties. Mr. and Mrs. Evans, with their eldest daughter; Mr. and Mrs. Pellett, an absent-minded old student and his very commonplace wife; Mrs. and Miss Featherstone, a fashionable lady and her daughter, the latter a great huntress; Mrs. Dixie, in magnificent sunset effulgence, and finally Arabella, who was staying with Lady Clevedon, and begged to be driven over to call upon her charming niece.

Arabella made a great many awkward though proper assumptions about Viola's supposed state of romantic bliss and her presumed distraction if Philip left her for a day or two; she was disposed to talk a little archly about 'somebody,' and to indulge in gentle raillery on the subject of 'honeymoons which lasted a good deal longer than one poor month.'

Viola, unhappily, could not extract the cream of the situation and enjoy it, such as it was, in spite of its grim satire on her real position; it hurt without amusing her.

'Whom the gods intend to destroy,'[48] Harry Lancaster had once remarked, 'they send into the world with a sensitive spirit, *minus* the sense of humour. Whom the gods intend to torture, but to keep alive for further sport, they endow also with a sensitive spirit, but add to it a sense of humour abnormally strong.'

The neighbours discussed the new mistress of Upton Castle with perfect freedom, but upon the whole not unfavourably. The Evans family were even enthusiastically favourable; perhaps because Dick, the family oracle, had pronounced, when he met her at Clevedon before her marriage, that she was 'a nice, unaffected sort of girl, and very good form.'

Geoffrey, who was a frequent visitor at his sister's house, used often to hear, at second hand, the criticisms of the neighbours, and sometimes he would repeat them to her.

'I say, Ila, my dear,' he announced one day, 'Mrs. Pellett thinks that you are sinking into a decline.'

'She must have been comparing notes with Mrs. Barber, then,' said Viola; 'that is also her opinion.'

'Then you have certainly found your way to Mrs. Barber's heart,' observed Philip; 'it is her highest compliment. If she loves you, she represents you with one foot in the grave.'

'A good attitude to be photographed in,' Geoffrey suggested, with a boy's extravagant foolishness. 'Happy thought! We could arrange you artistically, with cross-bones, you know, and an extensive churchyard for a background. You might be toying elegantly with a skull!'[49]

Viola smiled, and drew her hand across her eyes, as if to erase the heavy lines beneath them.

Geoffrey wanted to know how she liked her new neighbours. Her judgments were indolently charitable. The only person she actively objected to was Mrs.

Pellett, the lady who originated the 'decline' theory. The others were all 'very pleasant.'

'You'll have to go and call on them, you know,' said Geoffrey. 'You *would* go and get married, and you must take the consequences. Does a woman promise to pay calls in the marriage-service? Rather rough on you, isn't it? Calling doesn't seem in your line.'

'That is probably the reason it is given me to do,' said Viola, in all seriousness; 'it is a discipline.'

Philip having gone to town for a fortnight, Viola managed to cajole her brother into sharing the 'discipline' with her.

'Only two calls to-day,' she said;' and it will be such a relief to me.'

She was a little over-hasty in this last conclusion, as she afterwards found, to her cost. The first call was on Mrs. Pellett; 'to get it over,' Viola said. That exemplary lady lived in a small red-brick house, which lay on the outskirts of Upton, smothered among trees, and very damp and dark.

Ushered into a musty drawing-room, where the blinds were down, the visitors had an opportunity of inhaling the heavy atmosphere, and of surveying the beauties of the room, before the owner appeared. The table was in the exact centre, and in its own centre it wore, like a weight on its heart, a heavy china bowl, which stood on its head and supported (as a father acrobat, upon the soles of his feet, his little son) a second smaller bowl, this one in the normal attitude.

The glacial severities of the marble mantelpiece were softened by pastoral groups in pink china; gallant swains and bashful shepherdesses, with dispositions of marvellous sweetness. Let the world growl and grumble as it might, these delightful creatures smiled on untiringly. On the wall beamed the portrait of a lady, with pale glossy hair and a pink face, smooth as a pebble, small blue eyes and attenuated eyebrows, high up out of reach of the eyes, as if they were intended by nature to break the interminable expanse of the forehead which rose majestically above them. In spite of that forehead, no one would have had the temerity to suggest that the lady was a person of intellect. Anything more blandly and blamelessly feeble than that face, with its thin nerveless lips, would be hard to picture.

'I believe she had the top of her head shaved and thrown into that forehead,' Geoffrey declared; 'and I believe Mrs. Pellett follows her example. Hers is just as fine; it's quite grand, – one feels in her presence like looking up at Mont Blanc.'

'O Geoffrey!'

'It ought to look well in a sunset, but wants ruggedness. I wonder' –

The door opened at this point and Mrs. Pellett entered the room.

Geoffrey, who had absently fixed his eyes upon the owner's forehead, woke with a start to reply to her polite greeting. Mrs. Pellett was a good deal like the portrait of the pale pink lady, which she said represented her mother, whose sweetness of disposition and admirable character were but feebly reproduced in the picture. The parent surpassed the child in meekness: Mrs. Pellett had not given herself to district-visiting and village affairs without acquiring some decision of character. This applied, however, only to her own walks of life; in relation to the world in general, she was obedience itself. She who terrified the schoolmistress with a glance of her eye, and made herself dreaded like the Day of Judgment among defaulting scholars, told Viola that she could not travel alone for however short a distance, and never left home without her husband.

When Viola saw that kindly but absent-minded old husband, she wondered how his presence could inspire any sense of security. He might have seen his wife run over by the slowest of waggons, and never have awakened to the melancholy fact till all was over. He was a scholar, a man who had distinguished himself at college, and who now carried in his handsome old face the stamp of thought and cultivation. He spent his days buried among his books, whence he emerged with eyes still turned inwards, and an unconquerable tendency to answer the frivolities of visitors and of his own family entirely at random.

'My dear, this is Mrs. Philip Dendraith,' explained Mrs. Pellett, in a louder tone, for the second time, as her husband, though extremely polite and cordial in a blindfold sort of fashion, was evidently settling into a contented state of ignorance as to the name and condition of his guests.

'Yes, my dear, so you said; – so you said. It is a strange thing that one can live for years in a place and yet remain quite ignorant of one's neighbours. Mr. Philip Dendraith is a name upon everybody's lips, and yet never before have I had the pleasure of meeting him.'

Geoffrey's face was a study.

'My dear, you make a mistake,' began his wife; 'this is not Mr. Dendraith; it is' –

But the old man was not listening. He was asking Viola if she liked the neighbourhood, whether her father and mother were in good health, and how were all her sisters.

'Brothers, dear,' remonstrated Mrs. Pellett.

'And brothers?' added her husband blandly.

'Your husband looks younger than I expected,' he went on pleasantly.

'Charles!'

'Well, my dear, I looked for one rather more mature – not quite so boyish' –

'I don't look my age, I know,' the audacious Geoffrey broke in, seeing that Mrs. Pellett had given up her husband in despair and turned to Viola. 'My wife often complains about it, but I tell her it is a fault that will mend.'

'Yes, yes,' said the old scholar, nodding his head; 'quite soon enough, quite soon enough. Very interesting old place that of yours – fine example of later Norman work; but I fear the sea is fast undermining it. My friend Foster there tells me that the water is working its way under the keep, and that he doesn't think it will last for many years longer.'

Geoffrey sadly shook his head. 'I fear it is too true,' he said. 'I thought of building a breakwater to receive the brunt of the battle just at the point, but I am told that the plan is not feasible. The tide runs too strong round there.'

'A sad pity,' said Mr. Pellett in a musing tone; 'we are losing all our fine old monuments, between the ferocity of the elements and the greater ferocity of the Vandal Man. But I must not get upon this subject – it is a sore point with me.'

'Ah! then we shall sympathise,' cried the unprincipled youth, with much feeling'; I too wage deadly war against the destroyers of history, the devourers of the past.'

Upon this Mr. Pellett, all unsuspicious, took the serpent into his bosom; but the serpent, untrue to his normal character, underwent conversion in that citadel of honesty and kindliness, and left the house feeling extremely uncomfortable, for the old man had evidently taken a fancy to him, and had given him a friendly invitation, in parting, to come again.

'*Geoffrey!*'

'Yes, yes, I know,' said that youth, with a frown and a blush; 'let's say no more about it.'

'But how *could* you? It was really too bad; I don't know what I was saying to Mrs. Pellett; I quite lost my head in my dismay at your behaviour. What possessed you?'

'Don't know, I'm sure,' said Geoffrey, scratching his head uncomfortably. 'Thought it would be a lark, – once in the mess, couldn't back out; – worst of it is, Mr. Pellett asked me to go and see him – dashed if I know what name to go under.'

'Your own, of course,' said Viola rather severely, at which her brother made a grimace.

He promised to behave like an archangel during the call at the Rectory, and he followed his sister, hat in hand, into the presence of the Evans family, with an expression that would have done credit to St. Sebastian.[50]

Mrs. Evans was a tall, indefinite sort of woman, in nondescript attire; each year of her busy, careful, rather wearing existence had left its stamp upon her, not so much in signs of age as in a certain dim and colourless quality often to be observed among women who have passed their whole life in a small country village.

Married very young, she had missed her girlhood altogether, and had to endure the troubles of a woman's life before she had had time to realise any of its possibilities. She had a large family and a small income, and she had lived at Upton from her girlhood. Two and two generally make four. Mrs. Evans at fifty was as narrow and dim and petty in thought, as she was patient and irreproachable in action. Her opinions might be accurately guessed before she had uttered a word, because those opinions did not grow from the depths of her own being, but had settled upon her, like dust, from the surrounding atmosphere.

A sort of dull tragedy (though the neighbours knew it not) was being acted before their eyes in the picturesque old Rectory, with its red-tiled roof and warm lichen-covered walls. Mrs. Evans never from year's end to year's end knew the meaning of that benign and radiant word: health. Headache, back-ache, neuralgia, weakness, weariness, and a thousand nameless oppressions were her cruel and constant companions; yet a word of complaint scarcely passed her lips, and her husband, though he acknowledged in words that his wife 'enjoyed weak health,' was as blandly ignorant of the actual meaning of those words as though he had spoken in an unknown tongue.

It was in *his* service, in the grim cause of wifely duty, that she had surrendered so much, and he did not even know it. Among other things which she had had to surrender was her woman's power of attracting. That had entirely departed. She was excellent, admirable, but she was quite without charm.

Her fellow-creatures, at whose behest she had thus despoiled herself, now turned away from their obedient servant, rewarding her heroism with neglect, veiled under words of cold approbation.

Society has no reward for the faithful; only curses and stoning for the heretics.

The daughters of the Rectory were pleasant, large-limbed, fresh-looking girls, apparently unlimited in number, and somewhat wanting in variety. They respected their mother, but they worshipped their father: a singularly plain, pepper-and-salt-coloured[51] man of clerical appearance and manners. Quite unmistakable were the deep lines from nose to chin, and the shape of that triangular portion of the face bounded by the cheek- lines, the nose and the upper lip. He had also a clerical habit of rubbing his hands together when he did not clasp them behind his back and tilt himself forward at intervals on his toes.

Like many of his cloth, the Rev. Richard Evans enjoyed more than most men the usual privileges of his sex. His position was patriarchal; wife and daughters sat at his feet; his lightest word was law. So absolute was his rule that he never required to assert it. He was jovial, agreeable, but firm – very firm. His wife characteristically admired him for being firm with her and the family in matters wherein, in point of fact, he had absolutely no right to interfere.

Dorothy, the wild, auburn-haired youngest daughter, was the only one of the sisters who gave no promise of following in her mother's footsteps. She tore more frocks in one summer than any of her sisters had torn in their lives; she resented gloves, and would not keep her hair tidy. Sometimes she was disobedient, even – awful thought! when her father had commanded, and finally (most ominous sign of all of a lawless disposition) she hated and loathed the admirable

Mrs. Pellett with the whole force of her young soul. To hate Mrs. Pellett was to hate law and order, to hate duty and worth personified. According to Dorothy, it was also to hate primness and propriety, to hate officiousness and cant and dunderheadedness, not to mention ugly caps and horrible Sunday bonnets, and all the subtle forms of prim ugliness that a woman of her type can collect around her. Mrs. Pellett had once interposed with an ill-advised homily when Dorothy had been discovered in one of her many escapades, and the girl now cherished for her a hatred so strong as to be an absolute passion.

Admirable Mrs. Pellett! She was destined by her virtues to excite such evil feelings in the breast of more than one young and misguided creature.

Dorothy, like most good haters, was also an ardent lover. When she loved at all, she loved with her whole heart.

During the first call of Viola and her brother, this young scapegrace with a girlish horror of being 'caught' by visitors, had retired hastily to the farthest corner of the room, from which vantage-ground she sat and stared with all her eyes at the strangers. Geoffrey, now in the ardent phase of a fresh convert, was looking like a chorister. It seemed absurd to expect him to do anything but sing divinely.

Mrs. Evans remarked, after he was gone, what a beautiful expression that young man had, and one of the daughters feared that he was going to die young.

Dorothy regarded him with little interest, but Viola's face filled her with a new emotion: she had never seen any one – out of a picture – in the least like her. What eyes she had! And with what a strange, wistful expression they wandered from face to face.

She was not a bit like a married lady, Dorothy thought. She had no little airs of importance, no accustomed little phrases, no proper sentiments.

What unusual quality was there in her voice, that made her seem miles apart from every one around her?

Of all vulgar errors, that is the vulgarest which supposes young women to be interested and attracted solely and chiefly by young men. There is no feeling more intense and romantic, in its own way, than the devotion of a girl to a woman a little older than herself. No lover ever admired more enthusiastically or worshipped more devoutly. Dorothy had already entered upon the first stage of such an experience.

She begged to be taken to call at Upton Castle, much to the surprise of her brethren, for Dorothy would usually undergo any penance rather than submit to this vexatious social usage. If Viola spoke to her she flushed up and her eyes sparkled; if Viola addressed some other person, Dorothy watched her every gesture and absorbed her every word. The object of all this devotion was absolutely unconscious. She never had the opportunity of forming those happy friendships which play so large a part in a girl's existence, and which sometimes last on through the more sombre years of womanhood as a never-failing solace and joy, whether the life be smooth or stormy. Girls to her were strange and wonderful creatures, not to be understood. She felt shy of them and very envious, recognising in their lot what she had missed herself.

Mrs. Evans said that she hoped Mrs. Dendraith would come over to the Rectory whenever she felt inclined; tennis was always going on, and they would be delighted to see her.

Viola blushed and thanked her hostess, and wondered if she would ever have the courage to avail herself of the invitation. She had a vague yearning to take part, though only as an outsider, in the bright thoughtless life that went on in the Rectory household. Perhaps she felt instinctively that without some such medicine for the spirit, she must break down altogether.

She did venture, after much hesitation, to call one afternoon, and the welcome she received was so hearty that in a moment she felt how absurd had been her fears. The ice once broken, intercourse became quickly established between the two houses, and Dorothy was in the seventh heaven.

For Viola, however, there was always a feeling of constraint in her relations with the family; she could not throw off her reserve, though she made herself much liked among her companions by her sincerity and by the wistful gentleness of her manner. She was still very far apart from them, even while she entered into their pastimes and tried to understand the mysterious ease and freshness of their lives.

How pleasantly the talk ran on among them, interspersed with little disputes and little bursts of laughter! How simple and spontaneous it all was!

As for Geoffrey, he established himself on almost brotherly terms with the whole family; and the family quickly had to reconsider their views about him in the capacity of chorister and the probability of an early grave.

'He is one of those people who will live to be a discipline to their friends, to an aggravating old age,' said Dick.

Strange to say, Dick was the member of the family with whom Viola found that she had most in common. He was inclined to be confidential, as young men often are with a sympathetic woman; and Viola, in spite of her outward coldness, was essentially sympathetic. She had suffered too much to be lacking in that womanly quality. Dick, in the innocence of his manly heart, never for a moment suspected that his companion had her own heart-breaking problems to solve, and that, where he was in perplexity and trouble, she was in despair. He cherished an ardent desire to engage in scientific pursuits, which his father thought slightly impious and distinctly unremunerative. Dick's wishes had been opposed, and he now found himself harnessed for life to an uncongenial occupation, which left him no leisure of body or mind for the work in which he felt that he might have excelled. He was conscious of a falling off in aptitude and a falling back in knowledge, and his soul at times was full of bitterness – a bitterness which no one at home could understand. Viola did understand, or at any rate she understood what it meant to have biting regrets, and Dick found great relief in pouring out his troubles to her. The fact of communicating his trouble partly assuaged it, and he began intuitively to turn to Viola on all occasions when he desired consolation. To be thus appealed to was the one redeeming circumstance of her present life, saving her from the egotism that invariably threatens the victim of a trouble such as hers, by calling her thoughts away from herself and summoning her sympathies to the rescue of another person.

From her childhood Viola had been trained under a system of restraint and arbitrary rule. Chilled, stunted as her nature had been, it now began to put forth pale little shoots towards the light; a piece of audacity which society, in alarm, set to work at once to punish and to check. Faithful servants are never wanting to carry out such decrees.

Finding that Viola and Dick were generally companions during the long rambles which the girls and their brother used to take on Saturday afternoons across country, the judicious mother thought fit to check the growing intimacy.

Mrs. Pellett, to do her justice, had been the first to notice it, and she had considered it her duty (never had human being duties so many and so various as Mrs. Pellett) to give a hint to the rector's wife on the subject.

'Mr. Dendraith is a good deal away,' said Mrs. Pellett, 'and although I am sure that your son is all that he should be, and dear Mrs. Dendraith is – ahem – a most highly principled young woman, it does not do to set people talking. There is nothing more unpleasant, and' –

And so on. Thus it happened that on Saturday afternoons, when Dick came to the Rectory from his work in town, Viola was seldom or never there.

'Why don't you ask Viola Dendraith to walk with us as she used to do?' he asked on one occasion.

'A married woman has other things to do,' said Mrs. Evans.

'She can't order the dinners all day long,' he objected. Mrs. Evans smiled: 'Do you suppose the mistress of a house has nothing to do but to order the dinner?'

'She has to row her maids, I suppose; but I can't imagine Mrs. Dendraith doing that.'

Mrs. Evans would have been wiser to let matters alone, for Dick now used often to walk over to Upton Castle on Sunday afternoons, and as Philip was seldom in, Viola and her visitor would take a walk by themselves, as if Mrs. Pellett had never been born! They used sometimes to spend a quiet hour in the ruins enjoying the sea-air and the wonderful changes in the hues of ocean and sky which could be so well seen from this romantic spot. Always they would knock at Caleb Foster's door in the old keep, to inquire for his well-being and to lure him from his stronghold for a talk. Had Mrs. Evans known what these walks and wanderings were to Viola, in her desolate life, perhaps she might have thrown off her judiciousness, at any rate for a moment of impulsive pity. The rector's wife never quite came up to Mrs. Pellett's standard of moral severity, and being conscious of this defect, she was in secret fear of Mrs. Pellett's criticism, often acting not quite on her own initiative in consequence.

'My dear,' said that bulwark of morality on one memorable occasion, when she had interrupted Dick in some confidence about a love-affair, and sent him away smothering terrific imprecations – 'My dear, excuse the frankness of a sincere well-wisher, but don't you think it would be wise to give that young man a hint not to come here quite so often?'

'Not so often?' repeated Viola in a dazed manner. Mrs. Pellett took her hand.

'You are inexperienced, dear Mrs. Dendraith; you don't know how careful one ought to be not to give rise to talk.'

Viola gazed at her visitor in stony silence.

'So very little will do it,' pursued the monitress soothingly.

'So it appears.'

'Of course I say this out of a friendly desire for your welfare.'

'You are very good.'

'I dare say,' pursued the lady, with delicate tact – 'I dare say you are glad to welcome even unsuitable visitors to your house, because you lead rather a lonely life, and no doubt feel dull now and then. But you know we must not allow our little trials to turn us from the strict path of duty and prudence – I am sure you will agree with me.'

Viola bowed.

'The only way to avoid being dull is to keep oneself always occupied,' continued Mrs. Pellett. 'Now, for example, *I* am busy from morning to night, and I don't know what it is to be dull.'

'No?' said Viola.

'It is right that we should all have some occupation, whatever may be our station. Do you take any interest in poultry?'

Viola shook her head.

'I think most people would be glad to work if only they were allowed to do what they can do well,' she said.

'Ah! but it is not for us to *choose*,' said Mrs. Pellett; 'we have to take what is appointed for us, and simply do our duty.'

Viola followed an audacious impulse. 'What *is* duty?' she inquired.

Mrs. Pellett looked startled and uneasy. Wherein lay the advantage of platitude if one was to be mentally knocked about in this manner?

'Our duty,' said the lady majestically, 'is the – in fact, the duty that has been given to us to perform by a Higher Power.'

Viola gazed at her in silence.

'Of course,' pursued Mrs. Pellett, waving aside the subject as now worked out – 'of course, dear Mrs. Dendraith, we all feel that your life at present is a little quiet and dull, your husband being so much away – but some day we hope that there will be quite a different state of things. No doubt in due time we shall hear the patter of certain little feet about the house, and then there will be no time to be dull, will there?' Mrs. Pellett's manner was archly encouraging.

Viola seemed turned to stone. She neither moved nor spoke. She only looked at her visitor with an expression of mingled loathing and defiance, which must have pierced any shell of self-complacency less adamantine than that of Mrs. Pellett. Viola knew too well what was expected of her; a pleased embarrassment at the mention of that which she was taught in the same breath to regard as the most blessed and desirable of contingencies.

The thought of that expected embarrassment filled her with fury, and sent the waves of angry colour to her cheeks, so that she had the additional misery of knowing herself to be apparently responding with the utmost propriety, exactly according to custom. The painful flush deepened and spread over neck and brow, while Mrs. Pellett smiled approvingly, and finally made some remark that filled the cup of disgust to overflowing.

As frantic prisoners shaking their prison-bars, the words came clamouring for egress to the closely-set lips: 'You are a fool; you are an idiot; you are *intolerable!*'

'Well, my dear,' said the unconscious Mrs. Pellett, smiling, 'we won't antici- pate these joys, if you would rather not' – (Viola drew a sharp breath) – 'but I thought you wouldn't mind it with me, you know, and of course it would be such a happiness and comfort to you.'

Still no answer. How could she speak to such a woman without making a more than ever detestable hotch -potch of misunderstanding? How could she tell her to mind her own business, and cease from her intolerable impertinence, without losing control over herself altogether? If she let but one word escape her, Viola knew that she would behave in such a way as to make Mrs. Pellett think that she had gone mad. With a strong effort she kept silent. She had not philosophy enough to thrust aside her disgust and forget the incident. Mrs. Pel- lett's plain, pompous face, with its look of respectable vacuity, haunted her long afterwards.

But Mrs. Pellett was not the only offender, nor was hers the only kind of offence. Viola had to learn that, as a married woman, she was expected to listen with calmness and amusement to anecdotes and allusions which were considered sullying to the innocence of a girl. Again and again she sickened with astonished anger and misery, dreading to meet her neighbours, because among them – as she considered – she was always liable to insult. Her womanhood, her very dig- nity as a human being was insulted. Her state of mind was such that, at times, she might have been considered on the verge of madness; indeed, if sanity has for its standard the condition of the average mind in similar circumstances, Viola must certainly have been pronounced to have gone far beyond that boundary-line. Marriage seemed to her nothing less than an initiation into things base and unlovely, desecrating and degrading all that in her girlhood she had been taught to reverence and to cherish. The blackness of her solitude made these wounded feelings doubly hard to bear, and the sense of humiliation became so terrible that even suicide – which her mother had taught her to place on the same level as murder – grew less heinous to her imagination, as the impulse to fling away the horrors and the indignities of life became more and more frantically importunate.

Not long after Mrs. Pellet's warning on the subject of Dick Evans, Philip happened to find him with Viola in the ruins. The look of suffering had gone for the time from her eyes, for Dick was talking to her about the sea and its silent ceaseless work of building and destruction, about the crumbling of the land along the coast, and the erection during long centuries, of great beds of chalk formed from the shells of myriads of tiny creatures, – little throbs of momentary sensation in the bosom of the ages.

The sea-breeze was blowing up fresh and blue; clouds overhead thronged across the pale sky as if inspired by some joy or passion.

Philip met Dick Evans with seeming pleasure, and the three stood talking together for a few minutes. Presently Dick went off to speak to Caleb Foster, who was at the door of the keep, sharpening a carpenter's axe upon a grindstone, and then Philip turned to his wife.

'My dear,' he said, 'do you know that this is the third time this week that Dick Evans has been here?'

'Yes,' said Viola.

'Though the very last man in the world to be jealous, I am also the last man in the world to allow my wife to be talked about. You will be good enough in future not to go out walking with Dick Evans. Of course he can call when he likes, but there must be nothing more.'

'Ah! I enjoyed those walks,' said Viola in a low voice, almost as if she were speaking to herself.

Her husband gave a slight, amused smile; the remark seemed to him so *naïf*.[52]

'You can get one of his sisters to go with you; that will do just as well, and better, from a social point of view.'

An expression of despair came into her eyes, but she said nothing. Philip looked at her fixedly, and his lips gave a curious twist as he turned away with a muttered remark that he was going to walk over to Upton Court, and would be back to luncheon.

Dick presently returned with Caleb Foster, who proceeded to give an instructive dissertation upon Being and Essence, with copious illustrations from Kant and Hegel, till the solid earth seemed to Viola to swim beneath their feet, the wind and sea and the steep white cliffs to grow alike imponderable. Dick's robust animal consciousness and his absence of metaphysical instinct roused him to violent rebellion.

'In the name common-sense, my dear sir' – Caleb gave a sigh.

'Common-sense,' he cried dejectedly – 'if you are going to appeal to common-sense, I have nothing more to say; we must at once drop the chain of logic.' He opened his thin fingers, as if actually letting go that ponderous object.

'But I deny that the two things are incompatible,' objected Dick.

The other shrugged his shoulders.

'Common-sense may be a crude sort of wisdom, but logical it is not, or I think this globe of ours would be rather less "distracted" than we find it.'

'Saved by a syllogism,'[53] observed Dick musingly.

Caleb shortly after this returned to his work, and then Dick proposed to Viola that they should go for a walk.

'I want to show you those Saxon barrows[54] upon the downs that I spoke to you about. You said you would like to see them.'

Viola coloured. Philip had forbidden her to go for a walk again with Dick. Her only strong pleasure, her only source of fresh and wholesome ideas, was to be surrendered, and at the thought, an impulse of rebellion sprang up within her, fierce and desperate. 'Do they all want to drive me mad? – or wicked?'

'Will you come?' asked Dick casually, expecting her assent as a matter of course.

'Yes, I will come,' she said, with set lips. But all pleasure in Dick's society had ceased. The sense of wrong- doing stalked like a spectre beside her, dogging her footsteps, go where she might. In vain the sweet wind blustered round her, in vain the untamed monster at the cliff's foot swung its vast bulk upon the complaining stones. A little fretting chain, holding her to the small and local elements of her life, pinioned her joyous impulses and sounded its familiar 'chink, chink' in her ears.

'You seem tired,' said the young man, checking his impetuous speed.

Had she answered as Nature dictated, she would have brought dismay into his manly bosom by bursting into tears. The wildness of the scene, the appeal of the lark's song overhead, and of the old old song of the sea; were almost more than she could bear. She felt like an outcast from all these elemental things, an exile from the world of reality and joy.

But though her heart spoke strongly; her training was loud-voiced also. Habit triumphed over impulse.

'I am a little tired,' she said; 'the wind is pushing hard against us.'

'Let us rest, then,' Dick proposed. 'The wind has long ago swept up all moisture; we can safely sit upon the grass,' and he flung himself down at full length, while Viola, tired rather in mind than in body, sank wearily beside him.

Her big retriever, Triton,[55] like an embodied Rapture,[56] was racing the wind across the downs. Viola called to him in her sweet vibrating voice, but he did not hear until Dick's shout joined issue with the gale. Then the dog turned and came tearing back, his brown body scouring the earth in its passage. He bounded up happy and affectionate to his mistress.

'If I must part with every other friend, at least I shall always have you, – till you die,' she said, with a pathetic little caress. 'But you will desert me and go away into the silent land, and then' –

'You will get another Triton,' said Dick, with a good-natured laugh.

'But these beautiful brown eyes will not be forgotten. Ah! where can you find a human spirit like this?'

'You are always a little hard on us poor humans,' said Dick; 'after all, most of us mean well enough, though perhaps we make rather a mess of the doing.'

'In men and women,' Viola returned, 'I miss the generous, faithful soul of a creature like this. If I could meet any one – man, woman, or child – one-half as noble, I would set him on a pedestal and worship him to my life's end.'

'Not a bit of it,' said Dick, laughing; 'you would long for a little amiable human weakness in your deity, and haul him down again – or worse still, poor fellow! leave him there in cold and solitary glory, like another Pillar Saint.'[57]

Viola shook her head.

'Look at those eyes; where can you find human eyes as beautiful?'

'Well, I know at any rate one man and one woman who surpass old Triton on that point, and curiously enough they possess just those qualities that you admire so much in him.'

'Do I know the people?'

'You know one of them: Harry Lancaster.'

'Oh!' said Viola abruptly.

'The other is his friend, Mrs. Lincoln. No doubt you have heard of her, as she has taken that little house belonging to your father-in-law on the coast – what is it called? Fir Lodge, or Fir Dell, or something of that sort.'

'Fir Dell,' said Viola. 'Yes, I know about her.'

'People here won't call upon her because she is separated from her husband, but I must say she seems to me a very refined, ladylike sort of woman, and I know Harry Lancaster thinks her little short of an angel; in fact, I sometimes fancy he is a little bit in love with her.'

'But – but she is married!' said Viola.

Dick smiled and shrugged his shoulders.

'He is just the sort of fellow to cherish "*a grande passion*"[58] for the unattainable.'

Viola threw her arms round her dog's neck and laid her cheek against his head, so that her face was turned from her companion.

'I think I am rested now,' she said presently. 'Shall we go on?'

The pause seemed to have indued her with amazing strength, for her pace now rivalled Triton's, and Dick laughingly asked her if she were training for a race.

'Am I walking fast?' she inquired abruptly, slackening speed.

'You look pale,' said Dick, in his kind, chivalrous way. 'Have I taken you too far?'

'No, no.'

'It seems to me, you might take the prize in a mile-race across country!'

They paced on in silence for some moments, then Dick said, 'You have never seen Mrs. Lincoln, I suppose?'

'Never.'

'She is a very curious woman, – dreadfully clever, but I like her. As for her opinions, I fear they would shock you, Mrs. Dendraith.'

'Does she dissent from the Church?'

Dick stopped and broke into a shout of laughter.

'My dear Mrs. Dendraith, Mrs. Lincoln cares as much about the Church as she cares about the Upton ladies! There are rumours afloat that she is a follower of Zoroaster, or a Buddhist!'[59]

Viola looked aghast.

'And that she worships those very ugly little figures that you see in Oriental shops. They say she buys them by the dozen.'

'Impossible!'

'It is also said,' Dick pursued, 'that she is building herself a little temple off her drawing-room, like a conservatory, and that she means to found a Buddhist monastic system and make Harry Lancaster high priest.'

'And he admires such a woman!'

'You would forgive him if you saw her.'

'Never,' said Viola.

Dick held out his hand to help her up the last few feet of the barrow, which stood beside two or three other hillocks on the highest point of the downs, commanding a view of the usual incredible number of counties.

Dick then began to discourse upon the probable history of these old relics of our forefathers, upon the different races that had peopled Britain: races with round heads, long heads, or coffin-shaped heads, each race having buried its dead in barrows of distinctive form, so that these burial-places told part of their story to the archaeologist at the first glance. Dick went on to relate some strange legends, full of the wild poetry of northern sea-girt melancholy lands, haunted by mist and storm.[60]

Viola leant back and listened dreamily. With her head pillowed upon the soft grass, she could watch the clouds drifting and melting and streaming, wind-intoxicated, across the heavens. Scarcely was the earth visible at all; she grew conscious only of a brilliant circle of blue hills and a shimmer of universal light. The sense of trouble faded away; Fate had granted a moment's amnesty.

Viola heaved a deep sigh. The vividness of her personality was dimmed; its edges lost their sharpness, and her consciousness seemed to spread out and extend into the outlying world of air and sunshine, and the unlimited ether that lay above.

The voice of the story-teller ceased, and the windy silence of the downs closed softly round about. Dick, after a few minutes, looked at his companion.

'Are you asleep?'

'Yes, and dreaming.' She did not move, but lay with closed eyes peacefully.

'May I know your dream?

'It was of wind and waves – of a world where there is romance and happiness and rest; – where' – Viola suddenly raised her head and sat upright, the peace all gone from her face – 'and where there are no Mrs. Pelletts.'

Dick laughed.

'Why, Mrs. Dendraith, you are not so good, after all, as I thought you! Mrs. Lincoln might rebel against Mrs. Pellett, but *you*! – and *apropos*[61] of that, I fear we shall have to be going; I see we have been out for three hours! Remember you have a public opinion to consider, a position to keep up, and Mrs. Pellett to confront.'

'If I committed a murder,' exclaimed Viola, as she sprang to her feet, 'I should not think it necessary to apologise to Mrs. Pellett!'

CHAPTER XXIV

GUIDE, PHILOSOPHER, AND FRIEND

As Philip was not home to luncheon on that day of iniquity, he did not discover his wife's act of insubordination till she took it upon herself to inform him; and though very angry at the moment of confession, he was disarmed by her frankness.

'Don't let this happen again, however,' he said. 'I seldom lay commands upon you, but when I do, I mean them to be obeyed.'

The walks thenceforth were given up, and Dick had to content himself with paying formal calls at Upton Castle, when he found Viola nervous and constrained, looking paler and more lifeless each time he came.

'I begin to half-believe in Mrs. Pellett's theory about the decline,' he said anxiously to his mother, who shook her head, and feared that the poor young thing had not long to live.

On one occasion Viola called at the Rectory immediately after Mrs. Pellett's departure, and found her devoted admirer Dorothy, fuming with indignation.

It seemed that Mrs. Pellett, with her usual enlarged views about duty, had just returned from an incursion upon the Manor-House, where she had been kindly mentioning to Mrs. Sedley what she and many others at Upton thought about dear Viola's sad appearance.

The Bulwark (as Harry Lancaster used to call her) had dropped in on her way back, to explain to her friends at the Rectory how much trouble she had been taking on Viola's behalf. Dorothy stamped her foot.

'I was burning to throw an antimacassar at her head!' exclaimed that impulsive young person; 'the way she sat there swelling with importance and propriety – ugh! I wish she had burst, like the frog in the fable – and then we should have heard no more about her!'

'Oh! consummation devoutly to be wished!' cried Dick.

'Fancy taking the trouble to go all that way just to see Mrs. Sedley and frighten her out of her wits – the old idiot!'

This last epithet appeared so pointedly to apply to Mrs. Sedley that Dorothy stammered an explanation.

'I suppose I ought to be grateful to Mrs. Pellett,' said Viola, 'but I am not. I – I *hate* Mrs. Pellett.'

Dorothy stared for a moment, and then broke out into laughter and embraces.

'Hurray!' she called out at the top of her voice. I thought you couldn't hate any one!'

Viola gave a little 'Oh!' that was very expressive. 'Can you hate with all your mind, and with all your soul, and with all your heart?' inquired Dorothy.

'I fear I can.'

'So much the better,' said Dorothy, after an astonished pause; 'people who can love can always hate.'

'But they oughtn't to,' said Viola.

Theologically, Dorothy agreed, but humanly, she didn't.

'If people are nasty,' she argued, 'they are made to be hated.'

Viola rather demurred at this, but Dorothy urged that (for instance) sheep and cattle, being good to eat, are meant by a considerate Providence to be eaten (her father had explained that in his sermon last Sunday); therefore, by analogy, people who are suitable for being hated are meant to be hated. No one could love a black -beetle, and no one could love Mrs. Pellett (except her husband). Dorothy, in an awed whisper, even went so far as to say that she didn't think God Himself could love Mrs. Pellett!

The girl's expressions of devotion to Viola were as energetic as her denouncement of her *bête noir.*

'I do love you so, there is nothing in the world that I wouldn't do for you. I wish you would try me.'

'Supposing I did something very wicked.'

'You *couldn't*!' cried Dorothy.

'But suppose it for a moment.'

'Still I should love you and stick to you through thick and thin. It is impossible for you to be you and for me not to love you.'

'Then I am not quite alone in the world! 'Viola exclaimed.

'Alone in the world! Why, every one that knows you thinks you are an angel!'

'Dick, for instance?'

'Oh! Dick *loves* you so,' pursued Dorothy with ardour.

'Do you love Dick?

'Almost,' said Viola, with a smile; and Dorothy thenceforth went about imparting the interesting information that Dick and Viola loved each other to distraction.

Mrs. Pellett's interposition (interference, Dorothy called it) was, of course, effectual in raising Mrs. Sedley's fears. Her daughter found it very difficult to lull her suspicion that something was wrong, however careful she might be to seem in good health and spirits.

'I assure you I am quite well,' Viola used to say again and again, but her looks belied her words.

Mrs. Barber's compliments fell thick and fast. The two never met but the housekeeper would exclaim in sepulchral tones, 'Well, ma'am, you *do* look ill-disposed, that you do!'

Though Dorothy's assertion, that every one in Upton thought Viola an angel, was not quite accurate, her quiet, unassuming manner and gentle expression had disarmed the criticism even of that village, severely just!

'The present topic of conversation here,' Adrienne Lancaster wrote to her brother, who was now with his regiment in Ireland, 'is Mrs. Philip Dendraith. She is thought nice-looking and ladylike, but too quiet. She certainly is quiet, but I feel sure there is something in her a little out of the ordinary. I am determined to know her better; it will not be difficult, as she is so often at the Rectory. I doubt if she is quite happy; though, if she is not, it is probably her own fault; some people lack the right temperament for happiness. Perhaps you will say that she lacks the right *husband*, but I fancy happiness is a thing which a husband can neither give nor take away.'

Adrienne subsequently carried out her intention of becoming more intimate with Mrs. Dendraith, but the manner in which the friendship was cemented differed materially from her own forecasts.

Matters had been going rather slowly, for Viola's reserve seemed invincible, when something happened which shook things out of their sluggish course.

'Since my last letter, dear Harry,' wrote Adrienne, 'a most astonishing event has happened; *I have had a proposal*! – and from whom do you think, of all people in the world? – from – I wish I could see your face when you read this – from Bob Hunter! Think of it: Bob, with all his jokes and his acres, at my feet! Perhaps I oughtn't to tell you, but it was too comic an episode to keep to myself. Augusta says it would scarcely be Christian.'

Bob Hunter was a wealthy young man with a property at about eight miles from Upton. Most people said he was mad; a few said he was clever, perhaps because he had attained so much celebrity as a skilful baffler of designing mothers. These doomed ones he so overwhelmed with quips and quirks and mad sayings, so confused with pun interlaced with pun, meaning hooked into meaning, that they lost all hope and presence of mind.

At one of the Rectory tennis-parties Viola found her mental horizon much enlarged by an introduction to this incredibly eccentric creature. There is nothing to equal an abnormal human being for putting to rout one's narrow preconceptions. Bob was a lank and weedy young man, with a long pale ugly face, colourless hair and eyelashes. Life to him was one long farce. Viola felt as if she had come in contact with a being from another sphere. She had an opportunity of watching him 'confounding the knavish tricks'[62] of Mrs. Featherstone, a county lady with a hunting daughter to marry, both veterans retiring from the field utterly routed.

'She that captures Bob Hunter,' that agile person remarked after a little caper of jubilation on the tennis-court, 'must be swifter than Atalanta.'[63]

'Ah! Mr. Hunter,' said Adrienne, 'if some aspirant were only wise enough to avoid pursuing you, you would come and tamely lay yourself down at her feet!'

Bob looked at her gravely, pirouetted slightly, according to his custom, and danced off to the other end of the lawn.

Later in the afternoon Adrienne and Viola were strolling together in a retired part of the garden. Adrienne had been trying to draw Viola out, and Viola was showing a perverse inclination to give her new acquaintance the benefit of her ideas about the difference between the temperature of to-day and the temperature of the day before yesterday.

They were not too much engrossed in their meteorological discussion to become aware of the approach of Bob Hunter. He came forward, stepping it in little triplets and hailing the two ladies, as they established themselves on a rustic-seat at the end of the path, with an appropriate quotation from the poets.

This was all in his usual manner, and caused Adrienne no surprise, but what followed fairly took her breath away, and made Viola grow hot and cold from sheer amazement.

'Wise and lovely one,' said Bob, addressing Adrienne, 'your words are full of the wisdom of the Egyptians. She that pursueth not arriveth at the goal;[64] she that hunteth is taken in the snare of the fowler, and the birds of the air laugh her to scorn. Julia Featherstone, that accursed damsel, shall be humbled. Adrienne Lancaster, because that she hath passed by on the other side, verily she shall be exalted. Not she, but her adorer taketh the lowest place. Even according unto his word he layeth himself (irrespective of a clay soil) at her feet.' And before a remonstrance could be uttered Bob Hunter was sprawling at full length on the ground.

'Mr. Hunter, for Heaven's sake, get up!' exclaimed Adrienne. 'You are really too ridiculous!'

'Nay, cruel one, but I love you,' remarked Bob in an explanatory manner. '(No, don't go, PLEASE, Mrs. Dendraith, I prefer to have an umpire on these occasions). Adrienne, at your feet, I lay myself and all that I possess. Will you have me and my appurtenances?'

'Do get up, Mr. Hunter.'

'Give me your hand, then?'

'Supposing some of the tennis-players were to come and see you in this ridiculous attitude.'

'I thought it was graceful,' said Bob, craning his neck so as to get a view of himself. 'Oh, you who abound in grace, yet have no grace for me, I will arise and go to my Featherstone!'

'Pray do.'

'What! a woman and not jealous!'

He sprang ardently to his feet. 'Still more am I yours; still more must I worship this rare and charming bird!'

He began to skip about and execute elaborate steps, talking all the time, and showering puns, quotations, and allusions upon his astonished audience. He kissed Adrienne's hand, he called her 'adamantine,' he became like Irving in 'Hamlet.'[65]

'Heavens!' exclaimed Adrienne, 'was there ever such a proposal before in history?'

By this time she was laughing helplessly, and the more she laughed the more extravagantly Bob Hunter behaved.

Yet he managed to make her understand that he meant his proposal seriously, and intended to persevere in his eccentric suit till she gave in.

'Of course it is a "splendid chance" for me,' said Adrienne rather bitterly, when her wooer had at last consented to pirouette back to the tennis-ground. 'Miss Featherstone and her mother have been angling for him for years, and Miss Featherstone has a dozen "chances" (as they are flatteringly called) to my one. Mother would be wild if she knew I had refused him, and all my counsellors, male and female, would hold up hands of dismay at my folly. I wonder whether they are right, or I. If I don't marry, I shall live on in this dead, foolish, gossiping little village, trying to make two ends meet and talking empty nonsense with my neighbours. I have no place in life, no interest; my time is swallowed up in a mere struggle with petty household details, a struggle to keep up appearances and to live "as becomes our station." My mother's whole existence has become absorbed in that effort, and mine too. If I married' –

She paused and sighed.

'If I married, I suppose petty details of another kind would take up my time; I should have to gossip and talk nonsense perhaps on a larger scale, and then' –

'And then you would have to learn to smile when people insulted you,' Viola put in, 'and to smile again when they took you by the arm and whispered loath-some things in your ear; and again to smile when' – her voice broke – 'when you realised that you had given up all right to resent what they said, for in accepting your position you had accepted all these things, and as many more – this side of madness – as might present themselves for your endurance.'

Viola was almost breathless when she stopped speaking.

'*Mrs. Dendraith*!' exclaimed Adrienne in indescribable amazement.

'Miss Lancaster!' said Viola, and the two women stood facing one another in the pathway.

'I don't think you take things in quite the right spirit,' observed Adrienne at length, her theories getting the better of a first sympathetic impulse; 'a woman can make marriage into a holy of holies. Think how sacred an office it may be; how a woman may serve and minister, and make her life one long, lovely self-sacrifice.'

Viola was shivering from head to foot, so that she could not answer.

'Believe me, there is no position in which opportunities for heroism do not exist, but the position of wife and mother has always been, and surely always will be, the best and noblest and holiest that a woman can fill.'

Viola shuddered.

'I am very wicked, I know,' she said; 'I can't be patient under insult, and to be married seems to be the endurance of one long insult, and to rob one of the very right to resent it.'

'I don't understand,' cried Adrienne. 'I dare say people are vulgar and imper-tinent, but what does that matter, after all?'

Viola turned away. She could not speak of it further, and Adrienne's suc-ceeding remarks were received without opposition, but without response. This conversation, however, was the beginning of a closer acquaintance. Adrienne studied her new friend, and soon formed a neat compact little judgment about her which satisfied herself, and was very serviceable for everyday use, since Viola never showed enough of herself to invalidate the theory.

Miss Lancaster thought that she might have influence for good over her new friend, and being always zealous in well-doing, she tore herself occasionally from her numerous home duties to spend a day or two at Upton Castle. The mentor then noticed with approval, Viola's continual self-suppression, her cheerfulness in her mother's presence, her disregard of headaches and other signs of ill-health, and her evident determination to do her duty.

But this was mere stoicism and power of will, not the smiling acceptance of troubles, the sweet welcoming of tribulation, which delighted Adrienne's dutiful soul.

'It is a great comfort,' said that adviser judiciously 'it is a great comfort to think that, however one may be placed, duty is never far to seek. Life is full of bitter disappointments' (the speaker sighed heavily), 'and there is much pain and anxiety to bear, but if we keep up a brave heart, and do well what lies to our hands, we shall assuredly feel a quiet joy and satisfaction which nothing else in this world can give. Do you not find it so?'

'A quiet joy and satisfaction?' inquired Viola, turning her hungry, melancholy eyes upon her companion.

That look seemed to be answer enough, for Adrienne took her hand and said earnestly, 'I fear, dear Viola, that you are not so happy as you might be; I see there are sad things in your lot, as there are in most lots; yet I think there are elements of happiness too, if you would take advantage of them. Your husband is fond of you' –

The speaker paused, in case Viola should have anything to say on this head, but she answered nothing, and Adrienne continued –

'He is ready to give you anything you desire; you have a comfortable, even luxurious home, and no anxiety about money matters. Ah! no one knows what that means except those who *have* such anxiety. Viola, I sometimes, in my weak moments, feel inclined to ask if it is worth while struggling on, with these never-ceasing little economies, these never easing efforts to make one shilling play the part of two. But then come little solaces and pleasures, and after the fit of depression, you pluck up a brave heart again and go on. After all, it is your duty, and that makes it possible and right.' Viola assented.

'I don't tell you about my own petty griefs except to let you see that you have companions in trouble all around you.'

'I never doubted it for a moment.'

'And that you are spared a very great deal of ceaseless worry by having no anxiety with regard to these odious pounds, shillings, and pence.'

There was a long pause. Then Viola made a remark not at all in the spirit which Adrienne had intended to call forth.

'I really don't see what is the use of our all coming into the world to struggle and battle in this way; it is so very – ridiculous.'

'I don't think so,' Adrienne returned hastily; 'there is not one of us but can do some little good in the world, if he will only use his opportunities.'

'If we all *can*, we all don't; I mean, we don't all,' said Viola, 'I and the few that do a little good are overbalanced by the many that do a little harm. Of course one must do one's duty, but I feel sometimes as if it was altogether hopeless and useless.'

Adrienne's orthodox views on this point had ferreted out of their hiding-places Viola's secret heresies. She was alarmed at herself as soon as the words were uttered, and meekly accepted Adrienne's next argument without a word of dissent.

'It is not a hopeless struggle, dear Viola, if once we realise the beauty and the blessedness of *sacrifice*. That is the key to all the terrible problems of life; that alone makes us understand – if but dimly – that the highest good is to be got out of pain, and that the most blessed life is the life of sorrow.'

Viola had it on her lips to say, 'Then we ought to inflict upon one another as much sorrow as we can, in order that we may all quickly attain blessedness,' but she changed her mind and gave a hurried murmur of acquiescence.

Adrienne little guessed what demons of doubt and fear she had raised by her 'judicious' feminine influence.

All this time Bob Hunter, in the most persevering manner, was pursuing his eccentric suit. Before long Mrs. Dixie became joyfully aware of what had happened, and she was now making her daughter's life a burden to her by urgent entreaties to accept the advantageous proposal. When Adrienne sadly but firmly refused, the old lady sought and obtained sympathy from the rector's wife, in her bitter disappointment. As for Mrs. Pellett, she thought Adrienne's conduct was wanting in principle. If her poor dear mother's death were to be hastened by this ridiculous refusal, Mrs. Pellett hoped that Adrienne would not be overwhelmed with life-long remorse – she sincerely hoped that she would not suffer in that excruciating manner! Adrienne was deeply troubled. Her mother had worried herself ill, and Bob kept coming and coming to open the sore afresh.

'Very likely it is your last chance,' said Mrs. Dixie tearfully;' we see so few people in this retired village; and what is to become of you after I am gone if you do not make a home for yourself now? O Adrienne! you know the fate of an unmarried woman who has to make her own living! Don't sadden my declining years by the thought that I must leave you alone in the world, and penniless.'

Adrienne shivered. All that her mother said was so ghastly true! Marriage without love, or –

'Viola, under any conceivable circumstances, would you have married Bob Hunter?'

'Yes, under *some* conceivable circumstances,' Viola replied, 'and I expect so would you and most women. My husband says that every woman has her price.'

'But you don't believe that, surely!' exclaimed Miss Lancaster, much shocked.

'I am afraid I do,' said Viola.

Her companion gazed at her searchingly.

'You mean that every woman would marry for money or position if only she were offered money and position enough?'

'Oh no; different women sell themselves for different things: some for money and position; some for money and position for their relatives, some for the highness of another person – yes, I think that every woman has her price.'

'It seems almost a crime to marry without love,' said Adrienne gravely.

Viola paused.

'It may sometimes be a crime to refuse to marry without love,' she suggested.

'Never – unless perhaps some one's life were at stake – and even then – Well, it is a difficult question. If it *is* a crime to marry for money, the punishment must be awful.'

There was a long significant pause.

'How difficult it sometimes is to clearly see one's duty!' exclaimed Adrienne. (Only a few days ago she had talked so glibly and comfortably about duty). 'Is it purity of motive or is it egotism that makes a woman shrink from marrying to please her relations?'

'Well may she shrink!' cried Viola.

'Yet I do believe firmly,' said Adrienne, 'that the domestic life and its interests call out a woman's best qualities; that before she marries she has scarcely lived.'

Viola was silent.

'If one could only be married without having a husband!' exclaimed Adrienne. He is the drawback! Poor Bob! he would keep one in jokes, wouldn't he. But oh! the awfulness of having that creature perpetually about one! I like to be able to look up to a man.'

'Yes; but it is so difficult,' said Viola naively, at which her companion laughed.

Time went on, and Bob continued to press his suit.

Mrs. Pellett, the indefatigable, one day electrified Upton by the information that she had seen Mr. Hunter going up the avenue of Fir Dell to call on 'that Mrs. Lincoln.'

'This comes of not saying "yes" when she had a chance,' said Mrs. Pellett. 'Perhaps she'll see how silly she was now that it may be too late.'

'Viola, the necessity for decision has been removed from me,' said Adrienne. 'Bob Hunter has deserted me for Mrs. Lincoln.'

Viola turned pale.

'I wish that woman had never come here!' she exclaimed.

'So do I,' assented Adrienne, 'for more reasons than – Bob Hunter. It is strange how unprincipled women seem to have a hold over men which good women seldom achieve.'

Adrienne ran over the list of good women: Mrs. Evans, Mrs. Dixie, Mrs. Sedley, Mrs. Pellett, – and shook her head.

'You wouldn't suspect my brother Harry of being led astray by a bad woman, and yet he sits at Mrs. Lincoln's feet; at least he used to do so. I am thankful to say that they have not met for some time, as far as I know, for Harry's regiment has been quartered in Ireland. I sadly fear he is deeply attached to her; – of course, this is between ourselves. It has long been a great trouble to me. Poor Harry! he is such a fine, generous, passionate creature that when he once loves, it is like tearing his heart out to deprive him of his ideal. I, like you, wish to Heaven the woman had never come here!'

'She must be very wicked,' said Viola.

'Very wanting in womanly feeling at any rate,' Adrienne amended. 'I cannot understand a self-respecting woman allowing herself to be talked about in the way Mrs. Lincoln is talked about. I would undergo tortures rather than that.'

'You would rather submit to be talked *to* as a woman is talked to (and about) after she is married,' suggested Viola, with a vivid flush. 'I can't say that I think, as far as the talking is concerned, that one gains so much by being thought respectable.'

'Oh! my dear Viola, for Heaven's sake don't say such things; it grieves me to hear you!'

As Adrienne herself had not been guiltless of little vulgarities which Viola disliked and resented, no answer was forthcoming to this remonstrance.

Things were going on very badly at the Castle just at present. Philip was always at home, and this for Viola meant a greater amount of suffering. There was no respite. The day was dull and weary, and filled with a thousand annoyances, great and small; but the night – the time for solitude, stillness and repose, the time to build up strength and draw in new hope and peace – the night was a living hell!

She might never be alone, never feel that she absolutely possessed herself. Her very thoughts were scarcely free. Freedom was an unknown word; the only words that ruled in that red-hot Purgatory[66] were right, duty, submission.

What inmate of the harem, she used to wonder, endured slavery more absolute than this? If she could but tear out heart and soul, so that she remained a mere shell, animate but not sentient, and let *that* stay and be housekeeper, wife, mother, whatever was wanted. It would play the part better than she played it, and there would be none of this hatred and loathing, this sinful, invincible shrinking from her accepted duties. What, heaven could be worth such a price? what hell worse than the hell which now devoured her?

She felt as if she must shriek or blaspheme; as if her very personality must blaze up and be consumed in the flames of a swift-developed madness.

She was utterly alone – cut off from human help; for even Harry's interest had been led elsewhere. The protecting hand whose finger-tips had been slowly slipping away, was now quite withdrawn. The solitude was profound. A punishment this, thought Viola, for daring to let her mind dwell upon the memories of those scenes before her marriage, when Harry had tried so hard to save her. The longing for unconsciousness, for death, became unappeasable: to be mercifully wafted away to some quiet region where there was no heartache, no indignity, no altar where the souls and bodies of women were offered up in sacrifice, while the honourable and the respected of the earth danced round, singing psalms of triumph. What though that gentle world were canopied with clouds shutting out the sunshine of the earth? What though vapours still and sullen hovered there, lulling the spirit in a dreamless rest? The sweetness of life, the glory of the world, was not for her; welcome then, the land of shadows and of silence, where sorrow was laid to sleep and the throb of misery ceased. Not even the fear that it was wicked to long so for what Heaven had not willed, could overcome the yearning.

It seemed at times as if things *could* not go on much longer in their present course, and yet it was evident that there could be no sudden break. Mrs. Sedley had done her work too well.

There were at this time many small difficulties of the petty and worrying order to contend with. Mrs. Barber was perpetually coming to Viola with discouraging stories about the household affairs, stories always given in the most majestic language, which, like all other luxuries, had to be paid for, and Mrs. Barber's language was paid for ruinously in that commodity of undetermined value that we call time. Instead of trying to set matters right, she talked about how they went wrong, and the domestic machinery began to groan and creak unpleasantly. This did not tend to improve matters between husband and wife; Philip was not used to lying upon crumpled roseleaves, and he frankly told his wife that if she could make herself neither agreeable nor useful, he really failed to see what she was there for.

'Not for my own pleasure, assuredly,' Viola had once been goaded into replying.

'I'll be damned if it's for mine, then!' cried Philip, with a snarl.

'Then let me go!'

'Where to, may I ask?' He gave a loud laugh.

He had a newspaper in his hand, which, with insolent coolness, he was reading at intervals.

'That does not matter, so long as I may but go.'

He gave a contemptuous shrug of the shoulders.

'How difficult it is to make you realise your position!' he said. 'Do you think that you have only yourself to consult? Let me remind you that you bear *my name*; that, in fact (to speak so that you can understand), it is branded upon you, and by that brand I can claim you and restrain you wherever you may be, so long as you live. *Now* are matters clear to you?'

She turned very white, but answered seemingly without emotion, 'Quite clear; you hold over me a power of more than life and death. You can treat me as you choose, for open resistance (even if I could resort to it) would mean for me – ruin. I am at your mercy. I think, however, that, in common fairness, all this ought to have been explained to me before I married.'

'My dear,' said Philip, 'a man can get a woman to marry him on any terms. It is her own look-out if she doesn't know what marriage involves. She ought to find out. But do you suppose finding out would stop a woman from marrying? Not a bit of it; not if she found out that she would have to throw herself on her husband's funeral pyre like an Indian widow![67] These are plain facts, my dear; and any woman of the world will tell you the same thing. Besides, who are you, to be discontented with what satisfies other women? But I am tired of this subject. Be good enough to give a little attention to your household duties for the future, and spare me further hysterics.'

He turned away and buried himself in the paper.

For a moment Viola stood before him hesitating, as if she intended to say something more, but apparently changing her mind, she walked slowly away.

If Philip had brought all the powers of his mind to bear upon the subject for the next year, he would never have guessed the feeling that made his wife at once seek Mrs. Barber and consult with her seriously as to the means of effecting an improvement in the state of the domestic affairs.

It was the first time that the mistress of the house had actively used her authority, and it greatly startled Mrs. Barber. That high functionary of course thought that any suggested change was impossible, but in course of time she became convinced that it had to be made, and reluctantly set about the task.

Philip, some time later, noticing that his wishes had been carried out minutely, gave an approving nod to his wife, and remarked that he was glad to see that she had taken his advice to heart and turned over a new leaf.

'How shall I reward you for this sensible conduct, my dear?'

'I want no reward, thank you; I am glad you are pleased.'

'What *do* you want, then?' demanded Philip, with a frown.

'Nothing.'

'So be it. I had a little present I was going to give you, a present that would make the eyes of most wives glisten; but since you want nothing you shall have nothing.'

He put back the red leather case which he had brought out of his pocket and went on with his breakfast.

'If you would condescend to ask me for this confounded trinket, and take a little interest in it, I would give it you even now,' said Philip after a long silence. 'I am not a bear or a tyrant, whatever you may say.'

'I never said you were either.'

'Well, will you ask me for this thing.'

'I cannot accept it as a reward for anything I may have done that pleases you,' said Viola, flushing.

'What a mad woman you are! And pray why not?'

'I have only done what I thought myself bound in duty to do.'

'But if I choose to show that I am pleased with you' –

Viola shook her head. Unluckily for herself she had the old Puritan spirit largely developed. She understood principle but not compromise, duty but not diplomacy. She had no perception of character, and therefore no instinct to adapt herself. It never occurred to her that a man like Philip could be wounded as well as angry; and that she was inflexibly rejecting the only overtures of peace which he knew how to make.

'As a reward I cannot accept it,' she repeated.

'Idiot!'

Philip took the case again out of his pocket, opened it, and laid it on the table. It contained a star of magnificent brilliants, gleaming and scintillating upon their bed of sapphire velvet.

He watched her face.

'Do you like it?'

'It is lovely.'

'Do you wish to have it?' She shook her head.

'And what if I say that you *must* have it?'

'You have already clearly explained to me that I have no choice but to obey you; moreover, it has always been my desire to obey you to the best of my ability.'

'Very well then; take it, and wear it, if you please.'

He handed her the case, which she took.

'I am tired of this sort of thing, let me tell you, Viola,' he went on. 'It is time that you should clearly understand your position as my wife, and then perhaps you will see that your best policy is conciliation, not defiance.'

'I have never been defiant.'

'You have certainly never been conciliating!' he exclaimed. 'A woman can generally get her own way with a man (within limits) if she knows how to manage. You are not half-clever.'

Viola gave a wintry little smile and a faint shrug of the shoulders.

'Now, you understand that I want you to *wear* that star. I don't give it you to be locked away in some old drawer and never seen. It will look well in your hair.'

'I will do what you wish,' she said.

Philip made an impatient movement.

'I don't understand you,' he exclaimed. 'You are as pig-headed' – Viola looked up.

'You talk about making me understand my position,' she said, 'but it seems to me that I understand it very well. I am – in your own words – branded with your name. It gives you a claim over me so long as I live. I understand that quite clearly. If I were to leave you, you could make life impossible to me; I have no more illusions. I see and understand. It is just because *I do* see and understand that I offend you. You would have me act two parts at the same time. That cannot be, even at *your* command. You are my husband – you married me in the face of my repeated assurance that I did not wish to marry you – you have thus become my master, and, if you choose, my tyrant – I am at your mercy. In these circumstances, how can you expect from me anything except deference and obedience? If you are my master now and for ever, you cannot hope to establish any other relation between us. You take your stand on your authority, and there you must remain.'

Philip rose slowly and went to the fireplace.

'It may surprise you to learn that you talk damned nonsense, my dear,' he said in his suavest tones.

'Then perhaps I had better hold my tongue,' she answered.

Philip shrugged his shoulders.

'It is to be hoped that you will have children,' he said, with an intonation that made her shrink as if she had been touched with hot iron. '*They* would soon bring you to your senses.'

'Do you find you are generally able to foretell how circumstances will affect me?' she asked coldly.

'I have some knowledge of human nature,' he replied, 'and I have kept my eyes open. A married woman who has no children may give her husband trouble, but the first baby infallibly drives the nonsense out of her. After that the game is in his hands. She has to behave rationally for the child's sake.'

Philip gave a slight smile as he said it, which was subtly, profoundly wounding.

'If you are determined to deprive me of every grain of self-respect, if you are resolved to humiliate me to the very dust,' said Viola, in a low voice full of suppressed passion, 'it may please you to know that I recognise my utter helplessness to resist you even in *that*. While my mother is alive' – she stopped abruptly.

'While your mother is alive you are afraid to make a scandal in her respectable family,' said Philip. 'Very right and very wise, my dear. I drink to your respected mother's very good health, and may her days be long in the land.'

CHAPTER XXV

THE WEST WING

A large portion of Upton Castle had remained uninhabited. Sir Philip made various jocular allusions to the size of the family which might find accommodation in the great deserted rooms of the west wing, and these allusions were, for some recondite reason, considered exceedingly amusing. In fact, the west wing had become a sort of standing joke among the people of Upton, who generally made one last a long time, and took care that it should not be of a subtle or impersonal character; *that* might cause an epidemic of headaches. A pleasantry which required one to think was as bad, in the eyes of the Upton circle, as a play that made demands on one's pocket-handkerchief.

Of course, Viola was not allowed to miss the sweet savour of the Upton joke. Philip repeated it to her with an insolent laugh, and added one or two apposite remarks, which Viola would willingly have burnt out of her brain with hot irons, so that their imprint might be eternally erased.

That vast deserted wing over which Upton made merry, had become her favourite haunt in the winter afternoons, when the closing in of the light made work or reading impossible, and the stillness of the dusk creeping over the sea brought a tired lull to the sense of unappeasable misery.

The west wing was nearest to the ruin, and from the windows of its vast old rooms one could look almost into the keep, where Viola often used to see Caleb working before his doorstep, until the darkness crept up and forced him to desist. Sometimes she would go out and have a talk with him, which she always found a great relief, for Caleb could arrest her own painful thoughts, and carry her away into his cold, clear, sorrowless world of 'pure reason.' But often Viola was too wretched to seek this respite; the solitude which was driving her troubles deeper and deeper into her soul was becoming daily more and more of a necessity. She shrank at the approach of her fellow-creatures, from whom something hurtful, foolish, detestable, might, it seemed, always be expected. Like some animal accustomed to rough handling, she flinched even when no blow was intended. The old rooms of the west wing were dark and dim, as if with the shadows of many years. They seemed to Viola to conceal a haunting danger, an unknown mysterious danger, hanging like a curse over the house.

No one knew of her visits to this region of silence and shadows; she was supposed by the household to have gone out with Triton or perhaps with Dorothy Evans, who sometimes accompanied her on her interminable rambles. She kept her secret jealously, stealing in unobserved by the door leading on to the terrace, and creeping up the great staircase, till she found herself, safe and alone, in the long corridors out of which opened the innumerable dusty, musty rooms. She scarcely dared to breathe as she moved with careful footsteps over the oaken floors, half-expecting to see some form emerge from the gathering shadows or rise up from the great four-post bedsteads, whose dark canopies must be embellished (as she fancied) with the phantasmagoria of human dreams. Among the old rooms was one called the Death Chamber, which especially fascinated her. Here, generation after generation, the Dendraiths had died, sometimes calmly under the shadows of the great black bedstead; once by violence.

In examining a fantastically carved cabinet which stood near the mantelpiece, Viola discovered a number of old letters, written in the last century by the unhappy lady whose story Philip had told on that fatal day long ago. Many other musty treasures came to light: a bit of faded ribbon, a silver thimble and a piece of dim silken embroidery, with one of its miraculous flowers of unknown genus half-finished, the threaded needle stuck into the silk, as if the work had just been laid down. What were the fifty or a hundred years that had passed since the skilful fingers touched that dainty piece of embroidery? A mere fiction, an unreality.

The two realities: the life of that bygone lady, and that of her not less unhappy successor, – seemed to annihilate between them the empty phantom Time and to touch each other closely. The little relics of everyday occupations which had lain there undisturbed since their owner passed away, spoke of her so loudly that Viola felt as if she had known the woman who had slept and dreamt and, alas! wept in this old room; who had woven her sorrow into silken devices, and died with the grief still in her soul, the embroidered flowers of Paradise still uncompleted. Viola took possession of the key of this cabinet, and mastered the secret of the hiding-place of the treasures. On one windy afternoon, in the twilight, she stole up to the old room, taking with her a small narrow packet. She went first to the window and looked out. The waves were rolling one after the other over the expanse of grey waters: ocean's battalions making onslaught against the shore. How calm, how beneficent these same waters had looked on a certain summer afternoon! – that afternoon when she might have averted her fate, had she been willing to fling off the claims of conscience; Could it be that she regretted having done her duty? She leant her head desolately against the window-sill. Adrienne had spoken of the quiet joy and satisfaction that follows duty performed, but Viola felt nothing but a passionate misery to which she saw no possible end. Even if release came to-morrow, she felt that her soul was seared and branded for life, and that at best there was nothing left for her but to die. Never since her childhood had she been hopeful or light-hearted: now it was impossible to expect relief. There were no stores of garnered joy to fall back upon in her present trouble. This was like a sudden savage tightening of a cord that for years had been cutting into the flesh, wearing away the powers of rebound and the powers of enjoyment, just at the time when these should have been growing and accumulating.

Mrs. Sedley's long life of persistent self-neglect and self-deterioration was bearing its fruit, twenty and a hundredfold: the inevitable punishment, when it came, was heavy, and it fell on innocent shoulders.

Viola remained at the window watching the waves as they rolled over, melancholy, dreary, unceasing. Such were the movements of human destiny, the restless everlasting labour without aim or hope. What was this ceaseless turmoil of the ocean but a weary response to the perpetual stimulus of a blind necessity? What did these eternal waves achieve, as they rose and sank and rose again, expending their force merely upon their own birth-element, effecting nothing? Caleb Foster said that in the course of ages they wore away the land by their ceaseless fretting, and added thus a few miles to the dominion of the ocean.

Perhaps the human waves were also wearing something away with their repeated onslaughts, adding thus to the dominion of – *what?* That was the awful question. And in any case was it worth while?

Another dangerous thought came: What if all that we are told about Providence be the offspring of human imagination, part of our blind response to the goad that drives us all to live and think and feel and strive, till the breath goes out of us and the life-fever is stilled?

Oh! what would her mother say to such wild questions? What would even Adrienne say? Viola felt as if she were sinking deeper into some black nightmare gulf whence there was no returning; an ante-chamber leading by a long narrowing passage to the regions of the damned. She looked round her at the sinister dusk gathering and thickening in the corners of the silent room, at the vast oak bedstead and the carved cabinet, with its grinning faces.

She touched the packet she held in her hand with a singular gesture, and stood looking down at it steadily. A wave of colour spread over her face, and her eyes lighted up. She drew away the paper wrappings and disclosed the knife which Harry Lancaster had given her on her wedding-day, and her husband had forbidden her to keep. Evidently in this one particular she had failed in obedience. She looked at the ornament attentively, examined it this side and that, and ran her finger along the steel. Viola thought of Harry's impassioned words of warning before her marriage, and it occurred to her swiftly in passing, that he might have given her the thing not quite without a purpose! But the idea was dismissed as preposterous.

Harry! How suddenly he vanished into the great silence which engulfs so many who seem to have made themselves part and parcel of our lives: What was he doing, and thinking? Scarcely a word of his had been forgotten. He had succeeded in weaving himself into Viola's memories, as the bygone Lady Dendraith had woven her troubles into her silken impossible flowers. And he too had left the threaded needle in the silk, and gone away and left the work unfinished. Did he ever think of her now? Did he still – Viola frowned and hurried away from the window, trying to banish that question from her mind. Did he love her still? Of course not; she was no longer free; he had ceased loving her as soon as she became Philip's wife. Harry would not be so wicked as to let his passion cross the adamantine marriage boundary. No; she must go through the world without his love, as she had elected to do; it was the maddest folly to permit her thoughts to wander back to the old times which could never be recalled. She wondered how she would feel if Harry were to walk into the room at this moment. Her heart beat fast at the thought, and then faster as she discovered how much it had moved her. She was alarmed. Of all forms of sin, that of loving one man while married to another had seemed to Viola the farthest removed from the sphere of possibility. She had always turned from the idea with disgust and horror.

And now! –

Now she could at least guess how such dreadful things *might* occur, and what a weight of guilt and misery the wretched woman must carry at her heart, until the sin was expiated by some frightful suffering or cast out by the grace of Heaven.

Restlessly the lonely figure began to pace the room, up and down, up and down; the knife in her hand, its tiny gems gleaming in her face.

'Surely he will not find it here,' she muttered half-aloud, going over to the cabinet and opening the drawer containing the letters and embroidery.

Taking the knife in both hands, she laid its point for a moment against her breast, pressing the handle a little. She let it rest there for a moment, as if questioning her ability to press it still farther should conscience permit. She was about to place it beside the other treasures; when a sound through the dusk made all the blood rush to her heart. She looked round in terror, but could see nothing. Her impulse was to rush out of the room, but she dared not move. Some terrible form, she felt sure, would meet her from every darkened corner, and as she passed the bed a figure would rise up out of the shadows and clutch her. She braced herself for a great effort. The whole width of the room had to be crossed; the door was at the farthest corner, the bed occupied the middle of the wall opposite the window, and must be passed in order to reach the door. She set her teeth and moved forward rapidly. Thank Heaven! in another moment the ordeal would be over. But oh! if the door did not open quickly she thought she would go mad! Her eyes were fixed in fascinated horror on the bed as she prepared to make a rush. She had taken two steps forward, when suddenly she staggered back with a sick gasp, for out of the shadows of that bedstead – merciful Heaven! it was no fancy, but a ghastly fact! – a figure *did* rise up and a pair of arms *did* stretch out to clutch her! Viola uttered a shriek of terror. She saw something dark standing above her, a white face and two white hands approaching. She tottered back, struggling blindly, towards the window, ready to tear it open and fling herself out; then her power of movement failed her as in a nightmare and the room swam round. She felt the white hands on her neck, the dark arms close round her, and then something within her brain seemed to give way.

She knew no more.

When she awoke to consciousness the canopy of the carved bedstead was above her head, and she was lying on it weak and helpless.

She could see the demon faces of its carving by the light of a flickering candle which stood on the cabinet.

'Do you feel better now?'

Viola started and trembled. It was Philip's voice.

'Yes.'

'Hold your tongue, then, and take this.'

He gave her some brandy, then let her lie quiet for ten minutes. At the end of that time he came to the bedside. 'You are easier to frighten than I thought,' he said, moistening her forehead with eau-de-cologne.[68] 'You might have stopped to think for a moment before you fainted. You surely don't suppose that I didn't know of your frequent visits to this blue-beard chamber.'[69]

'You knew?' repeated Viola.

He smiled.

'Naturally. I thought you were coming too often, and began to suspect that something was up, – secret assignations, for all I knew. So I concluded it was time to reconnoitre. I reconnoitred from the convenient depths of my great-grandmother's four-poster. I didn't mean to give you such a fright, though. How you did shriek! But I confess I thought a little start would be salutary. It's uncanny to have a wife who spends hours in disused rooms, looking as if she were going to commit suicide from an upper window. Not that I am afraid of her ending her days in that fashion. It pleases young minds of a certain order to dally with such ideas, but they seldom come to business. I don't expect to be a widower yet awhile, my dear.'

Philip smiled urbanely as he bent over the figure of his wife, whose closed eyelids and exhausted attitude pleaded vainly for a moment's respite from his sneers. He thought she was shamming, or at least yielding unnecessarily to the effects of the shock.

'You would like to know, perhaps, how I became acquainted with your visits here. In a very simple way, Caleb Foster had seen you at the window, and without knowing he was betraying a secret, happened to mention the fact to me. As there is a staircase leading from this room to the terrace, I thought perhaps you were making ingenious use of it. Women with a Puritanical training are generally the most enterprising, when they get the chance.'

Viola raised herself for a moment, but her strength failed her and she sank back exhausted, the angry tears, to her intense disgust, welling up into her eyes. She hid away her face that Philip might not see them.

But he was not to be deceived.

'Oh! if you are going to resort to weeping, I have no more to say. You had better let me carry you to your own room, and I can send Mrs. Barber or the maid to you. I dare say women know better the etiquette in such matters than I do.'

'I can walk,' said Viola, as he began to lift her from the bed.

'Try,' he said.

She managed to totter only a few steps towards the door. Philip lifted her in his arms.

'You can leave me here, and send Mrs. Barber to me,' she said. 'Put me down.'

'Nonsense; I shall take you to your room, as I said.'

'I should much prefer to stay here. Philip, put me down,' she repeated sharply, struggling to get free.

But he paid not the slightest attention. She was carried down the long empty corridors to her room.

As he laid her on her bed he bent down over her, his arms still round her, as if enjoying the sense of her helplessness and his power. He was smiling into her face. 'Now,' he said, 'for the ministering angels and sal-volatile.[70] I think this afternoon may be an instructive one for you, my dear. You observe that your doings are not secret from me. I have ways and means of finding out everything that I want to know. It would take a much subtler person than you are to baffle me, and one who is rather more of an adept at telling lies. Let me advise you, for your good, to be open with me. It is your best policy. You have plenty of opportunities, if you would only use them to your own advantage. I am quite open to womanly wiles, my dear, if you did but know it.' He gave her a little careless, insolent caress and walked off smiling.

'If you only knew how I *hate* you!' Viola exclaimed, with a sob of passion.

'My dear, I know it quite well. People generally hate their masters, if they are mad enough to oppose them. Again I say in all good-fellowship – try the *other* policy!'

CHAPTER XXVI

SIBELLA

Viola was seriously shaken by the shock which she had sustained on that afternoon in the west wing. She shrank from going about alone; especially after dark, and merely to look at the window of that dreadful room from outside would make her turn cold in full noontide.

'Dorothy, I wish you would introduce me to some of your villagers,' she said once; 'my life is so utterly useless that I think I am reaping the punishment of all cumberers of the ground. My own society is becoming unbearable to me.'

Dorothy, though much surprised, gladly did as she was asked, but added that really there were not enough poor people at Upton to supply the needs of the already existing district visitors.

In spite of disappointment and difficulties Viola did make a determined effort to lay the energies of her wounded soul at the feet of fellow-sufferers.

She was coming back from a round of visits at Upton one afternoon, feeling sad and disheartened. It was late, and she felt a nervous dread of being alone at Upton Castle for two hours at dusk. She decided to take a longer way home, so as to make the time of solitude shorter. The house was becoming almost intolerable to her, and the strain of mind and nerve had begun to show only too clearly in her face. Viola bent her footsteps towards the sea. Arrived at the cliff's edge, she paused and peered over. A man was standing on the beach throwing stones into the water. If only it were Caleb! A good wholesome talk with that amiable encyclopedia would be like a tonic to the overwrought brain. It must be Caleb: who else would be on the shore at this time?

Viola determined to descend. The way was steep, but not difficult to one who knew the windings of the path. She lost sight of the figure on the beach and when she arrived there somewhat, breathless, he was far away in the distance, looking very small and very dim. She broke into a run, but on coming closer she began to feel doubtful whether it were Caleb after all. Nevertheless something impelled her to go on. The sea ran hungrily upon the beach, dragging the stones back and forward with each pulse-beat. Viola continued her reasonless pursuit. The power that drew her on seemed irresistible.

Suddenly the man, who had been walking at a brisk pace, Came to a standstill, and looked up towards a pathway that led from the beach to a little wind-shorn wood nestling in a hollow of the downs. From the heart of the wood a tiny column of blue smoke rose out of shelter, to be buffeted by a boisterous sea-breeze and driven inland.

Viola paused with beating heart, still instinctively keeping out of sight. A strange idea had taken possession of her that this man was – Harry Lancaster!

She started violently, and shrank back into the fissure where she had concealed herself, for her suspicion was confirmed. Her heart gave an excited bound and then seemed to stand still altogether. What had brought him thus suddenly over from Ireland? She watched his movements breathlessly. After looking up at the pathway to the little wood for some seconds; Harry turned away and walked to the verge of the sea. Viola could hear the great stones crunching under his footsteps as he plunged across them. He stood and watched the waves rolling up, and the hissing back-rush of the water over the small pebbles.

Occasionally he would turn and take another expectant look at the pathway, but ten minutes passed and nobody appeared. For whom was he waiting? The tide had just turned, and every tenth wave brought the line of wetted pebbles farther towards the cliff, causing Harry to step back gradually in the same direction. He came at last to within a dozen yards of Viola's hiding-place. Yes; there was no mistaking that upright soldier-like figure, that peculiar pose of the head. There was a very sombre expression on his face; the lips were set and hard, as if their owner suffered pain.

The temptation to reveal her presence was very strong, but Viola, resisting it, held her, breath lest she should betray herself. Interest, yearning for sympathy, dramatic curiosity, all battled with the nervous horror of being discovered. Finally conscience, as usual, turned the scale.

Then came a scorching thought!

Fir Dell lay among the trees just up here: could Harry be waiting for Mrs. Lincoln? It seemed impossible – Mrs. Lincoln, a married woman, and not a good one. No! Harry was not that kind of man. His character was too deep for such mockery of true love.

Then came a chilling consciousness: what was unforgivable in. a woman, a man might do without ceasing to respect himself or to command respect from others. Whatever he might do or feel, however, Viola was sure that she ought to avoid him. Since the line where sin begins and innocence ends did not coincide in the two cases, her *rôle*, in the event of a meeting, might prove beyond her powers. It would be like a game wherein one player was bound by the rules and the other was not.

Again Harry turned to look at the pathway from the wood, and this time he hurried forward, raising his hat with a relieved smile.

'I feared you were not coming,' he said.

'I very nearly did not come,' returned a voice singularly soft and rich, – a woman's voice, implying many things, as voices do.

Viola drew in her breath, too excited and bewildered to realise that she had now assumed the part of eavesdropper.

'Max Hoffmann and his followers have just left me,' the voice continued, 'or I should have been here before. Not been waiting long, I hope.' She gave him another hearty shake of the hand. 'How nice it is to meet again after all this time! I see you have a great deal to tell me, if you choose.' She looked anxiously and affectionately in his face.

'You are right,' he said. 'You always know, Sibella.'

By this time the two figures had moved a little, and were walking forward side by side along the shore.

Viola saw a graceful figure, clad from head to foot in rich dark red. Against the grey of the sea and sky and the white cliffs, that touch of warm colour was most cheering. Instinctively Viola glanced at her own ladylike gown of nonde-script tint, and was dimly conscious that the difference of attire indicated some radical difference of temperament.

Firm and fearless was this woman's gait, and the same spirit showed in the upright pose of the head. It was scarcely possible in the dusk to discern the fea-tures. The hair and eyes were dark, and this, with the red cloak and little cloth cap, gave the wearer a rather gipsy-like appearance:

During the few seconds in which all this had passed, Viola stood motionless in her hiding-place. She was scarcely capable of movement, for there was a strong paralysing pain at her heart. It was not figurative or poetical; it was an actual physical pain, as if the stream of life being blocked up, were struggling in vain for outlet.

'Harry, you don't look well; what is troubling you?'

'More things than one; but I want to hear about you. Tell me everything. You have haunted my thoughts as usual, Sibella. I don't like these long partings.'

'Nor I,' she said; 'but life is full of partings – perhaps in preparation for the last and the longest one of all. What was that?'

She paused suddenly.

'Did you not hear a sound of footsteps over the stones?' Harry shook his head.

'Surely! Ah, yes! I see a figure running by the foot of the cliff there, looking like a moving shadow against the white.'

Harry also could see something that might be a figure.

'We must have been overheard,' he said.

'The good people of Upton take a more than Christian interest in their neighbours,' observed Sibella, with a laugh.

'Confound them!' Harry exclaimed. 'Well, I hope our eavesdropper was interested.'

'*I* hope that she may catch cold,' said Sibella.

CHAPTER XXVII
CONSPIRACY

As the afternoon went on, the wind began to rise, and the sea became perturbed as if with premonitions of storm.

Sibella shivered.

'It is going to be a wild night,' she said. 'Do you hear that ominous muttering in the sound of the sea; not loud, but deep and malignant? The wind is very keen and angry,' she continued, as Harry did not answer; 'let us go home. I should like to show you my little house in the wood; it is so pretty and cosy.'

They walked on quickly together.

'Harry, I have often wished that your sister would come and see me, but of course she won't.'

'I fear not,' said Harry, with a shake of the head. '"A mad world, Horatio!"[71] Adrienne,' he continued, 'is a woman to go through fire and water at the call of duty. She has a theory ready made to fit anything that happens, so that she and Fate stand obstinately confronted; they devour each other, tails and all, while Adrienne, gradually diminishing, still cries out, "Uncomfortable, but for the best!"'

Sibella smiled.

'What hope have I of indulgence from such a woman?'

'Or what hope has she,' said Harry, 'of evading her own theories? She belongs to that vast band who suffer from what I call the disease of *words*; who are eaten up by words, as some wretched animal is devoured by parasites. Adrienne pronounces to herself (for instance) the word 'duty,' or 'right,' and lets it fasten upon her soul and feed there as a leech.'

'Is it curable?' asked Sibella.

'Not when it is far gone.'

'Your sister?'

'Half her substance is already devoured. Speak to her out of the fulness of the heart, and she balks you with a *word*. Try to vault over it, and you leave her far behind on the other side; she sits upon the partition and shakes her head, and perhaps sighs. And that ends everything.'

Sibella laughed a little sadly.

'And the word that partitions us – she and I, is – 'respectability.' And I used to be *so* respectable! There was really something extra superfine about my respectability, if she only knew it; it was a respectability as of the Medes and Persians!'[72]

'Foreign virtue,' said Harry, 'is unsatisfactory to the truly British mind.'

'Say instinct,' she suggested. '"British Mind", is a phrase that seems to me too enterprising.'

'I think you are pretty well,' he observed; 'you don't run amuck in this way unless you have some surplus energy. You are only quixotic when in good health.'

'I haven't been laughed at since I saw you last, except behind my back. It is quite refreshing! No, I am not well, however, in spite of my energy – and I have been very ill indeed – in the summer.'

'And you never told me!' Harry exclaimed, reproachfully. 'It was cruel to keep me in ignorance.'

'Well, well, perhaps I won't next time. No, I would rather not talk about it just now; it's a miserable subject. I thought I was going to die, quite alone, without a word of farewell to any one, and' –

'*Sibella!*'

'Don't look so horrified. It is over. Peace be to the past. Come back, and see my home; why do I keep you shivering here? And we can talk out our arrears by my study-fire. Such a dear little room, Harry, looking on to the sea, with a group of sighing pine-trees for a foreground.'

She led the way up the path by which she had descended to the beach, and the talk drifted on till they reached the house.

Sibella led the way into a pleasant little room, where tea and toast and a friendly kettle awaited their coming. Books and work lay about, and there were sundry antique vases and glass bottles of strange shape.

'I see you still have your prehistoric things in bronze,' said Harry, standing near the fireplace while Sibella made the tea.

'What should I be without my *memento mori*?[73] I think of the fellow-men who fashioned these images, and I know that all is vanity.'[74]

'Tea is not vanity,' said Harry; 'tea is an eternal verity; I am sure Carlyle[75] would admit that.'

'In one of his paroxysms of silence,' added Sibella fantastically. 'Sugar?' she inquired.

'You have forgotten!'

'Sugar it must be, and many lumps,' she said. 'He that takes no sugar, secure in the consciousness of innocence, says so boldly at once.'

Sibella laughed and pushed a low chair before the fire.

'Now are the conditions of masculine amiability fulfilled? Stay! *buttered toast* – some men become fascinating after buttered toast – though it is more usually indicated in the case of maiden ladies, not without cats.'

'Oh, please don't do that!' Harry exclaimed, bending down to take the slice of bread which she was toasting. 'You'll be roasted alive. I want no buttered toast.'

'But I want you to be amiable – go away, let me alone; I am happier than I have been for many a long day. It is the old instinct springing up again, of the woman to wait upon the man. That happens – a reversion to some hereditary instinct

– to all of us. Hence our inconsistencies which people throw in our teeth. Ah! the bread begins to steam and to emit sweet odours. This, let me remark suggestively, is the stage at which the flush of dawning amiability begins to appear – in the average patient.' She looked up and smiled.

Sibella's was one of those faces which indicate the high-water-mark of human development. Thus far has man gone upon the path of progress; thus far is he removed from the animal. Still it was not the face of a saint; for that, the smile was too brilliant and sometimes too mocking.

'Why do you talk of everything except yourself, Sibella?'

'I want to hear how you like Upton, what you are doing, whether you know any one here, whether' –

'I like Upton extremely,' she said; 'the neighbourhood is charming, and the sea – ah! that goes to my heart. But it is very tragic; there is something tragic in the air of this place, I never felt anything before to equal it. It quite depresses me sometimes.'

'You are as impressionable as ever, I see,' said Harry. He seemed about to say more, but hesitated.

'Do you ever see Philip Dendraith now?' he asked at length.

'Oh yes; he comes pretty often.'

'I want to interest you about his wife,' said Harry. 'I told you how I tried to save her from the marriage, and how I failed. She knows nothing of the world; she is intensely sensitive; judge for yourself whether she is happy.'

Sibella had risen and walked to the window. 'It seems almost as if this deadly oppression in the air of this place had not been without meaning. I wonder if the trouble of this girl could in any way have communicated itself to me.'

'I think it is more than probable,' Harry returned. 'Sibella, I have roused your sympathy, but I want more.'

'My help? What can I do?'

'I don't know, but I want you to watch your opportunity. What you mean to do you *can* do.'

She gave a dissenting gesture.

'How one must pay for one's victories!'

'Yes, one must pay for being stronger than our neighbours,' said Harry.

She gave a long sigh.

'One beats up against wind and tide, not for a moment daring to relax, lest the current sweep one back upon the hard-worn way. At last, after a hard fight, a little temporary shelter offers itself for a moment's breathing-space. Do you fondly imagine that the luxury will be allowed? Pray undeceive yourself. Your friends crowd round congratulating, "How well you are placed! What a charming and convenient spot! Fate has been kind indeed – the shade, how grateful!

the sun, how warm! – truly Fortune smiles upon you." What you win with your heart's blood is counted to the gods!'

'If you are tired out, I have no more to say,' Harry rejoined, rising and going to the fire.

'Go on,' she said; 'I speak one way and act another. You know me.'

'I know that when people have had to fight and to suffer, they do one of two things:, either they develop the instinct to push others back as they have been pushed back themselves, or they become eager to rescue and to warn. I thought that you would belong to the second class.'

'You always think over-highly of me, and at one time I was nearer to deserving it than I am now. I fear I have lost hope. The misery of people overwhelms me, sickens me. How can one rescue individuals who expiate the sins against Reason of the forefathers of the race? It is all written in the Book of Doom.'

'That is fatalism,' said Harry.

Sibella paused, and her eyes wandered out to the mournful fir-trees, themselves like Fates standing dominant over the fast fading scene.

'A woman brought up in such a manner as to make her at once intensely sensitive and intensely conscientious is a ready-made martyr; nothing can save her. She is predestined.'

Harry bent down and stirred the fire with vicious vehemence.

'I think women like Mrs. Sedley ought to be' – he smashed a large piece of coal into splinters by way of finish to the sentence.

'You ask me to help this girl,' Sibella continued. 'Why not suggest that I should forbid to-morrow's dawn? The whole machinery of doom is in motion; can I stop it?'

Harry felt himself grow cold.

'She is a woman; she is human,' he said.

'She is the child of her generation,' returned Sibella. 'Woman is the scapegoat of society. Upon her head are piled all the iniquities and the transgressions and the sins of the children of Israel, for an atonement; and then 'by the hand of a fit man' – as the Scriptures have it – she is driven forth into the wilderness.'

'We must save her!' cried Harry hoarsely.

'"But the goat on which the lot for Azazel fell, shall be presented alive before Jehovah, to make atonement with him, to let him go to Azazel in the wilderness,"' quoted Sibella slowly.

'But if she should rise in revolt; if she should refuse any longer to be made into a scapegoat?' cried Harry excitedly.

'She cannot revolt; she must accept the ceremony as sacred. She is the child of her fathers, and a spell is laid upon her. Conscience is the most tenacious of human attributes, provided it has its root in prejudice. You can deliver a prisoner who will run when the gates are open, but what can you do with one who draws the bolts and turns the locks against his would-be saviour?'

'If you will not help her, she has no helper upon this earth!' Harry exclaimed.

'I thought your sister was her friend.'

'My sister!' he cried impatiently; 'she only cheers on the victim; feeds her on a soft warm spongy sort of doctrine, perfectly ruinous to one of her temperament.'

'Are you unable to help her yourself, – since you believe in the possibility of rescue?'

Harry passed his hands through his hair, with a gesture of desperation.

'Her husband hates me and suspects me. I could not go to his house. Before their marriage I was his rival – his determined and obstinate rival. I thought on that day of the wedding, when I saw her standing there by his side, as if I must either break in between them and tear her away, or go mad on the spot. I did neither, of course. I am capable of killing that man if I saw him ill-treat her.' He bent his head, buried in his hands, upon the table. 'I would die for her, I would commit a crime for her; – what do I care?' he went on excitedly. 'Her eyes haunt me day and night; I am almost desperate, – if only she would listen to me – if only she would leave him and come with me! We *could* do it if only she *would*!'

Sibella looked at him with pity in her eyes.

'I know what you are thinking, though you don't say it,' he cried – 'that still her fate would pursue her, making happiness impossible because of the eternal visitations of remorse. Yes; and I know it is damnably true. The curse is upon us to the end!'

Sibella laid her hand tenderly on his arm, but made no immediate reply.

A strong gust of wind that went sobbing round the house seemed like the wild and grimly sincere answer of the elements.

She had said that she believed in Fate, and her belief was strengthened as she stood mournfully by the side of the man who had been to her for the best years of her life her devoted and unswerving friend. What could she do to unravel the Gordian-knot,[76] tied and drawn tight by the force of generations and the weight of centuries?

Perhaps the melancholy in the sound of wind and wave, the dark loneliness of the swaying pine-trees, uttered gloomy prophecies and forbade the rising of the star of hope.

Her knowledge of the force of emotion in this man made her tremble the more.

'To have the capacity for extreme suffering in this best of all possible worlds,' she said bitterly to herself, 'is to attract it.' She paused, deeply considering. Then she touched him on the shoulder quietly –

'Harry, I will do what I can.'

He stretched out his hand and pressed hers without speaking.

The silence continued for some minutes, the wind cannonading outside, and tearing and snarling in savage temper at every victim branch exposed, by ill-luck, to its fury. Sibella gave an excited shiver. From familiar association, some favourite lines ran in fragmentary snatches athwart her hastening thoughts: –

> 'Pain, ah! eternal pain!
> I hear Aeolian harpings wail and die
> Down forest glades, and through the hearts of men.
> Pain, pain! eternal pain!'[77]

She rose and walked restlessly to the window, and then back to the fire.

'Why are you not a man of faint desires and half-developed nerves? Why are you not quietly wise with the wisdom of the world, taking things as you find them?'

'I suppose our nature is our fate, and can't be evaded,' said Harry.

'Then pray for a new nature,' cried Sibella. 'The gods are cheats! What is the use of giving us a commanding watchword, an 'open sesame' at which all doors fly back, if the eternal hunger is to be awakened by the splendour of our visions? Every human possibility they fling recklessly at our feet – yes, but just to show us that there is a green land and fair cities beyond the desert which we can never cross!'

There was a loud ring at the bell: Harry sprang up. 'A visitor on such a night! I will go.'

'No,' said Sibella hastily; 'you may get indirect help or information; one must not neglect such chances. Stay and keep your ears open.'

The door was thrown back and the maid announced, 'Mr. Dendraith.'

One glance passed between Sibella and Harry, and then she went quickly forward.

'How good of you to come on this wild evening, Mr. Dendraith! You are indeed a chevalier *sans peur*' –

'Don't stop abruptly, Mrs. Lincoln!' exclaimed Philip.

'Oh, no man wants to be *sans reproche*;[78] it is not "good form." Do sit down and warm yourself. You know Mr. Lancaster, of course; he too has come against wind and tide to break my solitude.'

'What! Lancaster! Didn't recognise you for the moment – a thousand pardons. When did you return, to these delirious parts? I don't wonder you act the moth; our local lights are dangerously brilliant.'

'Of course Mr. Lancaster has filial duties to perform at Upton,' said Sibella.

'True,' said Philip. 'I hope you have found your mother and sister well.'

'Pretty well,' said Harry laconically.

'Are you making a long stay?'

'That is undecided.'

'I fear,' said Philip, 'that you are rather a rolling stone – no stability. There is nothing that gives more weight to the character than a permanent address.'

'Weight, but not charm,' put in Sibella; 'for that one does not need the more solid virtues. Whoever loved a man for his punctuality?'

She had a bright flush on her cheeks, and Harry saw that she was talking at random to keep the conversation going.

'I believe,' she continued, 'that Lord Chesterfield[79] completely estranged the affections of his son, and that Madame de Sevigné[80] made an enemy for life of her daughter, simply and solely through the alienating effects of good advice.'

'I must be going,' said Harry abruptly. He would not be persuaded to wait for the rain to cease.

Sibella went with him to the front-door.

'Come and see me to-morrow if you can. I want to talk this matter out with you. Keep a firm hold over yourself with' – she threw back her head towards the study. 'Don't let him guess that you are otherwise than indifferent. I can see he enjoys your suffering; this is an enemy who must be warily fought – he is keen and strong. Good-night and good-speed.'

She hastened back to her guest.

'At last!' cried Philip.

'At last?' she repeated.

'At last I have you to myself.'

'As far as talking was concerned, I think you had that privilege from the beginning.'

Philip smiled.

'Our friend was not so eloquent as usual; he didn't quite appreciate my intrusion, I fancy.'

'Do draw your chair near the fire,' said Sibella.

She had established herself comfortably, with her feet on the fender, looking the picture of idleness, and now and then a little secret smile flitted across her face as she listened to her companion's compliments. Philip drew his own chair closer to the fire, as he was bidden, keeping a pair of searching and admiring eyes fixed upon Sibella's face.

He studied her intently. He wished to find out whether he had made any kind of serious impression upon her; whether he sufficiently interested her to remain in her thoughts after he had left; whether she noticed the lapse of time between his visits. This was always the unsolved question in his mind. To-night his excitement began to rise.

'I wonder sometimes,' Philip said, drawing his chair a little closer – 'I wonder what Upton would be like if you were to leave it.'

Sibella's head bent lower for a moment, and Philip saw a smile spreading over her face.

'I really don't think it would be endurable,' he added in a low voice.

'The value of property would go down,' she remarked.

'Oh! but I mean seriously.'

'So do I, very seriously.'

'Mrs. Lincoln, you know well how dependent I; am upon you for' –

'Amusement,' she said. 'Yes, I know it well; I study up old *Punches*[81] so that you may not come to me in vain.'

'I come to you for something more than this' –

He watched her face keenly for something that might encourage him to go on, but the motionless attitude, lowered eyes, and: the slight smiles, like wandering fires, playing round the lips told him nothing. He was too wary to venture further. He knew that he had expressed his meaning, but not so definitely that she could openly resent it, if her mind lay towards resentment.

There was a long pause.

'The elements are conspiring in my favour,' said Philip; when presently a heavy gust shook the window. 'My visit is long beyond all hope of indulgence, but my excuse is the storm. Were it *between* instead of around us, I should treat it with little respect.'

'You seem to confound me and the storm in your imagination,' said Sibella, looking up for a minute.

'Ah! how can you say that? Have I not waited long enough? Have I not obeyed your merest hint and wish? Have I not again and again been silent when I longed to speak?'

She gave a little shudder.

'Well, we will not pursue this subject,' she said; 'there are things which appear to us under aspects so different that we have no common language in which to discuss them. In so far as you mean, and feel disrespect, I bitterly resent every word you have uttered. Don't protest. You are a man of the world, and think of these things as men of the world think of them. That is enough for me. You don't understand? No, and you can't.'

Philip frowned.

'I must have further explanation; it is my right.'

She shook her head. He came towards her eagerly. The excitement of the experiment was near to carrying him away, cool-headed as he was.

She broke into a laugh. She too had been trying an experiment, and the result entertained her.

Philip looked angry. He felt that he had made a miscalculation; the affair had drifted on to a wrong footing – drifted? Had it not been skilfully guided by

Sibella, whose will quietly and subtly opposed his, deliberately blunting the point of the episode to which he had been leading up? He was puzzled and amazed.

'It's that confounded fool, Lancaster!'

He felt too angry to stay longer, especially as Sibella was looking exasperatingly amiable.

'I fear I have outstayed my welcome,' he said, taking her hand; 'perhaps some other day, when you have not had a more attractive visitor, you may treat my poor feelings with less disdain.'

She laughed a little, and said politely that she never treated anybody's feelings with disdain, least of all Mr. Dendraith's.

'Oh, that's mere arabesque,'[82] cried Philip; 'I would really prefer downright impoliteness.'

She gave a little gesture of horror.

'I should expect to be struck dead on the spot by a vengeful thunderbolt, if to you I could be guilty of impoliteness!'

CHAPTER XXVIII

'THE HUMAN COMEDY'

The elements had stormed themselves tired; with the dawn came a slowly growing peace, and the sun rose over a sea still perturbed, but with the movements of a past agitation, no longer with the riot of present passion.

All the changes of the night Viola could have described, detail by detail. She lay in the great carved bed, listening to the roar of wind and wave, following with wide-awake intentness every rise and fall in their voices, every shift from boom to shriek, from blasphemy to lamentation, as, with a baffled drop, the sea-gusts swerved from the castle wall and went searching and blustering among the trembling battlements. As the storm grew less violent, the wind seemed to be playing hide-and-seek through the windows, through *that* window where Philip had sat and fallen so many years ago.

Always on these wild nights the memory returned to haunt her, and to remind her of the wickedness that lay at the bottom of her heart, ready at any time to rise in volcanic rebellion against principle, against conscience, against all the long faithful teachings of her childhood. She had formed a strange habit of torturing herself with this memory, as if she felt it a talisman against sin. To-night the talisman had been mercilessly used, for she was frightened at the tumult that had been roused in her by that scene on the beach. What business had she to care whom Harry went to meet on the shore, or whom he loved?

But the pain throbbed on none the less, gnawing, corroding ruthlessly. It seemed as if by morning her, very heart must be eaten away, and then, thank Heaven! there would be nothing more to suffer!

In the bewilderment of these stormy night-thoughts, she half-believed that the dawn would really find her calm and insensible. When the first signs of it crept about the room she rose and looked out, leaving Philip safely asleep. The sea was bleak and wan.

> 'By the lone shore
> Mournfully beat the waves.'[83]

It was Sunday morning, promising well for a day of rest.

Kneeling by the half-open window, her dark hair flowing about her with an abandonment that she never permitted to her own heart, Viola leant her head upon her hands and prayed. As her eyes fixed themselves upon the point in the grey sky where the flush of dawn had just appeared, there rose an unconscious worship in her soul for that coming sun, at whose glance the leaden waters awoke rejoicing, crying aloud at the glory of their resurrection.

The scene was one of deep religious significance to Viola; her soul wrestled in prayer, soared in adoration to the God of Nature, whose works were so great and fraught with terror, yet so marvellously beautiful.

Her own griefs appeared not less bitter but more bearable, since they were imposed by the hand of the All-powerful, who had promised to lead His obedient children safely through the darkest places, would they only have faith in Him. It was but for a little while, and then rest. Viola had been so often tempted to cry out in her misery, 'Why THIS trial of all others?' but to-day she thought she understood that it had been inflicted just *because* it alone seemed quite intolerable to her, because by this means alone could her soul be purified in the agonising passage through fiery gulfs of humiliation. The shame of conscious sin was not spared her; she was doomed to look into her own soul and see there – struggle as she might – a guilty love for one who was not her husband, a man who had done his utmost to lead her away from the path of obedience, and who – God forgive him! – had made her waver in secret with the awful force of the temptation.

Perhaps the tempest that had raged within her all through the night had left her exhausted in mind and body, and therefore the more ready to be touched by the optimistic influences of sunrise over a calming sea.

It seemed to her as a distinct message; the gentle yet spirited little waves, foam-crowned and tinged with the splendour of the morning, brought tidings of peace as they rolled in, each with a little sigh, upon the shore.

When at last Viola returned from the window prepared to take up the burdens of the day, there was a look in her face such as is seen sometimes in the faces of the dying; very calm, beautiful, and unearthly.

Philip was in one of his most biting moods this morning; every incident was the signal for a sneer, or for some remark that to Viola was worse than any sneer.

Philip's coarseness – though he knew how to conceal it when convenient – had attained a high stage of development.

This morning, after various remarks which Viola felt on their way, and dreaded as if they were so many blows, Philip fell to talking about Harry Lancaster. He alluded to his former conduct in no measured terms, and informed his wife that he had now turned up again, and was philandering at the heels of Mrs. Lincoln, the improper but agreeable young person who had become tenant of Fir Dell. It was well he had thus transferred his attentions, as Philip had no notion of having the fellow loafing about *this* place on any pretext.

'We shall probably be meeting him now and then,' he said, 'and I wish you to let him see clearly that my wife is a different person from Richard Sedley's daughter.'

'I hope that I know what is fitting for your wife,' said Viola, who was more ready than ever in her present humour to allow her individuality, as a woman, to be swallowed up in her wifehood and daughterhood.

When she went upstairs to dress for church, the thought that Harry might be there, filled her with unrest. Would he see her? Would he speak to her, and if so, in what manner? Would it be distantly and formally, or with the old ring in his voice that meant so much – ?

When Philip and his wife entered the church, the school-children and labourers were in their places, as well as a few of the farmers and their families.

The brilliant morning light fell in slanting beams across the building, and through the Norman windows unattentive worshippers might watch the trees waving in the wind or white clouds sailing across the sky.

The pew belonging to Upton Court was in the chancel, and thither with echoing footsteps marched Sir Philip, following in the humble wake of old Lady Dendraith, in purple silk, and bonnet tilted to one side in a rollicking fashion, of which the innocent wearer was quite unconscious.

To Viola's surprise, Geoffrey – now returned from his year at Sandhurst[84] – appeared and came to his sister's pew.

'Have you walked?' she whispered.

'Across country! dead beat – couldn't stand "Sunday at home" – the mother's laying it on hotter than ever – the governor's simply intolerable. Look at my boots!'

They betrayed recent contact with Mother-Earth.

'Came through all that to get away – wouldn't have let me go if I hadn't said I was coming to church.'

'I'm glad you have come,' said Viola.

Geoffrey kept up a running commentary on the people as they came in.

'Caleb Foster! What does *he* come to church for?'

'For the same reason as every one here present,' said Philip, 'to propitiate Mrs. Grundy.'[85]

'*I* come to propitiate my mother,' said Geoffrey in a stage whisper.

'Mrs. Grundy masquerading,' said Philip; 'a man never pays her so much attention as when she bespeaks it through his mother, or his sister, or his cousin, or his aunt!'

'Mr. and Mrs. Pellett! Hurrah!' exclaimed the excitable youth, hoarse from speaking *sotto voce*.[86]

Mrs. Pellett wore a bonnet which alone might have been a passport into heaven, if proved indifference to the pomps and vanities will suffice for that purpose. But clearly Mrs. Pellett had no notion of trusting solely to her head-gear for her heavenly prospects; her expression, as she walked up the aisle, could not have been surpassed, to say nothing of her books of devotion, whose size was prodigious.

Her white-headed husband slowly followed. Among his musty folios, the old scholar was happy and at home, but out in the light of day, among a host of staring fellow-creatures, he felt bewildered. The smallest boy in the school might have bullied Mr. Pellett beyond the walls of his study. His wife's signs to him to get out the books confused him, and made him shift his hat from one place to another, knock down the umbrellas, and finally propel the entire body of volumes on to his wife's person when she was kneeling for a preliminary prayer.

There were few hearts in that church which did not leap for joy at the sight! Dorothy Evans was visibly enraptured.

The Clevedon party arrived next with several visitors, among them Arabella; and finally Mrs. Dixie appeared, followed by Adrienne – Viola held her breath – and – *not* Harry!

Why did he stay away? Had he gone to Mrs. Lincoln's? Was *she* keeping him from church?

The whole place seemed to have grown suddenly dark and bleak. How cold the pillars looked! how hard and rough the stonework! how repellantly uninteresting the faces 1 how horribly ugly Mrs. Pellett's Sunday bonnet!

Mrs. Dixie and Adrienne caught Viola's eye, and Adrienne smiled across at her.

Then the congregation rose and the service began.

Viola heard the familiar words reverberating through the church, and heaved a sigh of something between relief and desperation. She looked round at the bent heads of the labourers, dull, patient creatures bowing under the yoke of toil all through the week, and trooping on Sunday to praise the God who so ordered their soul-destroying lives. Yet it was with a sense of envy that Viola studied the vacant, bucolic faces.

She tried to follow the service as usual, but her thoughts were too quick and her heart too disturbed. She found herself absently turning over the leaves of a great Bible. The first words that attracted her attention were: 'So I returned and considered all the oppressions that are done under the sun; and behold the tears of such as are oppressed, and they had no comforter; and on the side of the oppressors there was power, but they had no comforter.'[87]

Always the tiny white clouds flitted merrily across the little stage formed by the arch of the window opposite, and through it danced the light of the spring morning.

'I will sing of mercy and judgment: unto thee, O Lord, will I sing.'[88]

The people, in a slow, toiling manner, beat out the words of the psalm.

Viola felt heart-sick and bewildered.

Things spoke with many voices; there was a confusion of tongues; life was hedged round with mysteries black as midnight; yet out of every gulf came some vivid lightning-flash for a quivering moment, through the rolling vapours of the darkness.

'The Lord executeth righteousness and judgment for all that are oppressed,'[89] sang the industrious people.

Geoffrey, who was not musical, wandered about tentatively among the lower notes, but came out enjoyingly with the verses: 'I am like a pelican in the wilderness; I am like an owl in the desert.'

'I watch, and am as a sparrow alone upon the housetop.'[90]

The picture of the forlorn sparrow seemed to attract him irresistibly. What a medley it all was, of the comic, the pathetic, the dull, the commonplace, and the tragic; a world in miniature!

By this time Lady Dendraith's bonnet had slipped so hopelessly out of position that Sir Philip rashly interfered, causing her to lose her bearings altogether, and reach a state of confusion in which he was powerless to help. There seemed to be no method in the madness of that bonnet, no apparent claim in any part of it to be more to the front or to the back than any other part – a fatal difficulty in a head-gear with whose topography one is not familiar. Lady Dendraith spoke piteously of an aigrette[91] as a landmark, but Sir Philip washed his hands of it inexorably. The bonnet kept the schoolboys and Geoffrey happy for the rest of the service, and gave the old lady a severe qualm of dismay when she went home and consulted the mirror. She looked like an elderly Bacchante,[92] just returned from a revel! Meanwhile she settled herself in a dark corner and went decently to sleep.

The text of the sermon was from the Book of Job[93] (Lady Dendraith gave a peaceful sigh when it was given out). The weary, passionate words thrilled through the shadows of the church, and every heart capable of suffering stirred responsively. Job, cursing the day of his birth, longs to be where 'the wicked cease from troubling and the weary are at rest.'

'Wherefore is light given unto him that is in misery, and life unto the bitter in soul; which long for death, but it cometh not; and dig for it more than for hid treasures; which rejoice exceedingly, and are glad, when they can find the grave?'

Mr. Evans undertook to show that Job's sentiments were reprehensible; that in no possible circumstances is the creature of God justified in desiring to evade the trials that He has appointed.

'Oh! my brethren, we must bow to the will of Heaven without repining; we must accept, we must even welcome, the trials that come to us, though we may be stricken with disease, and lonely and deserted as job was. Resignation is the lesson at once of life and of religion. It may, be, my brethren, that we fancy ourselves better able to understand what is good for us than our Heavenly Father, who tempers the wind to the shorn lamb.'

(A phenomenally thoughtful shepherd in the congregation here felt the fatal opposition between religion and science, boisterous weather having set in immediately after shearing on more occasions than one that he could mention).

'We know that more will not be given to us than we can bear,' pursued Mr. Evans, and his robust and prosperous appearance seemed to justify the opinion, though a glance at his worn-looking wife might have bid him pause before making so quite sure of his doctrine.

Mr. Evans preached for about twenty minutes, and in that time he had succeeded in taking all the passion and force out of the character of his hero, and in reducing to commonplace the utterances that have come ringing down to us through so many ages, fresh and hot from the soul of one who cried aloud in anguish of body and anguish of soul.

As soon as the sermon was over and the organ began to fill the church with triumphant strains, the old clerk set open the doors, disclosing a view of the sun-lit churchyard.

As the worm-eaten side-door was flung back, Viola caught sight of two figures among the graves: – those of Harry Lancaster and Mrs. Lincoln. Mrs. Lincoln had on a blue cloak and a hat of the same colour, in which was twined a wreath of real ivy. She was sitting on the top of a flat tomb, and Harry stood beside her, looking down. Viola thought she had never seen so attractive a face.

How could a bad woman look like that? And there was something in the expression that filled Viola with an astonished belief that, however she might have sinned, Mrs. Lincoln was a person to be implicitly trusted.

As the notes of the organ poured through the open doors Sibella rose, and she and Harry strolled away together, as if to avoid encountering the people when they came out.

The church-door was the scene of many greetings. Every one said, 'What a lovely morning!' unless he remarked, 'What a gale there was last night!'

Dorothy and Mrs. Pellett waylaid Viola.

'Good-morning, Mrs. Dendraith. I *hope* you are feeling better than you look.'

'Oh, much!' Geoffrey answered for her.

'Your dear mother is feeling very anxious about you, my dear.'

'Thanks to your kind interest in my sister,' said the irrepressible one, 'my mother has scarcely had a wink of sleep for three weeks.'

The rector came forward to shake hands all round.

'Mr. Evans, I must congratulate you on your sermon,' cried Mrs. Pellett. 'It was excellent – so *sound*.'

'Well, I trust that it was, perhaps, *sound*,' returned the rector. 'I have always endeavoured to – in short, be sound. There is so much to be deplored in these materialistic days as – as regards – in fact *soundness*.'

'Ah, so you may say, Mr. Evans!' exclaimed the lady sadly; 'so you may say.'

Mr. Evans shook hands with Mrs. Dixie.

'Charming morning, Mrs. Dixie. And what a gale we had last night! By the way, I have to congratulate you on the unexpected return of your son.'

'Yes; we are indeed glad to have the dear fellow back again.'

Viola was greeted effusively by Arabella. How long it was since they had met! She really must try and get over to see Mrs. Dendraith, but so much always went on at Clevedon. There was to be a large gathering there on the 12th – everybody invited. And so that dear Mr. Lancaster of whom Augusta was so fond had come back. Had Mrs. Dendraith heard of it?

Mrs. Courtenay's sharp little brown eyes, fixed upon Viola's face, were like two gimlets.

Yes, Mrs. Dendraith had heard of it from her husband.

'You have not seen him yet, I suppose.'

The moment was a crucial one for Viola, to whom an untruth seemed almost impossible. Perhaps Arabella saw that she was perturbed, and scenting a mystery, perhaps an improper mystery (Oh, joy of the proper!), she pinned her dear Mrs. Dendraith unwarrantably to the point.

'You have seen Mr. Lancaster, perhaps. I hope he is looking well.'

'I hear that he is,' said Viola.

'Oh, then you have *not* seen him?'

This was cruel.

'Yes, I have seen him,' said Viola at last, in desperation, not perceiving any loophole of escape. But nothing would induce her to continue the conversation. She plunged after her husband and brother in the hope of persuading them to leave, but when she appealed to Geoffrey, Arabella bore down upon Philip.

'Charmed to meet your wife again, Mrs. Dendraith,' said Arabella, with one of her most irresistible wriggles. 'I am always accusing Fate for her unkindness in putting fourteen miles between our houses.'

'Nobody could regret that more than I do,' returned Philip.

'Oh! Mr. Dendraith, you are as bad as ever!'

'I fear that in your society I shall become considerably worse,' he replied.

'Dear, dear; what will your wife say if I let you go on like this? Is she jealous? I really hope not, for she would have much to suffer. *You* don't know what it is to be jealous; I am sure. How nice that must be!'

'It is,' said Philip.

'You are a spoilt child of nature, Mr. Dendraith; all the gilt without the gingerbread – no, I don't mean that quite, but all the plums without the cake – no, that won't do either; but you know how excellent are my intentions. Now, haven't you some Upton news to tell me? – somebody has surely died or got married since I left. I hear that charming creature, Mr. Lancaster, has returned; quite the pet of the village, isn't he?'

'Oh, quite,' said Philip.

'Your wife tells me he is looking so well.'

Philip gave a slight movement of the eyebrows.

'Nobody heard of his arrival till last night,' he observed.

'Really! and yet I thought she told me that she had met him – a mistake, no doubt, on my part.'

'If you never make a mistake of greater importance, Mrs. Courtenay, you have my sincere congratulations.'

'Now, Arabella,' interposed Lady Clevedon, 'you have chattered long enough. Philip, I want you and Viola to dine with us on the 12th. Will you?'

'Charmed,' said Philip; 'I have nothing on the 12th.'

'We have some people coming – a good many of the neighbours – and there are one or two staying in the house who can sing and play, so we shall have some music. If you can perform, bring your instrument.'

'The big drum,' said Philip; 'it shall accompany me.'

Geoffrey returned with his sister and her husband for luncheon. On the homeward way they fell to discussing Harry Lancaster's sudden return.

'It must be just over two years since you saw him, Viola,' said her husband.

She did not answer.

'Or is it longer? No, the last time was at our marriage.'

'Oh, if you are going in for this style of discussion *à la* maiden aunt' – cried Geoffrey, 'I shall put cotton-wool in my ears. Let us not recall the past.'

'It has been said that no man would willingly react his part in it,' observed Philip.

'Certainly no *woman* would!' Viola exclaimed.

'Woman is an adorable and ill-treated being,' said Philip; 'quite immaculate, as ill-treated creatures always are. It's constitutional with them. Arabella seems in good form – tricksy as ever. Adorable Arabella!'

'Grinning idiot!' exclaimed the irreverent Geoffrey.

'She has a graceful habit of putting her foot in it which I cannot enough admire,' pursued Philip, with one of his short sudden voiceless laughs. 'She cheerfully informed me to-day that Viola had already seen Harry Lancaster, and thought him looking well. As Viola had heard of his arrival only this morning from my own lips, I was obliged to reprove Arabella for inaccuracy.'

'What on earth put it into her head that Viola had seen him?' cried Geoffrey.

'Arabella's is not a head that I should like to have to account for,' returned Philip, watching his wife's face furtively.

She was very pale.

'What had you been telling her, Viola?' cried her brother. 'You know it won't do to let a woman like Mrs. Courtenay go about saying that you have seen Harry Lancaster before any one else had heard of his arrival; it doesn't sound well.'

Philip's cat-like instinct found full indulgence this afternoon. Nearly, but not quite, Viola found herself a hundred times confronted with the alternative necessities of telling a falsehood and confessing where and how she had seen Harry. To admit it thus late in the day, implying the previous concealment, was distasteful. On the other hand, Viola thought it probable that Philip had *not* really believed Mrs. Courtenay to be inaccurate, and that he now amused himself by this slow torture of his wife, whose secret was no longer hers to tremble for or to keep.

'Upon my word, Viola,' said Geoffrey, with an air of worldly wisdom worthy of his promised moustache, 'I must take an opportunity skilfully to put Mrs. Courtenay right about that matter. Lancaster used rather to dangle after you before your marriage, and there's nothing too ridiculous for people to say. Ah; Triton, my boy, how are you? I say, that'll do now; down, good dog, down. Ila, you don't train him well. Your visitors will have to sacrifice their best clothes as the price of your acquaintance. Sir Walter Raleigh[94] got off easily in comparison!'

Geoffrey received no reply.

Standing before the door of her home, Viola was seized with a frantic impulse to turn from that great iron-bound portal and run away, no matter whither, so only that she need never again cross the threshold. A strong excitement held her; it seemed that her one chance of averting some hideous catastrophe lay in the desperate act of immediate flight; it was hers to decide upon it now, or to follow the fatal path to the end.

The hot sun pouring down upon the gravel and on the grey stone steps darted madness into her brain (or was it supreme wisdom?).

Why did God, she asked herself wildly, forbid His forsaken children, whom He had permitted to be degraded, to wash out stains and memories unendurable in the waters of death? Why did He force them to return to be tortured anew, with indignity heaped on indignity?

The sunshine was blinding; Viola put out her hand to steady herself against the stone balustrade, for she was faint and slightly swaying. She gave a terrified start.

Ah pitiful God! she *dared* not cross that threshold, for – or was she dreaming? – there was blood upon it! Yes, *blood*; a stream which seemed to be oozing slowly under the door, stealthily moving forward to the steps till it dripped, dripped –

'By Jove! Philip, look-out – quick, lend us a hand – Viola has fainted!'

And so across the threshold, over the phantom bloodstream which she alone had seen upon the doorstep, the unconscious burden was carried into the house.

END OF VOLUME II

THE WING OF AZRAEL

by
Mona Caird

Yesterday, this Day's madness did prepare
To-morrow's Silence, Triumph or Despair.

In THREE VOLUMES.

VOL. III

LONDON:
TRÜBNER & CO., LUDGATE HILL.
1889.

CHAPTER XXIX

A DANGEROUS ACQUAINTANCE

When Viola regained consciousness she was lying on her bed; Mrs. Barber, with a portentous array of *eau-de-cologne* and *sal volatile* bottles, stood over her, looking unutterable woe.

She fell to rubbing Viola's hands, and to applying vast quantities *of eau-de-cologne to* her forehead.

'Well, I *am* glad to see you restored, ma'am! I thought you was dead and gone, that I did! Permit me to apply some more *eau-de-cologne*, just above the temples.'

'Thank you, Mrs. Barber, not any more at present,' said Viola, who was already sopping just above the temples, in consequence of the housekeeper's amiable enthusiasm. 'If I might have a dry handkerchief, – the *eau-de-cologne* is running into my eyes.'

'I expect the walk was too long for you,' Mrs. Barber continued – 'on a hot day like this too. I never did think those long walks was quite conducive' (the word as she understood it being entirely self-contained).

Viola longed to lie back and rest and be silent, but Mrs. Barber talked on, till at last Philip and Geoffrey came up, and the housekeeper retired, in answer to a nod from Philip.

'All right now, Viola?' asked her brother.

'Yes, I am better,' she said.

'Who do you think has been calling? Harry Lancaster! But we thought it well not to let you come down to see him. He was sorry to hear of your not being quite up to the mark.'

'Oh!' She seemed but little moved.

'And he was very sorry to miss seeing you, and other things polite. I don't think he looks well. Are you going to get up again to-day?'

'Yes; I am all right now.'

Viola dreaded that as soon as Geoffrey left, Philip would speak to her about her meeting with Harry. The house seemed to stifle her. She hurried out and away across the gardens to the cliffside-pathway leading to the beach. The sea was just growing calm with the sinking of the wind, and gleaming with the mellow tints of afternoon. There was a whisper of spring in the air; little white clouds

overhead were carrying the sweet message from land to land. In a few minutes
Viola was on the lonely shore, the waters sweeping to her feet. She lay against a
long wave-like ridge of pebbles which the tides had flung up to stem their own
advance upon the land.

At times of strong excitement, human feeling is not simple but infinitely
complex. Nothing is too trivial to consider, nothing is too alien to the central
emotion. Viola lay watching the overlapping curves of the little waves which
raced one another to the strand, watching the fretwork of foam spreading
between ridge and ridge, and the brilliant reds and browns which the touch
of water revealed in the 'so-seeming virtuous'[1] pebbles – like the unsuspected
things which tears will summon forth in human hearts.

> 'Wave after wave for ten thousand years has furrowed the brown sand here
> Wave after wave, under clouds and stars, has cried in the dead shore's ear.'[2]

Thus for centuries, the sea had beaten, just as to-day, on the crumbling coast,
and probably for centuries after would beat so; while the joy and the anguish of
human souls came and passed away as the shadow of a cloud over the sea, or as a
tremor in some salt pool left by the resilient waves.

When the human being fully realises how utterly he is swallowed up and
lost in the world of infinities, the moment is always vital and terrible, though it
has been felt and described so many times before. The realisation seldom comes
until, seeking in vain for help, the sufferer finds himself shouting to a deaf universe, and hears his own voice dismally echoing through its unending spaces.

Viola, who had hitherto been shielded by religious teaching from this conception, felt the horror of it come upon her to-day overpoweringly. There was
pain, look which way she would – pain in her own little world of being, exquisite, unbearable; pain in the thought of the vast, soulless, indifferent universe,
– a giant machine grinding on for ever, 'without haste and without rest.'[3] Where
were the previous morning's faith and peace? All gone, and in their place: doubt,
hatred, disgust, wounded dignity, wounded affection, devouring anxiety, and
over all a consciousness that this hot emotion mattered nothing and availed
nothing; that presently the waves would be beating and retreating, with only the
cliff and the gulls for audience. Religion spoke warningly, but the familiar voice
was not heeded. Viola turned her face to the hard stones, and broke into deep,
silent, terrible sobbing. Some heartstring seemed to break with each sob.

So still she had lain there that the sea-gulls – cold-hearted birds! – came
sweeping quite close to her and over her head.

At length the crisis of the passion came, the wave broke and passed on. There
was one tight stifled cry, and then Viola, changing her attitude, fell into a sort
of lethargy.

She was dimly conscious of the stirring wind and the unresting sea-sound, dimly conscious of the golden glow that began to light up the sky. The waves sounded hoarse and desperate. Deeper and deeper grew the blood-red stain upon the waters, and the land seemed to have caught fire. The swiftest cloud-streaks were overtaken and their cool white turned into gold.

At the wet wave-line upon the sands a figure, clad in sunset-red, was slowly strolling, stooping now and again with swift movement to snatch some feathery sea-weed from the tide. A large brown dog accompanied her, barking when she flung a pebble for him into the sea, that he might swim out in pretended search, to return and shake himself, and bound and bark again for another mimic errand.

The two figures worked their way gradually along the shore. Viola, lying against the ridge of pebbles, presently opened her eyes and found the dog standing beside her, dripping from tail and legs and ears, and threatening at any moment to shake himself with vigour. But a voice recalled him. Viola started up; she felt as if she ought to rise and flee from it; it was the voice of a siren, luring from the ways of righteousness. She felt that instantly.

Sibella, turning to pick up a stone for her tyrannical dog, found herself face to face with Viola.

Both women coloured deeply, and for a moment there was silence.

'I beg your pardon for unknowingly disturbing you. I thought myself alone.'

Sibella hesitated, coloured again, and then said almost shyly, 'I have been very anxious for this meeting, Mrs. Dendraith. You observe this is not the first time I have seen you.'

Viola, too excited and bewildered to know what she thought or felt, continued to gaze at her companion in silence. Perhaps Sibella saw or divined her feelings, for she sat quietly down on the shingle by her side and began to talk. She spoke without personal reference, but with a subtle implication of comradeship which touched Viola's loneliness, as the glow of the fireside is welcome to one shivering and belated. Then, more fancifully, she spoke of the sea, of its perpetual variety, its endless range of expression and meaning. She went on to speak about the down country inland, contrasting it with the tame fields and pastures among which she had spent her childhood and her married life. Viola grew interested, and the more Sibella told her, the more breathlessly interested she became. There was a strange resemblance to her own experience in the story that Sibella told. She too had been strictly and watchfully brought up; she too had begun life with a store of 'principles' – enough (Sibella said) to stock the Bench of Bishops.[4]

Before half-an-hour had passed Viola was speaking as she had never before spoken to human being; her cheeks were flushed, her eyes burnt with excitement. The unwonted utterance had thrown a confused light upon her own emotions, while the comments of her companion, flinging brilliant cross-flashes, frightened and allured at the same time.

'But what do you mean? I don't understand; it turns things topsy-turvy,' Viola cried, with a sort of terror-stricken excitement. She stretched out her arm as if trying to grasp again the bulwarks of her creed.

A firm, gentle hand was laid in hers.

'Don't be frightened to open your eyes and to use your reason. If the creeds of our youth are true they can bear the light. We have both been taught, as we imagined, to worship God. I fear that we have really been taught to worship the devil! We were trained to submission, to accept things as they are, to serve God by resignation – yes, even the resignation of our human dignity – whereat the devil laughs in his sleeve, and carries off the fruits of miserable lives to add to the riches of his kingdom.'

'Oh! I can never believe so!' cried Viola.

'No; we are both well grounded,' said Sibella, 'but you are naturally more conscientious than I. The better the soil the richer the harvest for the devil. I always questioned and doubted, though from force of circumstances I obeyed. But there came a crisis in my life, and then I broke away. I don't say it is a success, but in refusing to submit to what was degrading I have at least rescued myself from the unbearable self-loathing which a woman' –

The speaker paused, as Viola drew in her breath sharply. Sibella laid her hand upon her arm.

'It is better to face things,' she said gently. 'You have not suffered quite alone; I told you in what circumstances my marriage took place; a mere child, brought up without knowledge of life, of my fellow-creatures, of the very laws and customs which were to rule my destiny. Everything in my surroundings was untrue, unscientific, groundless, fabricated. In my cramped painful little world, there were a thousand invented crimes, a thousand invented tortures, and in the close motionless atmosphere, these things grew more monstrous and unwholesome every day. This process of education and subsequent marriage, through which so many sensitive girls are made to go, always reminds me of the torture that the Romans inflicted upon one of their generals who had offended them; they cut off his eyelids and then compelled him to sit in the blazing sun.[5] I, having been worked up through years of training to a state of overwrought sensitiveness, was asked to give my hand in marriage to a man whom I scarcely knew, and for whom I cared nothing – a man who regarded women as his lawful prey, let them fill what position in life they might. The family was eager for an heir; to provide one, and afterwards to devote to him my whole life and energies, was to be my sacred duty and privilege' –

Viola gave a slight movement, and Sibella tightened the grasp of her hand.

'I, of course, did not understand all this: how could I? My pastors and masters had exhausted the Dictionary for terms to express the blessedness and the poetry of what they called a woman's destiny. How was I, a bewildered girl knowing nothing of the world, trusting that my parents had my welfare at heart, – how was I to know that legalised insults and indignities were in store for me?'

'You must think wrongly of it!' Viola broke out. 'It is God-ordained – don't take that belief from me or I shall go mad!'

'My poor girl, you have already lost that belief – I am not taking it from you.'

Viola turned away, not denying. After a moment of silence she said, 'Please go on; this has a terrible interest for me!'

'My parents must have known that the marriage was unsuitable, but they had brought up their daughter with the strictest and most admirable principles, and they trusted to *that* to keep things straight and the family honour (as they humorously called it) intact. As a rule the method answers; society is founded upon the success of such exploiting; but in my case it failed.'

'I ought not to listen!' Viola murmured.

'You ought to listen and then to judge,' said Sibella. 'The story is so painfully obvious, and yet nobody sees it or admits it, and so the hoary old hypocrisies are kept up, the threadbare cant which yet holds bravely together and is thick enough still to hide the truth from our crops of fresh young victims as they spring up year after year.'

Viola pushed back the hair from her brow in a sort of desperation.

'Most women,' Sibella pursued, 'spend their energies in making all these time-honoured iniquities possible and successful, encouraging the repetition of these profitable old crimes apparently for all eternity! The fortitude and goodness of the victims are relied upon – and not in vain – to ward off from their perpetrators the natural punishment. It is for the victims to pay the price of the iniquity and to make it socially successful, and this they must do and keep silence on pain of excommunication. If the fortitude breaks down, ah! then what a hue and cry! The woman is hunted, scorned, ruined; there is no mercy.'

Sibella turned suddenly to her companion. 'Are *you* going to make successful another of these old villainies? Are all women who come after you to be worse off, to be heavier-hearted, because of you?'

Viola half-rose, as if to leave her dangerous companion. But she did not go. 'If you are right, Mrs. Lincoln, the best and noblest women I have known are all wrong. Their goodness and their suffering has been in vain.'

'And so *are* the virtues and the martyrdoms of good women in vain. That is why the devil finds our planet such a happy hunting ground. I assure you he enjoys himself immensely. He is full of humour. What's that?'

There was a sound of footsteps over the shingle. She raised herself to look over the pebble-ridge.

'Is any one coming?' asked Sibella.

Viola had turned white. 'My husband,' she said.

'Oh!' Sibella's expression changed. 'He will be angry at finding us together – I understand. It was my fault, if fault there be. Remain passive. Say as little as you can, and keep as much as possible your usual manner.'

Philip raised his eyebrows slightly on seeing his wife's companion.

'Mrs. Lincoln! what fortunate star directed my steps towards this spot?'

'Then you are glad to see me here?' Sibella observed, looking up into his face with a singular smile.

'Do you throw a doubt upon my good taste?' he inquired.

'I cannot be guilty of that mistake since meeting your wife.'

'I bow for us both,' returned Philip. 'I never can get my wife to bow for herself.'

'She has an admirable model always before her eyes. I am lost in admiration of your bows; I wish you had lived in the last century.'

'Thanks' said Philip. 'Your compliment is intoxicating.'

'You would have been perfect in a minuet, Mr. Dendraith. We have none of that delightful dignity of movement in these days; stateliness and grace have died out.'

'Pardon me' –

'Oh! this is *too* much!' laughed Sibella; 'my worst enemies have never yet called me *stately*. Graceful?' she pursed up her lips and raised her eyebrows – 'perhaps; – I have studied that a little – but stately! I should die in the attempt.'

'You do not leave a bewildered creature time to catalogue your attributes, Mrs. Lincoln; he can only think of you as a delightful and dazzling whole.'

'I am glad you don't think me unfinished,' said Sibella, dismissing the subject. 'How glad I am to have made Mrs. Dendraith's acquaintance. One never really knows a man till one knows his wife. Mrs. Dendraith throws, unconsciously, a flood of light on your character – most becoming,' she added.

Philip's lips looked rather tight about the corners, but he smiled, and said suavely, 'It is very kind of you to take my wife in hand, Mrs. Lincoln; to know you is a liberal education.'

'You overwhelm me.'

'If you stay much longer in this position, I fear the sea will do that,' Philip returned. 'Viola, my love, do you contemplate restoring the grace of your presence to my humble abode before nightfall?'

'I am ready to come now.'

'Then my house will be a home once more,' he said, drawing Viola away to the side farther from Sibella.

'Mrs. Lincoln, you will permit me to walk back with you.'

'Thank you, no; I do not require an escort.'

'Once more, then, let me express my deep gratitude for having interested yourself so kindly in my wife.'

He looked Sibella full in the face as he said this, holding out his hand.

Laying hers in it, she returned the look point-blank, and replied, with a little smile and bend of the head, 'please don't thank me; I feel myself so unworthy. Though I am interested in all that concerns you, my interest in Mrs. Dendraith has arisen quite independently of any such sentiment, and thanks weigh heavy on my soul, as ill-gotten treasure. Once more good-bye.'

She turned with a significant bow and smile, called her dog, and walked quietly away. A challenge had been tacitly given and accepted.

'Was this prearranged?' Philip asked.

'No, accidental.'

'Perhaps you had other fish to fry,' he suggested.

She did not answer.

'I need not observe that our fascinating friend is not fit society for you, my dear.'

Although this had been Viola's own opinion until this afternoon, she flushed painfully.

'You must intimate politely but firmly that you feel obliged to forego the pleasure of her further acquaintance. Better avoid the shore in the afternoon, as she seems inclined to make it a promenade.'

'What is she accused of?' asked Viola.

'A mere friskiness,' returned Philip; 'culminating in a trifling elopment, scarcely worth mentioning. Lancaster's bosom-friend, Elliott, was the happy man.'

'Did she leave her husband to go with this man?'

'Well, no; she went away alone, but it is supposed that he followed her afterwards. Anyhow she did not break with him, as a prudent woman would have done in her slippery position. There was no divorce, of course, but her character is gone. No woman can associate with her and keep her own in good feather. I wonder a young person of respectable instincts like you would be seen speaking to her. It must not happen again.'

'What has become of – of the man?'

'Elliott? That is a delicate question, my dear. What does happen to men who run after other men's wives? Scripture is mute upon the subject. Elliott is now expiating his misdeeds in another, but, alas! I dare not affirm with confidence, a better world. Perchance he is doomed to a cycle of never-ending flirtation with his neighbours' wives, till he wishes he had never been born.'

'He is dead?' said Viola.

'You are a trifle bold, my love, in your expression. Say, rather, he has departed; he has gone to another sphere; he is at rest. Of course the last is rather euphonious than instructive.'

'Has any one a right to condemn Mrs. Lincoln when her sin is only conjectured?' asked Viola.

Philip shrugged his shoulders.

'Possibly not. I merely explain to you that to associate with her is to take the bloom off your own reputation, and I have no notion of possessing a wife in that bloomless condition. Now, I hope I have explained myself clearly, my dear. Not a breath, not a whisper shall go forth against the woman to whom I have given my name. Take care that you do nothing to give rise to it. You will see nobody, man or woman, without my knowledge; you will make no acquaintance, man or woman, without my knowledge. You will receive no letter that is unseen by me. And now' – Philip held open the gate into the garden gallantly – 'now to the home of which you are the sunbeam.'

CHAPTER XXX

A TOUGH BATTLE

Sibella sat in a low chair before the fire, with a blotting-pad and writing materials on her knee. She had abandoned her ruddy-tinted gown, and wore a fashionably made dress of dark cloth, neatly braided. Mrs. Russell Courtenay herself would not have felt unhappy in the attire.

Several sheets of writing-paper lay on the table, each with the commencement of a letter abruptly abandoned. Sibella was now struggling with another letter, writing a few words between long intervals of gazing into the fire. She wrote to the end of the first page, and then, with an impatient movement, tore off the half-sheet, crumpled it in her hand, and threw it into the flames. The next few minutes were spent in sketching fabulous creatures on the edge of the blotting-pad, and writing under them the names of common domestic animals. Sibella appeared to devote herself heart and soul to this occupation, looking at her sketch from this side and from that, adding brightness to the eye and spirit to the tail, by means of deeply considered touches. The being under which she traced the letters D. O. G. had a strange, square-looking jaw and an appalling grin; his tail when unfurled must have been available as a weapon at a distance of several yards, and along his backbone the hair stood up in a ridge, indicating a spirit sorely aggrieved. Facing this work of art was a creature of the panther order, thin and strong and agile, with a watchful eye and a look of stealthy swiftness. Under this image the artist wrote, somewhat inconsequently, 'Philip Dendraith.'

'DEAR MRS. DENDRAITH, – It will surprise, and, I fear, displease you to receive' –

'DEAR MRS. DENDRAITH, – Please believe I am actuated by a friendly spirit' –

'DEAR MRS. DENDRAITH, – Could you meet me to-morrow afternoon on the shore at three o'clock? I want very much to' –

Sibella pushed away the paper in despair, and supporting her chin on her hands, sat looking steadily into the fire.

The door-bell rang.

'Ah, if it were only that poor girl!'

Sibella gathered together her papers and awaited the announcement of her visitor. A maid brought in a card.

'The lady wished to know if you could see her, ma'am.' The shadow of a train of thought seemed to pass through Sibella's eyes in the second of silence that followed.

'I shall be glad to see Miss Lancaster.'

Adrienne, looking rather pale, but very composed, was ushered into the room. Sibella had risen and bowed.

'I have to apologise for this intrusion' – began Adrienne.

'Please don't apologise. Will you take a chair near the fire?'

'Thank you; I prefer to avoid it; the wind is sharp outside.' Adrienne sat down, wondering if there were anything in her manner to show that her heart was beating so hard that she could scarcely draw her breath.

'I think it well to plunge into my business at once,' she said, when Sibella had drawn her chair facing her visitor, and placed herself in a calm attitude of attention.

'Please do so.'

'I came on behalf of my friend, Mrs. Dendraith.'

'She has sent you?'

'Not exactly. Yesterday afternoon I called at her house, and found that she had just returned from a long interview with you on the beach. Mrs. Dendraith told me all that you had said to her.'

Adrienne looked her hostess full in the face, as if she expected her to flinch from her righteous gaze.

'She told you all I said to her,' Sibella repeated, with the gleam of a smile in her eyes; 'and what did you think of it?'

Adrienne flushed with indignation.

'Since you ask me, Mrs. Lincoln, I must confess that I think it is the most extraordinary, the most unprincipled advice that I ever heard in my life. I listened to Mrs. Dendraith in incredulous amazement. I know that you have long been my brother's friend, and therefore I have hitherto felt ready to believe well of you' –

Sibella gave a little bow.

'But when I hear that you not only hold such views yourself, but actually try to poison with them the innocent mind of a young wife, then I feel' –

'That the innocent mind calls for your protection. I admire your championship and self-sacrifice; I fear this interview must be painful for you.'

'I should have imagined that *you* might have felt it painful,' said Adrienne, with a gasp.

'Oh no,' returned Sibella politely; 'not at all.'

The visitor was silent for a moment, collecting her energies.

'I come here to-day to make an appeal to you, to rouse your sense of justice and mercy, to represent to you what a terrible injury you may do to that young wife. She is not happy, as a person of your penetration would quickly see. But she is supported by high principle. She is noble, she is self-sacrificing, she is pure; faith is her sheet-anchor, and I consider that any one who robs her of it, or shakes it by so much as a passing doubt, is guilty of a cruel, an accursed deed.'

Adrienne paused, breathless with disgust and anger.

Mrs. Lincoln's steady look was full of judicial attention; her expression was almost sympathetic.

'I have believed,' Adrienne went on, curbing her indignation, 'I have always believed that no human being is wholly devoid of good.'

'Not even such as I, Miss Lancaster?'

'Not if you will give the better impulses fair-play,' Adrienne returned severely, at which the other smiled.

'Oh! Mrs. Lincoln, if you had seen that poor girl yesterday, as I saw her, you would not smile! It was terrible. She came to me entreating and imploring that I would make her believe again, that I would reconvince her of her own principles, and of the love of God. Everything seemed to have gone from her; and it is *you*, Mrs. Lincoln, whom she has to thank for this! I wish you had seen her fling herself upon the sofa, crying that she could not endure to live; that she was lowered and humiliated for ever; that it was intolerable to be herself! Of course it is a very morbid idea, but I cannot get it out of her head.'

'Ah,' Sibella said, 'to feel so is to endure the tortures of the damned.'

'Are you quite heartless?' Adrienne said, bringing down her little clenched hand upon her knee. 'Have you no pity, no forbearance? If you *must* have disciples, if you can't rest satisfied with flinging over every law of God and man on your own account, why, in the name of reason, must you pick out for your followers sensitive creatures who suffer in this dreadful way?'

'You care for this girl very sincerely, I think,' said Sibella.

'I would do almost anything for her.'

'It will surprise you when I say that I too would do almost anything for her.'

'No, it does not surprise me; nothing that you might say or do could surprise me any further. A woman who dares to advise repudiation of the most sacred duty to one so pure and sweet as Viola Dendraith would hesitate at nothing!'

There was a pause.

'You do not even defend yourself,' Adrienne exclaimed.

'Because, Miss Lancaster – to follow your example of limped[6] sincerity – I do not see my way to make you understand.'

Adrienne bowed.

'It is, then, owing to my inferior intelligence that I differ from you,' she said. 'I never before felt occasion to bless my stupidity.'

'Then your experience has not at all resembled mine,' Sibella answered. '*I* have blessed my stupidity again and again! When I am dead there will be found written on my heart, "Blessed are the stupid, for they shall never be confounded."'

Her eyes sparkled in spite of her cool manner; her words, quiet, swift to the point as hailstones, stung as they fell.

'Alas! you are *not* stupid, Miss Lancaster, if you will excuse my saying so.'

'A compliment from *you*' – murmured Adrienne.

Sibella gave a shrug.

'A compliment from me is nevertheless worth having,' she said.

'I can bear your good opinion of my intellect, but for Heaven's sake don't tell me you approve of my principles!'

'I am not going to,' Sibella answered, 'for I don't.'

They sat looking at one another for a second in silence.

'Am I to understand that you intend to pursue Mrs. Dendraith's acquaintance?' Adrienne at length asked.

'A question I scarcely feel called upon to answer,' said Sibella; 'but this I will say, that whatever seems to me best for your friend that I shall do.'

'Perhaps you are not very well acquainted with her husband?' Adrienne suggested.

'I have had some opportunity of studying his character.'

'If so, you know what it means to oppose him.'

Sibella bent her head.

'And that he has absolutely forbidden his wife to meet you, or any one, without his knowledge?'

'Having appealed in vain to my better feelings, you now appeal to my fears,' said Sibella. 'Yes, I know all that.'

'And you intend to measure your strength with his?'

'He having on his side nine-tenths of the law, to say nothing of his wife's conscience and the powerful alliance of highly principled friends! – it is madness, is it not?'

Adrienne looked at the speaker from head to foot.

She was slight, graceful, soft in outline and in attitude. Her pose was rather indolent, though there lay in it a subtle hint of large reserve force. Her face at this moment wore a peculiarly soft expression.

Adrienne felt interested; she was vaguely conscious of something incomprehensible in this unprincipled woman. Sibella must be inherently bad. If a character failed to catalogue itself under one's own familiar headings, there was nothing but badness to account for it, – unless, indeed, it were madness.

'Miss Lancaster,' said Sibella, suddenly turning her eyes from the sea, 'it is childish for you and me to sit here bandying words. That will not avail either of us, and we forget our sisterhood in foolish opposition.'

Adrienne did not appear to care to acknowledge the sisterhood.

'But we *are* sisters,' Sibella pursued, answering the unspoken thought; 'we are separated only because we can't see clearly into one another's minds. That is all. It is only dimness of sight that holds us back. You think of opinions, things social and things of rule, of names and shadows, and you turn coldly away and deny our common nature which makes us sisters against our will. We stand as the poles asunder; but that is only in words, believe me! We are one, we are human.'

Sibella again turned her eyes seawards.

'We stand shivering between two eternities; we came out of the darkness, and we see the darkness waiting for us a little way ahead – such a little way! And we have to pick our steps among rough stones, and our feet bleed, and we try to roll some of the stones away! And they are too heavy for us, and we are lonely, and the Place of Stones[7] where we toil is very bleak, and we cry out that we must have love and hope or we die. And love comes, and our hearts leap up, and every stone at our feet breaks into colour, and every wave and every dewdrop gleams. Then a cloud comes into the sky, and dims all the glory, and love goes away shivering; and with him go joy and sympathy and brotherhood hand in hand. But we yearn after him still, and we seek for him all our days. That is your story and mine. There is no real difference between them. Opinions, things of rule, haunt us like Phantoms, and we bend the knee to them, and let the incense that they swing before our faces mount to the brain and deaden it. And when, in our wanderings, we come across a fellow-struggler, the Phantoms crowd round us and shake him off, saying "This creature is accursed; do not commune with him; *us* he will not acknowledge. Touch him not, accost him not, he is no brother of yours;"' and we pass on. But our hearts bleed and cry out for the love and the brotherhood that we turn from. We want it, we droop and pine for it; but the Phantoms assure us that all is well, and we try to crush down our longings, and march on obediently, Phantom-led, into the darkness.'

Sibella paused for a moment, and then went on in a tone still sadder: 'And each one has his life-struggle to go through, and death to face; each with his attendant Phantoms must pass from mystery into mystery. Believe me, only the Phantoms hold apart soul from soul.'

There was a long silence.

At last Adrienne said, with a changed expression, 'I suppose you will say that I am under the influence of my Phantoms?'

'As more or less we all are.'

'Do *you* acknowledge to that?'

'I am under the influence of all things,' Sibella replied, 'no one more so.'

Adrienne looked thoughtful, but after a moment she drew herself together.

'I think, Mrs. Lincoln, the differences between us have little to do with what you call Phantoms. They are very real indeed. Our ideas seem to represent black and white, positive and negative, good and evil!'

Sibella made no reply. She took up, in evident absence of mind, the pen that lay beside her on the table, and began to trace outlines on a scrap of paper. A procession of grim but shadowy forms followed close upon the heels of a more substantial figure, and from every side troops of shadows crowded up out of the dimness in attitudes of command, or exhortation, or entreaty, or sadness. Far away was a range of high-peaked mountains, but the shadows were very near and loomed large, so that only now and then for a brief moment could the human being, so close beset, catch a glimpse of the eternal hills, and when he did so, the vision was so strange and new and startling, that he felt afraid, and thought that he had gone mad. Then the shadows bent down comfortingly and closed up their ranks, till the vision was forgotten.

Sibella looked up at last.

'Tell me,' she said, 'the doctrine that you hold, wherewith alone one can be saved.'

'I am sorry that I can't put my ideas of what is pure and right into a nutshell,' said Adrienne; 'all I can say is, that they are very unlike yours. Am I to understand, Mrs. Lincoln, that you intend to seriously attempt to lead Mrs. Dendraith to throw aside her duty, and repudiate the ties that she has formed?'

'That have been formed *for* her, let us say, for the sake of accuracy.'

'Excuse me,' said Adrienne, 'in this country no woman can be forced to marry against her will.'

Sibella shrugged her shoulders.

'Wide is the infernal kingdom, and perfect its form of government! You do not know the story of Mrs. Dendraith's girlhood and marriage?'

'Whatever her story may be, I cannot see that any hardships or any other person's fault can justify her in evading the simple laws of right and wrong, merely because they happen to press her rather closely.'

'Nor do I see,' returned Sibella, 'that the daily unpunished sins of society against its women should continue to be expiated by their *victims* instead of their perpetrators, for ever and ever, Amen! The girl has suffered more in a couple of years than her amiable father could suffer in a lifetime. Let *him* suffer now; it is his turn.'

'Then you would advise her to leave her husband and disgrace her family?'

'I have not yet said what I shall advise her to do.'

'And her good devoted mother; is she not worthy to be considered?'

'Her good devoted mother sacrificed the girl open-eyed, in the name of all that is sacred. It is interesting to remember that – for instance – Druid priests used to cram great wicker images with young girls and children, and then set fire to them,[8] – also in the name of all that is sacred!'

'What has this to do with what we are speaking of?'

'History repeats itself,' said Sibella. 'No doubt any interference with those sacrificial rites would have greatly pained a sincere and conscientious Druid; but I confess that I should quite cheerfully inflict upon him that pain, if I could thereby save the imageful of victims, even if he regarded his honour and the honour of his whole family for ever sullied!'

'You scoff, then, at family honour?'

'I confess,' said Sibella, 'that I am not very tender about the honour that nourishes itself on the fortitude, the pain and suffering of others.'

'I fear that appeal to you will be in vain, Mrs. Lincoln. You fling over with a light heart, the creeds and the traditions of centuries, all that our forefathers have taught us, all that our mothers have prayed and suffered for. For my part, I am old-fashioned enough to believe that our ancestors may have been as wise as ourselves.'

'That I never disputed,' Sibella threw in.

'And I do not feel competent to decide anew for myself every question under the sun.'

'A very creditable humility,' said Sibella; 'but if you regard it as presumptuous to reject the doctrines of your forefathers, you must possess a vast and varied store of opinions, for which you are very much to be envied, – especially if you succeed in keeping the peace among them.'

Adrienne grew impatient.

'Of course I don't mean that I take every idea without exception.'

'You take only those that please you. Then, after all, Miss Lancaster, I do not see that your humility so very much transcends mine.'

Adrienne, who was accustomed to rule the not very brilliant conversational world of Upton, felt angry and bewildered. She had a complete and dignified confidence in her principles, an underlying satisfaction in her powers of insight, of language, and of judgment. To-day all these seemed at fault. Sibella was, of course, profoundly mistaken, but it was not very easy to make the fact appear. Adrienne's cause, although that of Heaven, did not triumph as so righteous a cause ought to have triumphed. The usual comfort of the baffled advocate of Heaven was denied her, for Adrienne did not regard herself as weak in argument or retort; if, therefore, under her guardianship Heaven lost ground, the look-out for Heaven was very serious.

No one sooner than Adrienne would have laughed at the position thus boldly presented, but so mysterious are the workings of the mind, that all are capable of taking mental attitudes, which the sense of humour would alone forbid, were it only summoned to the rescue.

'I fear I have not won you over to my views,' said Adrienne; 'therefore it seems useless to continue the interview; though I shall leave you with a heavy heart, as I feel that my poor friend has an insidious and a powerful enemy, just when she has most need of allies. I, at any rate, shall spare no effort to counteract your influence.'

'A declaration of war?' asked Sibella, rising and going over to the fire.

'You leave me no alternative. I cannot stand by and see that girl disgrace herself, and every one connected with her. I consider not only Viola herself, but her people, especially her mother and father. If any disgrace were to befall his name, I know it would kill him.'

'She must save his elms and his honour,' said Sibella; 'she has not frizzled in her wicker cage long enough to satisfy her friends.'

'I entirely dispute the analogy between Viola's case and these Druidical sacrifices,' said Adrienne.

'Therein also history repeats itself,' returned Sibella.

Adrienne, who had half-risen, paused undecidedly. Something in Mrs. Lincoln's face made her go up to her as she stood leaning against the mantelpiece in a dejected attitude.

'I ask you to have pity, Mrs. Lincoln,' said Adrienne. 'I ask you – a woman – to help me to save this sister from the worst fate which the world has to offer. Never mind whether or not the world is justified in so punishing her; all that you need consider is, that it *does* so punish her, and that the punishment means *absolute ruin*. Think of it! a girl sheltered as Viola has been sheltered, accustomed to refined society' –

'Her father's, for instance,' Mrs. Lincoln suggested.

'Accustomed to be protected from all slight or insult' –

'Her husband's, for example.'

'To be cared for and saved from all offensiveness and vulgarity' –

'Mrs. Pellett's; Mrs. Russell Courtenay's' –

Adrienne paused reproachfully.

'Think of the fate of this girl – cut off from all her friends.'

'Would all her friends desert her?'

Adrienne coloured. 'A woman's good name must suffer if she remained her friend.'

'Oh!' said Sibella shortly, 'go on.'

'Then, to be practical, what can she do? Where could she go to? What would she live upon? It makes me shiver to think of it! She could not go into a family and teach. Who would take a governess who had run away from her husband? And what else offers itself to a woman of Viola's training? Have you considered all this? Have you really thought what you are doing?'

'Miss Lancaster, I can only reply that I have your friend's welfare at heart fully as much as you have, and that I have thought of everything. Myself and all that I possess will be at her service. We have each of us to act as we think best, since we fail to convince one another. As long as I live, Mrs. Dendraith has at least one devoted friend who will never desert her.'

And with that assurance Adrienne had to be content. She left Mrs. Lincoln with an uncomfortable sense of failure, and walked home vividly thinking.

CHAPTER XXXI

THE SHIRT OF NESSUS[9]

To die, to be unconscious! The longing for it was like a gnawing hunger in the soul. To be mercifully wafted away into a great silence, where there was no heart-ache, no passions to struggle against, no indignity! Whatsoever Viola's lips uttered as she knelt in prayer, that was the cry of her heart.

The day arrived for dining at Clevedon, a day to which Viola had looked forward with uneasy joy mingled with dread. Harry would be there! Her nerves quivered; she felt as if she were visibly trembling. The evening found her worn-out and haggard with excitement.

'Viola, you have been out so little since our marriage that your wedding-dress must be quite fresh still, especially as you never put it on – in consequence, it would seem, of my having once admired it. I should like you to wear it to-night, and also the diamonds I gave you, which you also appear to despise.'

White gown and diamonds were awaiting her when the hour for dressing arrived. The dress lay gleaming on the sofa; the diamonds on the toilet-table. Anything that symbolised her marriage, she shrank from touching as if it had been fire. And to-night she must array herself in that glistening garment, feel it clinging to her like a shirt of Nessus, close and firm, burning, burning.

'You look well,' said Philip critically, when his wife appeared in her glisten-ing satin and soft lace, 'and the diamonds are very becoming. But you are pale – however, that is pardonable with dark hair. You wear no flowers. Is that from design?'

She looked down at herself.

'You want that finishing touch,' said Philip. He went off and brought some azaleas from the conservatory. 'Here is the very thing, a spray for the dress and a spray for the hair.'

He advanced to arrange them for her, but she drew back, scarcely perceptibly, and held out her hands for the flowers.

'Thank you.'

Philip turned on his heel, walked over to the other end of the room, and laid them quietly on the fire.

'If you won't take your adornments from me, you can go without. You certainly have a habit of straining at a gnat, my love, having swallowed the camel.'[10] He laughed, looking her in the face, with an expression that made her sick with fury.

The delicate azalea petals were shrivelling as he spoke, helpless in the savage hunger of the flames. The sight was full of parables.

The eyes of husband and wife met.

Have you not learnt wisdom?' he asked. 'Are you always going to play the *rôle* of obstinate child?'

'I am as I was made and as I was taught!' she exclaimed. 'I can't adapt myself, – I can't alter myself, – I am helpless. Things are too much for me; I cannot bear it!'

She walked to the window, repressing the blinding tears that welled into her eyes.

'My dear, you choose your time for a scene admirably. I hear the carriage just coming round.'

Viola was struggling for composure, and dared not trust herself to speak.

'Sulky!' he said, with a shrug of the shoulders. 'That, I hope, will give way before we join your aunt and her guests. Come, I hear Cupid on his way to announce the carriage. In his presence, at least, don't be emotional, I pray.'

The butler (or Cupid, as Philip called him) entered at the auspicious moment, and found the husband helping the wife on with her cloak. Cupid thought his air was most devoted, but to Viola the act seemed like an assertion of right, the signal of victory, a careless victory, as if he had overcome the will of a tiresome child.

Her eyes were quite dry as she took her place beside her husband. He glanced at her, and seeing that she was calm, settled himself in his corner with a satisfied air.

The irreproachable little brougham[11] trundled along over the bleak downs, its lamps sending in advance a flying shaft of light, chasing the darkness which closed up behind it, as waters close behind a moving ship.

Heine[12] might have written a bitter little poem on that well-appointed equipage, with its sleek coachman, sleek horses, smart footman, moving daintily through the darkness, gliding discreetly across the wide solitudes, with their eternal sea-chant beating through the salt wind of the downs. The mysteries of nature, the mysteries of the Human, confronted one another cynically.

Perhaps, after all, a well-appointed brougham and a creditable coachman are matters as deeply mysterious, in their way, as any we find to ponder upon under heaven.

When presently Clevedon came in sight Viola's heart gave a throb. Harry's face rose up before her and his voice sounded in her ear.

The shuttles of her fate were flying fast and furious!

Would she have strength to get through the evening, with this iron hand clutching her heart and stopping its beating?

'Mr. and Mrs. Philip Dendraith.'

The assembled guests in the drawing-room at Clevedon watched with interest the entry of the new-comers.

'Well, Viola dear, how are you?' said her aunt cordially. 'Cold, I suppose, after your drive. Take that chair by the fire. Mrs. Featherstone, I think you know my niece – oh! yes, of course, you have exchanged calls. This other lady I need not introduce, I think.'

The other lady was Mrs. Sedley, who had greeted her daughter with an anxious glance at her pale cheeks.

'Mr. and Mrs. Russell Courtenay.'

Arabella was resplendent to-night. She entered, with some vivacious remark on her lips, slightly inconsequent perhaps, but very sparkling. She then serpentined round the room, with arching neck, recognising her friends and emitting exclamations of joy and surprise.

'And Mrs. Sedley! I am *so* glad to see you again; it seemed as if we were never to meet. And dear Mrs. Dendraith here I am glad to see. I am so deeply interested in your daughter, you know; I have made myself quite a nuisance in calling on her so often.'

Mrs. Sedley gravely felt sure to the contrary.

'Ask Mrs. Dendraith and she will tell you how I have pestered her,' said Arabella. 'She is looking rather pale to-night, but the white dress – her wedding-gown, I see, so prettily altered to the fashion – becomes her admirably.'

(It clasped her close, burning, burning –)

'What a lot of people there are here to-night! Augusta told me she was going to ask the whole county. I see that delicious Bob Hunter in the other room, and the Pelletts, and the Evans party' – Arabella looked all round curiously. 'Of course, Sir Philip and Lady Dendraith will be here. Ah! yes, there they come. Oh! do look how Mr. Sedley is devoting himself to Miss Featherstone; I should be quite jealous if I were you! I always keep a watchful eye on *my* husband; I find it is quite necessary; men are all alike in that way' – Arabella laughed – 'and I

don't think we should care for them much if they weren't a *little*, just a little bit
– don't you know – ?'

'Mrs. Dixie, Miss Lancaster and Mr. Lancaster,' announced the butler.

'Then you don't care for hunting, Mrs. Dendraith?'

Hunting; no – I – not hunting, – I don't care for hunting, – very much.'

Mrs. Dixie entered the room looking like a schooner in full sail. With her
healthy-looking ancestor still at her throat, and a large proportion of the jewellery
that had been saved from the wreck mustered upon her person and overflowing
onto the person of Adrienne, who followed, the old lady swept forward, with
head held very high, yet graciously. Viola presently found herself shaken by the
hand and talked to about something that she did not comprehend, and then she
became aware that Adrienne was speaking to her, and there was a sort of whirl in
the air and a flicker of the candle-light, – and the next moment her hand was in
Harry Lancaster's. And she felt nothing! no, she felt nothing, except this whirl
in the air and this ebb and flow of light. Her hand might have been a block of
wood. He was looking at her fixedly – holding her hand tightly in his. Presently
she became conscious that he held it no longer.

She *did* feel something, then! something hot and desperate, – a leaping up of
the heart, a wild yearning to feel that touch again! What was righteousness, duty,
heaven or hell? – nothing, nothing! Be it right or wrong, she cared only for one
thing in the whole world, and for that she cared madly.

'Mrs. Dendraith, ahoy!'

From one end of the long room to the other Bob Hunter had half-skipped,
half-skated across the floor, pulling up opposite to Viola. He then proceeded
with perfect gravity to perform a few steps, fixing her intently with his eye and
keeping his body steady, while his legs moved with extreme nimbleness.

He seemed to expect her to break into steps likewise, and she even began to fear
that he would take her by the hand and insist upon her dancing, perhaps as a substitute for conversation. He knew that she did not understand that difficult art!

She saw Geoffrey on the broad grin, watching the little scene from the fireplace – Mrs. Dixie putting up her eyeglass to observe the conduct of her would-be
son-in-law.

Adrienne, with flushed cheeks, stood beside her, trying to talk to an unwilling neighbour, who wanted to watch Bob Hunter.

That athlete came suddenly to rest, remarking that exercise was better than
any tonic.

'Charmed to see you here to-night, Mrs. Dendraith – I address you without
ceremony, you see. Ceremony is the bane of genius.'

'*You* ought to know, Mr. Hunter,' said Arabella enchantingly.

Bob Hunter swung round and made her a bow. Then he swung back again to Viola and asked her what was the difference between a windmill and a Dutch cheese.

Viola blushed distractedly, and said she really had not the slightest idea. There lurked in her mind an uneasy fear that he thought of Arabella as the windmill!

'Oh! come now, this is weak,' remonstrated young Hunter; ' try and think.'

'I can't guess riddles,' cried Viola; 'I never could.'

'Use your intellect,' urged the tormentor.

'I haven't got one!' exclaimed Viola in desperation, at which Bob gave a chuckle.

'This is becoming serious; *I must* have that riddle answered,' and to Viola's intense relief he danced off to the other side of the room, going from group to group, asking what was the difference between a windmill and a Dutch cheese.

'My court-fool,' said Lady Clevedon, with a shrug of the shoulders.

Adrienne gave a curious little movement and a spasmodic smile. The vision of a warmly furnished room, with a view of sea through its long windows, was before her at that moment; of a dainty figure and a face with curving lips; she seemed to hear in turn quiet words of scorn and irony, words of sympathy, words of defiance. What would Sibella Lincoln think of a woman marrying Bob Hunter in order to be settled in life?

Adrienne frowned and tried to shake off the recollection. Had the woman whose character could not bear investigation actually been able to make Adrienne Lancaster feel her attitude towards Bob Hunter degrading? The idea of accepting his offer had not been regarded as quite out of the question. To sell herself was therefore not quite out of the question!

'Ah! Mr. Lancaster at last!' exclaimed Arabella; 'the hero of the evening! I thought I was never to have a word with you; every one has been crowding round you so. Tell me, is it really nice to be a universal favourite?'

'I thought that *you* would have known all about that, Mrs. Courtenay.'

'I? Oh dear no! quite an obscure person. I want to know whether you enjoy being a cynosure[13] – don't you know?'

'A – ?'

'A cynosure of every eye.'

' Depends painfully upon the eye, Mrs. Courtenay.'

'Oh, you are horrid! You won't give a plain answer to a plain question.'

'No; I give a plain answer to a beautiful person.'

Mrs. Courtenay wriggled, and Adrienne looked at her brother in amazement. As Geoffrey said, Arabella would squeeze compliments out of a boot-jack!

'And now, Mr. Lancaster, come and sit down on this sofa, and tell me everything you have been doing since you left us all lamenting. You can't think how dead and alive Upton has been without you!'

'Indeed, Mrs. Courtenay, I can.'

'Come, I can't have you conceited; that would be to spoil perfection.'

'Am I to regard myself as perfection?'

'Oh no! for then you would no longer be perfect.'

'As long as I continue to believe I have faults, I shall know that I remain fault-less. It is worth crossing the Irish Channel to discover this.'

'Now, no more badinage; I want to hear the serious truth about you. You don't seem in the least ill, Mr. Lancaster; I believe you are a fraud, and that you just got up a little scare to secure sympathy. Well, you have succeeded in your wicked design: all the Upton ladies are prepared to protect and cherish you, and to insist upon your taking their medicines and going to their pet doctors. Won't that be nice?'

'Delicious!' said Harry.

'That sweet Mrs. Dendraith seemed quite concerned about you. By the way, do you know I have been envying her for getting the first sight of you after your return. She *was* highly favoured.'

'I don't know exactly what you mean,' said Harry, not without a feeling of suspicion and uneasiness. 'I see her to-night for the first time.'

'Oh, come, Mr. Lancaster, that won't do!' cried Arabella, laughing. 'Why, I had it from her own lips! If you wanted to keep it dark you ought to have engaged her not to tell.'

'I don't understand,' said Harry.

'Well, let's go and ask her about it; she will explain.'

'I don't think it's worth explaining; questions of date do not interest me.'

Oh! but this is more than a question of date,' said Arabella meaningly.

But as Harry would not follow her to Viola, she had to content herself with asking how he thought her looking.

'Pretty well,' he said.

'She is so very quiet, is she not? I sometimes fear she is not happy. Yet her husband is very nice, and handsome beyond expression.'

The announcement of dinner sent people hunting for their appointed part-ners. Viola was allotted to Dick Evans; nearly opposite to her sat Geoffrey, radiantly happy by the side of Adrienne Lancaster, with whom he had fallen ridiculously and suddenly in love. Adrienne had been conducted to her place by Bob Hunter in his maddest humour. Viola saw that he was proposing to her at intervals during dinner, and poor Geoffrey's happiness fearfully diminished as he became aware of these untoward circumstances.

Harry Lancaster and his fate, Arabella, were also on the opposite side of the table; Mrs. Dixie had been introduced to an old gentleman called Bavage, whose name she caught imperfectly, but whom she at once declared she had met twenty years before, and so worked upon the feelings of Mr. Bavage that he too had recollections of that far-off divine event.

Now and then Viola caught sight of Harry in conversation with Miss Featherstone. Miss Featherstone was cold and calm and fashionable, and Viola found herself growing more and more antipathetic towards the hard, handsome face. Loneliness was not a new sensation to her, but as she glanced round the table at the rows of polite faces, she thought that never in her life before had she felt so cut off from human help and fellowship.

Harry was there. Yes, but it might have been his ghost; he had neither look nor word for her now! Well, no matter! Nothing could matter any more. That was one comfort. Things had come to a climax; old faiths had been shaken, cherished principles held from childhood were growing dim; in thought she could sink no lower; heaven had drifted out of sight. She loved guiltily, – it had come to that! – and she loved in vain.

Viola caught the admiring eyes of her adorer, Dorothy, fixed upon her, and turned away her own with a sickening sense of shame and misery.

'O Dorothy, if you knew!'

Dick Evans was talkative. He told Viola all about some interesting excavations that were being made upon the barrows on the downs, and he wanted to know if she really wouldn't be persuaded to go for walks with him again. What was the objection? Did her husband think Dick would run away with her?

'Heaven knows!' said Viola.

'You look as if you wanted exercise,' pursued Dick. '(I don't mean that you had better run away with me on that account). You seem paler than you used to be.'

'Do you think I am going to die?' she asked, with a little laugh.

Oh no, no! Only you ought to be careful of yourself.'

What have I to be careful of?'

Dick looked at her. 'What is the matter with you to-night? You are not like yourself.'

That evening's conversation brought Dick to the conclusion that women are flighty sort of creatures, not to be counted upon or understood; that they don't quite know what they want; and if they do, by some strange perversity of nature, they refuse to take it when the chance comes. There was something not quite sane, he thought, about even the best of women.

A little farther down the table, sublimely ignorant of the many little dramas that were being acted around him, sat old Mr. Pellett who had been rapt, still warm, from his studies and brought, much against his will, to the festive gathering. He was in a state of absent-minded amiability, listening very humbly and a little bashfully to the remarks of a young lady of seventeen who was talking to him about lawn-tennis. Mr. Pellett, in Upton society, was a truly pathetic figure. On her left, Viola had a grey-headed person who appreciated a good dinner and a young woman who forbore to nag him with trivial chatter during the sacred hour. She was therefore often at liberty to watch the others, and to busy herself with her own excited thoughts. Once or twice, looking up suddenly, she would find Harry's eyes fixed upon her as if he had been exerting, consciously or unconsciously, some subtle magnetic power. There was an expression in his face that set her heart beating furiously; he used to look so in the old days!

The next moment he was relating some anecdote to his neighbour which created a shout of laughter; Philip capped it with a second, and Mr. Sedley with a third; Bob Hunter bringing the series to a climax and setting the table in a roar.

Mrs. Sedley sat in her black dress gravely looking on, and wondering why every one was laughing. Her face was deadly white, and there were deep black borders under the eyes. She had told her husband before starting that she felt almost too unwell to accompany him to-night, but he had insisted on her coming, and as the painfulness of the ordeal induced her to regard it as a duty, she gave in. Once an intervening head was moved aside, and Viola caught sight of her mother's suffering face.

In an instant there was a rush of fear and shame at her own unholy thoughts. What unspeakable grief if that mother knew how the daughter had changed in these two short years! Was there nothing in this world for her but sorrow and disappointment? Her sons had caused her grief after grief, and her daughter – ? Scarcely half-an-hour ago that daughter had been ready to fling over everything on earth for the sake of a passion which Marion Sedley's child ought not even to know the meaning of!

Roars of laughter awakened the echoes of the old dining-room; except Mrs. Sedley's, there was scarcely a grave face at the table. Her husband was talking about the peculiar attractions of widows, and their extreme fondness for the 'dear departed.'

'A man never knows how devoted his wife is to him till he dies,' said Philip; 'it must be sweet to die.'

'Death is undoubtedly the great whitewasher,' Harry asserted.

'Or the great endearer,' suggested Adrienne.

'He that would be loved, let him make haste and die,' said Harry.

'We shall all be loved some day let us be thankful,' cried Bob Hunter.

Dorothy Evans shook her head vigorously. Her brother saw that she had Mrs. Pellett in her eye.

'I am sure there are *some* people that one *couldn't* love even after they were dead!'

My dear!' remonstrated Mrs. Pellett.

'Not if they died ten times over,' said Dorothy with emphasis.

'My dear child, so unchristian!'

'Not if they didn't wake up at the sound of the last trumpet!' cried the young woman doggedly, piling up the agony. 'You would feel everlastingly grateful to them for dying, but you could never love them – *never*!'

'Perhaps you don't know how to love, Dorothy,' said Dick, with a half-warning smile.

'Oh, don't I!' Dorothy ejaculated, with a glance at Viola.

'Do you love *me*, Miss Dorothy?' inquired Philip indolently. 'Man and wife are one, you know!'

'No, I don't,' said Dorothy briefly.

'Would you love me if I were dead?'

'No.'

'Can you imagine any circumstances in which you would entertain that feeling towards me?'

'Nobody ever loved anybody who asked questions,' Dorothy retorted.

'I feel crushed,' said Philip; 'it is evidently time for me to die!'

'Then why don't you do it?' asked the ruthless one beneath her breath.

He caught the words and laughed.

'All in good time, cruel but fair one!' he said.

Mrs. Sedley, who was leaning back in her chair saying nothing, made a slight spasmodic movement, but no one noticed it.

'Don't talk of dying in that flippant manner,' said Lady Clevedon; 'it is uncanny.'

When she gave the signal to the ladies, Mrs. Sedley rose with an effort and moved from the table giddily. She recovered herself, however, and passed into the drawing-room with the others.

Viola characteristically lingered behind, allowing more self-confident ladies to precede her, and, alas! by these tactics falling into the clutches of the watchful Mrs. Pellett, who took her by the arm encouragingly and led her out with the faintly rustling procession.

In the drawing-room every one drew round the fire and began to talk, chiefly of local matters and domestic details.

'You are not well to-night, Marion,' said Lady Clevedon, leading her sister-in-law to a low chair.

'Not quite well,' Mrs. Sedley confessed.

Viola had deserted Mrs. Pellett and was standing by her mother's side.

'It is nothing,' said Mrs. Sedley, catching sight of Viola's anxious face.

I often feel so – very often.'

Viola tried to persuade her to go home at once.

'Oh dear no; your father would be annoyed. I shall get on all right – if you will hand me that bottle of smelling-salts.'

Viola gave it, and repeated her persuasions, saying that she would return with her mother to the Manor.

But it was of no avail. Mrs. Sedley was determined to remain to the end.

'Only another hour and a half,' she said, with a faint smile.

The other ladies, having discussed all local matters, were now engaged upon a recent scandal which had been making a stir in the fashionable world.

Viola was sitting apart, pale and exhausted with excitement.

'Oh, Mrs. Dendraith,' cried Arabella, 'you lost that anecdote! It is for your private ear – quite too shocking to relate in public.'

'I fear it will be wasted on me,' said Viola, shrinking back.

'Oh! you can't fail to enjoy it; it is really too good, isn't it, Miss Featherstone?'

Viola drew away quickly. 'Please don't trouble, Mrs. Courtenay; I *hate* such stories!'

She said it with such a fierce vigour that there was an awkward silence among the ladies, the silence that always falls when any strong expression of opinion is given in society. Viola set her lips, as she played with the blade of a paper-knife, and felt a wild impulse to hurt physically these well-dressed complacent beings who seemed incapable of being hurt in any other way. It was incredible to her that women could be so vulgar and so ignoble.

Presently Bob Hunter appeared as a forerunner of his colleagues who were lingering over their wine. Viola's heart began to throb. Last of the train Harry Lancaster came into the room, and was immediately waylaid by Sir Philip and by Mrs. Featherstone. He seemed to be in a lively vein to-night, for wherever he went there was a stir and a burst of laughter.

Viola had to clutch her paper-knife very tightly to prevent herself from visibly trembling.

'Oh! Mr Lancaster,' Mrs. Courtenay was saying, 'I have heard such shocking things about you. I hope they aren't true.'

'I hope not, I am sure,' said Harry.

'I hear that you call upon this dreadful Mrs. Lincoln who has come to live here. (I tell Sir Philip it is encouraging immorality to let her rent his house).'

'Clearly,' said Harry, 'any one who lets his house connives at the misdeeds of his tenant, past, present, and future.'

'No; but really,' urged Mrs. Featherstone, 'I think it is so bad for the neighbourhood; I hope you haven't been weak enough to call upon her!'

'It is very kind of you to take so much interest in me,' said Harry. 'You can't imagine me frequenting any but the most irreproachable society, I hope? Are not *your* severe doors open to me?'

'Oh! I am not so particular about my *men*,' retorted Mrs. Featherstone, with a laugh. 'I used to know Mrs. Lincoln a little before the scandal: I can't imagine what she comes here for. The man she ran away with is dead, isn't he?'

At this moment Viola, who had been receiving the homage of Dorothy Evans, was sitting alone on a sofa, Dorothy being summoned by her mother to have her sash re-arranged. As usual, it had worked itself round from the back to the front.

Harry managed to break away from Arabella, and went straight to the vacated seat.

'I thought I was never to have a word with you,' he said, in a low, hurried voice. 'There seems a fate against it.'

Philip's eyes were resting on them, and they both felt it.

'I want to give you a letter presently. Don't start; look as if I were telling you that the weather in Ireland for the last month has been extremely changeable. The letter is from Mrs. Lincoln, not from me. You never in your life had a more sincere friend than she is. The shock-headed little girl who has just left you is equally sincere, but not a whit more so. Trust them both, and oh! Viola, do as Mrs. Lincoln asks you.'

She raised her eyes for a moment. Suddenly her head swam; she grasped the back of the sofa, breathing quickly.

'What is in the letter?'

'There is no opportunity to tell you now: I shall be suspected – Viola – one word, or sign' – Harry bent towards her, with his elbow on his knee, his hand half-hiding his face. 'Drop your handkerchief for "yes"; touch the lace on your dress for "no."'

There was a rustle of silk close beside them. Viola gave a gasp.

'However, we had plenty of gaiety,' said Harry, in a conversational tone; 'the Irish are a very hospitable people.'

By this time Mrs. Pellett had passed on.

'Now for my question, Viola. Do you trust me? and will you do as Mrs. Lincoln asks you in this letter?'

She dropped her handkerchief, and Harry stooped to pick it up.

Mrs. Russell Courtenay was approaching.

'And Mr. Evans really is thinking of restoring his church? I hope they won't make the usual gaudy monstrosity of the old place.'[14]

Harry rose to yield his place to Arabella.

'Oh, please don't get up; you two looked so comfortable and happy there; I wouldn't disturb you for the world.'

'Thank you. Well, we were very comfortable and happy, as you say,' said Harry, who had become rather white, 'but our joy would be still greater if Mrs. Courtenay would bestow upon us the light of her countenance.'

'Flatterer, avaunt!'[15] cried Arabella, glancing curiously at Viola's pale cheeks. 'Mr. Lancaster,' she said impressively, 'I don't believe you!'

The two looked for a second in one another's eyes.

'Scepticism, Mrs. Courtenay, is the curse of the age.'

'Oh! there are other curses besides scepticism,' said Mrs. Courtenay. 'Things are coming to a dreadful pass in society – people running away from their wives and husbands, and all that sort of thing. You know this case in all the papers[16] – really it makes one wonder who *is* to be trusted; as if one might expect one's nearest and dearest to be in the divorce-court to-morrow! I am quite unhappy about it, really I am.'

'That is very good of you,' said Harry.

'You speak in riddles, Mr Lancaster. Do you know' – (Arabella lowered her voice) – 'Mrs. Dendraith got quite angry when we were discussing this divorce-case after dinner. She evidently dislikes the subject; she is so good and sweet, is she not?'

A pause.

'Don't you think so, Mr Lancaster?' Arabella repeated.

'That follows from her sex,' he said, with a sort of jaded politeness.

'Oh! will you never cease these flatteries?'

'England expects every man to do his duty.'

'Mr Lancaster, I don't think I like you to-night. I believe you are tired of me, and want Mrs. Dendraith to yourself. Well, I will not detain you.'

She looked into his eyes as she said it, and then swept away, leaving Harry watching her with an absorbed expression.

'She guesses,' he said to himself. 'Well, I have to play a game against the world – an Arabella more or less makes but little difference; one can't cheat these carrion crows of their natural food.'

He returned to Viola, keeping a watchful eye upon Philip and Mrs. Courtenay. He began to talk about indifferent matters, and then, without change of attitude or manner, he said, 'Will you take the letter?'

She looked at her mother. Harry bent closer.

'*Viola*,' he repeated in a pleading tone.

She gave a sign of assent.

'I will put it into your hand as we say good-night; it is very small; be careful not to drop it. There are many suspicious eyes round us. Burn the letter as soon as you have read it.'

'We are being watched,' said Viola nervously.

'I will leave you,' returned Harry; 'but as soon as you find an opportunity go into the conservatory; – it is cool and pleasant; you are looking very tired.'

He left her without further hint.

After a few minutes of bewildered struggle with herself, she rose and entered the conservatory. The cool green of the leaves and the sound of dripping water were grateful indeed to her tired nerves.

She sank into a low chair, and a sensation of languor crept over her, mind and body; a longing to give herself up to her fate, to resist and strive no longer.

Soft music crept in from the drawing-room; a gondolier's song, rhythmic and indolent.

Viola heaved a sigh, a deep long sigh and lay back among the cushions. The tears of pleasure and relief welled up under her closed eyelids.

CHAPTER XXXII

DAUGHTER OF THE ENDLESS NIGHT

The music mercifully did not cease, and Viola lay there like a tired child resting.

It was no surprise to her when presently a figure stood by her side and a voice sounded in her ear. She did make one desperate effort to escape the danger of this interview, but Harry laid a hand upon her arm, and she was helpless. Indeed she was physically too exhausted to make any successful attempt to oppose his will.

'There is no time to lose,' he said; 'let me give you the letter while I have the chance. It is to ask you to meet Mrs. Lincoln at Caleb Foster's to-morrow. Caleb is a friend of Mrs. Lincoln, and he is absolutely trustworthy. Gossip is impossible to him. And now I want you to think deeply over our position. Everything depends on you. We – Sibella and I – are ready for all risks. But we can do nothing unless you help us.'

'Why was I ever born?' she exclaimed.

'Don't despair,' he said gently, taking her hand. 'No one need despair who is loved as you are loved.'

She turned away.

'Viola, be reasonable. My love for you before your marriage was as it now is, the homage of my whole being; it is of the real and lasting kind, and it is ready – it has shown itself ready for sacrifice.'

She was passing her hands over her eyes to force back the tears of joy. He loved her still – her fears were all unfounded – the horrible loneliness was gone. The sense of wrong for the moment was drowned in the flood of joy and relief.

'I am not pleading now that you should return my love – though I passionately long for that – I want you to understand that you have at your service one who is ready to risk anything for you, but who would despise himself if he tried to build up a claim upon you through that service.'

(Ah! if she might only tell him!)

'Nevertheless, I want you to reconsider your views on these questions, and to ask yourself if a true and passionate love *can* be a wrong to any woman. I want you to ask yourself if mere external circumstances can turn right into wrong in a breath. I know, and Viola, my darling, you *know*, that your husband's love for you is not as great or as reverential as mine, and yet his is legitimate. Is this rational? Is this just? No, it is wrong, from beginning to end – accursedly, infernally wrong!'

He was kneeling beside her, clasping her hands, though she made a sort of spell-bound effort at resistance. Some instinct seemed to hint to him that his words no longer fell on stony ground. She shivered at his touch.

'Love is its own justification. Every one capable of real love *knows* that it is.'

'If all believed that – ah! don't touch me – I can't think when you touch me – if all believed that, everything would fall into confusion.'

He leant forward eagerly.

'And do you really think that society rests safe and sound upon its foundations of misery and martyred affection?'

'Oh! I don't know what to think or say. If your ideas are right, what becomes of purity and truth?'

He looked at her for a moment in mournful silence.

Sibella's words still rang in his ears: 'Such a woman is foredoomed. We cannot save her.' Was it true? He felt a gloomy foreboding that it was. The past seemed to be too strong for her, the attitude of feeling to be changelessly fixed, in spite of all the suffering she had endured.

'Adrienne says I ought to obey the call of duty, to regard myself as placed and dedicated for life. I am Philip's wife; I can't get out of that, can I? I can't get out of the obligations which it implies, however terrible they may be, except by shirking.'

'Listen to me, Viola; if there is such a thing as justice, I say that no woman is morally bound to a man when she is married to him as *you* were married to your husband. You do no good to any one by submission. You only add to the anguish of other women in your own position, and of men in mine.'

The words seemed full of the sophistry of passion; they made her heart beat, attracting, tempting, and at the same time repelling. Emotion, and the ingrained results of long training, were at variance. The heart stirred beneath its crust of acquired sentiment, but she felt as if she could curse the man and the woman who had disturbed that crust, and awakened her to new and more exquisite anguish.

Harry began to wonder whether, after all, it would not have been wiser to leave Viola with her convictions undisturbed. It seemed a hopeless task to free her from them so entirely that she would be ready for action. And without action it was worse than useless – so far as her own fate was concerned – to see clearly. Just in proportion to the additional knowledge would the suffering increase.

'Viola,' he said, 'you make me fear that, after all, I have only added to your misfortunes instead of saving you.'

She hesitated for a moment, then she shook her head.

'You have made me suffer, but you have saved me from suffering quite alone. Adrienne is good and kind, and a true friend, but oh! she does not know, she does not understand.'

'If only I could take you in my arms and carry you away from all this misery, and comfort you and heal you as only the ministries of love *can* heal. Will you not come? I plead for something more than life.'

'And I,' said Viola, 'have something more than life to defend.'

'And how will you defend it? By remaining in your present position?'

'O Harry! you torture me.'

He took her hand and kissed it.

'Viola, do you love me? You *do!* I know it!'

In a moment he had drawn her to him and laid her head close down upon his shoulder. She could not move without a strong effort, and she did not make the effort. She seemed half-stupefied. He stooped and kissed her on the lips, and Viola knew that her fate, whatever it might be, was sealed.

'I was certain this would come some day, but it seems too wonderful to be true.'

Two or three never-forgotten moments of silence passed, and then Viola said, with a sigh, 'But, Harry, this can only bring unhappiness.'

She tried to draw away, but he held her tightly.

'Don't talk to me of unhappiness when I hold you for the first time in my arms and know that you love me! You will come with me, Viola,' he pleaded; 'you will hesitate no longer!'

'Oh, let me go! let me go! You mesmerise me; you bewitch me. I did not mean to give way like this; I am light-headed; life is too hard for me – I can't cope with it – its temptations are terrible.'

'Thank Heaven you feel them! Now it all seems plain to me. You will not sacrifice everything to mere prejudice any longer. You care for the *thing*, not the *name*; you care for the honour that the heart recognises, not the honour of the world. It may be good to suffer martyrdom, but your cause must be worth the cost. What *you* are asked to suffer for – though it counts its martyrs by the thousand – is not worthy of the sacrifice.'

'But I have fears, so many fears,' said Viola. 'You want me to leave my husband. That means to disgrace my family.'

'Who have deliberately sacrificed you to their worldly interests.'

'My mother believed that she was acting for the best; and as for my father, he only did what hundreds of parents are doing every year.'

'I think it is high time that the other hundreds had their eyes opened a little,' muttered Harry. 'It would break my mother's heart,' said Viola. I *cannot* do it; it is impossible! And my father – my brother' –

'Viola!' he pleaded, taking her hand and drawing her towards him, 'you think of everybody except the one person who loves you more than all the rest put together – a thousand times more. It would break my heart to lose you and to know of your wretchedness, but you never think of that. Perhaps if I had destroyed the happiness of your childhood and handed you over to a misery for life, you might have been careful about *my* heart too. As it is, I suppose I must expect always to come last.'

'O Harry! you know I am struggling with temptation, struggling to do right – but all these ideas are so new to me, so appalling!'

'I suppose it would surprise you to hear that to me the *old* ideas are appalling.'

'I see their hideousness, and how awful it is to be a woman – yet' –

'Then why will you not act? Sibella and I are pledged to support you and protect you through thick and thin.'

'I understand that; you are both far too generous and too good to me. Give her back her letter, Harry; tell her I thank her with all my heart, but – but it's of no use. I am beyond help. Why should you both trouble to rescue a vacillating, foolish woman who has not the strength of mind either to submit silently to her fate, or to break free from it boldly?'

'We do it because we love her,' said Harry. 'Will she not make us happy by consenting to put herself in our faithful hands?'

Viola shook her head.

'I dare not – I dare not – for my mother's sake. I don't fear anything for myself, but for her – no, I dare not.'

'Is that your sole reason?'

'I only know that while she lives I must endure it as best I may. I *cannot* deal her such a crushing blow! She would die, indeed she would!

As the last words were uttered Adrienne entered the conservatory hastily.

'Viola dear,' she said, 'will you come with me? Your mother is going home. She feels unwell, and wishes you to know.'

'Unwell!' Viola turned pale and hastened away.

'I am afraid it's serious,' Adrienne said in a low voice to her brother as she passed out.

Mrs. Sedley was lying on a sofa in her sister-in-law's boudoir, whence Lady Clevedon had banished every one but Adrienne and her own maid.

'What is it? What is it?' cried Viola.

'I think it is a bad faint,' said her aunt; 'she is much better now.'

Mrs. Sedley was struggling as if for breath.

'Take me home, Viola,' she gasped.

'I don't think you ought to be moved till you are better, Marion,' said Lady Clevedon.

Mrs. Sedley's brows contracted painfully.

'Take me home,' she repeated.

'Very well; you shall go if you wish it. Gibson, will you go and ask Mrs. Sedley's coachman to get his horses in as soon as he possibly can? and tell James to ride over and ask the doctor to go at once to the Manor-House.'

Before the carriage arrived Mrs. Sedley seemed a little better, so that when her husband came in to know what in the world was the matter she was just able to answer cheerfully that it was only a fainting-fit, and that she was almost well again now.

'I am sorry to hurry you away, but I am so afraid of being laid up away from home. If Philip will allow her, Viola is coming back with me.'

Adrienne had gone to tell Philip what had happened, and she returned with a gracious message of permission to Viola to accompany her mother home. Adrienne laid an accent on the word *permission*, as implying a right and dutiful spirit on the part of Viola, and commendable relations between the husband and wife.

The stars were all ablaze as the ramshackle old vehicle trundled homewards across the downs. Mrs. Sedley lay back with closed eyes, Viola beside her, while Mr Sedley and Geoffrey sat opposite, occasionally speaking in undertones. Mr Sedley had begun with his usual bawl, but on Viola's remonstrance he had reduced himself to a hoarse whisper.

One of the windows was open, admitting breaths of soft air, imbued with the marvellous sweetness of spring.

Holding her mother's hand Viola sat looking out into the night. Creeds, doctrines, social laws, all seemed to lose form and substance in that wild darkness; they trembled and waned when brought thus face to face with nature, face to face with the inexorable facts and the unutterable sadness of life.

Harry was right; these stars, this darkness, that unappeasable sea, confirmed him; this pain, this failure and disappointment, confirmed him. He pinned his faith to realities, and he flung conventions to the winds. He would, have *things*, not names; only people who build their faith on 'common-sense' were mad enough to lay down their lives for the sake of words and phrases, to bid farewell to love, happiness, all the best and sweetest things of life, at the bidding of a shadow.

Viola shivered with foreboding. In the dim starlight all the occupants of the carriage looked strange and white, but her mother's face was ghastly.

Death seemed to be already of the party. They could feel his presence among them. The pain-stricken, toilsome, joyless existence was nearing its end. It might be a matter of months, or of weeks, but the end was in sight. The brutal pitiless demon of human destiny was about to put his last touch to the ugly work. And now to Viola, for the first time since her marriage Death seemed awful instead of beneficent. For the first time, almost in his very presence, her heart rose in passionate anger against him and his clumsy solution of the human problem: destruction in default of cure. A vision of the glory and splendour of life had been given her, and she felt desperate, for very pity, as she looked at the white face of the woman who had never known that glory even for a moment. To have lived for all these years and tasted so few joys; to have known nothing but care, anxiety, self-denial, cruel suffering and disappointment, and nothing but ill-treatment from the man for whom all had been endured; to lose one's life thus, and at last to die and leave no passionate regret in any heart, to be forgotten just because of the meek dutifulness which left no room for the more vivid qualities which give colour to the personality, and attract the love of others, even though they be more like faults than virtues! Would she find in heaven the love that she had missed on earth? If not, she had missed it for all eternity; she had missed everything – life itself; she was like a blind person in a world of colour, one deaf in a realm of music; and to complete the irony of this woman's fate, the moral that her child was drawing from it now was in direct opposition to every principle for which the painful life had been given wholesale, as a willing sacrifice to God and duty. In vain, Sibella had said, was the suffering of good women.

There was a solitary oil-lamp burning in the hall when they arrived at the Manor-House. The place struck chill as one entered, and had the musty scent of old rooms seldom visited by the sunlight.

After Mrs. Sedley had been carried upstairs and laid in the great four-post bedstead, the watchers began to look anxiously for the arrival of the doctor. When he did come, hope seemed for the moment to revive. He had attended the family since Mrs. Sedley came to the Manor-House, a bride, and they all looked to him for help in time of trouble. He was a grave man, with iron-grey hair and beard, and of highly respectable appearance.

With much solemnity, he felt the patient's pulse, asked a few questions, and then sat down to write a prescription.

When he left, Viola followed him from the room.

'Tell me the truth, doctor,' she said.

He looked at her doubtfully.

'I want to know if there is any hope.'

'Well then, there is not,' he answered quietly. 'There has been no hope for the last year and a half; the disease that your mother is suffering from has been coming on for a long time, but, with her usual stoicism, she said nothing about it till it was too late. She begged me so urgently not to reveal the truth to any of her family that I yielded, not seeing what good it would do you to know.'

Viola had turned aside sick at heart. Life was one long tragedy!

'Then my mother has known for a year and a half that she was dying.'

'Yes; and she suspected the truth some time before that. She has had troubles in her day, and that has hastened the mischief – in fact, I believe has induced it. But your mother has no fear of death – she is a sincere Christian, and can face it without flinching.'

'And nothing can be done?' asked Viola, ignoring the consolation.

'Nothing can be done, I am sorry to say, except to relieve some of the suffering.'

Viola turned hastily away. 'Thank you,' she said, 'thank you for telling me the truth.'

* * * * *

Two anxious days passed. Lady Clevedon drove over to help in the nursing, but Mrs. Sedley would not hear of it. A trained nurse was procured to relieve Viola, and then commenced long days of anguished watching. The suffering became more and more acute, till at last day and night there was no rest, scarcely a moment's respite from pain.

'Oh! can't you give me something to relieve it?' Viola used to ask the doctor with desperate eyes.

'I have done what I can. There is one other strong remedy I might try, but that would hasten the end. We must not do anything to anticipate by a second that appointed time. It would not be right.'

The same answer was given each time that Viola renewed her appeal. She felt at last a passionate hatred of that stolid word 'right.'

'I detest people who think more of doing right than of being merciful!' she exclaimed in exasperation, unconscious what a mental revolution the words revealed. She had been sitting for eight hours by her mother's bedside, watching the paroxysms of anguish, helpless to relieve them.

The doctor took her outburst quite calmly, merely giving orders that Mrs. Sedley should be tended more constantly by the nurse for the future, and that Mrs. Dendraith should be with her mother only for two or three hours at a time.

'You will make yourself ill if you are not careful,' he said.

'What does that matter?'

'One patient in a house is quite enough. Besides, you could not then nurse your mother at all.'

Viola gave in.

Visitors now began to come from far and near to inquire for Mrs. Sedley. Adrienne, always to be found where there was trouble and her help might be needed, managed to drive over to the Manor-House to relieve Viola and to cheer

her, more than once a week. Mrs. Evans lent her a pony-carriage, which sometimes Harry, sometimes Dorothy, used to drive.

On several occasions, when Adrienne had gone up to see Mrs. Sedley, Viola
and Harry found themselves alone. But not a word passed between them about
their last interview at Clevedon, not a word about Sibella, except on Harry's
part, when he delivered a letter from her expressing regret and sympathy. Once
Viola came down looking white and almost desperate.

'Your mother's suffering is worse!' Harry exclaimed, coming over to her and laying his hands on her shoulders, as if he thought that would, in some way, help her.

'Oh, it is too horrible! How can she live through it? The power of endurance is really ghastly! Why can't people die before it comes to this? The doctor
says there is a struggle between a strong constitution and a determined, disease.
The disease has got the upper hand, and they are fighting it out – and we can do
nothing – nothing, but wait for the certain victory of the disease!'

She sank upon the nearest chair with a gesture of exhaustion, lying back for
a moment with closed eyes.

Harry bent down and kissed the thin little hand as it lay passively upon her
knee. It trembled, and she drew it away.

'When they know there's no hope,' she said presently, 'when they know that
it is merely an affair of days or weeks, why don't they give the sufferer everything
and anything that will put an end to the torture, though it does shorten the life
by a few days? What can it matter?'

'What indeed!'

'If I knew what that medicine was I would give it myself,' Viola said, rising
excitedly. 'Why not? – why not?' Then the impossibility of the thing overwhelmed her, and she sank down again. 'If only the doctor would consent to
give it, and mother to take it!' But she shook her head with a hopeless sigh. 'The
doctor would never consent. He is like all the rest of us, very respectful of the
last few laboured breaths when existence is only a torture, but careless how the
life-stream is poisoned while there is yet the precious gift of health to save! That
is just our way of doing things!'

'Viola, you are worn out – you are killing yourself!' Harry exclaimed, hastening to her side, for she looked as if she were about to faint.

'Not I,' she said; 'I wish to Heaven I were! That would solve the whole problem; I know no other solution.'

'*I* do,' said Harry in a low voice.

'Don't!' she exclaimed, turning away with an expression almost approaching
to dislike. 'I am inconsistent, I know, but in *this* house such words seem to burn
and brand my very soul – even to see you makes one feel – oh! if you only knew
how hateful it all is to me! – to think of my mother upstairs dying – trusting me
absolutely – believing in me absolutely – and to meet you like this, under her

roof, in this room, after – after what has passed – I must not do it – if I could tell you the anguish of self-contempt that I feel when I think of it all.'

She was standing by the window with her arms raised to her head in very desperation.

'You still feel my love – our love – to be guilty, then?' he said, not daring to approach.

'Oh! yes – no – I don't know what I feel – but I can't talk of it now! Oh! why did you disturb the certainty of my beliefs? Why did you throw me into horrible conflict like this? I have nothing now to cling to! When I follow the old faith I no longer feel calmly certain that I am right. I seem to be like the doctor and the rest of them, sacrificing others to my prejudice, to the good of my foolish soul; but if for a moment I dare to adopt your ideas, then the old feeling comes rushing back torrent-like; my mother's spirit seems to stand before me, pleading, exhorting, reproaching, and then – then I fling the sweet, hideous temptation from me, as I would hurl away some venomous serpent.'

It struck Harry as he watched her, and listened to her with bleeding heart, that she was a symbol of the troublous age in which she lived, a creature with weakened and uprooted faith, yet with feelings and instincts still belonging to the past, still responding to the old dead and gone dogmas.

He felt appalled at the conflict he had raised. Sibella, with her keen insight, had partly foreseen it.

Not without a severe struggle with himself, Harry promised Viola that he would not come here again, since his presence caused her so much pain, and he was rewarded by seeing a shade cross her face.

'Yes, it is better,' she said, shaking her head angrily to throw off the inconsistent feeling of disappointment 'it will be much better.'

'Then this is to be our last meeting for some time?' He paused irresolutely. 'Come out with me into the garden. We will drop all difficult and painful topics – I will not distress you in any way, if I can help it. Whatever else we may be to one another, we are at any rate two human beings in a mysterious and disastrous world, ignorant of our fate, ignorant of pretty nearly everything except "that grief stalks the earth, and sits down at the feet of each by turns,"[17] as some Greek poet says. On that ground at any rate we may meet without a sense of guilt, whatever be our creeds.'

He opened the low window, and together they passed from the musty smells and dimness of the damp old drawing-room into the radiance of a sweet spring morning.

The may blossom was not yet out, but every tree and bush was sprinkled with tender green; the tangled shrubberies were alive with tiny leaves. Overhead the windows of Mrs. Sedley's bedroom stood open to admit the sunshine and the balmy air.

Hearing footsteps on the gravel, Adrienne came to the window and looked out. 'What a perfect morning! Viola, you look like the genius of the spring in your white dress.'

('Oh! if you only knew, what would you think?' Viola inwardly exclaimed).

'And what do *I* look like?' inquired Harry.

'Oh! you look like a prosaic sort of Summer,' said Adrienne; 'one can't expect to look symbolic in a tweed suit. Harry, I wish you would go and get me some primroses, I see myriads of them in the park.'

'All right; will you come too, Mrs. Dendraith?'

She assented. The primroses grew, as Adrienne had said, in myriads. Viola found herself taking more pleasure in the simple occupation of gathering them than she could have believed possible, considering the burdens that lay on her heart. How often, in the old days, had she and Geoffrey and Bill Dawkins gone wild over the flowers and the wonders of the spring! How sweet they were! How their very scent spoke of simple and innocent delight and the wonder of childhood! The throb of bewildered misery ceased under the gentle ministry of sunshine and flowers, and the unspeakable freshness of the rejoicing meadows.

When a vast bunch of primroses had been amassed, the clean, yellow trunk of a felled tree was chosen for a resting-place, where the chequered shade of young limes tempered the sunshine. It was the site of Viola's little sylvan temple of the days of yore; here the ruthless Thomas had stood with his pruning-knife to desecrate and destroy, and now the little wood, once more in festival array, was chanting its song of spring, forgetful of the freight of the years.

Harry saw that a more peaceful look had come into Viola's face, as her eyes wandered over the flowery meadows and followed the movements of the white, hurried clouds.

She lay back resting, with a look in her eyes as if they were seeing something beyond the clouds and the blue of the heavens. The look was not one of joy, but there was neither fear nor grief in it. It was calm and penetrating. She and Fate seemed to be looking into one another's eyes steadfastly. Motionless and silent she lay thus, apparently unconscious of the flight of time.

The birds began to come close to the two still figures, and a couple of squirrels bounded after one another up the nearest tree, chattering and crying excitedly.

'When I was a little girl,' Viola said at length, scarcely moving from her position, 'I had a temple here; the walls were made of briony, and the pillars of eglantine. The high altar was an ivy-bush, and for incense I had the breath of flowers. It was the Temple of Life. Roses I carried in handfuls to my shrine (that was for delight), and as the seasons went by all the sweetest flowers of the field – honeysuckle and wild-briar and violets; and then for splendour scarlet poppies, and for love and constancy forget-me-nots, and for happiness the big wide-eyed daisies of the corn-fields. I had also the enchanter's night-shade, which meant witchcraft or fascination, and then there were dead leaves in shoals for melancholy, and the harebell for grief, and for faith the passion-flower.'

She paused for a moment, and then went on with a still more dreamy look in her eyes, a still more dreamy calmness in her voice:

'And I worshipped in that temple. At church, on Sundays, I prayed, but before my own little woodland altar I adored. All beautiful things were there; hope, truth, faith, happiness, and love. It is hard to explain in words what it was I worshipped. I worshipped the earth and all that is in it; I worshipped the loveliness of life.

'One day, when I came to my shrine, the beautiful temple was in the dust; I found Thomas, with his knife, cutting the briony and laying low the walls of eglantine. The high altar was flung down. After that I had to live without a temple or an altar. Once thrown down, they can never be set up again; the deed is done for ever; the sacredness has gone, and all new temples are half-shams. And all that, item by item, happened to me afterwards in life. It was a prophecy. Now I have no temple.'

A squirrel on a branch above peered curiously and timidly at the speaker, and then darted up the tree in hot haste.

'I think that I knew – child as I was – what was coming. I knew that my temple and its destruction were symbols of the future. It seems to me as if the shadow of Fate were always upon me, and that in some secret chamber of my heart is written what is to come – I see – I feel rather – shipwreck and disaster.'

'That is a dangerous fancy,' said Harry, gazing anxiously at the melancholy face; 'it will make you yield to circumstances instead of erecting your own will into a circumstance dominating all the rest.'

'There are big powers at work,' she said, still in the same dreamy tone. 'I can see the wave rolling in, centuries old – high, resistless, unbroken; my will and yours are mere pebbles on the shore – Hush! do you hear that?'

She raised herself and sat listening. Harry knew what she meant. It was the deep woeful sound in the breaking of the waves.

He tried to persuade her that such a sound was inevitable in certain states of the weather, and that he had heard it often when no disaster had followed its warning.

'Disaster will follow this,' said Viola; 'I feel it. I don't mean about mother. What has to come soon to her will be no disaster, but a release. There is something else coming.'

Harry felt, with an inward shudder, that this was only too probable. Matters could not continue long as they were; but what turn were they to take? That was the dreadful question. With a woman of Viola's temperament there was much to be feared. She had not the habit of good fortune.

Viola presently rose abruptly.

'It is time to go.'

'And must I not come again?' he asked wistfully, taking her hand and looking at her with pleading eyes.

As they stood thus they became aware of a stealthy footstep behind them. Their hands parted, and Philip Dendraith stood before them smiling.

Viola turned very white, but she did not move. Harry's attitude was quietly defiant.

'I have been to the house expecting to find you with your mother, my dear,' said Philip; 'Miss Lancaster, however, has taken your place. It is very kind of Miss Lancaster.'

'I was just going in,' said Viola.

'Ah! I thought very likely, when I first saw you, that it would turn out that you were just going in. I have come to propose to stay for a day or two here. I thought you would miss me if we were parted too long' (this with a brilliant smile). 'Shall we stroll back together?'

Philip did not allow the conversation to flag for a moment, and when Harry and Adrienne were sitting, ready to start, in the pony-carriage, he said affably, that he hoped they would soon drive over again and see them.

'You may be sure I shall come whenever I can,' said Adrienne as they went off.

Philip and Viola stood watching them down the carriage-drive.

'Pious occupation, nursing one's mother,' observed Philip, twirling his stick.

Viola did not answer.

'You are a deeper young person than I thought, my dear,' continued Philip; 'flirtation and filial piety form a remarkably judicious combination. Who could object to a young wife's going home to nurse her mother? No one but a monster, of course; and if a young man happen to hover about the place at the same time – even though he *is* a former lover – who can object? Only the monster base enough to suspect unjustly his highly-principled spouse. Primroses – what could be more innocent? Viola,' said Philip, coming closer to her, 'do you really think that you can carry on a flirtation with this man under my nose without my suspecting it?'

'No, I do not think so for a moment,' she replied.

'Then may I ask you why you make the attempt?'

'I did not make the attempt. I came here to nurse my mother, certainly without a thought of Mr. Lancaster's coming here.'

'Injured innocence,' sneered Philip.

'Not so,' said Viola; 'I do not call myself innocent.'

'Oh, really! – a pretty confession. Then are you allowing this man to make open love to you, and have you actually the audacity to tell this to *me*?'

'I have tried hard to remain true to my old principles, but I do not feel that I have succeeded. I tell you frankly that my sense of duty and allegiance to you is no longer what it was. I have not entirely cast it off – it is too much part of my being for that – but certainly I have ceased to feel as I used to feel about it, so I suppose there must be war between us. You need not trust me; I don't ask to be trusted, for I no longer regard it as a point of honour to follow your wishes in all things, or to make my wifehood the sole pivot of my existence. I feel that it is a false relationship, into which I ought never to have entered, and I do not now regard it as binding in the sense that I used to consider it binding – holding sway over my every deed and thought. I repeat, do not trust me now. You must watch me, frustrate me. I am no longer yours – body and soul. I belong partly to myself at last. Half of my soul, if not the whole, is liberated. Do you understand?'

'I understand that jargon? Certainly not! I only understand that if this sort of thing goes on much longer there will be nothing for it but to keep you a prisoner, with a hired attendant to watch you every hour of the day. You know that I should stick at nothing if necessity prompted. By Heaven! I would swear you were mad (I don't think I should have to perjure myself either), and have you kept under lock and key, if it came to that. You evidently don't know me yet. Meet this man again, and I promise you that will be your fate. Don't imagine I am using idle threats. That sort of thing doesn't answer with a mule-headed woman like you. I speak without hyperbole. You shall not put my honour and my name in jeopardy though you die for it. Now go to your mother – I wish to Heaven you had never left her!'

* * * * *

Mrs. Sedley was in great pain during all that night; Viola and the nurse took turns in watching by the bedside. The invalid had been asking anxiously for her sons, and a telegram had been despatched summoning the eldest and Geoffrey, the only ones within reach. The second was with his regiment in India.

The two arrived next morning, and it was strange to see the look on Mrs. Sedley's face when she heard their footsteps. Viola was a well-beloved child, but never had her presence evoked such a light of joy in her mother's face as shone on it now, at the sight of the young scapegrace whose extravagance had helped to bring the family to the brink of ruin, and through whom the sister had been doomed to the most terrible form of sacrifice which a woman of her type can endure.

Viola felt that after all the years of companionship between mother and daughter, this stranger son was more to her mother than she was – she who had watched by the bedside, feeling the anguish of every pang to her heart's core, knew that the last look of love would be turned not on her but on him.

And so it proved.

The exaltation of feeling caused by her son's return caused a rally in the invalid, but before evening the watchers saw that she was weaker, and that the alarming symptoms were increasing.

The doctor was summoned, for the second time that day, and every one waited in suspense for his coming. There was a hush all through the house which seemed the deeper from the heavy mist that hung about the park; the white, familiar mist so characteristic of the shut-in, gloomy unhealthy old house, over which the hand of death was resting. What could be more appropriate than death in that atmosphere of fog and stagnation? Not the faintest stir was in the air; the movement and tumult of life had no place here. It was a spot where the most vigorous, if forbidden to return speedily to the outer world of hope and effort, might feel ready to lie down and die.

The sound of the doctor's phaeton broke through the stillness.

His verdict was decisive; the patient had not many hours to live. Seeing what she suffered, her family were to be congratulated.

A terrible five hours passed before the end came – hours which seemed to Viola like so many years of cruel experience. Mr. Sedley, when he was at last made to understand what must happen, became almost distraught. He knelt at the bedside sobbing like a child, entreating his wife to stay with him, declaring that he should be lost without her, that he had always adored her, even at his worst, and imploring her to forgive him for his past ill-conduct.

'My husband, if I have anything to forgive, I forgive it freely; I would have borne from you whatever you might choose to inflict. Was I not your wife?'

'I have been a brute,' he groaned.

She laid her thin long hand on his head and said a few words in his ear.

'I will try,' he said, sobbing;' I will try.'

Her voice was growing very weak; the last moments were evidently drawing near.

'Ah! you have ever been a good and dutiful child,' she said, as Viola, with quivering lips, bent down and kissed her. 'God has been very good to me. You will be faithful to your life's end.'

At the last a great peace seemed to fall upon the dying woman; she murmured texts from the Bible, interspersed with words of exhortation to follow Christ, to walk with Him to the end, to seek Him, and lose all for His sake.

'He has given me rest and peace; He has saved my soul with His precious blood.'

A woman of one mood, of one motive, one thought, she died as she had lived, with her eyes fixed on the same image; the aspect and perspective of all things still unchanged. She spoke in gasps: 'Viola, you will be faithful to the end – my husband, God will forgive – we shall meet again – God be with you, dear ones! To Him I commend you, till our blessed reunion in Christ – Christ my God, save and forgive!'

A last long kiss, whose memory remained vividly to Viola's dying day, the final pitiful farewells in the fading light of that dreary fate-laden afternoon, and then all was over.

Viola felt herself being drawn away by a firm kindly hand as the dying agony drew to its crisis.

'Do not grieve – I am thankful – so thankful.'

The last look was for the son, the last prayer for his salvation.

The long martyrdom was over. As far as earthly prescience could decide, the tired woman was at rest. The agonising wheel of life had ceased to whirl, and where there had been pain and striving there was a black unconsciousness. Oh! to pierce for one moment that veil of mystery! to follow the soul through these gates of darkness!

CHAPTER XXXIII

DUST TO DUST

Those were ghastly days at the Manor-House which succeeded Mrs. Sedley's death.

The dull fog still clung about the park and shrouded the avenue, and on the second day a sullen rain began to fall, making everything sodden and unspeakably dreary. Mr. Sedley appeared to be perfectly stunned by his loss. He had never believed in illness, unless it were a case of scarlet or typhoid fever. That any woman could go about with a mortal disease gnawing at her life, performing her ordinary duties, was an idea quite out of his range and it seemed almost impossible for him to realise that the old order of things which his wife had for so long maintained at the Manor-House was over and done with for ever. Mr. Sedley very soon set up a fiction that he had been a devoted husband, and that his loss had utterly broken him. His bewilderment, discomfort, and the profound disturbance of long-established habits were all placed to the account of grief for the loss of his wife. The workings of remorse which had assailed him on her deathbed were not yet stilled, so that altogether the man's state of mind was truly pitiable.

Viola never knew how those dreadful days before the funeral were lived through. There was no sympathy between her and her father; she felt resentment against him for his conduct towards her mother, and could scarcely listen in patience to his eulogies and lamentations, now that she was dead and his tardy appreciation could avail her nothing.

With her second brother, who had been abroad during the greater part of his career, Viola felt almost like a stranger, but she and Geoffrey drew nearer together during that funereal experience. He was strongly affected by his mother's loss, not so much because he deeply felt it, as because he found himself for the first time in the presence of death. He began to confide some of his difficulties to Viola, when they sat alone by the fire in the evenings, perhaps after passing together the door of that closed room where the dead woman lay, cold and peaceful.

'Viola, they say that in another fifty years nobody will believe in the immortality of the soul.'

They were sitting in the drawing-room towards evening, the curtains not yet drawn. Outside was the same greyness and mist that had hung about the place since Mrs. Sedley's death.

'I haven't thought much about these things, to tell you the truth; I imagined that I believed in immortality and God and religion, but now' – he paused with a look of awe on his face; – 'what do you think, Viola'? I suppose you think as we were all brought up to think in our childhood.'

'O Geoffrey, I don't know! 'Viola exclaimed, thrusting her hand through her hair and crouching lower over the fire. 'I have been so much shaken lately. I begin to feel that our old beliefs will have to be learnt and believed all over again, if they are to be of any use to us. They don't answer to one's call when one is in dire extremity. They leave you – O Geoffrey! I believe they leave you more lonely and hopeless than professed unbelievers are left in the presence of their dead! I can't tell you what a sense of despair comes to me when I look at our mother's face – peaceful as it is. I can't help thinking of her life, and the utter ruin of it, and the mistake of it – and nobody understands! I feel, when people *will* console one and talk about heaven and all that, as if I would rather they told me brutally that there is no hope: that it is all a silly delusion; that there is no ground for our faiths, no pity for our love, no answer to our yearnings – anything would be better than this cant consolation which you know only springs from custom and not from conviction.'

Geoffrey looked amazed.

'I had no idea' –

'No, of course you hadn't,' she interposed hastily. 'I am frightened of it myself; and yet I feel as if there were some faith more real than the faith of our childhood; – only I can't find it.'

The conversation was an epoch in Geoffrey's life, and the strengthening of a new impetus in Viola's. It was also the beginning of a friendship on fresh foundations between brother and sister, which entirely altered the direction of development of Geoffrey's character.

The day of the funeral was cold and damp. It seemed a singularly appropriate day for the burial of one whose whole life had been pitched in that low tone of colour. Side by side Geoffrey and Viola watched the gloomy procession draw up to the door, the silent decorous bustle of black-coated mutes, and then the lifting of the coffin into the hearse.

Some feeling which Viola could not have explained induced her to witness every cruel detail. Among the rows of ghostly trees the black procession moved solemnly to the park-gates. Alighting from the coach at the churchyard steps, Viola was carried back in memory to her wedding-day, when she had passed between rows of villagers and over garlands of fresh flowers to the clanging of the noisy bells.

In another few minutes they were all in their places, Mr. Sedley and his two sons, Philip and Viola, side by side in the chancel.

Every family in the neighbourhood and all the Upton people were represented, and among the congregation were the Manor-House coachman, Thomas the gardener, and 'old Willum,' a little more bent, but otherwise just the same as of yore. At the sight of him, for the first time Viola had to force back threatening tears.

But the trial was yet to come.

The first part of the ceremony over, the procession moved out to the grey churchyard and wended its way through the tombstones to the open grave. Viola's heart gave a sick throb.

Cold, gloomy, gruesome! There was not a gleam of hope, not a ray of sunshine or of triumph in the whole depressing scene! It seemed as if, in life and in death, Mrs. Sedley were alike incapable of evoking such a passionate note. Her Christian's faith and her Christian's trust were equally destitute of inspiring force. 'Ashes to ashes, dust to dust.' Never in her life had Viola doubted so profoundly, never had she plunged into such an abyss of far-reaching despair, of religion, of God, as when she stood by her mother's grave and watched the coffin with its white wreaths being lowered into the earth. How greedy it seemed, yearning to close up over its prey! She turned aside with a sick heart.

The bystanders were flinging flowers on to the coffin; primroses and violets and the first-fruits of the garden. As through the mists of a dream Viola saw familiar faces round the grave. Mr. Evans was there, and Dick, and Sir Philip and Lady Dendraith, and Thomas, and 'old Willum,' and Mr. Pellett (how kind of him to come!); and there was Caleb, looking solemn and argumentative, in the background.

At first sight of his face Viola was seized with a mad impulse to laugh. A disposition to philosophic utterance seemed to be contending in him with a sense of propriety, but a single glance was enough to convey to his familiar friends that he regarded death as no evil, and that, consciousness being involved in the ideas of pain and pleasure, Death might, in fact, be looked upon as the great Emancipator! As Viola's eyes turned away from the countenance of the philosopher they lighted unexpectedly upon another and even more familiar face!

She had been told by Mrs. Evans that Harry Lancaster was not to be at the funeral, but Mrs. Evans must have been misinformed, for there he stood, half-hidden by Sir Philip's stalwart form, and partially eclipsed at intervals by Mrs. Pellett's new funereal bonnet. Viola gave a visible start, and at the same instant, as if in grim comment on the nature of all human affection, the first clod of earth fell with a dull thud upon the coffin. The sweet flowers lay crushed and stained beneath it.

'Earth to earth, ashes to ashes, dust to dust' – (Viola's eyes contracted with a look of terror) – 'in sure and certain hope of the Resurrection to eternal life.' She looked up piteously, as if she were asking whether that hope were real and trust-worthy, or utterly empty, as it seemed to her to-day in this grey churchyard amidst the black-gloved respectability that hung its head decorously round the grave.

'In sure and certain hope of the Resurrection to eternal life.'

'Eternal Life!' Harry was not more hope-inspired than Viola at that moment. His thoughts followed a melancholy impulse: for that dim defrauded unrespon-sive spirit what would life eternal have to offer? Growth, discovery, creation? a tapestried experience making richer the possibilities of all human existence? Not this, but only a stagnant gazing at the same monotonous group of images, a repetition *ad infinitum* of the same dull idea! That surely was not *life.* With all her sanctity, with all her religious enthusiasm, the dead woman had no breadth of spiritual outlook; it was to little local things that her mind held relation; to changing temporal institutions that she clung, flinging over them the mantle of religion.

An existence entirely composed of spiritual experience, an eternal life, in which no small observances or earthly things had part, was utterly impossible for such a nature.

Less reasoned, but none the less profound, was Viola's doubt of the promises of the burial-service. Oh! for a moment of blind unquestioning belief – anything to still the horrible fear that possessed her, as she peered down into the black abyss of Death, and felt the spirit departing from her for ever!

Harry divined that she was passing through a great mental crisis. What might the new wave of emotion sweep away in its course? These thoughts of death had touched her closely indeed.

What if some day she had to stand beside *another* grave and hear that dull thud upon the coffin-lid as the greedy earth closed round it? What would she feel then, if she had allowed the beloved and loving soul to go from her, perhaps for ever, into the great darkness, still thinking that his love was but half-returned, still grieving and sore at heart because of her? Would any one of the motives for which she had done this thing seem worth a thought at such a moment? Ah! no; desperate and heart-stricken, she would feel only that she had been false to the one good in life, and that now the bitterness, sorrow, and hopeless remorse had come too late!

In the presence of Death she was conscious of the unutterable pathos of all affection, the tragedy that comes sooner or later in the train of every intense human emotion.

Harry, watching her intently as she stood with her eyes fixed upon the grave, felt a growing conviction that the battle with Fate which he and Sibella were waging for the possession of this woman's soul, had entered upon a new phase. She looked up, and their eyes met.

He drew a long breath. Viola was awake at last; loving to her utmost, hating to her utmost; reckless and well-nigh desperate. She was ready now for anything. They were on their way to the crucial moment. Had she sufficient force to hold on to the end? Once resolved, would she fling behind her all weak remorse, free herself from the clinging remnants of abandoned motives? Would she eschew fatal hesitations, and prove herself to be made of the stuff which produces great deeds of heroism or of crime? Would she act boldly and consistently, as she had resolved, or would she show herself the child of her circumstances, stumbling fatally under the burden of her sad woman's heritage of indecision, fear, vain remorse, untimely scruples? No marvel if she did so, but woe to her and to all concerned, if she failed in courage at the critical moment!

A short time now would decide everything!

CHAPTER XXXIV

IN GRIM EARNEST

Yes, she was ready for anything! She moved as one in a dream; the people around her seemed like shadows. She played her part among them, but even as she spoke that grey churchyard, with its open grave, was before her mind's eye; she heard the thud of earth upon the coffin-lid, while the clammy mist seemed to be clinging round her, and the words went out mournfully over the tombs, 'Ashes to ashes, dust to dust.'

Sad, hopeless, terrible, seemed the game of life; the thought of it created a recklessness that Viola had never known before.

Scruples, hesitations, seemed ridiculous in the gaunt presence of Death, who mocks at human effort and cuts short the base and the noble at their work with grim impartiality. Yet as soon as she left the Manor-House to return to her cliff-side home, the daring spirit suddenly departed from her, as if by magic. On the instant that she crossed the threshold, she felt the strange gloomy will-destroying influence of the place descend upon her pall-like. Philip's dominant spirit seemed to pervade the whole house, even in his absence.

Though he was often away from home, he used to appear at uncertain hours during the day, and Viola never knew when she was likely to be alone. He seemed to take a delight in haunting her, and in turning up when and where she least expected him. He used to come in stealthily and appear at her elbow before she knew of his approach. This custom had the effect of making her intensely and miserably nervous. After that experience in the west wing she had been very easily startled, and now she lived in a perpetual state of strain and dread, and had contracted a habit of perpetually looking up in expectation of her husband's panther-like approach. Her power of resistance and initiative seemed to be charmed out of her by the mere atmosphere of the place; it was almost as if Philip possessed some mysterious magnetic force, so overwhelming was the influence which he exerted over all within his reach, especially over those of nervous temperament.

In spite of the associations of the room in the west wing, Viola was still attracted to it, and she felt, moreover, that she could never rest until she had found, and put back in its place, the precious knife which she had let fall in her terror. But she dreaded that Philip should find her there again, and for that reason put off, day by day, her intended visit to that haunt of shadows.

Once Philip announced that he was going out for the whole afternoon, and Viola resolved to choose that day for her quest. It would not take more than a few minutes to replace the knife in the oak cabinet; if she went immediately after her husband left the house, surely even *he* could not discover her.

She watched him out of sight, and then looking nervously round, she crossed the dark hall, avoiding the smiling eyes of the portraits, and passed through the door leading to the west wing. The stillness of so many empty rooms was oppressive. Stepping as quietly as she could, Viola passed the closed doors until she came to the death-chamber, whose lock she turned with beating heart. After a moment's pause she entered.

There was the great black bedstead, sombre and solemn; there stood the oak cabinet, with its carved door half open, just as it had been left on that dreadful afternoon. Viola sickened with reasonless terror. She felt as if she must turn and leave her errand unaccomplished. But she resisted the impulse, and went forward with her eyes fixed on the floor seeking the fallen knife.

Is there, after all, some Fate that guides the footsteps of men and maps out their path for them from birth to death? Viola had always been convinced that she was thus guided; she had given up all expectation of rescue, and looked into the eyes of Destiny mournfully and hopelessly. Every movement, every act, every thought, was preordained to lead up to misfortune.

She stooped suddenly and picked up the knife from the floor, where it lay just as she had dropped it. She was thankful to hold it again in her hands, to know that it was safe. When last she held it thus she was battling fiercely against herself, against the supreme passion of her life; and now – ! now the battle had been lost – conscience was defeated, faith and hope abandoned. She laid the little dagger passionately to her lips, looking round, with her quick nervous glance, as if dreading every moment to see the form of her husband looming through the dusk. Then she laid the knife carefully in its hiding-place, beside the other treasures, locked the cabinet, and with a sigh of relief turned away.

A qualm of fear passed through her as she approached the bed, but this time no figure emerged from its shadows.

She reached the door safely, went out, and turned the key.

Thank Heaven the ordeal was over! On turning her heart gave a great bound, for she found herself standing face to face with – Mrs. Barber. She uttered a little cry of dismay, and put out her hand to steady herself against the lintel of the door.

'Mrs. Barber,' she said at last, 'what are you doing up here?'

Mrs. Barber set her lips.

'I am here, ma'am,' she replied with dignity, 'in the performance of my duty. I come to see that the rooms are kept in order.'

'Oh!' said Viola.

'Your tea is waiting for you;' added Mrs. Barber, who felt that she had the best of the situation; 'it has been in the morning-room for half-an-hour.'

'I will go and take it,' said Viola hurriedly.

She hastened down the echoing corridor, crossed the hall, and shut herself into the little ante-room where, as Mrs. Barber had reproachfully announced, the tea was standing untouched. But the tea had yet longer to wait.

Viola went down on her knees on the hearthrug, absently taking the poker and goading the already willing little fire into a brighter blaze. Maria, who was basking in the warmth, set up a loud purring and rubbed herself against the arm of her mistress.

Viola knew now for certain what she had often before vaguely suspected: that in Philip's absence she was watched by the housekeeper! Again and again she had found reason to fear it, and to-day's instance confirmed the suspicion. There remained not the shadow of doubt in her mind that Mrs. Barber had followed her this afternoon to the west wing; in fact, Mrs. Barber was her jailer. Who would Philip employ next? Possibly the kitchen-maid! The walls of her prison seemed to be coming nearer and nearer. Viola was reminded of the gruesome old story of the prisoner shut up in a tower, whose walls encroached a foot each day, till at last they closed in and crushed him to death. When would the catastrophe arrive? She would rather it came at once, than hang back and keep her perpetually on the rack of expectation and dread. She gave a nervous shudder and looked round the room suspiciously, as if fearing that she was even now not alone. The whole household might be spies, for aught that she knew! There was no evading Philip's vigilance. It seemed as if her most secret thoughts were at his mercy.

Feeling nervous and overwrought, Viola was just moving into a low chair before the fire, when a faint sound caught her ear. She started and looked round, expecting to see her husband. But there was no one in the room. The sound came again: a faint tapping on the window-pane.

Viola's heart began to beat. She listened anxiously. In another second, again came the stealthy tap upon the glass.

It was raining, and there was a slight beating of rain-drops on the panes, which Viola tried to think she might have mistaken for the other sound; but when this was repeated a third time she rose, summoning all her courage, and went towards the window. Then out in the dusk she saw a man's figure, and a man's face looking in. She clutched the nearest chair, turning very white. The man signed to her to open the window. She hesitated for a moment, and then, with a sort of blind courage, she went close to it and peered out.

'Who is it?'

'Don't be afraid; it is Caleb Foster,' a voice replied. 'Open the window.'

In an instant the roar of the sea smote loudly on the ear, and the soft west wind and rain were blowing into the fire-lit room.

'What is it? Will you come in? or' – she hesitated, looking back nervously over her shoulder.

'Come out to me,' said Caleb. 'I won't detain you a moment. Oh, it is raining; you will get wet.'

'No matter – no matter.' She snatched up a rug from the sofa and stepped out on to the gusty terrace. The waves were dragging the stones savagely back and forward just below, the terrace almost overhanging the sea at high tide.

'I was directed to give you this,' said Caleb calmly, bringing a letter from his pocket, where it had evidently not gained in cleanliness or smoothness, 'and I was told to bid you be of good cheer, and brave and determined, for you have faithful friends.'

'Are you in their confidence?' asked Viola, flushing.

'I know nothing,' said Caleb; 'private affairs are not my business. I am called to deliver a note and a ridiculous message, and I deliver them. If other people take pleasure in emotional excesses, I regret it; but, on the principle that the individual is at liberty to do what he pleases, on condition that he does not encroach upon the liberty of others, I offer no obstruction to the errors of our friends. They employ me as a messenger – I am willing to oblige; I ask no questions. Should you consult me I might be ready to give my opinion; otherwise I abstain from interference. Good-evening. The sooner I am off the better. One word of unasked advice, however – don't act on impulse; think everything out calmly from all sides; count the cost before you take any decided step, and don't fly in the face of the world if you can avoid it. Socrates' – but Caleb thought better of it, and retired without mentioning what Socrates had to say on this point.

Viola hastened into the house to read her letter. It was from Harry, asking her to meet him at a spot on the downs, about a quarter of a mile from the coast-guard station, on the following afternoon at four o'clock. Sibella was expecting a visit from Philip at that time, so there would be no difficulty. Harry would be at the appointed spot in any case, if Viola did not come, he would know that something had happened to prevent her.

Viola pressed her hands to her brow distractedly. The time for decision had indeed come! Every fear, prejudice, faith, principle, superstition which she had ever known, rushed back upon her in a mighty flood, forbidding a response to the appeal of this letter. The secrecy was revolting to her instincts, the deceit and plotting intolerable. She realised, nevertheless, that she had to choose between that and life-long endurance of her present fate. These left her no alternative. But there was no time now to think it out, for she heard a soft footstep in the corridor.

Flinging the letter into the fire, she stood awaiting her husband's approach. He had returned very soon. Maria got up and slunk away.

'Well, my dear,' he said, with his wonted smile, 'what have you been doing this afternoon? You are flushed' – (She put her hands to her cheeks). – 'I see too that you have not taken your tea.' He looked at her keenly.

She felt that he would read every secret in her eyes. 'I am not a great tea-drinker,' she said.

'Still you do generally take it. Have you had visitors?'

'No one has been in the house.'

'Oh! have you met some one *out* of the house?'

'I saw Caleb,' she answered, struggling against the benumbing sensation of powerlessness which Philip's presence always created in her.

'You and Caleb seem to have a great deal in common,' he remarked. 'Were you out, then, in all this rain?'

'Yes, for a short time.'

'Talking to Caleb?'

'Yes.'

'Would it seem impertinent if I were to inquire the subject of your collo-quy?'

She hesitated.

'I think you may just as well tell me,' said Philip. 'I shall find out if I wish to know.'

'Are you going to cross-question Caleb?'

'That is a matter of detail,' said Philip. 'I only remark that if I wish to know I *shall* know. How have you been spending the rest of the afternoon?'

'I am tired of answering questions,' she said, with a sudden flash of rebellion.

'Oh! something up evidently this afternoon. That too I shall find out. Your affairs seem to be getting into a very complicated condition, my dear; I can't say that I think you have the head to carry through an elaborate system of plots and deception. It seems also a little inconsistent with your upbringing and your "principles." I suppose, however, it is the natural weapon of the weaker vessel Women take to it by instinct.'

'By necessity, you might say.'

'From preference, my dear. I know your adorable sex.'

Philip established himself in the easy-chair and stretched himself leisurely.

'An unusually good fire,' he said, leaning back and crossing his legs. 'You have been burning something I see.'

Viola looked round with a start, and Philip smiled.

'There is a little bit of charred paper sticking to the side of the grate.'

He took the poker and turned it down, and as the heat caught it the lines of handwriting were visible in little glowing spots across the notepaper. 'Put two and two together. H'm. Did Caleb bring a note?'

'I have already explained that I would rather not answer any more questions,' said Viola. 'If you are so certain of finding out all that you wish to know, why catechise me? Find out what you please; I don't think I should care very much what you found out!'

She was thinking of a grey churchyard and an open grave, and the thought of it brought a delicious sense of rest. If the worst came to the worst –

'My dear,' said Philip, 'excuse my saying so, but you are losing your looks.'

She raised her eyebrows slightly, but did not answer.

'All this plotting keeps you anxious – it is not becoming.'

She smiled.

'You do not seem to take much interest in your dress, either,' he went on. 'Now there is no greater folly a wife can be guilty of than to neglect her appearance. Her husband is apt to follow after strange gods' –

'The stranger the better,' Viola muttered between her teeth.

'You may treat all these matters with disdain, my dear, but I can assure you your conduct is most foolish. A man expects his wife to make some effort to attract him.'

Viola was silent.

'To be frank, my dear, you have in every way turned out unsatisfactory: as an investment (so to put it) I may say that you are, in point of fact, more or less of a fraud; pardon my crudeness. I bargained for a wife who would behave as other wives behave, and also I naturally expected that she would do what you have hitherto failed to do, provide the family with an heir.'

'A duty and a privilege indeed!' Viola observed.

'Why you sneer I know not,' said Philip. 'I could have had women by the dozen who would have been only too delighted to fill your position at any price. Perhaps you will understand that I feel a little "sold" under the circumstances.'

'I understand only too well everything that has to do with our fatal marriage. Why won't you let me go?'

'And have a scandal attached to my name! No, thank you, that won't suit me at all. It will suit me better to bring you to reason. I have tried fair means, and they have failed; now I shall try foul. I am tired of all these childish conspiracies with your former lover and his *chère amie*,[18] who, you may not be aware, is carrying on a flirtation with that gay Lothario[19] at the same time that she makes love to me.'

'To you!'

'Yes, my innocent one, to *me*.'

Viola looked at him coldly. 'You are very clever,' she said; 'but there are some women whom you could not understand if you studied them for a thousand years! Mrs. Lincoln is one of them.'

'Then *you* understand this Sybilline[20] creature!'

'No; but I am not so hopelessly at fault as you are, for at least I am *aware* that I do not understand her.'

'Well, if a man of the world doesn't know when a woman wants to flirt with him, he ought to be ashamed of himself.'

Viola could only look at her husband in bewilderment. Why was he telling her this? Did he really believe what he said, or was it to arouse in her mind distrust of Sibella? Surely Philip could not be attempting to excite her jealousy! He was too clever for that; yet what could be his motive for such assertions? If Sibella had given any reason for them, it was certainly for some object connected with Viola's own fate. Harry's letter said that Philip was expected to call at Fir Dell to-morrow afternoon. What did this mean? Viola was puzzling over these things when Philip broke the silence once more.

'Now, my dear, I should like you to try to understand what I say. I have stood a great deal of nonsense from you, knowing how absurdly you were brought up, and how ignorant you were of the ways of the world. But it is really time that you knew a little more. Perhaps you are not aware that before our marriage my father advanced a large sum of money to your father, to enable him to pay his debts and to stay on at the Manor-House, which otherwise he would have had to leave. Liberal settlements were made on you, and in fact, your father, knowing my infatuation, availed himself of the opportunity to make a good haul. I, of course, thought so charming a bride ample indemnification. I believe that your father did pay some of his debts and he continued to live at the Manor-House, but he also began to contract fresh debts, on the strength of his alliance with our family, and it is morally certain that we shall never see a penny of that money again. You will pardon my remarking that, all things considered, your father got decidedly the better of us.'

'It would be more reasonable to complain of these matters to him, then,' said Viola. 'I, being not the seller but the thing sold, can scarcely be held responsible. The object of merchandise called to account for its owner's delinquencies? – surely that is very business-like! If you allowed yourself to be imposed upon you have no one but yourself to blame. Such accidents will happen even to the cleverest of purchasers.'

'Still, I think that the matter concerns you more closely than you are disposed to allow,' said Philip. 'If a man buys a pointer who will not point, he has either to send him back to where he came from, or to train him into better ways – with the help of the whip, if necessary.'

Viola's eyes flashed.

'You can go too far with me,' she said.

'Possibly; but up to now it seems I have not gone far enough.'

'I don't see what remains for you to do as regards insult and insolence.'

'Oh! I assure you we are only beginning. I have been playing hitherto, and playing very badly. In future it shall be in grim earnest. I shall exact what is due to the uttermost farthing.'[21]

CHAPTER XXXV

A PERILOUS PROJECT

Adrienne Lancaster disturbed husband and wife at their *tête-à-tête*. She was in a state of great anxiety, for she had just learnt that her mother stood in imminent danger of losing the little pittance on which they had hitherto been struggling to live and to keep up appearances. What was to become of them if the blow did fall Adrienne dared scarcely conjecture. She was in the utmost distress, for her mother had been urging her to accept Bob Hunter's proposal, resorting to tears, commands, reproaches, and finally to 'wrestlings in prayer' in her daughter's presence.

Adrienne was looking ill and worried.

'Everything seems to come at once,' she said; 'Harry also is a great anxiety to me.'

She said that her brother went perpetually to Mrs. Lincoln's, who was doing him incalculable harm; he seemed perfectly infatuated, and would hear no word against her.

'At this very moment,' said Adrienne despairingly, 'he is sitting in her library at Fir Dell, listening to one knows not what wickedness and folly.'

Had Adrienne been present at Fir Dell she would have been astonished indeed! It was worse even than she thought.

'I wish to Heaven we could do this without so much plotting and conceal-ment,' Harry was saying. 'Viola hates it, and I fear at any moment, she may do something desperate which will upset all our plans.'

'The sooner we make our attempt the better,' said Sibella; 'but, for my part, I have no scruple about using the only weapons left us by the enemy. A pris-oner has to use such means as he can find. If he takes his jailer honestly into his confidence, his chances of regaining his freedom are, to say the least of it, inconsiderable. Picture to yourself a man bound hand and foot, and at the same time cunningly persuaded by those who have bound him that he must make no deceitful and underhand attempt to liberate himself. That man is evidently an idiot if he does not laugh at such teaching, and employ any method that offers itself – subterfuge, stratagem, what you will, in order to oppose the brute force which has been used against him.'

'I wish you could persuade Viola of this.'

'I can never persuade her,' Sibella answered. 'The grim necessities of her posi-tion may force her to use distasteful tools, but she will never lose her scruples. She will never see that these hesitations, this half-heartedness in the struggle for freedom, tend as much as the direct force of the enemy to make it unattainable. But this is the work of centuries; it is in the blood; arguments are unavailing. We must trust to the force of the *personal* impetus in Viola's case. She will never change her feeling rapidly enough through the suasion of ideas. What are ideas in the face of prejudices? Stars at midday.'

'Do you think she will keep the appointment to-morrow afternoon?' asked Harry.

'I would not count too surely upon it. Her feelings are at present chaotic. She may at any moment have a relapse and determine to "do her duty," as she calls it, to the end. If you have any news to tell me, come to the beach below my house to-morrow morning. Come in any case, as I may have something to say to you. Try and keep your sister away from Viola, if you can. She is a dangerous foe to us. We could scarcely have one more formidable.'

Harry shook his head gloomily.

Everything seemed to be going wrong. The pending family calamity was not only most unfortunate in itself, but it happened at a most unfortunate time. His mother was incessantly urging Adrienne to accept Bob Hunter's proposal, and Adrienne seemed at her wits' end to know what to do. She said she would try to find employment in teaching if the worst came to the worst. If it did come to the worst, Harry felt that he could not desert them, and then what was to become of Viola? It was, however, decided that plans for the flight should be made with her on the following afternoon, as if nothing had occurred. If she agreed, Sibella was to be informed at once. Viola and Harry were to leave the country as quickly as possible, beginning life over again, and making up their minds to face all possibilities.

'Don't forget at any time that you *did* decide to take the risk,' said Sibella. 'Viola risks more than you do, and whatever troubles you may have to bear, they must inevitably fall harder upon her. She gives up everything for your sake – always remember that when the time for feeling what *you* have sacrificed begins. I need scarcely tell you this, but even the best of men are sometimes forgetful.'

'I hope I shall not be forgetful in this matter,' said Harry gravely, 'though I am not among the best of men.'

Sibella undertook to do all she could to detain Philip next day as long as she could, though she felt it impossible to answer for him. She harboured a suspicion that he had guessed their whole plan, and was quietly watching them, ready at the right moment to frustrate it. There was something about his expression and manner that was not reassuring. He never breathed a word hinting at suspicion, but Sibella feared that he did suspect. On that day when they had met on the beach, a challenge was tacitly given and accepted between them. Philip Dendraith was not the man to forget that challenge, and he knew that Sibella's memory was at least as long as his. They were thus in a state of secret war; though they always met with compliments and smiles, and fenced with one another with never-flagging energy and skill.

'We never tire,' said Sibella. 'He is resolved, and I am resolved. I am not like Viola. I fight such an adversary with the first best weapon. I will oppose force with fraud till justice has delivered us. What do I care? Injury and insult to a suffering sister shall not be allowed to succeed for want of a little frank transgression. I will fool him to the top of his bent if I can, as he would fool me. What man can stand flattery? I flatter him. Sometimes I think I have made way, but possibly his submission is only a ruse to deceive me – one can never tell. Still the man is vain; the heel of Achilles![22] – he is used to the homage of women! That gives me a handle. If he thought I was falling a victim to his fascinations, I believe even *his* astuteness would fail him! Well, we shall see! Everything hangs on the next few days. Much depends on to-morrow's interview being safely achieved and the arrangements carefully made. Give Viola written directions in case of mistakes, and make sure she understands them thoroughly. And don't be so excited at seeing her again that you forget to be cautious. Philip may have discovered Caleb's visit, for aught we know. You can't be too careful. Play your part bravely and cautiously. Everything depends on trifles. Meanwhile I shall be anxiously thinking of you, while I and my visitor will entertain one another with our usual flow of badinage and compliment. There are few things I would not do in order to defeat this man.' Sibella's lips set themselves firmly. 'A fierce struggle lies before us now. See if (as Pope says) "you don't find me equivocating pretty genteelly!"'[23]

CHAPTER XXXVI

THE WHIRLPOOL OF FATE

The force of circumstances prevailed. Mrs. Dixie, overpowered by anxiety and vexation, became sufficiently ill to work upon her daughter's fears, and when next morning the dreaded blow fell, Adrienne became thoroughly alarmed at her mother's condition.

The old lady was now perpetually alluding to the Workhouse[24] as the final destination of the Lancaster family, and Adrienne was given to understand that this declension of their fortunes was entirely her doing. Mrs. Dixie even descended to particulars regarding their future existence at the expense of their country. Adrienne, knowing that they were in truth quite penniless, and that her mother's life depended upon careful nursing, was in secret despair. At this crisis Fate decreed that Bob Hunter should appear again at the Cottage to repeat his periodic proposal. Adrienne, tired out with trouble and perplexity, ended by accepting it.

From that moment Mrs. Dixie began to recover, and Bob Hunter pirouetted in triumph. This was far from being the happiest time of Adrienne's life! She thought of Sibella and wondered what she would say when she heard of the engagement.

'But what is that woman to me?' she angrily asked herself.

On that same eventful morning Adrienne went over to Upton Castle to announce the news. She was anxious not to allow it to reach her friend through side-channels of gossip.

Viola's congratulations were not effusive. '*Adrienne*! how could you be so mad?'

Adrienne had not mentioned the loss of their income. She coloured a little.

'Bob is a good fellow at heart, you know – and I do think it is all for the best – and I mean to do my utmost to make him happy; and then – well, you know there is my mother ill, and wanting all sorts of things we can't get her, and she feels so terribly our position. You know it is as we feared. She got a letter this morning. Things could not be worse.'

'O Adrienne, I am grieved! What a curse the want of money seems to be! And you have to – to sacrifice yourself because of this.'

'Am I to watch my mother dying and know that there is nothing before us in the future but genteel starvation? Indeed I don't see how it can be even genteel.'

'I think,' said Viola, growing very white, 'that it is better to be in your grave, than alive and – a woman.'

Adrienne was shocked.

'Oh no, dear Viola. A woman always has a noble and a happy sphere in her home, wherever it may be: we must not take despairing views of life.'

'This ought not to be,' cried Viola, clutching her hand. 'Can't your brother help you? Can't you work? Can't you –

'And my mother ill, our home broken up, and not a penny to call our own? After all, I am going to do my duty to Bob, and I always think it is a woman's fault if her home isn't happy.'

Adrienne did not meet with much more encouragement when she told her brother of her engagement.

'I believe it to be my duty,' she said.

'Oh! in that case – ! I have sometimes wondered how these things come about; the process seems very simple.' Presently he laid his hand on her shoulder, softening. 'So the burden is laid upon you,' he said, with a sigh; 'why can't I bear it instead?'

She shook her head. 'That is impossible, as you know. Don't grieve, dear Harry; I am not unhappy. I feel that I am doing right, and that I shall have strength to perform my task.'

Harry thought that his sister had had enough tasks to perform already. What she needed was the radiance of a great joy to warm and expand her whole being. Always in the shade, she was becoming pale and poor, like a flower grown in a cellar. In course of time she would perhaps become a second Mrs. Evans, busily adding to the depression of an already low-spirited world.

'I am satisfied that it is my duty,' said Adrienne.

'Oh! confound this everlasting duty!' Harry exclaimed.

Adrienne did not at once reply. She had noticed that her brother had become quick-tempered, not to say morose, of late, and she wondered if Mrs. Lincoln had anything to do with this change for the worse.

'You may say, "Confound duty," dear Harry,' said Adrienne, 'but you know that you feel its sacred call in your heart, and dare not disobey it any more than I dare to do so.'

'I assure you, you are mistaken,' said Harry, who in his present mood regarded 'duty' with much acrimony and ill-will. 'I would dare to do anything. No good comes of prudence, or duty either, that I can see.'

Adrienne was much concerned at her brother's frame of mind, and again put it down to the evil influence of Mrs. Lincoln.

'I wish I could get you to look upon my engagement in a different light, dear Harry,' she pleaded.

'Pray mention the light,' said Harry affably, 'and I shall be charmed to oblige you.'

She shook her head.

'Don't you recognise that duty' –

'Look here, if you mention that word again,' said Harry, 'I shall emigrate.'

'No, no,' interposed Adrienne hastily. 'You *must* see that for a woman' –

'Timbuctoo or the Wild West,'[25] he murmured threateningly.

'A woman's lot in life is different from a man's,' Adrienne persisted.

'Very,' said Harry. 'She can't go off at a moment's notice to Timbuctoo.'

'Upon her shoulders is laid the beautiful and sacred cares and responsibilities of married life, and I believe that upon these rest the very foundations of society.'

'Once upon a time,' said Harry grimly, 'it was the custom to build a living creature into the foundations of every city and every city-wall,[26] for without that little formality – as our thoughtful ancestors supposed – the city could not stand. This premature interment, with such unpleasantness as might ensue to the chosen instruments, was intended to make firm and solid the foundations of society. Perhaps it did. The foundations at any rate seem to be exceedingly solid and firm! When is the marriage to be?'

'As soon as possible. Bob wants it at once, and mother too. We should not go away for more than a week, or perhaps less, so that mother could come to us almost immediately. We thought the wedding might be in ten days. Of course you will give me away.'

'If you wish it – in ten days,' he repeated thoughtfully to himself. After that he fell into a reverie from which nothing could permanently rouse him. Even when Adrienne recurred to the topic of 'duty' he let it pass unchallenged. That this mildness was the result of profound preoccupation, was proved a little later in the day when he and Adrienne strolled together to the beach, Harry flinging himself at full length against the pebble-ridge below Fir Dell, and throwing stones into the water. Deceived by his previous calmness, Adrienne had been trying to show him how mistaken he was in his views of life, and especially in his interpretation of the natural destiny of woman.

'Her most sacred duty, dear Harry' –

'*Damn!*' The monosyllable was breathed *sotto voce*, but with suppressed ferocity, into the shingle. Then the culprit hastily pulled his hat over his eyes, and rolled over out of earshot.

Adrienne had not caught the smothered "language of imprecation,"[27] but she was none the less alarmed at his behaviour. He continued to lie at full length on the shingle, with his cap pulled over his eyes in a manner that Adrienne thought denoted a shocking state of self-abandonment. What had come to him? She looked up to the distant castle for inspiration, but the long rows of high windows only reminded her of another strange and perturbed spirit, imprisoned therein. Suddenly Harry sat bolt upright, his cap still very much awry and his hair extravagantly ruffled. Adrienne followed the direction in which he was gazing. A figure was seen descending the pathway through the pine-woods from Fir Dell. Harry shaded his eyes and strained them anxiously.

'Who is it?' asked Adrienne.

'Mrs. Lincoln.'

'Oh, let me go!' exclaimed Adrienne, hastily jumping up.

Harry gave a grim smile. It amused him that his sister shrank from meeting a woman who had dared the enmity of the world rather than remain in the position which Adrienne was about to accept deliberately, with her eyes open.

'You had better come and speak to her,' said Harry. 'She will enlarge your mind.'

'I will never willingly enter that woman's presence again!' Adrienne cried. 'Good-bye. I am going home; won't you come? *Do* come.'

'I want to see Mrs. Lincoln,' Harry answered.

Adrienne sorrowfully left him, and when she was quite alone, she gave way to a fit of ladylike weeping, in a neat methodical manner, afterwards drying her eyes and putting aside her handkerchief in good time before reaching the village. Meanwhile Harry and Sibella had met and were moving together closer to the sea.

'It is as we feared,' said Harry. 'The blow has fallen; my mother and sister are penniless.'

'I was sure of it. And your sister is engaged to be married to Bob Hunter; you need not tell me. I am grieved. Fortunately your sister has an obedient soul. The marriage service – strange to say – will reassure her. For her own sake this is devoutly to be wished. How does all this bear on your own affairs? Must you wait for the wedding?'

Harry explained that it was to take place in ten days, and that he must, of course, be present. He felt that he ought to stay with his mother till the couple returned to their home. After that Mrs. Dixie would go to them. Bob had fortunately accepted his mother-in-law with a light heart.

It was accordingly arranged that Harry should go to town as soon as the bride and bridegroom returned, that he should come back next day, not to Upton, but to a little country station farther along the coast called Shepherd's Nook. Thence he could easily walk by the shore to the castle, reaching it at the time appointed. Sibella – who had found out from Philip that he was to be absent for three days at that time – was to obtain from Caleb the loan of his boat: the very boat in which Viola and Harry had made that other less momentous journey before her marriage, – and in that they were to put off, under cover of the dusk, and evade pursuit, if any should be offered. They would land and take the train to Southampton, and thence get over to France, if possible, on the same evening.

The details of this project were further discussed and all things arranged, subject to Viola's consent, even to the day and the hour.

'This unexpected delay worries me,' said Harry. 'It seems ill-omened.'

'It is not very long,' Sibella answered cheeringly. 'The time will soon pass – sixteen days; why, it is nothing!'

'One does not know what may happen in sixteen days.'

The twilight was creeping round them, the waves beating monotonously on the patient shore. A belated gull floated overhead, uttering its shrill cry. There was an expression of feverish anxiety in Harry's face as he raised his eyes toward the dim outlines of the castle, which the darkness was gradually obliterating.

'Caleb said this morning, that though it may be good to resist evil laws and conventions for the sake of others, the rebel himself inevitably gets trampled on, and generally by those whom he tries to rescue. Are we preparing martyrdom for Viola?'

'Remember what she now suffers,' said Sibella.

'If I but knew what these slow, endless days would bring about!'

'If we knew all that was coming in our life, how many of us would consent to live it out? You will see her this afternoon, remember.'

'If she is not there' –

'I think that she will be there,' said Sibella.

* * * * *

The big stable-yard clock struck four. The appointment was at half-past four. Philip sat in the library writing letters; he had said nothing about intending to go out, and looked as if he had settled down for the afternoon. Viola, like an uneasy spirit, wandered from room to room and from window to window, unable to keep still for a moment. It was a grey afternoon, and a mist was streaming inland from the sea. Maria, purring before the anteroom fire, looked the emblem of placid contentment.

'O Maria! why can't I take things as you do, you sensible animal?'

Maria blinked.

'He has hurt us both, but you blink and purr before the fire, and make the best of things, while I let the thought of it eat into me and drive me mad. Foolish, isn't it, dear? You are a model of what a respectable cat or a wife should be, and the more there are who follow your example the fewer the broken hearts! Wise Maria!'

Viola was down on the hearth-rug with her arm round the sleepy animal, who purred a soft acknowledgment of the attention. A step on the carpet made the cat dart deftly away, to hide behind the sofa – wide awake now and wary.

'I am going out for a short time this afternoon,' said Philip. 'I hope you won't feel lonely in my absence.' This was said with an abundant display of white teeth.

'No, thank you.'

'You had better fill up the tedious interval till my return with a round of calls.'

'I don't think I have any calls to pay.'

'Excuse me; Mrs. Russell Courtenay reproaches you every time we meet her for not having been to see her, and I am sure there is a long-standing debt to Mrs. Pellett. I will order the carriage for you.'

'Oh no, please don't,' said Viola; 'I can get on for another day or two without seeing Mrs. Courtenay or Mrs. Pellett.'

'If you don't care to do it for your own sake, you might remember that your neglect of social duties is a great handicap to me.'

'Some other day I will call,' she said.

'Well, I warn you not to be up to any mischief. You will regret it if you do.' And with that he left her.

Did he know? Viola hastened upstairs for her hat, and on the threshold she encountered Mrs. Barber.

'What do you want?' Viola asked sharply.

'Excuse me, ma'am; only to know if Maria was with you?'

'Yes, of course she was with me; you know she always is at this time. Be kind enough not to intrude on such trifling pretexts another time.'

She evidently was not to be allowed to leave without the housekeeper's knowledge. Would it be wise to go at all? It had now begun to rain heavily; her leaving the house in spite of the bad weather would excite suspicion. Viola weighed the matter in her mind very carefully, and came first to one decision and then to another. Inclination insisted clamorously that the appointment should be kept. She trembled with happiness at the thought of it. But a thousand fears and scruples still pulled the other way. At last she flung them all aside in desperation, and made a firm resolve: come what might, she would go. There was danger and misery in each direction. Boldness might best solve the problem after all. Anyhow she would go. She determined to leave the house by the door of the west wing, as that led on to the terrace and was more secluded. She might thus escape the vigilance of her jailer. She glided down the stairs in her black cloak, ghostly and white with excitement. At the foot stood once more the sentinel of Fate – Mrs. Barber! Viola gave an angry exclamation.

'Going out, ma'am, on such an afternoon! Do you really think, ma'am – excuse the liberty – as it's quite conducive?'

'Be good enough to let me judge for myself,' said Viola, too excited to smile.

'You will at least take an umbrella, then,' said the housekeeper.

Viola accepted the suggestion, and hurried out. Either she must have lost her head in her excitement, or she had, in good earnest, resolved to dare everything and take the consequences, for without finding out whether or not Mrs.

Barber were watching her still, she walked straight towards the appointed spot, in the direction of the coastguard station. It seemed to her, as she moved rapidly across the wet grass, with the rain in her face, that she was being driven by some external power to her fate, and had nothing to do with her own act or its consequences. The downs stretched far away, with their veil of rain drifting with the wind, the sea-sound mourning on for ever. These wild bleak stretches were like the Eternity into which Viola felt that she was hastening; the sense of personal identity half-swallowed up in some larger sense which made her despairingly resigned to whatever might be on its way to her through the mist. Excitement ran so high that it had risen to a sort of unnatural calm; she was in the centre of a cyclone; everything was unreal, vision-like; the whole scene and action appeared as a dream from which she must awake to regain the power of will. As she came in sight of the appointed spot in the hollow of the downs, behind the shelter of a group of furze-bushes, she strained her eyes, in hopes of discerning the expected figure. Expected as it was, however, there was a thrill of joyful and unreasonable surprise on seeing what she looked for. From motives of prudence, Harry did not advance to meet her, but when she came drifting up to him, shadow-like, through the, now driving rain, he held out his arms, without a word or a moment's hesitation, and drew her into his embrace.

At his touch something in her heart seemed to snap; the strain yielded, and she broke into deep convulsive sobs, perfectly silent.

He soothed her, very quietly, very tenderly, saying little, for he saw how overstrained and excited she was. He drew her head down on his shoulder, and made her rest there; Viola absolutely passive, as if she had lost all power of will. The sobs gradually ceased, and she lay resting quietly exactly as he held her, listening still in a dream, to his words of comfort and love and hope. He told her that in a very little while the misery would be over; that for her sake he was ready to face anything; the whole world was before them, and, hard as it was and cruel as it was, his love should stand always between her and the worst that lay in its power against her. Let her only trust to him. He explained the plan which he and Sibella had made, and finally he suggested the day and the hour for the flight.

She lay quite still, listening to him, the tumult and feeling of guilt all gone, and in their place a sense of peace, and of deep, almost fathomless joy.

All around them across the downs the rain was sweeping, the wind rising each moment and lashing the sea into angrier storm. The gloom and passion of day seemed like an echo of their own fate.

'Come what may, these moments have been ours,' he said, looking down into her eyes, which were dark and soft with the ecstasy of self-abandonment. 'You will hesitate no longer?'

'No longer,' she answered. 'When I am with you it seems right and true: the sin of it vanishes. I feel that nothing is of any value without you. I leave behind me no loving heart to be crushed and wounded; with you I fear nothing; for you I would do or risk anything. Are you satisfied now?'

His arms tightened round her and their lips met in a long never-satisfied kiss. At that instant, as if in sympathy, the wind leapt up with a fresh gust and swept furiously over the downs. They could hear, the next minute, the breaking of a gigantic wave against the cliff's foot, the scattering of the spray, and then the hoarse resurgence into the deep. To Viola it all spoke in parables.

'If anything happens to part us' – she said dreamily.

'Don't talk of such a possibility.'

'Still there will always be the memory of to-night; it will be enough for me even – even if we see each other for the last time. It seems now that I have known the supreme earthly joy, and what more can one ask for?'

'That it should not be so fleeting! Viola, you must not speak about seeing each other for the last time; I can't face such a thought. I am greedy for happiness. As for you, you need it as a flower needs sunshine, and I mean that you shall have it!'

Suddenly a human voice rang above the sounds of wind and rain; the dream abruptly ended, and they found themselves confronted by a pair of startled, bewildered blue eyes.

'*Dorothy!*'

The girl turned alternately very red and very white, and began to stammer some confused remarks about coming to call at the castle, – Mrs. Barber had directed her here – she was very sorry – didn't know – couldn't imagine; and then she fairly broke down.

Neither Harry nor Viola looked in the least like a surprised culprit.

'You know our secret,' said Harry; 'what do you mean to do with it?'

Dorothy burst into tears.

Viola stood beside her, looking troubled, but scarcely realising yet what had happened. Strangely enough the idea of the secret being disclosed did not distress her much. She had been so deeply hurt and wounded, so miserable and desperate, that the thought of a public scandal, and even of Philip's vengeance, did not fill her with extreme terror. It was just another misery that would have to be borne. But when it became clear that she had lost Dorothy's friendship, the sorrow began in good earnest. To forfeit the girl's love and respect, to fall from the giddy pinnacle where the little hero-worshipper had placed her, down to the lowest depths of infamy – this was to Viola beyond all comparison more painful than the prospect of the scorn of all the outer world put together. As for poor Dorothy, she was weeping as if her heart would break.

If every human creature, man, woman and child, had accused her idol of this sin, Dorothy would have contemptuously denied and disbelieved the accusation. Viola could do no wrong – and now! – it was unbearable, unbelievable. The storm of tears broke out afresh.

'Have I not warned you, Dorothy? Have I not told you that I was capable of wickedness?'

'This is no wickedness,' interposed Harry.

'And you would not believe me.'

'But I never thought of such a thing as – as this!' she cried tearfully. 'Oh! how *could* you? how *could* you?'

'If you knew our story and understood things a little better,' said Harry, 'you would perhaps come to see that your friend is true to herself in acting in defiance of the world; anyhow it is not for you to reproach her or to judge her.'

Dorothy swung round upon him like a tigress.

'It is you, it is *you*, you wicked, deceitful man! How dare you tempt her to do wrong? I think men are all fiends!' cried the girl, almost choked with her own vehemence. 'It is all your fault; every bit of it. You are a villain – a black-hearted villain! I hate you! I believe you are the devil!'

'Whether or not I am the devil,' said Harry, smiling slightly, 'I certainly am the person to blame in this matter, if blame there be. I should like to know how you intend to use your knowledge of our secret. If you mean to divulge it, it is only fair to prepare us.'

'Oh! let her tell everything!' Viola exclaimed. 'What does it matter? There is no real hope for the future. Let the end come quickly.'

For the first time Dorothy allowed her eyes to rest on her friend's face. 'Do you repent? Are you sorry?' she asked plaintively.

'No,' Viola answered with decision. 'I am glad. You will soon forget me, Dorothy; you will find that after all Mrs. Pellett is a safer person to have to do with, and you will cease to grieve for me.'

'I hate Mrs. Pellett!' cried Dorothy ferociously, 'and I never was so miserable in all my life! – *never*! I wish you were dead – and good – rather than this! Why didn't you die while you were good?'

'Rather, why was I ever born?' cried Viola impetuously. 'What does God want with creatures foredoomed to misfortune, foredoomed to sin, foredoomed to be torn in pieces between faith and doubt, impulse and tyranny, duty and passion? Why does He plant feelings strong as death in our hearts, and then call it sin when we yield to them? Why does He fling wretched, struggling, bewildered creatures into an ocean in full storm, and then punish them fiercely because they don't make way against the tempest? It is cruel, it is absurd, it is unreasonable! He drives His creatures to despair! He asks what is impossible, and He punishes like a fiend. God can never have suffered Himself or He would not be so hard and unmerciful! No one is fit to be God who has not suffered.'

She stopped breathless.

Dorothy, with the tears still glistening in her eyes, was gazing at her friend in alarmed bewilderment. A Vicar's daughter might well tremble at such an outburst! She began, however, to perceive the desperation in Viola's mood – nothing short of it could have driven her to such utterance – and to recognise that there were secrets in her life which had brought her to her present sin and disobedience. She had been sorely beset and tempted. What right had any one to judge? She would repent and return to her duty; she was too sweet and noble to forget it for long. Dorothy felt her heart beginning to overflow again towards her friend.

'Oh! tell me you repent,' she 'said imploringly; 'only tell me you repent.'

'I do not repent,' said Viola, with a sad little headshake.

'Well, I can't help it!' exclaimed Dorothy, going up to her and flinging her arms round her neck. 'Good or bad, right or wrong, I love you, and I can't stop loving you. You are always my dear beautiful one, and I will never desert you, let them say what they will. I will defy them all. If you have done wrong, you are very miserable; and you may be very lonely, and I will always come to you. I don't care!' Dorothy went on, apostrophising an imaginary audience who were remonstrating – 'I don't care; she is more worth loving, sin or no sin, than all the rest of you with your virtues, put together! If Mrs. Pellett says nasty things, I will – I will *trample* upon her,' pursued poor Dorothy, grinding her teeth.

'Oh! my dear, faithful little friend, you don't know what you are saying; we can never see one another again after – after people begin to speak ill of me. They would speak ill of you too if we were ever to meet.'

Her voice trembled, and her kiss was long and tender and sad, as a kiss of farewell in which there is no hope.

Dorothy returned it passionately.

'It is *not* the last; it *shall* not be the last! You will repent and everything will blow over. But if you don't, I shall stick to you and love you always, whatever you may do. Remember that if all the world deserts you, if Mr. Lancaster deserts you, I shall never desert you. Send for me whenever you are sad or lonely and I shall come to you. You don't know me; you don't know how I love you. To-day when I found this out I was so miserable, only because I loved you. But whatever you may do, I shall always love you and be true to you! And this is not good-bye; I won't consent to say that hateful word till we die, and even then I won't believe it is parting for ever. Heaven would be no heaven for me if you were not there! – not with all the harps and the psalms that they could get together! If it's wicked, it's the truth – and I can't help it.'

It was some time before Dorothy calmed down sufficiently to yield to Harry's suggestion that it would be well for her to return home before it became too dark.

The lateness of the hour made Viola give a little start of alarm. She ought to have been home before now. If Philip had returned, the danger of discovery would be increased by the delay.

Viola laid her hand in Harry's in farewell.

He bent down and kissed her, disregarding the presence of Dorothy.

'It is all settled, then,' he said, under his breath. 'You will make no mistake. Wednesday, the 24th, at ten o'clock, at the door of the west wing, unless we send a message through Caleb to announce any alteration of plan. If you should wish to communicate with me, do so also through Caleb. Be brave; almost everything depends upon you. My whole life is now in your hands, as well as your own future.'

He looked white and haggard as he bade her a lingering good-bye, and watched the two figures hurrying side by side across the uplands. He saw them part at about a hundred yards from the castle, Dorothy trending off to the right towards the village.

Viola looked back just before entering the house, and Harry knew that her eyes were straining through the dusk to where he stood; then she turned and passed across the threshold out of his sight.

* * * * *

Viola found tea awaiting her in the anteroom as usual. Maria welcomed her with much purring and arching of the back. On her way downstairs, after changing her wet clothing for something dry, she saw the library-door standing open, and concluded that Philip had not returned. When lie did return he would question her. What answers could she give? She felt a strong inclination to own frankly that she had met Harry. She had once made a declaration of war to Philip and warned him not to trust her. Why might she not say boldly, 'Yes, I have met Harry Lancaster'?

Then came a qualm of fear. Philip had said that if he found it necessary he would not shrink from placing her under lock and key. He would swear that she was mad; he would put her in charge of a keeper; he would do anything, in short, which her conduct made necessary; so lie had plainly told her. Dangerous work indeed to openly defy Philip Dendraith, and not less difficult to defy him in secret.

Half-an-hour later the front-door opened, and closed; Philip entered, and Maria left the room.

Viola felt a thrill go through her from head to foot.

Philip seemed preoccupied. What had Mrs. Lincoln been saying to him, that he, of all people, should become absent-minded? He sat down to the table and poured himself out cup after cup of tea. It had been standing so long that it was black and bitter, but he did not seem to notice it, *connoisseur* though he was.

He roused himself presently, and asked what Viola had been doing all the afternoon.

'I have been out,' she said.

'Calling?' he inquired.

'No; it was settled that I was not to call to-day.'

'Oh! was it?'

'You have been longer than you expected, have you not?' said Viola, with a
glance at his preoccupied face, over which, now and then, a pleased smile flitted.

'Perhaps I have – what's the time? Dear me, six o'clock! I had no idea it was
so late.'

He poured out another cup of tea and drank it off. Then he rose.

'I shall be in the library till dinner,' he said.

Viola could scarcely believe that the dangerous interview had passed off so
easily. At dinner, to her relief, the subject was not resumed. Husband and wife
spent together another of the long gloomy evenings which Viola always so much
dreaded. How many more of them were to come? Exactly sixteen if – Ah! that
terrible 'if.' She paled at the thought of all that it implied.

Facing one another at their solemn dinner-table, waited on by the ever-faith-
ful Cupid, exchanging now and then a few indifferent remarks, they pursued
their own thoughts, and lived their divided lives, while the eyes of fading portraits watched them, always with their look of cynical amusement.

After dinner Viola passed across the echoing hall to the vast drawing-room,
Maria, as usual, gliding in after her. The window was open, and let in the salt
wind from the sea. Gazing out into the darkness, Viola struggled to realise that
her fate was now actually decided; that the crisis of her life was close at hand;
that every detail of conduct and circumstance might at any moment change the
course of the whole future.

Memories of the afternoon jostled one another in her brain. Her heart-beats
quickened at the remembrance of the interview, with all its dream-like joy and
bewilderment. Harry could not complain now of a want of return to his devotion.
Viola did nothing by halves. Once fully roused, her love was strong, passionate
and unchanging. A transitory affection was not in her nature. Whatsoever had
been taken once into her heart was taken into it for ever. The same elements of
character which made her capable on occasion of a fury perfectly blind in its
vehemence, gave her also the capacity for an infinite devotion and for absolute
constancy. Harry had reason to rejoice. Viola was shaken completely out of herself; the magic chord had been struck, and her whole being was set in vibration.
Doubts, hesitations, were swept away; feebler currents daring to approach the
edges of the tempest, were caught and overpowered and utterly destroyed.

The depth and passion and sadness of the sea had perhaps taught their lesson
to the sensitive spirit; there was something in the strength and untameableness

of her emotions, when once excited, that strangely resembled the ocean in its gloomier moods. Her intense love of the sea, whose voice was in her ears day and night, whose every aspect was familiar, could not have played so large a part in her life without leaving an indelible mark upon her character. Her instinctive fatalism might have been the lesson of unresting tides, of the waves, for ever advancing and retreating, blindly obedient, in spite of their resistless power and their vast dominion.

Viola leant out into the darkness and stretched out her arms, as she used to do in childhood, longingly towards the ocean. She was a child again in spirit, in spite of all she had passed through since that midnight years ago, when she sat by the open window peering into the mysteries, and yearning to throw herself down by the water's edge and let the waves come up to her and comfort her. Now she had just the same wild longing to fling herself upon the bosom of the great sea, the same childish belief in the healing-power of that tameless giant in whom might and gentleness were so strangely blended.

And now she was to leave this life-long friend; the hoarse voices of the waves would haunt her dreams no more. Tears of regret came into her eyes. Even this vault-like old house, with its cavernous echoes, its gaunt passages, its unutterable melancholy, had become strangely, almost unwholesomely attractive, as such places will to the spirit that they are destroying. The mere fact that it had been the scene of so much torture, so much struggle and conflict, endowed it with a sort of sinister fascination. Every nook and corner of the house, and outside, every cleft and cranny where the little sea-plants nestled out of the wind's pathway, had burnt into her brain, etching itself thereon with marvellous fidelity through the corroding action of pain. The simplest objects and harmonies became poems and pictures: the curves of the ivy-tendrils that climbed over the palings of the garden, the movement of the seabirds, the quivering of a slender little weed that grew high up among the weather-beaten stonework, in a crevice of its own, solitary, pathetic, a deserted, delicate spirit shivering sensitively when the giant winds came sweeping across the entrance of its tiny sanctuary. If some day the shelter should crumble or be destroyed, if some day the fragile exquisite little plant felt upon it the full blast from the west, would it strengthen in resistance, or would the slender stem snap and the flower be whirled away on the breast of the storm?

Viola's thoughts wandered strangely this evening. Every incident of the afternoon was in her consciousness, while a thousand thoughts and memories danced in will-o'-the wisp fashion hither and thither through her mind.

Suddenly however, with such vividness that she knew she had never realised the idea before, she saw and understood her own position, with all its peril and its possibilities. The awful uncertainty hung like a cloud of terror over her head. Would the plan fail or succeed? If it failed, what then? And if it succeeded, still what then? It was dark and mysterious as this windy night! What lay hidden in the future, divided from her now by only sixteen dawns and sunsets, yet almost as mystically unknown as the realms beyond the grave?

As her eyes continued gazing into the dusk, a strange change seemed to come over the face of the waters, and she felt herself thrill with nameless horror. This great grey tossing ocean appeared to be moving rapidly from west to east in volumes indescribably vast, as if it were being sucked away by some distant whirlpool; and it went sweeping on and on, with dreadful steady swiftness, till of a sudden it came to the edge of a bottomless abyss, into which it rushed headlong with a wild roar, dragging after it the waters from all the seas and all the rivers in the world. And as it fell down and down into the black Infinite, the awful roar gradually died away, and the water fell and fell, in perfect darkness and perfect silence – for ever!

CHAPTER XXXVII

LAST DAYS

'Love not pleasure; love God. This is the everlasting Yea, wherein all contradiction is solved; wherein whoso walks it is well with him.'[28]

Through what freak of memory had these words been stirred up in the mind where they were resting apparently harmless and inactive?

'*This is the everlasting Yea.*'

It was as if a prophet stood in the pathway warning back. No matter! she would go on. Harry was there beckoning; there was a desperate delight in risking all for him. If she had to suffer for it, the suffering would be for him! She *had* loved God once, or she had tried hard to do so, but there was always something unreal about this loving God; Viola did not believe now that she ever *had* actually loved Him after all.

The promises her mother used to speak about had all proved empty and hollow; her own fault, no doubt; but she knew not how to mend it. If she had to be punished for refusing to submit to what was to her beyond endurance, for choosing, in defiance of law, the supreme earthly happiness – well, she must look her fate in the face and accept the inevitable. A woman stands always between the devil and the deep sea. She must make her choice.

> 'I myself am Heav'n and Hell,
> Heav'n but the vision of fulfill'd Desire,
> And Hell the shadow of a soul on fire.'[29]

Viola's belief in Hell was far more absolute than that of many who fancy that they hold the doctrine in all firmness of orthodoxy. She, who had known the atrocious torment of a soul bound close and fast to the Intolerable, had no difficulty in believing in eternal punishment. Had she not herself known the pains of hell in that long torture whose memory clung round her burning and blazing, only to be quenched with the consciousness of personal identity? The dreadful sixteen days were slowly creeping on; but oh how slowly! It rained incessantly – steady drifting rain, sweeping over the grey sea, and beating a perpetual summons on the westward window-panes. The only break to the feverish monotony was a visit from Dorothy, who came to assure Viola once more of her unalterable devotion.

'I warn you again not to believe in me,' said Viola; 'even your faithfulness will falter at what I am capable of.'

Dorothy shook her head.

'I hope you will do nothing dreadful; but if you did, it would make no difference, not even if you murdered a few people!' she added, laughing. 'I should know that they deserved it.'

Once Adrienne and Bob Hunter called when those deliberate sixteen days had marched past to about half their number; eight behind and eight yet to come. Adrienne was absorbed in the wedding preparations, or seemed to be so; Bob evidently proud and happy, and more than ever liable to athletic sports, though he now sometimes stopped abruptly and apologised. Adrienne had apparently been cruel enough to discourage his pirouettes.

'And you won't be late on Friday, will you?' she said in parting; 'and, Viola dear, I am looking forward to having you for a long, long visit as soon as we return home. You will be sure to come, won't you?'

'Oh, you won't care to have me so soon,' said Viola, paling a little.

'Nonsense; that's just what I long for. For one thing, I don't want Bob to get tired of me!'

Bob pirouetted in a manner which expressed remonstrance.

'One of adamant, you fail to appreciate the good taste of him who adores you to distraction.'

'Come away, Bob,' said Adrienne, 'you are beginning to be tiresome again. Now *don't* stand on one toe; you are really too dreadfully like a *première danseuse!*'[30]

Bob, unable to resist the temptation, tripped lightly across the drawing-room, and arrived at the fireplace on tiptoe, with one foot in the air and a most engaging smile irradiating his pale primrose countenance. For this offence he was hurried away amid some laughter by his betrothed.

A couple of days later Bob and Adrienne were standing together before the altar of Upton Church. The bride was calm and quiet, and rather pale; Bob cheery and affable. Viola looked paler than the bride, and her pallor was the more remarkable from the fact that her next neighbour happened to be Dorothy, with her rosy face beaming – like a harvest-moon,[31] said her brothers. Mrs. Dixie, magnificent and gracious, her ancestor still at her throat, presented another extraordinary contrast to Viola, whose white face, framed by the carving of the old oak stalls, had a look of sad aloofness almost unearthly. Harry, lifting his eyes to hers for a moment, read with a pang of bitter pain the story that was written in the face. It was a momentary glimpse into the depths of a soul; a glimpse such as is vouchsafed to us, fortunately perhaps, only at rare intervals. He felt that he had never really understood her grief, her conflict, and all the darkness and lonely horror of her life until this moment. The attitude and the expression told the whole history in a flash. A fierce desire burnt in him to do some bodily injury to Viola's father, who stood, a serene and comfortable wedding-guest, between Mrs. Pellett and Mrs. Russell Courtenay, occasionally whispering pleasantly into the ear of Mrs. Courtenay. Philip, handsome and exquisite, excited in Harry an even greater yearning to inflict a summary punishment. Philip looked deliberately round on one occasion, as if he felt the vengeful impulse directed against him; he gave a cool stare, and just at the end a singular little gleam of a smile which made his adversary feel uncomfortable.

'Till death do us part.'

Philip looked across at his wife. She felt the look, but would not meet it. She knew that it was a taunt, a reminder that she was his till death; that no plots or efforts within her power were sufficient to release her. She knew his delight in making her feel the fruitlessness of resistance. The instinct to torture was strong in the man. He belonged to a type which flourished in appalling perfection at the time of the Italian Renaissance. Possibly it was part of his policy to frighten Viola into a belief in his ability to frustrate any design that she might form. He knew how paralysing to effort is such a belief, and how far more easily his wife would betray her secrets if she were overwhelmed with a baffling conviction that it was useless to try to conceal them.

After the service Mr. Evans mercilessly gave the bride and bridegroom a homily at the altar, in which he enlarged eloquently on the wife's mission, the duty of subordination to her husband and devotion to the sacred cares of home. He spoke of the duty of the husband to cherish and love his wife, to guide, direct, and strengthen her, supplying the qualities which she lacked and making of married life a duet of perfect harmony.

Then came the signing of names, the usual congratulations, and the return to the Cottage before the departure of the wedded pair. The little drawing-room was crowded with guests, Mrs. Dixie doing the honours with indescribable pride and delight. Viola looked round at the familiar faces, feeling that she stood among the actors of her little world for the last time. In the future they would know her no more. Their part in her destiny was over for ever. Before another week had ended she would be on the other side of an impassable gulf, deep and dark as life itself! She sat leaning back, watching the crowd with a strange interest. It

was incredible that what had been planned could come to pass. These wedding
-guests reduced the whole scheme to dreamland; they banished into the vast
realms of Impossibility all things which wandered out of the line of their daily
pathways. One could scarcely look at them and continue to believe. Arabella was
there, stylish and writhing, and Mrs. Pellett still busy making virtue repulsive;
Mr Pellett, dragged to the festivity against his will, looked, in the glare of pub-
licity, as unhappy as an owl at midday. Mrs. Evans was present, and supremely
uncomfortable in that strange assortment of garments wherewith she did heroic
honour to the weddings and garden parties of the Upton world; her husband
indulged in clerical jocularities with some of the livelier members of the party;
while Dick and Geoffrey (who was just home on leave) talked about trout-fish-
ing in a corner.

The last time; the last time!

Dick came up for a talk (the last talk), friendly and frank as usual.

Dorothy was watching Viola with great anxiety. Harry, from motives of
prudence, had held aloof, but the girl was evidently afraid that, sooner or later,
somebody would guess their dreadful secret.

There was no doubt that Arabella still had her suspicions. She talked a great
deal to Harry, and very often about Viola. But Harry might have been discussing
the attractions of the Queen of the Cannibal Islands[32] for all that Arabella could
gather from his replies.

She presently transferred her notice to Philip.

'I always think a wedding is so depressing. Don't you, Mr. Dendraith? I am
sure your sweet wife agrees with me.'

'My wife, I am convinced, agrees with you in everything.'

'Oh! now, Mr. Dendraith, you are too bad; I am sure she regards me as very
frivolous; but about weddings I do think she would support my view.'

'I am sorry to see you so cynical,' said Philip.

'Oh, I am not so much cynical as observant,' Arabella retorted. 'When I look
round among my friends and acquaintances, I cannot find more than one or
two happy marriages in the whole circle. I believe it's because men *will* smoke
so much.'

'The whole secret,' said Philip. 'My wife won't let me smoke more than two
cigars a day.'

'Really! How wise of her, and how nice of you to be so obedient! Men are
generally so very wilful, you know. I shall really have to consult Mrs. Dendraith
about her system of management. You seem to be in perfect order, and yet not
crushed.'

'Not at all crushed,' said Philip. 'My wife says she doesn't like to see a man's
spirit broken.'

Arabella laughed. ('He rules her with a rod of iron,' she said to herself, 'and she lives in deadly fear of him.') 'Oh, Mr. Dendraith, I want you and Mrs. Dendraith to come over to tea with me next Tuesday. There are one or two people coming whom I should like you to meet.'

'Thank you,' Philip answered. 'I should have enjoyed it immensely, but on Tuesday, Wednesday, and Thursday I shall be in town. I have had engagements for some time.'

'Now, I am certain they are of mushroom growth,' cried Arabella;' it is very unkind. You and Mrs. Dendraith never *will* come and see me.'

'I assure you I am speaking the literal truth; you might have known that from my dulness. How can you be so suspicious? Cynical again. Viola, my dear, Mrs. Courtenay declares that I am manufacturing engagements. Can't you testify to the antiquity of my appointments for Tuesday and Wednesday of next week?'

Viola confirmed her husband's statement.

Well, I suppose I must forgive you, if that's the case; but it's very tiresome of you. I am glad to find you tell your wife of all your engagements: without, as you say, breaking your spirit, she is evidently very firm with you.'

'She is,' said Philip; 'but I know it is for my good.'

The bride now began to bid farewell to her fiends before departing in her ladylike grey dress which every one said was so becoming. She behaved with great self-possession, though one could see that she was moved. Mrs. Dixie folded her in a vast embrace, from which Adrienne emerged rather less exquisitely smooth than when she entered, leaving her mother weeping with great assiduity and much lace pocket-handkerchief. They were genuine tears that she shed, although this was one of the happiest days of her life!

When the bride came to Viola she gave her a long heart-felt kiss.

'Be brave and true to yourself, dear,' she whispered.

'Good-bye, good-bye!' Viola returned.

'We shall soon meet again,' said Adrienne, with a cheerful nod, passing on to Dorothy.

'Good-bye,' repeated Viola.

In how short a time was Adrienne to look back at that parting with a shudder of disgust; in how short a time was the memory that once she had called Viola Dendraith friend to be thrust aside, whenever it intruded, with horror and dismay! A life of smooth prosperity and domestic contentment was the reward of Adrienne's action at this crisis of her career, and every day of her well-appointed existence sent her drifting farther in spirit from the tortured, desperate, bewildered creature whose straying footsteps she had so earnestly sought to guide in straighter pathways, whose faults she had so conscientiously striven to correct. Adrienne had the consoling thought that she had, at any rate, done her best to save her erring friend from the abyss of guilt and ruin towards which she had been drifting.

After the departure of the bride and bridegroom the guests began to leave. Dorothy came up to Viola and folded her in a Herculean[33] embrace.

'You are worth all the rest of them put together!' she exclaimed. 'I have been watching them and all their airs and graces.' Dorothy gave a gesture of contempt. 'They look so silly!' she said, with severe energy. 'They mince and wriggle, and snip and sniggle, and go on like marionettes who have got wires where their souls ought to be! And you! – you seem like a beautiful calm statue among all these fidgeting dolls!'

'O Dorothy, you *are* extravagant!' Viola exclaimed, with a sad little smile.

'No, I am only telling the exact truth,' said Dorothy.

'Are you coming, dear?' her mother called to her.

Mrs. Evans shook hands with Viola, and said she hoped that she would come and see them soon at the Rectory; it was so long since she had been there. Then she passed on to collect the rest of her daughters.

'Good-bye,' said Dorothy, with another fervent embrace. 'You won't do anything dreadful, will you?' she whispered pleadingly. 'Please, please don't. But if you do it will make no difference. I shall love you always.'

'Dear Dorothy, you must – Ah! good-bye, and go,' cried Viola, with a break in her voice, as she kissed the girl and thrust her hastily away, for she felt her self-command begin to fail.

Dorothy gave a parting look and smile and followed her mother from the room. And in a few days even that loving and faithful heart had turned against the miserable woman who now watched her depart, knowing that they had met for the last time, and that love itself would presently stand back and pass by on the other side. The time was at hand when Dorothy would tear the memory of her idol from her heart with horror and anguish. The time was at hand when she would catch her breath at the mention of Viola's name, turning aside in miserable silence as it was tossed about from mouth to mouth with insult and execration.

Suddenly, as Viola remained with her eyes fixed on the spot where she had seen Dorothy for the last time, that strange image of hastening waters appeared again before her mind's eye, almost as vividly as when she had stood at the window looking out to sea. Again there was the mysterious stir; again the whole ocean seemed to be drawn away and away from west to east, towards a bottomless gulf, which was drinking up all the seas and rivers, sucking in, attracting, constraining, for ever insatiable and for ever empty. With awful tumult and distraction, the waters rushed to their doom, boiling, seething, rebelling in vain against the power that drew them with ever accelerating speed, onwards to the inevitable verge. And then once more, with a bound like that of some wild creature hunted to his death, they leapt over the brink, pouring down and down and down, in one smooth mighty stream, into the infinite darkness and infinite silence for ever.

Viola awoke with a sudden bewildered start, to find Geoffrey standing before her laughing.

'What's the matter, Ila?' he asked. 'Are you walking in your sleep? I have asked you a question three times, and you only stared at me with no speculation in your eye. I suppose a wedding *is* a thought-provoking sort of affair to the married.'

Geoffrey had by this time fortunately got over his passion for Adrienne, and transferred his affections to Dorothy Evans.

'You will come and see me, Geoffrey,' said Viola when, after some further conversation, he said that he must be going.

'Oh yes, of course, – in a day or two. The uncle has offered me some fishing at Clevedon, so I shan't be able to come till Tuesday or Wednesday. When I do I should like to stay the night.'

'Do come on Tuesday, then. I want *very* much to see you.'

'Why, my dear, of course I shall come as soon as I can. I thought I might perhaps have had an invitation to spend part of my leave with you. I don't wish to push myself – always was retiring. I've got a lot of things I want to talk to you about, Ila,' he went on more seriously. 'I have been reading Carlyle, and, by Jove' – well we'll talk it over later on. Good-bye just now. The governor's going. I shall probably call on Wednesday. Tuesday's rather busy.'

'Oh! do come on Tuesday,' said Viola, glancing swiftly round to make sure that Philip was out of earshot.

'Why do you so particularly want me to come on Tuesday?' asked Geoffrey.

'I would still rather you came to-morrow or on Monday.'

'Well, if you're so set upon it, I will try and turn up on one day or the other. Mustn't come on Wednesday on any consideration evidently. Something up on Wednesday. Well, I hope it will go off well and be a grand success. My blessing on you. Good-bye.'

Viola wished that Geoffrey's voice were not so exceedingly sonorous and hearty. Yet surely Philip could not have heard what he said from the other end of the room, through the hubbub of talk and laughter. The incident nevertheless made her feel uneasy.

'Now, Viola,' said her aunt, coming up and touching her on the shoulder, 'why have you never said a word to me all day? You haven't been to see me for three weeks, and now you have a chance of explaining yourself you neglect it. Well, how are you, and what have you been doing, and what are you going to do? You look pale, my dear. You shut yourself up in that old house and get dull. Now you must really come and see me. I have a friend I want you to know – Arabella's sister, Mabel Turner, but not so foolish as Arabella; one family can't be expected to produce two masterpieces. She is a great horsewoman, ready for anything. She is coming on Wednesday evening, and you must drive over in time for tea and stay the night.'

'I fear, Aunt Augusta, I can't do that,' cried Viola. 'I' –

'Now, my dear, I take no refusal,' said Lady Clevedon; 'you are getting into stay-at-home ways that are exceedingly bad for you. I simply insist upon your coming to me on Wednesday; so say no more about it.'

'But, Aunt Augusta, it is impossible.'

'Oh! stuff and nonsense; you have nothing in the world to do. Why can't you come?'

Viola shook her head and tried to turn the subject.

'Now, no more nonsense; you have got to do as you are told. Women are nothing if not obedient. I shall expect you on Wednesday not later than five o'clock. Now, good-bye, my dear.'

'Good-bye, Aunt Augusta,' Viola said, with a slight unintentional stress on the word. Every parting to-day had for her the sad solemnity of a last farewell.

Her aunt laughed. 'One would fancy that Viola was going to mount the scaffold to-morrow,' she said.

Before leaving, Lady Clevedon spoke to Philip about his wife's growing dislike to mingling with her fellow-creatures.

'It is really very bad for her, and you ought to check it. I wanted her to come to tea with me next week, but she says it is impossible, which (like a problem in Euclid)[34] is absurd. What can be her reason?'

'She may have Dorothy Evans with her, perhaps, next week, as I am to be away,' said Philip.

'As if she couldn't bring the girl! Tell Viola that I shall expect them both.'

Philip delivered the message when he and his wife were driving home across the downs.

'I suppose you will go,' he said indifferently.

'I decided not to do so,' Viola replied.

'Do you intend never to go anywhere again?'

'Oh no.'

'Then why will you not go to your aunt's?'

'Why, after all, should I go? The people there are all so lively and untiring; they oppress me. I am not meant for society.'

'I wonder what you *are* meant for.'

'A target for other people's wit and other people's cruelty.'

'A target that retorts is a novelty,' said Philip. 'A target has, or ought to have, the Christian's virtue; it turneth the other cheek also.'

They drove for the rest of the way home in almost complete silence.

The evening closed in with recurring rain which beat upon the windows of the house with mournful persistence for many stormy hours.

Viola sat by the big fireplace, a book, for appearance's sake in her lap, looking into the fire and thinking, thinking. And outside, the grey sea beat for ever upon the beach. There was no escaping from its voice. It was like a full-toned chorus to the drama of human life, mournful and prophetic.

Poor Adrienne! what were the waves foretelling for her? Would she have to grieve and suffer, or would she settle quietly down to her lot and forget how all the new ease and rest from biting anxiety had been purchased? It was not for herself, it was for her mother's happiness and peace of mind that she had consented. Would that console her? 'Every woman has her price,' Philip had said. Adrienne's price had been found and paid.

On Sunday morning Geoffrey appeared. 'You see I have come to-day,' he said, 'since you are having high-jinks on Wednesday, to which only the very select are invited. Philip says you aren't going to church, so let us have a talk.' Bringing out a tattered volume of Carlyle,[35] he opened it on his knee, drawing up his chair before the fire. He wanted to know what Viola thought of a celebrated passage in *Sartor Resartus* which he read aloud: "'Foolish Soul! What act of Legislature was there that *thou* shouldst be Happy? A little while ago thou hadst no right to *be* at all. What if thou wert born and predestined not to be Happy, but to be Unhappy! Art thou nothing other than a vulture, then, that fliest through the Universe, seeking after somewhat to *eat*, and shrieking dolefully because carrion enough is not given thee? There is in Man a Higher than Love of Happiness; he can do without Happiness, and instead thereby find Blessedness." Is all that true, do you think?' the young man asked wistfully.

'This,' said Viola, 'is really our mother's teaching in other words: that we ought to submit to what is sent us to bear, and to aim at something higher than happiness.'

'What is Blessedness, do you suppose?' Geoffrey inquired. 'Can't remember that I ever came across it. Don't know what to make of the passage. Ought we to try to be blessed, and never mind about being happy all our lives? And, Viola, how do you suppose one can set about being blessed? I don't know, for the life of me; and yet it seems as if that doctrine led one on to a high mountain and gave one a grander view of things. I don't know how to express it, of course, but you know what I mean.'

Viola looked very thoughtful as she sat gazing into the fire. Was it Fate that had sent her this second message from the great apostle of endurance and heroism?

'Love not pleasure; love God.' That was the first message. And now came this second one, 'Why shouldst thou be happy?' Were Harry and Sibella mistaken after all? Was it nobler to cast happiness to the winds – accepting the fact that

there is indeed no reason why one *should* be happy – than to rebel against circumstances divinely ordered, against the teaching of one's childhood, against the
laws of society and of the mighty past?

Viola was always open to teaching of this character; long years had worn a
groove in her mind where such thoughts flowed smoothly and familiarly. She
was haunted and troubled by them long after Geoffrey had gone. The ideas on
which she had resolved to act were not originally her own; she had not evolved
them for herself, she had not built them up from observation and thought, from
assimilation of the thoughts of others that were ready to mix with and fructify
her own. The ideas were in her mind still as things separate and distinct; they
had no long-tried supports to uphold them; they were isolated and unnourished.
Such are not the strong buttressed ideas to inspire bold and consistent action.
They may dissipate at any moment, and leave the actor lost and desperate, without light or motive, the slave of every impulse, of every turn of event.

The turn of event which helped to decide Viola's fate at this crisis was the
conduct of her husband. Philip was not a patient man, nor a forgiving one.
Viola's behaviour had exasperated him beyond all bounds, and he showed his
resentment by a system of subtle and refined torture, by playing upon his wife's
sensitiveness in a manner as ingenious as it was terrible. Every day the rack was
screwed tighter, till human endurance could do no more. Viola, whose power
of projecting herself into another mind was limited strictly to cases where the
mind somewhat resembled her own, had never realised how intensely annoy-
ing to Philip her conduct had been; she failed to understand that any conduct
on her part could seriously affect one so cold and strong and self-sufficient as
her husband. His contemptuous manner, his apparent determination to humble
and humiliate her at every turn and by every device, caused her to imagine that
she was powerless to make him wince in return. Had she known that under the
repeated evidences of her aversion he was suffering as keenly as a man of his
type is capable of suffering, it is possible that the history of her life might have
had a different ending. But she did not know, and the drama played itself out
inexorably.

Philip's studied insolence and insults after Geoffrey left – indeed before he
left – put to flight all effects of reading 'Sartor Resartus.' There might be something higher than happiness, but it was not to be attained under the same roof
with Philip Dendraith; it was not to be obtained by a woman, who for the sake
of food and house-room and social consideration remained his wife: unhappiness one could endure, but degradation and indignity never! Women in the
past had thought it no crime to take their own lives rather than submit to that.
Perhaps they were wrong, but Viola's heart leapt up in sympathy towards them.
They were her true sisters, in spite of all the years that raised a host of shadows
between them. She understood their desperation; she knew how their hearts

had burnt and blazed within them, how death to them had seemed the sweetest thing in all the world!

'Why shouldst thou be happy?' Perhaps there was no good reason. But 'Why shouldst thou live to be tortured and insulted?' Was there any better reason for *that?*

CHAPTER XXXVIII

DARKNESS

During these last slowly moving days Maria followed her mistress everywhere. She would scarcely allow her out of her sight. Perhaps Viola's restlessness may have warned this terribly intelligent animal that something unusual was in the air. The creature seemed to be striving, in her own eloquent fashion, to comfort her mistress and to assure her that under whatever vicissitudes of fortune, she might confidently count upon the support of her dumb and faithful friend.

'Ah! what shall I do without you, my dear?' Viola used to ask sorrowfully. 'If I could but take you with me!' –

Still the wild weather continued, rain and wind beating up from the south-west. There were rumours of wrecks along the coast, and at Shepherd's Nook the lifeboat had gone out to save the crew of a sinking vessel.

If on Wednesday it were still so stormy, how would they be able to effect their escape by sea? Well, no doubt Harry had thought of that, and would have some other plan. It was useless for Viola to trouble about details.

Monday was still stormy, though there were gleams of tearful sunshine light-ing up in patches an agitated sea.

'If this rain lasts,' said Philip, 'I think I shall give up my visit to London.'

Viola's face was half-turned from him, but he saw the colour rush into her cheeks.

'I can postpone it till next week if necessary. It will depend on the weather.'

Bright sunshine on Tuesday morning decided the question, however. Viola stood on the doorstep watching the phaeton which took Philip to the station growing smaller and smaller, till at last it disappeared in the distance of the sunlit downs. If all went according to plan, she had seen her husband for the last time! There was not one memory in the whole of her married life to make her think of that with compunction or regret! She stood there in the sunshine, with the wind playing round her, long after Philip was out of sight. When she did move, it was not to return to the house, but to wander out into the sunlit garden by the beautiful terraces, where the tendrils of the creepers were nodding and sway-ing, and the rain-sprinkled cobwebs fringed the pathway with brilliants. Maria was following, daintily picking her steps along the wet paths, nimbly springing on and off the parapet as her mistress strolled slowly, thoughtfully among the flowers. Only for short intervals during the whole of this day did Viola remain within-doors. In the morning she drove to the Manor-House, to pay the old place and its inhabitants a farewell visit. It was looking its serenest and sweetest. Terrible was the ache at her heart as she strolled once more round the familiar gardens, passed once more through the old rooms, where every nook and corner had vivid associations, where everything spoke of the dead woman who had borne so much and sacrificed so much, and all in vain. What would the mother think of her daughter *now* if she knew? Well, if she knew in good earnest, – not as a limited creature knows, who has only one or two little strings in his nature that vibrate responsively, but as a liberated spirit might be supposed to know, who overlooks the whole field of human emotion, – then Viola thought that her mother would not utterly condemn her.

No nook or corner was left unvisited to-day. Viola bade farewell to all her old friends: Thomas and the under-gardener, and, most heart-breaking of all, to old William whose eyes filled with tears at her words, and perhaps still more at the tone of reverent affection in which they were uttered.

'It always does me good to see you, Miss – Mum, as I should say! There, I don't believe as there's many like you, more's the pity; – the old place ain't been itself since you left. And never will be. God bless you!'

Viola turned away with tears in her eyes. Within the next few days would he recall his blessing? Would he be against her also? He could not know the how or the why and the impossibility of it all! Would he then take the usual simple course and condemn because he could not understand? Perhaps not. There was something large and generous in the tender old heart; though he might grieve and marvel and shake his head, yet perhaps he would not judge; he would simply leave the matter alone and go his own quiet way, reviling not, but trusting.

Another trying farewell was with Geoffrey, though, like so many pitiful things, it had its comic side. The young fellow was in one of his wildest moods; jovial, hearty, full of life, hope, and spirit. Utterly unconscious, of course, of what was impending, his 'Good-bye' was of the most commonplace description. He said that he was coming over to see his sister on Thursday, – not to-morrow, oh no; he remembered the mysterious high-jinks appertaining to Wednesday, and tactfully forbore to intrude. But on Thursday, when the excitement of the high-jinks had died away, he should claim a little sisterly attention while he a tale unfolded.[36] Geoffrey handed her into the phaeton with a fraternal nod of farewell, but Viola put her arms round his neck and kissed him.

'Geoffrey, dear,' she said, 'we have always been good friends, haven't we?'

'Why, yes, of course, we have,' Geoffrey returned, in astonishment. 'Who said we haven't? Because if you'll show me the fellow I'll knock him down.'

'Oh! I don't want you to knock any one down,' said Viola, with a sad little laugh; 'I want you only to remember always what good friends we have been and how fond I was of you, and always shall be. And – and think as kindly of me as you can. Good-bye.'

She kissed him again, and then before Geoffrey recovered from his astonishment the phaeton was half-way down the avenue.

Towards evening the weather showed ominous signs of a change for the worse. Black clouds were gathering over the sea, and the wind had a sound which the coastguard people knew so well betokened storm.

All promises were fulfilled. This last sleepless night in the gloomy home was wildly tempestuous. Viola, with every nerve on the stretch, shivering from head to foot, lay counting the hours as they were deliberately tolled out by the great courtyard-clock. She paced up and down her room, when it became impossible any longer to remain still, listening to the familiar sounds of the storm. The night wore itself out; but the rain and wind had only slightly abated by the morning.

Perhaps it was Viola's excited fancy that made her think that Mrs. Barber was more watchful than usual to-day. There was no evading her – or so it seemed. The talent which that respectable person displayed in finding excuses for her presence was as astounding as her admirable acting – if acting it were.

Viola was anxiously on the alert all the morning in case any message should come from Harry. Regardless of Mrs. Barber, she braved wind and rain, and went to the ruin, so that in case Caleb had any note for her, he might deliver it without difficulty. But Caleb was purely and freezingly philosophic this morning; he was absorbed in the Absolute, and had nothing to say on any other subject, unless it were a word or two on the Infinite. A stranger conveyer of a secret correspondence can scarcely be imagined. He appeared to have no curiosity on the subject whatever. For all one could tell, the philosopher may have thought that he was carrying letters on the subject of the differential calculus.[37] The day wore on, but no message came; the plan was evidently to be carried out as arranged.

The hours were like so many grievous burdens, heavy to endure; but they stole gradually away, the clocks announcing, with what seemed unusual emphasis, the passing of them one by one into eternity. The solitary evening meal was over, and darkness had descended upon land and sea. Viola decided to make herself ready to start, having hat and cloak downstairs, so that in a second she could fling them on and go. It would be well not to leave a moment too soon, because of Mrs. Barber. The moon was rising, but there was fear that the clouds might obscure its light at the critical moment. One thing must be done before leaving, and that was, to take her treasures from the oak cabinet in the west wing: Harry's gift and his letters. She had not dared to take these things before, for fear of Philip's discovering and confiscating them. Once possessed of these, she would hasten down the stairs to the door of the west wing leading on to the terrace, where Harry would be awaiting her.

Again and again Viola found herself overwhelmed with unbelief in the reality of the events which were passing panorama-like before her. It *could* not be true; it *must* be a gigantic and terrible dream. Presently she would awake and find herself going through the daily routine exactly as before, without hope of release. The hours were drifting on, the throbbing moments passing, passing, till the appointed time began to draw near. Maria was on the hearthrug purring softly. Viola stooped down and lifted the creature in her arms.

'Good-bye, you dear and faithful one, good-bye,' she said, burying her face in the soft fur and laying her cheek against it caressingly.

As she stood there with the animal lying in her arms, the door opened softly behind her very slightly, and then closed again as softly. No one entered, and Viola remained unaware of what had occurred. She glanced at the clock.

'I must go,' she said, giving the cat a last caress and laying her down again before the fire. Putting on her hat and cloak, she opened the door carefully, looked up and down the passage, and then hurried along past the cynical portraits in the hall, to the door leading to the west wing. Once on the other side of that, she breathed more freely. She hesitated for a moment, and then taking the key from the hall-side of the door, she locked it on the inner side and put the key in her pocket. At least she would be secure from Mrs. Barber's espionage. She had exactly five minutes to get her treasures and be at the terrace-door to meet Harry as appointed.

A gust of air greeted her as she entered the room. The storm apparently had blown in one of the lozenge windowpanes. Viola felt a superstitious thrill of fear, as if the gust had been a warning to her not to cross the threshold. But at the same moment she knew that no warning could retard her now, not even that too familiar moan in the sound of the sea. She advanced towards the cabinet, opened it, and took out the packet of letters and Harry's wedding-gift with trembling fingers. The light of the moon was sufficient to enable her to see what she was doing. She consulted her watch, longing feverishly for the end of this lonely suspense, longing to get once for all beyond the spell-like influence of the house, where she seemed to feel Philip's presence in the very air.

She put the letters in her pocket and took the knife from its hiding-place. How to carry it? She thought for a moment; and then thrust it into the coils of her hair, drawing the hair over it so that the sinister little weapon was almost concealed. She was hurrying towards the door, wondering if it could be possible that she would get safely away, when the doubt was horribly answered; for out of the darkness a tall familiar form emerged, and without apparent interval, her wrist was gripped by a hand, powerful and merciless. She uttered a stifled shriek, and then a low moan of despair.

'Very well planned for a beginner, my dear; shows a real bent in that direction, which if followed might lead to superior results. One would never suspect you of such things; therein lies your advantage.'

Philip still held her wrist between his fingers, which were closed upon it as a vice. The two stood confronting one another thus, Viola white as death, with the hard, set look of a determined and a desperate woman. Philip, with a smile on his face, prepared to enjoy himself.

'Pardon my detaining you,' he said, 'especially as you are keeping Mr. Lancaster waiting out in the cold on a stormy night like this; it seems inconsiderate. But you can lay the blame on me; say it was entirely my fault, and that I humbly apologise for any inconvenience I may have caused him.'

Viola made an effort to free her wrist, but the hard fingers closed round it more tightly.

'Not just yet, if you please; I have so much to talk about. This little plan of yours – I must really repeat my congratulations. I have watched it through all its incipient stages with unbounded interest. A plan like that is born, not made.'

He released her hand, but placed himself with his back to the door, so that she still remained his prisoner.

Viola's eyes were wild and desperate.

'What are you going to do?' she asked. 'What punishment have you in store for me?'

'Punishment! How can you talk of punishment – one who adores you' –

The smile with which he said it, of mockery, triumph, and conscious possession, made the blood mount impetuously to her very temples.

She looked round wildly for a means of escape. The window?

'Fifty feet from the ground, my love; and although no doubt adoring arms would be ready to receive you when you reached *terra firma*,[38] still I should not advise the attempt even in the cause of virtue.'

'Can't you say what you mean to do at once, without all these taunts? Surely the fact of your victory is enough for you.'

'Certainly; but your curiosity as regards the future seems a little morbid. However, I shall be happy to gratify it. During my visit to town I have secured the services of a most superior person, who will henceforth be always your cheerful and instructive companion. I hope sincerely that you will agree well with her, as the arrangement is permanent. All preliminaries are now settled, and the superior person will enter upon her duties to-morrow. You ask, perhaps, why I returned to-day instead of to-morrow, as arranged. Simply because I had my reasons for thinking that something was going on. I really am not in a position to afford to lose you thus prematurely. You see, my dear, you are an article of 'vertu'[39] which cannot be easily renewed, a luxury that a man can't afford to repeat too frequently. In point of fact, my dear, if you will excuse my mentioning it, you come rather expensive. The original consideration was heavy, but that would have been nothing had it stopped there. The truth is, however, that your amiable father still applies to me for money to get him out of disgraceful difficulties, and for the sake of avoiding a family scandal I allow myself to be thus bled with a sweetness of temper which borders on weakness. The outlay appears especially ruinous from the fact that still I am disappointed of an heir, a matter to me of serious moment. All things considered, therefore, my love, you will admit that you have been somewhat of the nature of a sell, and you will pardon my endeavouring to prevent your bringing the matter to a climax by disgracing yourself and me in this spirited manner. It will not do, believe me; and you must really oblige me by banishing the idea from your mind as an impossibility. I think you will have no difficulty in accomplishing this when you receive the able help of my superior person. After her advent I shall be able to leave you with every confidence and perfect peace of mind. This Pillar of Strength[40] has been accustomed to the care of what are pleasingly termed *mental cases*, and she is therefore as keen and quick as a detective. Charming and most clever is my superior person. I long to introduce her to you. I know you will love her.'

'Is your cruelty not satiated yet?' asked Viola at length. 'Will you not end this interview and let me go out of your sight? If I am to be a prisoner, show me my dungeon and leave me in peace. Only let me go. I can bear no more.'

Philip took a catlike step nearer to her.

'*Dungeon* is an ugly word, my dear; besides, I am far too anxious and devoted to let you out of my sight. No, no; husband and wife are one; there must be no separation. Now you will come with me, my love, not to your dungeon; far from it.'

He was looking into her face with a keen, vengeful enjoyment of her torture. Her shrinking movement and low cry seemed to rouse his worst instincts.

'Ah! you may shrink, my dear, but shrinking will not help you. What does it matter to me? You have got to learn once for all to whom you belong. I am not a man to be trifled with, believe me. What is mine is mine. You were about to make a vast mistake on that interesting point, which I am happily in time to rectify. Now is the moment for an impressive lesson, for there must really be no uncertainty in these matters. I am deeply grieved to keep our friend out in the rain all this time, but really, considering the circumstances, I think he can hardly be surprised. A fond husband parted for two days from his wife!' – He smiled in a particular way that always maddened her as he advanced quickly and took her in his arms, bending down to kiss her as she struggled violently to free herself.

'It's no use struggling, my dear,' he said, 'for I am considerably stronger than you are, and I intend to stand no nonsense. If it pleases me to kiss you, I shall kiss you. It is my right, gainsay it if you can. I am resolved that you shall understand. You are behaving as a fool, or as a spoilt child, and must be treated as such.'

Overcoming her frantic resistance, he kissed her long and steadily on the lips, partly because it pleased him to do so, partly it seemed, because it tortured her. Then he let her go.

She stood before him mad with fury, and for the moment literally speechless.

'Oh! I could tear myself to pieces,' she said wildly.

Philip looked at her and smiled. It was a game of cat and mouse.

'A very pretty and becoming little passion, my dear, which I must quench with kisses. You really can't call me a tyrant, when that is my only form of chastisement. Kisses till you are subdued.' He laughed at her desperation, as he advanced once more to inflict the tender punishment (as he called it).

She darted to the window and tried to tear it open, but he followed her, laying his hand upon her arm.

'Couldn't have a suicide in the family on any account, nor can I permit you to summon your lover to the rescue. Really your impetuosity is becoming dangerous. My superior person must hasten. Meanwhile I will cherish you under my own wing, enjoying all the lovely changes of your April moods. What! not subdued yet? More kisses required' –

'Oh! do you want to drive me mad?' cried Viola hoarsely, standing at bay, with her hand on the casement, leaning backwards away from Philip's arm.

'I am inconsiderate,' he said, 'to keep you parleying here at this time of the night; I will take you to your room. (Oh no, I can't trust you to go alone). Come with me. As I explained before, I am too affectionately anxious about you to let you out of my sight. And then my mood is tender – in spite of a slight coldness on your part, which I am always in hopes that my persistent devotion will be able to overcome. Allow me.'

He put his arm round her to lead her away.

'Don't touch me, don't touch me, I tell you, or I shall go raving mad!'

'I fear that I should be unable to detect the moment of transition,' said Philip, calmly persevering.

He stopped abruptly to examine something. 'Ah! what's this glittering bauble in your hair? This must come out, and at once.'

'Don't touch it!' cried Viola, and her hand was on the hilt of the knife almost at the same instant that Philip's words were uttered. She drew it out and held it behind her defiantly.

'Is the toy so precious? A dangerous plaything, and most unsuitable in the hands of a refractory pupil, undergoing much-needed instruction in the nature and duties of wifehood. Come now, give it up quietly; it will be far better for you in the end. We must have no violence, if we can possibly avoid it; that sort of thing really is very bad form, and you know my horror of bad form.'

He held out his hand for the weapon.

'Don't oblige me to take it from you by force. You must try to realise the situation. If I could make you understand, that somehow or another, by fair means or by foul, I intend to reduce you to submission and that *immediately*, you would save yourself and me a lot of fruitless trouble. Your conduct throughout our married life has been simply intolerable, and we must have an end of it. Women can't be reasoned with; they can only be governed autocratically. You have confirmed my opinion on that subject. Sheer will-force is the only argument that goes home to them. Now then, we understand each other. Give me that offensive weapon and come with me. I have been long enough in this musty and extremely depressing old room, where the family have died for generations; one can sniff death in the very air. Come with me. Let's have no more nonsense to-night. I have no doubt by this time our friend has become tired of waiting, and returned wiser and sadder to his fireside – perhaps also rather damper. But his mother, we all know, is thoughtful about gruel and a hot bath in such cases, so there is really no cause for compunction on your part. You did your best; he could not ask more. Come with me.'

'I will not come with you; I will not pass another night under your roof, though I die for it,' said Viola.

'And how are you going to avoid it, my dear?' asked Philip. 'The woman doesn't know when she is beaten! What power on earth can protect you now against me? You yourself have locked the door leading to the house, and cut yourself off from chance interposition. Besides, who would help a wife against her husband?'

She kept her eyes fixed upon him, watching every movement, desperate and defiant. He moved close up to her to take possession of the knife and to lead her away.

'Don't touch me, don't touch me, or' –

The rest of the sentence was lost in a sound of loathing and horror, for Philip had disobeyed her. Advancing till she was driven against the corner of the window and there was no possible loophole of escape, he took her in his arms deliberately.

'Don't make a fool of yourself,' he said; 'do what you are told. Give me that weapon at once.'

His touch, constraining, insolent as it was, forcing her in spite of all her resistance towards the door, excited her to very madness. He laughed, and bent down till his lips touched her cheek; his hand was seeking hers to seize the knife, while at the same time he was still drawing her away with him, steadily, resistlessly. He bent yet closer, and said something in her ear in a whisper, with an insulting laugh. Then in an instant – a horrible instant of blinding passion – the steel had flashed through the air with a force born of the wildest fury – there was a cry, a curse, a groan, a backward stagger, and Philip lay at his wife's feet mortally wounded. For a second – but ah! how interminable was that second! – there was silence within that chamber of death. The everlasting boom of the waves, with their moan and lamentation, sounded loudly outside – the distant chant of many voices mourning.

'May you be damned!'

Philip gave a groan and tried to raise himself on his arm, but fell back helpless. He tried again, with a fiercer effort, and a smaller success. The blood was flowing fast from the wound. His eyes were blazing with fury and hatred indescribable. He gathered his forces for a dying curse.

'May the gallows spare you for a more hideous fate; may you suffer all that your soul most abhors; may you be the tool and chattel and plaything of men, may they drag you to the lowest depths of humiliation; may indignity be heaped on indignity; may you be outcast, homeless, praying for death; may the pride of your soul be withered and utterly rooted out; may you die deserted in shame and misery; may your soul be damned for all eternity! The curse of the dying is said to avail much. May this curse stick to you and drag you down to hell, *Murderess!*'

His voice gave way and he sank back panting.

Almost at the same instant a man's step was heard in the passage outside. With a look of fury the wounded man struggled up for the last time, tried to utter some words – evidently of unspeakable passion – and fell back never to stir again. The footsteps stopped outside the door, which was thrown back upon its hinges, and Harry Lancaster entered the room. He paused abruptly, and there was a moment of dead silence. Viola was standing with head held high, the knife still in her hand, and in her eyes was a look that made the very heart stop beating. At her feet lay a human form, perfectly still, the white face upturned, one hand with the thumb pressed inwards conspicuous in the moonlight, which was tracing the outlines of the lozenge panes delicately upon the polished floor. Beside the prostrate figure was something glistening, something –

'Good God, what is it! What have you done?'

'Come and see,' she answered, with a wild sort of exultation. She went to him, put her arm in his, and drew him eagerly forward. It was a ghastly moment for him!

'You see I have killed him with this knife.' She held it aloft, and then threw it on the floor.

'Oh! you are mad!' he exclaimed. '*You* have not done this! Let me look at you.'

He turned her facing the full moonlight, and scanned the haggard features with an awful dread in his heart; yet almost a hope, so desperate was the crisis.

'Are you mad? Oh! tell me, are you mad, you poor tortured child?' he groaned.

'Mad? Oh no. I meant to do it. I knew it would kill him – I would do it again, I would do it again!' she cried in wild excitement. 'I leave a life behind me so loathsome, so intolerable – Yes,' she broke off fiercely, 'I would do it again.'

'Oh! spare yourself! Have mercy on yourself.'

'But it is true; it is the only thing that I can bear to let my thoughts rest upon, the only spot in my black life that is not black to me.'

She held out her right hand and looked at it, moving it in the moonlight.

'Call me guilty; it is sweet to me – sweet and clean and wholesome! I am guilty; I have murdered him.'

She drew an ecstatic breath.

Harry looked at her aghast. Say what she might, she was mad.

'His blood seems to wash away some of the blackness, the hideousness of the past – if that could be – but oh, no, no!' – (she thrust out her hands, shrinking back) – 'nothing can do that; there are no words for it; – the horror is in my heart, and it burns there; it burns – it will never cease burning – never, never!'

She flung her arms over her head, and then sank cowering to the floor, leaning against the wall beneath the window, and always shrinking, shrinking, as if in a helpless effort to escape from herself. Harry gave a gesture of despair. The horror of the situation became more and more appalling the longer he thought of it. What was to be done? Viola's guilt must be discovered with daybreak, and meanwhile where was she to go? what was she to do? The blood-stained knife lay at his feet: his own thrice-accursed gift! He picked it up and flung it out of the window, whence it flew in a long curving line, quivering with the intense force of the impulse, away over the cliff-side and down down to the greedy waves below.

'Will you come with me instantly?' he said. 'There is no time to lose, and I must save you.'

'Save me? – save *me*?'

For an instant – a horrible instant – a flicker of repulsion passed across his face! The scene, the circumstance, the ghastliness of the doom, seemed to have overwhelmed him.

Suddenly, as if she had been struck, Viola shrank away with a half-articulate cry which rang echoing through the room and made the very heart stop beating, and a sickening chill run through the frame from head to foot. It was the cry of a spirit hurled from its last refuge, cut off from human pity and fellowship, cast out from the last sanctuary of human love.

With that momentary flash of repulsion and horror, a fathomless abyss seemed to open its jaws, black as the grave, but infinitely deeper than that resting-place of the weary who have lived and died uncursed. For these lay waiting a haven quiet and reposeful; but for her whose every breath had been cursed, who was stained and tainted through and through with shame and crime – for her was only a bottomless grave where she would fall and fall, weighted with her crime and her curse, through the darkness for ever and ever!

The words of passionate entreaty which Harry was now pouring out seemed to strike on deaf ears. The conviction that the curse was to be fulfilled had already taken root, and it was fast becoming immovable.

'Viola, listen to me,' cried Harry, grasping her hand; 'rouse yourself and try to understand. Don't you realise that we must go away from here? I have just been explaining – only you did not seem to hear what I said – that we can put off in Caleb's boat, which lies about two miles on the farther side of the headland. The cliff is supposed to be inaccessible in that part, and so it was till a few days ago, when Caleb – but I will tell you about that afterwards; I want you to come away now, without more loss of time. Viola, Viola, do you hear me? I must save you.'

'But I can't be saved,' she said calmly, 'don't you see? I am lost and cast out for ever; his curse is upon me; the hand of Fate is upon me. What earthly thing can save me?'

'Love can save you,' he said.

'Love! – for *me*! Oh! you are speaking falsely; you are playing with me. I am not alive any longer. I have nothing to do any longer with human feelings and passions: I am dead. It is ghastly work playing with a dead woman!'

'O Viola, how can you torture me like this?'

'What do you mean? You shrink from me yourself. I saw the look in your eyes, and I know what has happened.'

'You are horribly deceiving yourself; but I have no time now to try to convince you – don't you understand that we must go?' he repeated hoarsely, 'and that I would die for you?'

She gave a heart-broken cry, pressing his hand hard and close to her lips. Then she thrust it aside and turned away.

He darted after her.

'I must go alone,' she said, without looking at him.

'You are quite mad! Where will you go to? What will you do? I must, I *will* go with you.'

She shook her head. 'That cannot be,' she said. 'You would see it yourself to-morrow. You think me mad, but I understand better than you do how things are. We stand facing one another to-night; but there is a deep gulf between us, and it will widen and widen, so that your voice cannot reach me – even now I hear it as a whisper; you will be cut off from me utterly and for ever. It is quite just and it is quite unalterable. We must bid one another farewell.' She moved away, covering her face as she passed the motionless figure on the floor.

Harry let her close the door behind her; but after waiting for a few seconds, to avoid her opposition, he followed her.

She had gone out by the side-door on to the terrace, and was hurrying, in the glimpses of the moon, along the narrow pathway that ran in and out by the winding cliff-side, and finally up to the distant headland and the ridge or hill on the highest point of the downs which marked from here the western horizon.

Though she moved swiftly, he overtook her almost at once. Hearing his step, she looked back and waved him peremptorily away. But he disobeyed her. 'You must not come with me; *indeed* you must not. Do not let your life entangle itself further with mine. I implore – I entreat you to go back. Let me think, hope, believe that you are not involved in this fate and this curse.'

'Viola, you don't know what love means. You don't understand that it can save and atone and protect from the direst curse that ever fell on human soul. In this black hour – which in truth I have brought upon you – am I to desert you? Can you ask it? It was all my fault, and you must let me save you.'

'You would do this out of pity,' said Viola, 'out of self-accusation; you would ruin yourself to atone for all the love that you have showered upon me, all the risks that you have run for me, all the opportunities that you have sacrificed for me. O Harry! do you not see that my one remaining hope and desire is to turn away from you the shadow of this doom?'

'But, my darling, we can turn away the shadow together. Whatever you think you ought to do in expiation, I will try and help you to do.'

'Ah! but if you were with me I could not expiate my crime; I should live enjoying the fruits of it – no, no, nothing can undo, nothing, nothing – and if we had eternity to work in! Go back to your own life; we are parted now; no power can prevent it. My punishment is sure, whether it come from man or from God. Love itself cannot help me now: I am beyond salvation. I am a lost soul, and every effort at rescue only makes my punishment the harder. Your love, in spite of all, has been the best and sweetest thing in my life. Don't you see how it will be its crowning misery, if you force me to drag you down with me – if I have to think of myself to the last as your evil genius, who from beginning to end, has brought you sorrow and pain and misfortune? I have no faith and no hope; if ever a soul was lost, mine is that soul. Something within me seems to have frozen; I don't hope – I don't fear – and I don't repent.' There was a strange light in her eyes as she recalled the terrible scene in the death-chamber. Repentance seemed to be as far from her thoughts as hope itself.

'Whatever happens, I must come with you,' said Harry doggedly.

'You might just as well take some creature out of her grave,' said Viola. 'I am dead; I am quite dead. The only thing that makes me alive again – through sheer anguish – is the terror that you will not leave me, that I shall yet bring some crowning misery upon you. If you have any pity for me, let me go!'

'But what will you do? Where will you take refuge?'

'No matter, no matter; only let me go!' and she moved on, signing to him not to follow.

Harry stood grief-stricken and desperate. His face was drawn and haggard almost beyond recognition. It was all his fault, all his fault! What in Heaven's name ought he to do? Should he let her go and return to take the punishment of her deed upon himself? If he did that, she would come back and give herself up; if he did not –

He saw her hastening away from him towards the distant headland, across the stretches of the downs, and his heart leapt up in wild rebellion against her decree of banishment. It was more than man could endure. He would not endure it.

Swiftly as she was moving, he soon gained upon her, the sound of the sea and rising wind preventing her from hearing him until he stood before her and uttered her name. Then she gave a miserable cry and stopped abruptly.

'Viola, your command is unbearable. I cannot leave you. It is not pity, it is not remorse that moves me; it is love – sheer desperate undying love. I will share your fate, whatever it may be, and glory in it.'

A quiver passed across her face, as if she were verging towards the realms of the living once more. But she shook her head.

'You think only of the moment; you don't foresee as I do.'

'I do foresee, and I foresee a means of easy escape to-night, if only you will be reasonable, if only you will be merciful. Beyond that headland, beyond the ridge of the downs, there on the horizon, Caleb's boat – as I told you – is lying moored and ready for our flight.'

'It is of no use; it is of no use,' said Viola.

'It *is* of use,' cried Harry, thinking she meant that the proposed means of escape were hopeless. 'Listen. Sibella and Caleb have arranged that the boat shall be waiting for us in that little inaccessible beach in order to avoid the risk of being seen or our means of flight suspected. Beyond that ridge you come abruptly – if you keep near the sea – to the western wall of the promontory, the place where the man rode over in the dusk and broke his neck. If we skirt the cliff close by that spot, and don't mind keeping pretty near the edge for another two miles – it is considered dangerous, for the cliff is breaking away in places, so we shall be absolutely secure from meeting anybody – if we take this slight risk we shall reach the boat in about twenty minutes, whereas we might take an hour to go round by the safer way. I am not a bit afraid if you trust yourself absolutely to my guidance. But this is not all (Viola, you *must* let me show you what our chances are before you reject them). Two miles along the coast, beyond the headland, Caleb discovered a part of the cliff which would have offered an easy descent had it not been for one steep little bit about midway, which was unscalable. It struck him that a few artificial steps cut in the rock would make it continuous with the slopes above and below, where one could scramble down without much difficulty. He made those few steps (Viola, hear me to the end), and now we can descend by this way to the beach and put off to sea. Do you see how many advantages that gives us? Nobody but ourselves, Caleb and Sibella know of the possibility of getting to that beach from inland; the cliff is thought unscalable for miles in that direction; our means of escape, therefore, will never be suspected until some chance adventurer discovers Caleb's steps. The course that we shall take will be quite different from any that their calculations could lead them to expect. Long before morning we shall be out of sight, and we shall have landed on French shores before they think of pursuing us by sea. Sibella and I had formed careful plans for our guidance after we reached the opposite coast (you know that she was to help us and stand by us wherever we went), and these – but I must tell you about them afterwards – I have no doubt whatever that I could save you, if you would only trust yourself to me and do as I ask you. Every moment is of value; I do not feel safe till I have left the land behind me. Come, darling, come.'

He put his arms round her to draw her away, but she resisted him.

'Viola, Viola, for my sake come.' His voice shook with the passion of his pleading. 'Remember how madly I love you! 'His lips were white and trembling, his eyes filled with tears.

She held her breath, wrestling with the might of the temptation to yield to his pleading, to seek rest and refuge in the eager arms encircling her, to lay her head on his breast and drift back to life once more, love-bestowed and tended. After the long conflict and self-suppression, after the gloom and grief and pain of her life, the thought of such surrender and protection was like heaven! The longing became so intense that she had to clench her hands and stand still and rigid in order to resist it. She must not, she *would* not yield to it; she must not, she *would* not inflict upon him this deadly injury. Murderess as she was, she had not the baseness to accept a joy, to seek to avert a punishment at his expense. There was no room for self-deception; it was as clear as noonday. It must not be. If she had to face the torture of wounding him now, when she must bid him farewell for ever, still the torture must be faced – even *his* torture, in order that he might be saved.

Harry was still desperately pleading, Viola with her hands clasped tightly, her eyes fixed on the clouds, resisting, refusing, entreating him to leave her.

'Don't look away from me like that, Viola!' he cried wildly. 'What have I done that you should treat me so? It will drive me mad!'

He fell at her knees sobbing. She steeled herself for the terrible moment.

'Good-bye! good-bye!'

In a moment she had darted from him, swift as an arrow. He sprang up and followed her along the cliff-side pathway. She was running with desperate haste, on and on towards the distant promontory. He was determined to keep her in sight whatever befell, though he thought it wise to seem to yield to her wish in the meantime. The moon was not yet high in the heavens, and the undulations and hollows of the downs cast great stretches of shadow, made yet more sombre by the groups of gorse-bushes, and here and there, farther inland where the slopes were more sheltered, by patches of wood and little wind-beaten copses.

What did Viola mean to do? Which direction would she choose? At present she was keeping along the edge of the cliff where the moonlight fell, as if bound for the distant ridge on the headland. She was in sight, and so far safe. But presently she must come to one of the great patches of shadow, and then a serious danger threatened. The shadows ran into one another, some spreading inland, some towards the ridge, some back to the castle and the country about Upton.

When once she left the moonlit spaces, Harry would lose sight and knowledge of her unless he kept close beside her at the moment of her disappearing into the darkness. That peril must be avoided at all hazards.

His heart stood still at the thought of what might happen if he let her out of his sight. If she did not fling herself over the cliff, she might wander about the downs till morning, to be then hunted as a murderess and brought back for the hideous ordeal. She had no thought of evasion or self-protection.

He quickened his pace, till he was close enough to the fugitive to overtake her if necessary in a few seconds.

She seemed to become aware of his presence, for she turned and waved him frantically away. At a short distance ahead of them, crossing their path, lay the broad mass of shadow which Harry regarded with so much dread. He dared not obey her gesture; the risk was too great. When he came up to her she looked absolutely distraught.

'Now, Viola, I am coming with you,' he said firmly; 'you *shall* not keep me back. Realise that it is useless to attempt it.'

In an instant she had gone up close to the cliff-side.

'If you advance a step beyond where you now stand,' she said, 'I throw myself over.'

He stopped appalled.

They stood facing one another, between them the imaginary line upon the grass, stronger to oppose him, as Harry bitterly realised, than any fortress-wall. She stood on the very verge of the precipice, well out of his reach. His heart stood still for fear.

'Viola, you are pitiless as death!'

He heard her give a low sob as she moved swiftly away keeping always close to the cliff.

His voice called despairingly after her, 'Viola, have mercy on me – let me come!'

'I cannot, I cannot – it is because I love you.'

'I *must* come!' he cried wildly.

She pointed silently over the cliff without looking back. In another second she had plunged into the shadow, and he could see her no more.

The blackness did not fall upon the edge of the cliff, and therefore Harry knew that she had left the perilous verge, and that he might pursue her. But which way had she gone? What did she intend to do? She seemed to be possessed with a feverish haste to cut herself adrift, to escape from the scene of so much misery. Hope sank within him as he ran on in desperate, clueless pursuit. The memory of her face and of her deed, her immovable firmness in spite of all his pleading, killed every vestige of it in his heart. If was almost worse than if she were mad. She was not mad – he had convinced himself of that; on the contrary, she was miserably sane, clear in her forecasts, in her grasp of the situation, in the certainty which she felt of hastening punishment. The notion of escape seemed to have no hold upon her; she would probably not deny her guilt if accused. Her one desire or necessity was to cut herself off from her fellow-creatures, even from those who would face all risks for her. She seemed to be thirsting for punishment, yet unrepentant.

Knowing that she had left the cliff's edge, Harry followed as swiftly as he could one band of shadow after another, faintly hoping to find the right one before Viola had time to evade him. But he could discover no traces of her. The shadows led away into the trackless downs and far into the country; it seemed hopeless to follow them at haphazard. All was dead and bleak and silent.

Surely she could not have gone back towards the castle or the village! That was the only shadowed route still unexplored. In the inland direction the quest seemed absolutely futile. There were belts of trees and hedgerows and thick copses offering shelter, – besides that of the darkness, – for a dozen fugitives.

Harry went hopelessly on, looking on every side, listening and watching intently. The breaking of a twig, the stirring of a leaf, made his heart beat feverishly.

Time passed, and he saw no living creature, except occasionally a bird startled from its rest; heard no sound but the movement of the tree-tops and the never-ending murmur of the sea.

More than an hour had gone by in this heart-wearing search, and all in vain. Once, had he but known it, he passed quite close to Viola as she lay hiding in the outskirts of a large wood, well out of sight among the thick undergrowth. She had heard her pursuer's footsteps along the road, and crouched down till he should pass by. She heard him come up, look this side and that, pause and listen intently. She thought that he must hear the wild beating of her heart. She clenched her hands to prevent herself from crying out to him. Then she heard the footsteps pass on, and a voice through the trees came floating back to her in heart-broken entreaty, calling her name.

Her plan had succeeded admirably – absolutely; but oh, how mournful was the victory!

The sound of the footsteps, pausing at intervals and then going on again, was dying away now in the distance. She could just hear herself being called by the beloved voice for the last time.

'Viola, Viola!'

Then only the winds could be heard lamenting, and the trees whispering in sheltered tumult.

Viola flung herself on the carpet of dead leaves and broke into a passion of sobbing. The paroxysm, long and terrible, passed over at length, and left her lying still and exhausted at the foot of the old beech-tree where she had fallen. The wind, passing on its way through the wood, mourned over her. She rose at last, and pushed her way out. With one long, last look in the direction which Harry had taken, she turned again seawards, retracing her steps and hurrying back to the shelterless downs. She directed her steps – sometimes walking very quickly, sometimes breaking into a run – towards the headland and the ridge on the western horizon. A great sweep of moonlit down led up to it. Here were no shadows, for the land rose in a long series of gentle undulations to the height.

Across this wide space Viola was hastening when Harry, hopeless with the failure of his inland quest, returned once more to seek her by the sea. He knew her love for it, and the fascination of its voice, and he thought that in this desperate hour it would perhaps lure her back to the cliff-side and the shore.

His conjecture proved true. When he descried the dim figure in the distance hurrying towards the headland, he gave a wild cry and raced madly after her, dazed with new hope and frantic with fear. Over the brow of that hill lay the western wall of the promontory, sheer and pitiless; would she remember and avoid it? Could he overtake and shield her from the peril? One thought brought relief to him: though the fatal cliff lay beyond the ridge, the boat lay beyond it also, and Viola knew of it. It seemed not improbable; – it was even likely that she would set herself adrift upon the waters, giving herself to the sea, and accepting without question its final inexorable verdict. Harry raced on.

A lost spirit indeed she looked, moving, unconscious of pursuit, across those bleak spaces, swiftly as if the west wind were driving her before it in scorn. Harry's speed was marvellous; the ground seemed to devour itself beneath his feet. And as he ran the stern, terrible words which Sibella had so often quoted were rhymically ringing, clear and hard as a peal of bells, in his memory, 'But the goat on which the lot for Azazel fell shall be presented alive before Jehovah, to make atonement with him, to let him go to Azazel in the wilderness.' Reaching the brow of the hill, the figure turned to look for the last time on the scene which held so many memories.

The dark outline was revealed against the sky, motionless, alone.

What feelings were in her heart as her eyes rested upon that stretch of shadowed, wind-haunted country?

The old familiar moan came up on the gale from the sea. How did it strike upon her ear to-night? Did she remember that by to-morrow her name would be in everybody's mouth, scorned and execrated? Did she realise that the hand of every man – except one – would be against her; that she was homeless, well-nigh friendless, with a hideous ordeal threatening, and a terrible death?

'What have I done? Oh! what have I done?'

The last flicker of hope died out; not a spark remained; there was no possible redemption. Harry saw that she was indeed doomed by fate, by circumstance, by temperament; that she was beyond the reach of salvation, even as she had said. Love itself stretched out faithful arms in vain. She could not even repent.

In the sky a phalanx of black clouds had been marching up stealthily from the west, so thick and heavy that the moonlight was threatened with extinction. Becoming suddenly aware of this danger, Harry darted forward in a panic. If the moon were covered before he saw which direction Viola had taken he would lose her again, and this time assuredly he would lose her for ever. He had to race the clouds. But he had no chance against them: he saw that clearly, with an awful pang of renewed despair, as he nevertheless put forth his utmost strength, and tore and strained, and struggled madly up the hill. The terrible effort seemed to rend him; he could not breathe; he was unable even to gasp; he felt rigid, paralysed. But he struggled on as one possessed. In a miraculously short time he had covered half of that inexorable space, but it was not within the power of man to reach the summit in the time. The strain was too much for him; he faltered, staggered, and half fell against the hillside; trying to drag himself up even then with his hands, his head spinning, a rush of blood filling his mouth. At that instant the solitary figure, with one last look over the moonlit country and the sea, with one glance upwards at the sky, passed over the brow of the hill and out of sight, while a second later the sombre procession swept over the face of the moon and plunged the whole landscape in darkness.

The scene was obliterated: darkness everywhere; over the interminable uplands, in their profound solitude, in the shrouded heavens, and over the sea: pitch-black, rayless, impenetrable darkness.

EDITORIAL NOTES

Volume I

1. Yesterday, this *Day's ... Triumph or Despair*: The epigraph is from *The Rubáiyát of Omar Khayyám*, translated by Edward Fitzgerald and first published in 1859, stanza lxxiv, ll. 1–2. Fitzgerald's is a free and rather impressionistic version of a selection of poems originally written in Persian and attributed to an eleventh-century Persian poet and mathematician. The *Rubáiyát* was highly popular with Victorian readers and well known across all social classes. Caird quotes again from the *Rubáiyát* below (see note 29 to Volume III, below, p. 328).

2. *Philosopher's Stone*: an object believed by alchemists to have the power to transform base metals to gold.

3. *'point a moral and adorn a tale'*: from Samuel Johnson, *The Vanity of Human Wishes* (1749), l. 222, a long poem written in imitation of Juvenal's Tenth Satire.

4. *Demosthenes*: Demosthenes (384–322 BC), widely considered to have been the greatest of Athenian orators.

5. *'The eye only sees ... power of seeing'*: It is unclear who Caird is quoting here. The original is Thomas Carlyle's quotation of Goethe in *The History of the French Revolution* (1837; ed. J. D. Rosenberg (New York: Random House, 2002), p. 6), but the exact wording used by Caird is from Charles Kingsley's (mis)quotation of Carlyle in *Alton Locke* ((1850; London: Chapman and Hall, 1861), p. 1).

6. par excellence: French: the best example of its kind.

7. *the question recently so much discussed*: this is presumably the question posed in the *Daily Telegraph*: 'Is Marriage a Failure?' in response to Caird's own article of August 1888, 'Marriage', *Westminster Review*, 130:2 (1888), pp. 186–201, where she describes it as 'vexatious failure' (p. 197).

8. *INTRODUCTION*: it is not obvious which source Caird is using for her information about Azrael. The name does not appear specifically in the Qu'ran, although there is frequent reference to the Angel of Death. The name appears only in one chapter of the Torah and the function of the figure is unclear, seeming to be more a general figure of sin or uncleanness than an angel. Judaism and Islam, however, do have strong religious and folkloric traditions that identify Azrael or Aazel (with many other variations in spelling and translation) as the Angel of Death. Typhon (or Typhoeus) is a huge monster in Greek mythology who was defeated by Zeus and imprisoned under Mount Etna. There is not such a strong identification with Azrael as Caird seems to suggest, though Typhon and the ancient Egyptian god Set are frequently linked and Set is, among other things,

the god of deserts such as the one into which the scapegoat is driven and where Azrael finds it.

9. *'eternal verities'*: permanent truths as created by God. The nature of such truths is debated by the philosopher René Descartes in his work *Meditations on First Philosophy* (1641).

10. *'conspiracies of tempest ... from within'*: Thomas de Quincey, 'Levana and Our Ladies of Sorrow', part of his unfinished collection of essays 'Suspira de Profundis', published in *Blackwood's Magazine* in 1845. See *Confessions of an English Opium Eater and Other Writings*, ed. G. Lindop (Oxford: Oxford University Press, 1985), p. 152.

11. *the workhouse*: an institution where the homeless and unemployed could go for lodging and where they were expected to work in return for accommodation. Although work-houses had existed as individual charities for centuries, the Poor Law Amendment Act of 1832 systematized their provision and governance. Conditions were harsh and they were places of last resort, much dreaded and feared by the poor, and the subject of much criticism by social commentators like Thomas Carlyle.

12. *turned black silk*: Miss Gripper is commenting on the shabbiness of Mrs Sedley's cloth-ing. The fabric of a garment which had become worn or faded could be reversed and resewn to extend its use.

13. *Mr. Mallock's question*: from William Mallock's *Is Life Worth Living?* (1879), an attack on Positivism and on the possibility of there being a scientific basis to religious faith. Mallock is best known for his satirical novel *The New Republic* (1878).

14. *charlock*: wild mustard, a weed with yellow flowers.

15. *'a weaker vessel'*: 1 Peter 3:7. The verse refers to women (specifically wives) as the weaker vessel whom men should honour. It implies that they should be more carefully treated because of their physical fragility.

16. *Cowper*: William Cowper (1731–1800), a poet of nature and of evangelical Christianity.

17. *Protean*: shape-changing, after Proteus, a figure in Greek myth who was able to change form at will.

18. *all the wisdom of the Egyptians*: this is the description of King Solomon from the Bible, 1 Kings 4:30.

19. *Marmion*: the rather anti-heroic title figure from Sir Walter Scott's poem *Marmion* (1808). The poem was very well known and sections were often learned by children for recitation.

20. *Albert biscuits*: a plain, round biscuit named after the Prince Consort, manufactured and sold by the company Huntley and Palmer from the mid-nineteenth century.

21. *a Radical*: a term from late eighteenth-century politics, but indicating at this point a person supporting parliamentary reform. After the first Reform Act of 1832, there were still many campaigning for further reforms, particularly the further extension of the vote to working-class men.

22. *'Palace of Delight'*: The central female character of Walter Besant's novel *All Sorts and Conditions of Men* (1882) founds a 'Palace of Delight' for instruction and entertainment in the East End of London. A real institution, the People's Palace, opened in the East End in 1887. Given the New Woman-type character in Besant's novel it is likely that Caird would have known it.

23. *weeping and wailing and gnashing of teeth*: proverbial phrase to suggest frustration and distress which originates in several references in the New Testament book of Matthew (8:12, 13:42, 13:50, 22:13).

24. *"the Unemployed"*: Caird's capitalization shows the appearance of 'the Unemployed' as a social category. Its use as a noun rather than simply as an adjective dates from the 1880s,

as does the term 'unemployment'. Lady Clevedon is joking in suggesting that intellectual work is not work at all.

25. *"you murder with a definition"*: The source of this quotation has not been traced.

26. *Mrs. Allen's hair-restorer*: one of the most familiar of nineteenth-century patent medical and cosmetic products, this was specifically advertised as restoring colour to grey hair.

27. *Momus*: a minor god in Greek mythology, Momus was persistently critical of the other gods and personifies complaint, ridicule and mockery.

28. *Quintilian*: Roman rhetorician Quintillian (AD *c.* 30–*c.* 96) was a famous teacher of principles of moral and technical efficiency.

29. *retain my commission*: the purchase of military commissions had been abolished in 1871, so Harry is a career soldier.

30. *It rose, like a rocket*: The proverbial phrase 'Up like a rocket, down like the stick' was in wide usage in the nineteenth century and Oscar Wilde's short story 'The Remarkable Rocket', based on the phrase, was published in *The Happy Prince and Other Tales* in 1888.

31. *"fine rapture"*: probably recalling the lines from Robert Browing's poem 'Home Thoughts, from Abroad' (1845), ll. 14–16: 'That's the wise thrush; he sings each song twice over, / Lest you should think he never could recapture / The first fine careless rapture!'

32. *the Unjust Steward*: a figure from the parable in Luke 16:1–8. The interpretation of the parable is agreed by biblical scholars to be problematic, but the figure of the steward is nothing like Lady Clevedon suggests.

33. *the rebellious angels*: the rebel angels were those who rose up with Lucifer against the authority of God. They were cast down to the lowest depths of Hell and imprisoned there.

34. *Nut-brown maid*: 'The Nut-Brown Maid' is the title of an anonymous late fifteenth-century ballad first printed about 1520. The ballad was reproduced in Thomas Percy's *Reliques of Ancient English Poetry* (1765) and much anthologized thereafter.

35. *"lumbering wain"*: the phrase is probably from George Crabbe's poem 'The Borough' (1810), letter xii, l. 88. A wain is a heavy wooden wagon and Harry is suggesting that he prefers the rough but genuine Sir Philip to his sophisticated son.

36. *Adonis*: a beautiful and much fought-over youth in Greek mythology.

37. *crochet antimacassars and crystal lustres*: anti-macassars were small pieces of fabric or cro-chet-work placed on the tops of chair backs to protect the material of the upholstery from the macassar hair oil used by Victorian gentlemen. Crystal lustres were intricate glass candlesticks designed to reflect light. The effect of these details is to indicate a fussy and over-furnished interior, and the 'keynote of existence' one of tasteless middle-class gentility.

38. *phaeton*: a light carriage drawn by one or two horses, it was considered a fast and sporting vehicle.

39. *card-case*: for holding the visiting cards that were essential in nineteenth-century eti-quette.

40. *'died in harness'*: like a horse or ox, while still working.

41. *conjugate your ζυπτο ... old Father Thames*: Sir Philip is asking whether Geoffrey is a dili-gent scholar who practises learning Greek verbs or a more sportingly inclined schoolboy who would rather go rowing on the river.

42. bête noire: French: literally, 'black beast', a thing or person particularly feared or dis-liked.

43. *the pew was large*: before the widespread church renovations of the Victorian period, private pews were often large and almost enclosed for privacy. They were rented or bought by wealthy families.

44. boudoir *is a term inconsistent with this lady*: boudoir is the French term for a woman's private room, but it also carries a suggestion of seduction or at least frivolity. Mrs Sedley's serious piety would certainly mean that she would never use the term herself.

45. *'Daily Meditations'*: There were numerous books of daily meditations published in the nineteenth century, usually consisting of a passage of the Bible for each day and some suggestions of the lessons to be learned from them. Caird is not referring to any specific volume but suggesting a familiar generic type of book.

46. *Balaam*: the story of Balaam is in the book of Numbers. It was a Bible story often told to children, perhaps because of the talking donkey. Theologically, however, and as Viola points out, it is a rather difficult tale to interpret.

47. *story of the young prince ... royal father*: it is not clear which particular story is being referred to, but there is much historical evidence for the existence of the 'whipping boy' in royal courts in Britain and Europe. The figure is also related to that of the scapegoat that Caird is using in the title of her novel: an innocent punished for the crimes of others.

48. *ormolu*: gilded metal used for decoration of furniture and ornaments, often very elaborate and ornate in form.

49. *sorrow is the nurse of virtue*: The source of this quotation has not been traced.

50. *Free Will ... by outward conditions*: The statement about free will is relevant to the theme of self-determination for women that Caird is exploring, as is the suggestion about the relationship between nature and nurture that follows.

51. *the 'Ego'*: this term is not being used in the psychoanalytic sense, which is an early twentieth-century translation of Sigmund Freud's original German 'das Ich'. The use that Caird might have been familiar with is from philosophy and refers to the essential self, but not with the implication of pride or self-centredness that is part of the modern understanding of the word.

52. *Realism as opposed to Nominalism*: Caleb Foster is referring to philosophical debates about the universal and the particular. Here, as in the discussion that follows, Foster is not apparently standing for any specific or new school of thought but is articulating familiar debates and positions.

53. *Nero*: Nero (AD 37–68), Roman Emperor 54–68, who has become an archetypal figure of the whimsically tyrannical ruler.

54. *action of the tins*: preserved food sealed in tins had first been produced for Napoleon's armies at the beginning of the nineteenth century. For a short time it was regarded as something of a luxury but had become widely available by the time that Caird is writing. It could be injurious to health through lead poisoning from the soldered seams of the cans, but this was slow, and more common illnesses, like botulism, were caused by imperfect canning processes.

55. *Philosopher's Stone*: not the same as the meaning above (see note 2). Here it is a joke, referring to the large stone that Harry and Caleb are sitting on.

56. eidolon: Greek: a phantom or an idealized imaginary figure.

57. *By the Lord Harry*: a mild oath expressing surprise or determination. It is of uncertain origin, though 'Old Harry' is one of the many terms used to refer to the Devil. 'By the Lord Harry' seems to have been in common use and can be found in the work of Lord Byron, Charles Dickens, Rudyard Kipling and Arthur Conan Doyle.

58. *tilting-ring*: Caird is mistaken here, thinking that the tilting ring is an arena in which a contest took place. In fact, in games which took place alongside jousting contests, the tilting ring was a suspended circle which the rider had to catch on the end of his lance as he rode towards it at speed.

59. *'ai ai'*: archaic Greek. Found in Greek tragedy, for example in Sophocles's *Electra*. Although sometimes translated as 'alas', this does not convey the full sense, which is a ritual cry of mourning and therefore more of a wailing sound than a word.

60. *'pale Philosophy'*: a typical personification of Philosophy as a pale and sometimes veiled woman. It is a figure found in a number of nineteenth-century poems, such as Anne Lynch's 'Byron among the Ruins of Greece' (1852), stanza ii, l. 4.

61. *'mon cher philosophe'*: French: literally, my dear philosopher, my philosophical friend. A *philosophe*, however, has a more specific meaning, which is a member of a group of intellectuals of the French Enlightenment who embraced reason and scientific method.

62. *like a Trojan*: heroically, courageously, in the manner of the citizens of Troy defending their city against the Greeks in the Trojan War.

63. *In the East ... presents her with a sword*: Caird may be thinking of part of the ceremony in some forms of Sikh wedding, but many wedding customs of both Hindu and Islamic tradition feature swords either as items of dress or in the ceremony itself.

64. *badly-dressed old sheet-anchor ... bourgeoisie*: a sheet anchor is a secondary anchor on a ship and therefore depended upon as a last resort. The bourgeoisie is the respectable middle class, therefore Philip's rather mixed metaphor depicts the middle classes as unfashionable and conservative, determined in their resistance to change.

65. *national Bulwark*: a bulwark is a defensive construction, either on land or on a ship, and is here another figure for the conservative middle class.

66. *Evil One*: the Devil.

67. *tied hand and foot like a Gulliver*: Jonathan Swift, *Gulliver's Travels* (1726). In the voyage to Lilliput, the shipwrecked Gulliver wakes to find himself tethered down by hundreds of tiny ropes.

68. *'pure reason'*: Harry is making a joke by suggesting the title of Immanuel Kant's massive philosophical work, *The Critique of Pure Reason* (1781). He is suggesting that Caleb does not treat Viola as a child, but addresses her in philosophical terms of rationality rather than emotion.

69. *Kant*: Immanuel Kant (1724–1804), German philosopher whose ideas were important to Enlightenment thought and to Romanticism. The rest of the line about Kant's ideas on religious belief is a much-reduced version of one of the positions that he argues through his three *Critiques*.

70. *Socrates*: Socrates (469–399 BC), Athenian philosopher, known for his method of dialogue and questioning. The Dialogues referred to below are his friend and colleague Plato's rendition of some of these conversations.

71. *'familiarity breeds contempt'*: a very familiar proverb that appears in English at least as early as the mid-sixteenth century and was also well known in Latin.

72. *resorted in despair to hemlock*: referring again to Socrates, who was condemned to death by the Athenian state, ostensibly for impiety and corruption of youth, but possibly for political reasons. Socrates drank a liquid containing the poisonous plant hemlock and died.

73. *Xantippe*: wife of Socrates, whose reported bad temper has made her the figure of a nagging wife. Harry voices a kind of feminist revisioning of her, in keeping with Caird's view of the destructive effects of marriage on a woman's character.

74. *'the symposium'*: The work of the great Athenian philosopher Plato (*c.* 428–347 BC) included the *Symposium*, which took the form of a discussion. Given the intellectual interests of Philip, Harry and Caleb, Caird jokingly gives their visits to Philip this title.
75. *'purple emperors'*: butterflies native to Britain.
76. *Derbyshire springs*: because of the limestone found in the geological formation of the Derbyshire hills, if objects were left in so-called 'petrifying wells' they would quickly become encrusted with carbonate of lime. Petrifying wells or springs were a tourist attraction, as was the activity of producing encrusted objects.
77. *Idol*: an image of a deity. Caird here personifies Duty as the god that women must worship, and the image of that god (presumably Philip Dendraith) is coming closer to claiming Viola.
78. *spoony*: foolishly romantic.
79. *"gravitation ought to cease when they pass by"*: The source of this quotation has not been traced.
80. *Manitoba*: a province in Canada. In the nineteenth century Canada was a popular destination for emigrants from Britain seeking to establish themselves in a better position, especially financially, by starting businesses there, particularly farming.
81. *cumberer of the ground*: Luke 13:7. The parable refers to a fruitless fig tree, therefore appropriate in Mr Sedley's mind when referring to an unmarried woman.
82. *'who looked as if the speed of thought were in his limbs'*: a description of a horse from Lord Byron's poem *Mazeppa* (1818), stanza ix, ll. 4–5.
83. *Japanese proverb*: the proverb is 'if you hate a man, let him live'.
84. *gigantic ancestor*: this is a large miniature, probably painted, of a deceased relative that Mrs Dixie is wearing on a ribbon around her neck.
85. finesse: French: refinement.
86. *'whatever is, is right'*: from Alexander Pope's philosophical poem *Essay on Man* (1733–4), Epistle I, l. 294.
87. *satisfied Faust ... 'Stay; thou art so fair'*: referring to the bargain in Johann Wolfgang von Goethe's drama *Faust* (1808 and 1832), where if Faust utters this phrase, thus acknowledging that fulfilment can be found in earthly life, the devil may claim his soul.
88. *'hideously serene'*: from Edgar Allan Poe's poem 'The City in the Sea' (1831), l. 41. It is an image of death-in-life, where he imagines a city ruled by Death, illuminated by an eerie light from the water, in a stasis threatened by destruction that does not arrive.
89. *'No swellings tell ... happier sea'*: from the same poem by Edgar Allan Poe, ll. 38–9.
90. *Caleb ... Williams*: Mrs Courtenay is thinking of *Caleb Williams* by William Godwin, published in 1794.
91. *Mrs. Carlyle ... not to state*: Jane Welsh Carlyle (1801–66) was the wife of the author and social commentator Thomas Carlyle, remembered as a prolific letter writer. Her correspondence was published and very popular. This quotation is from a letter of 10 August 1845. See www.carlyleletters.dukejournals.org.
92. *'fearfully and wonderfully'*: from Psalms 139:14: 'I am fearfully and wonderfully made'.
93. *'The Ambassador Extraordinary'*: *His Excellency the Ambassador Extraordinary*, a novel by Robert Kerr, was published in 1879. The name of the Ambassador is Viscount Malign and his character is exactly as his name suggests.
94. *'She was more ... single damn'*: from a poem 'Dedicated to Mrs H. Crawford by the Author', ll. 9–10. The poem is an epitaph for three turkeys and was written by the Scottish child prodigy Marjorie Fleming (1803–11).

95. 'respectez l'innocence': French: respect innocence. Mrs Courtenay is rebuking Harry for using the word 'damn' in front of Viola.

96. *'Lives there a soul so black'*: John Webster, *The White Devil* (published 1612), III.ii: 'I do not think she hath a soul so black'.

97. carte blanche: French: literally, blank paper, meaning full freedom to act in a matter as one sees fit.

98. *the Golden Calf*: the idol described in the book of Exodus. It was made by Aaron from the gold earrings of the Israelites while Moses was on Mount Sinai receiving the Ten Commandments. The Golden Calf is emblematic of false gods, and here the specific worship of money and expensive items is suggested.

99. *Mrs. Carlyle's maid*: Jane Welsh Carlyle's maid Helen is mentioned in several letters. This incident is described in a letter of 15 April 1841. See www.carlyleletters.dukejournals. org.

100. Entre nous: French: between ourselves. Caird uses several French phrases in Lady Clevedon's speech as an indication of her social position and sophisticated character.

101. savoir faire: French: literally, 'know how to do', meaning the ability to act appropriately in any situation.

102. *female suffrage*: women's right to vote. John Stuart Mill, during his term as a Member of Parliament (1865–8), spoke frequently in support of voting rights for women. At about the same time, suffrage societies were being formed around the country, notably by Barbara Bodichon in London and Lydia Becker in Manchester. Although there were some extensions of women's legal rights in other areas, in divorce and custody of children for example, the campaign for the vote was quite weak until the foundation of the National Union of Women's Suffrage Societies by Millicent Fawcett in 1897. Early suffragists are distinguished from the later suffragettes of the Edwardian period as the latter espoused militant direct action, while suffragists were solely political and social campaigners.

103. *pale lavender sprigs on a white ground*: a pattern of fabric worn by young girls. Lady Clevedon suggests that Viola's dress shows her to be both unfashionable and childishly naive.

104. *Professor Huxley*: Thomas Henry Huxley (1825–95), eminent biologist and publicizer of Charles Darwin's theory of evolution through natural selection. He was a great advocate of scientific education for all, including children and the working classes.

105. *'screws'*: swerving shots.

106. *'service'*: first delivery of the ball over the net. Tennis had become a fashionable pastime in the later nineteenth century and the placing of the technical terms in inverted commas indicates their relative newness at this time.

107. *'language of imprecation'*: the phrase was normally applied to the Bible, to describe the calls for destruction or curses such as are found in the book of Psalms. Caird makes a joke by describing Dorothy's language in these terms.

108. *Sir Roger de Coverley*: originally a character in Richard Steele and Joseph Addison's journal *The Spectator* (1711). He expresses old-fashioned values and, although amiable, is represented in the text as rather ridiculous.

109. *'offending against such … slower capacities'*: reported speech of Sir Roger de Covereley in the *Spectator*, 6 (7 March 1711), p. 12.

110. *'Watteau'*: Jean-Antoine Watteau (1684–1721). Fashionable in France in the early eighteenth century, he painted idyllic scenes of the aristocracy enjoying the countryside in an illusion of simple pleasures.

111. *lead the lamb to the slaughter*: Isiah 53:7: 'He is brought as a lamb to the slaughter', meaning meekly and innocently.
112. piquant: French: agreeably sharp, pleasantly stimulating.
113. *egg-and-breadcrumbed whiting*: whiting is a small fish and a common recipe for it was to tuck its tail into its mouth before dipping in egg, rolling in breadcrumbs and frying it.
114. *dancing dervishes*: a mystical Sufi sect founded in Turkey in the thirteenth century who employed dancing and particularly spinning around on the spot as part of their devotions. Their practices were known to missionaries and travellers from at least the sixteenth century and were largely regarded by them with suspicion and distaste. Harry's rational beliefs would see their practices as superstitious nonsense.
115. *fetishes*: in animistic religions, objects believed to possess autonomous power. The term had become familiar from ethnography and anthropology, particularly from Africa. Sigmund Freud's later use of the term carries a related but different sense.
116. *Teutonic races*: people of Northern Europe, including the British here.
117. *Borgias*: powerful family of the Italian Renaissance, notorious for violence and corruption. Lucrezia Borgia particularly was believed to have poisoned many enemies and rivals.
118. *'could not see the town for houses'*: proverbial phrase meaning to be unable to see the whole because distracted by its parts.
119. *wisdom of the Persians ... if you can lie*: this does not appear to be a Persian proverb. Mrs Courtenay (or Caird) is perhaps conflating a phrase that was in common use (though of unknown origin) in the nineteenth century with the legendary wisdom of the Persians and their believed propensity for luxury.
120. jeu d'ésprit: French: literally, game of spirit, a flight of fancy or witty phrase.
121. 'excelsior': Latin: higher, upward. The word was probably familiar to Caird from Henry Wadsworth Longfellow's 1841 poem of that title.
122. *Perseus to this Andromeda*: from Greek mythology. The hero Perseus, among other deeds, rescued Andromeda from the rock where she had been chained as a sacrifice to a sea-monster. Andromeda is an appropriate figure here, as she is being sacrificed as a consequence of the actions of her mother, thus one more innocent being punished for another's misdeeds.
123. *'the gladness is taken ... plentiful field'*: Isaiah 16:10.
124. *Like a cormorant*: the cormorant is a legendarily greedy bird.
125. *a couple of hundreds a year*: income derived from the interest on investments.
126. *camomile pills*: Norton's Camomile Pills were a well-known Victorian patent medicine, advertised as a remedy for 'Indigestion, Sick Headache, Bilious and Liver Complaints'.
127. tête-à-têtes: French: literally, head-to-head, meaning private and intimate conversation.
128. *'rather face a crocodile ... ladies' school'*: from a book published in the year before *The Wing of Azrael*: *A Sportsman's Eden* by Olive Phillips-Wolley (London: Richard Bentley & Son, 1888), p. 157.
129. *"he that fleeth ... in the snare"*: Jeremiah 48:44. The passage suggests that there is no escape from this particular danger.
130. *Talleyrand*: Charles de Talleyrand-Perigord (1754–1838), one of the most influential and successful diplomats in European history. He worked under five French kings and also through the Revolutionary period. He recommended to the French National Assembly in 1791 that women should only receive education in domestic matters, prompting Mary Wollstonecraft to dedicate *A Vindication of the Rights of Woman* to him in 1792.
131. *Agony Column*: part of a newspaper in which miscellaneous advertisements and requests for information were placed, often seeking missing relatives or friends. Although advice and

responses to reader's queries had featured in newspapers before the Victorian period, the term 'agony column' is only used to describe them from the middle of the century onwards.

132. *Niobe*: from Greek mythology, the mother of many children who were killed because of her insult to the gods. In pity, the gods then turned her into a block of marble that spouted water like tears.

133. *Briarean woe*: an adjective derived from the name Briarea, a Greek mythological figure with a hundred hands.

134. *Caudine Forks*: a battle fought by the Roman army in 321 BC in which two possible routes could be taken through a pass and both would lead to defeat. Here it suggests a dilemma.

135. L'art être belle: French: the art of being beautiful.

136. Au revoir: French: until we meet again.

Volume II

1. *'Youth at the helm'... Etty's famous picture*: William Etty (1787–1849), *Youth on the Prow and Pleasure at the Helm*, exhibited in 1832. The title for the painting comes from Thomas Gray's poem *The Bard* (1757), ll. 73–4: 'In gallant trim the gilded vessel goes; Youth on the prow, and Pleasure at the helm'.

2. *'the old lady'*: the implication that Sir Philip refers to his wife in this way is a further indication of his lower-class origins and his vulgarity.

3. *'chaff'*: slang word meaning to tease.

4. *'Divina Commedia'*: the Italian title of Dante's long poetic work, called *The Divine Comedy* in English. It is not clear why Philip refers to Sibella in this way, though the poem can be described as a moral edification and he is perhaps suggesting her progressive intelligence.

5. beux yeux: French: beautiful eyes.

6. Tant pis pour Upton: French: too bad, or more's the pity for Upton.

7. *a woman in the pillory restores the original bark to mankind*: slightly misquoted from George Meredith, *Diana of the Crossways* (London: Archibald Constable & Co., 1885), p. 15. The original text reads, 'A woman in the pillory restores the original bark of brotherhood to mankind'. The story is of an intelligent woman in an unhappy marriage who becomes involved in both political and sexual scandal. It sold very well and it is likely that Caird read it.

8. *bubble reputation*: Shakespeare, *As You Like It*, II.vii.152.

9. *"wait till the clouds roll by"*: a line from an older folk ballad, published in 1884 with words by J. T. Wood, music by H. J. Fulmer.

10. *the Salvation Army*: Christian organization for evangelical missionary and philanthropic work, founded by William Booth in 1865 and structured on a military basis with members wearing uniforms and having military rank titles. It worked mainly in the very poor East End of London.

11. *attempted the life of the Queen*: made an assassination attempt on Queen Victoria. There were several such attempts made during her reign.

12. *infernal machine*: a weapon, usually meaning a bomb to be thrown.

13. *'abominable idol'*: the spread-eagle lectern is a reading stand in a church with the book-rest in the form of an eagle with outstretched wings, symbolizing the spreading of the word of God. It is described as an abominable idol because it would have been among the

types of decoration condemned during the Reformation of the Church and subsequently associated with Catholicism.

14. *chaff*: not the same sense used above (see note 3). Here it means the husks that are left when separated from the corn in threshing. An 'old bird' would not be tricked by such worthless bait.

15. *"he that getteth up … in the snare"*: this is the same quotation as found above (see note 9 to Volume I, above, p. 320).

16. levée: an assembly of visitors. The word is French, meaning rising, and it came to be associated with a social occasion from the custom of French kings to receive guests as they were performing the elaborate tasks of getting up and dressing. Mrs Dixie's sense of grandeur is being evoked by using the word.

17. *"Uneasy is the head that wears a crown"*: William Shakespeare's *2 Henry IV*, III.i.31.

18. *fable of the man who invoked Death*: one of Aesop's fables, 'The Old Man and Death'. Versions of Aesop's fables had been published in Britain since the fifteenth century and they were a popular text for children.

19. à la: French: in the style of.

20. *eels get accustomed to skinning*: proverbial phrase of uncertain origin. Although many eels would be skinned (in order to be eaten) and therefore as a species might jokingly be suggested to have become used to it, it does not mean that each individual eel would be. The general suffering of people does not make individual suffering easier to bear.

21. *Russian knout*: a particularly vicious whip.

22. *"Cos t'other man's sick"*: The source of this quotation has not been traced.

23. *Bellerophon*: Caird confuses her Greek mythology here. Bellerophon was the hero who tamed the immortal winged horse Pegasus and was therefore the rider, not the horse as Caird seems to suggest.

24. *exordium*: Latin: a beginning or introduction, especially of a philosophical treatise.

25. *Loyola*: St Ignatius of Loyola, founder of the Society of Jesus (the Jesuits) in the sixteenth century. As a Catholic missionary and teaching order, Jesuits were the object of suspicion and distrust in Britain, as Harry's comment here shows. Jesuits were committed to teaching in the belief that childhood moulded the adult, thus 'playing the potter'.

26. *Valenciennes*: very fine and expensive lace, pieces of which would be 'inserted' (sewn as a strip or shape) into other fabric.

27. *Shelley*: Percy Bysshe Shelley (1792–1822), one of the Romantic poets. The Romantic movement saw the imagination as being of supreme importance to human life.

28. *Sheridan*: Richard Brinsley Sheridan (1751–1816), dramatist and theatre producer who later became an MP and society figure. Caird is referring here to Sheridan's reputation as a brilliant parliamentary orator.

29. une chaise de Sybarite: French: a chair for a Sybarite. Sybarites, from southern Italy, were renowned for their self-indulgence and taste for luxury.

30. 'Candide': a philosophical novel by Voltaire, published in 1759.

31. *George Herbert's … go with the hatchet*: George Herbert (1593–1633), poet. The proverb appears in his *Outlandish Proverbs* (1640; see *The English Poems of George Herbert together with his collection of proverbs entitled Jacula Prudentum* (London: Longmans, Green & Co., 1902), no. 566), which is collection of translated proverbs. It suggests that people are lazy, and will make an effort only after the work is done.

32. *"Where there is no honour there is no grief"*: Also collected in George Herbert's *Outlandish Proverbs* (see *The English Poems of George Herbert*, no. 186).

33. *silent Sphinxes*: The Sphinx is a common figure in Victorian literature, following the increased interest in archaeology in that period. There is a frequent confusion, however, between the Egyptian Sphinx found near the Great Pyramids at Giza, which is a symbol of royal power, and the Sphinx in Greek mythology. The latter is a monster that inhabited the area around Thebes, asking a riddle of travellers and eating those who failed to answer. The riddle was finally solved by Oedipus. Caird repeats the familiar confusion of the two figures.

34. *"Love and do what you will"*: St Augustine (AD 354–430), from the Seventh Sermon on the First Epistle of St John.

35. *latent self*: Caird is writing at a time when psychology as understood in contemporary terms was just emerging. She is not using the term in the Freudian sense, but in a way that shows the historical transitional stage in the development of the understanding of the mind, meaning the hidden or dormant part of the self.

36. *guerilla warfare*: the term is relatively modern, first used in the Peninsular War (1808–14), from the Spanish for 'little wars'. It means a series of small attacks, rather than a full onslaught.

37. *aides-de-camp*: officers acting as personal assistants to a commanding officer.

38. *Calonna*: powerful family in Renaissance Rome, suggesting a sinister and possibly murderous history.

39. *Lucrezia Borgia*: the second reference to the Borgias (see note 117 to Volume I, above, p. 320). Lucrezia is a familiar figure of the dangerous woman.

40. *lych-gate*: roofed gate at the entry to a churchyard. The first part of the funeral service was traditionally carried out there.

41. *Parr's Life Pills*: a best-selling and very widely advertised patent medicine, a kind of laxative tablet. It was owned by Herbert Ingram and Nathaniel Cooke, who founded the *Illustrated London News* on the profits from its sales.

42. *'Turk's Head'*: a Turk's Head is a complex knot with a wide range of uses both decorative and practical. As Caird is mentioning a duster or broom here, it is probably the handle that is made from a knot of this type.

43. *celebrity*: Mrs Barber misuses the word, she means celerity: swiftness. Her clumsiness with language marks her as socially aspirational.

44. *without form and void*: Genesis 1:2: 'And the earth was without form, and void; and darkness was on the face of the deep'.

45. *Brobdignag*: from the second of Gulliver's voyages in Jonathan Swift, *Gulliver's Travels* (1726), where he is in a country of giants.

46. *Cupid*: Cupid is the Roman god of love, but this is not the way in which the figure is being used here. Indeed, it would be highly inappropriate given the loveless household in which he works. Cupid was often depicted as a chubby boy child and the butler is being compared to this.

47. *mummied*: mummified. The unwrapping of Egyptian mummies had become a public spectacle even before the nineteenth century, but the defeat of the French in Egypt at the beginning of the century had greatly increased the trade in mummies. In this metaphor the version of Christianity taught to Viola is suggested to be dry, withered and from another age.

48. *Whom the gods intend to destroy*: Harry expands on the well-known phrase 'Whom the gods would destroy, they first make mad'. The origin of the saying is unknown, but versions of it can be found in ancient texts. It suggests, as does Harry's elaboration of it, that for some unlucky people suffering is extended and not permitted to be mercifully brief.

49. *We could arrange you ... with a skull*: Geoffrey is suggesting an arrangement familiar from Renaissance painting in which subjects would be depicted with such symbols of death in order to indicate their disregard for worldly matters and their pious focus on the life after death.

50. *St. Sebastian*: St Sebastian was a third-century Christian martyr. He is a frequent subject of painting, shown tied to a stake and pierced by many arrows. According to accounts, he did not die of his wounds but was later beaten to death. Caird uses him here as a figure of suffering.

51. *pepper-and-salt-coloured*: referring to hair colouring, meaning that it is a mixture of grey and the original, darker, colour.

52. naïf: naive. Caird uses both versions of the spelling in the novel.

53. *syllogism*: a form of reasoning where a conclusion is drawn from two given propositions, e.g. all trains are long, some buses are long, therefore some buses are trains.

54. *Saxon barrows*: ancient burial mounds. From the eighteenth century amateur excavation of such remains had become a fashionable pastime.

55. *Triton*: a sea-god of Greek mythology. An appropriate name for Viola's dog, given her passion for the sea.

56. *embodied Rapture*: a state of ecstatic delight in physical form.

57. *Pillar Saint*: a form of ascetic religious practice following St Simeon Stylites (AD 387–459), who lived on top of a pillar for over thirty years.

58. "*a grande passion*": French: a great and overwhelming love.

59. *follower of Zoroaster or a Buddhist*: Zoroaster (or Zarathustra) was the sixth-century founder of a monotheistic religion believing in the contest between good and evil, symbolized as light and darkness. Buddhism originated in India at about the same time and teaches that enlightenment can be reached through knowledge and practice of Four Noble Truths. Both belief systems had very small numbers of European adherents in Caird's time and signify an extremely eccentric lifestyle.

60. *haunted by mist and storm*: Dick's discourse is a mixture of relatively recent ideas on ancient British history derived from the developing discipline of domestic archaeology and reference to the mythology of the Icelandic sagas.

61. apropos: French: on the subject of.

62. '*confounding the knavish tricks*': a slight misquotation of the British national anthem, God Save the Queen (or King): Part of the second verse runs: 'Scatter her enemies, / And make them fall. / Confound their politics, / Frustrate their knavish tricks'.

63. *Atalanta*: huntress of Greek mythology, a legendarily swift runner who refused to marry unless her suitor could beat her in a race.

64. *She that pursueth not arriveth at the goal*: Bob's speech is not composed of any specific quotation but is a pastiche of a sermon that includes echoes of phrases from the Bible and deliberately archaic language.

65. *Irving in 'Hamlet'*: Sir Henry Irving (1838–1905), famous actor of the Victorian period. His appearance in *Hamlet* in 1874 was a theatrical sensation.

66. *Purgatory*: a state or location in which the souls of the dead suffer for a time until they are purged of their earthly sins.

67. *throw herself on her husband's funeral pyre like an Indian widow*: Philip is referring to the Hindu funeral custom of suttee (or sati), in which the widow would throw herself onto her dead husband's funeral pyre. As no similar custom exists for a bereaved husband, this is a literal example of the self-sacrificing wife.

68. *eau-de-cologne:* a perfume invented in Cologne in the early eighteenth century, used to refresh or revive fainting women.

69. *blue-beard chamber:* In Charles Perrault's 1697 collection of tales, *Histoires ou contes du temps passé*, Bluebeard goes on a journey and forbids his young wife to enter a particular room. Overcome with curiosity, she enters the forbidden chamber and finds the bodies of Bluebeard's former wives.

70. *sal-volatile:* ammonium carbonate dissolved in alcohol, also called smelling salts and used to revive people when fainting or exhausted. Women often carried small bottles in their pockets or bags.

71. *"A mad world, Horatio!":* This does not appear to be a precise quotation, but perhaps a conflation of the famous speech from *Hamlet* (a play much concerned with madness), 'There are more things in heaven and earth Horatio, that are dreamt of in your philosophy' (I.v.), and the title of a play by Shakespeare's contemporary Thomas Middleton, *A Mad World, My Masters*.

72. *the Medes and the Persians:* a proverbial phrase meaning something unchangeable, from Daniel 6:8: 'According to the law of the Medes and Persians, which altereth not'. Sibella is perhaps being ironic by referring to something assumed to be permanent but which is nevertheless subject to history and change.

73. memento mori: Latin: reminders of human mortality.

74. *all is vanity:* Ecclesiastes 1:2.

75. *Carlyle:* Thomas Carlyle (1795–1881), prolific writer of political, historical and social commentary who was very widely read and greatly respected in the nineteenth century. Caird may be prompted to mention Carlyle here because he quotes the phrase from Ecclesiastes in his *History of the French Revolution*, p. 15.

76. *Gordian-knot:* a difficult problem or task, named after an intricate knot tied as a puzzle by the king of Phrygia. Alexander the Great solved the problem by cutting the knot.

77. *'Pain! ah! ... eternal pain!':* from Edward Carpenter's long poem *Towards Democracy* ((London: George Allen & Unwin, 1917), p. 160), published in four parts between 1883 and 1902. Only the first two parts had been published in 1889. Carpenter was associated with progressive political and social thought and Caird's quotation of his very recent work indicates her positioning of Sibella as a free-thinking woman, as well as her own progressive politics.

78. sans peur ... sans reproche: French: without fear and irreproachable. The description is associated with the chevalier Bayard, a fifteenth-century French knight considered to be the epitome of chivalry.

79. *Lord Chesterfield:* The correspondence of Philip Dormer Stanhope, Lord Chesterfield (1694–1773) with his son was published by the son's widow in 1774. It contained advice to his son on a range of matters from etiquette to social and political success and became a handbook of good manners.

80. *Madame de Sevigné:* Madame de Sevigné (1626–96), whose correspondence, mainly with her daughter, was well known. It was copied and circulated in her lifetime and published in 1725.

81. *old* Punches: *Punch* was a satirical magazine, known for both comic writing and illustration, founded in 1841 and having a huge circulation in Victorian Britain.

82. *arabesque:* French: fanciful posturing.

83. *'By the lone shore ... beat the waves':* Charles Mackay, 'By the Lone Sea-Shore', ll. 5–6, published in *Songs* (1856).

84. *Sandhurst:* a military training college for officers.

85. *Mrs. Grundy*: originally a character from Thomas Morton's play *Speed the Plough* (1798), Mrs Grundy became the personification of rigid propriety and disapproval of any departure from such propriety. As this personification she was extremely well known in Victorian culture.

86. sotto voce: Italian: literally, under voice, in an undertone or aside.

87. *they had no comforter*: Eccelesiastes 4:1.

88. *'I will sing ... will I sing'*: Psalms 101:1.

89. *'The Lord executeth ... all that are oppressed'*: Psalms 103:6

90. *'I am like a pelican ... upon the housetop'*: Psalms 102:5–6.

91. *aigrette*: a plume of egret feathers worn in the hair or on a hat.

92. *Bacchante*: priestesses or female followers of the Roman god of wine, Bacchus, who were renowned for drunken and licentious behaviour.

93. *Book of Job*: In this Old Testament book God tests the faith of Job by afflicting him with dreadful suffering. Mention of it here echoes the many other references to long suffering that are made in the text.

94. *best clothes ... Sir Walter Raleigh*: Sir Walter Raleigh (*c.* 1552–1618), poet, explorer and soldier. A courtier and favourite of Queen Elizabeth I, Caird refers here to the probably apocryphal story that he laid his cloak over a muddy puddle to protect her shoes as they were out walking.

Volume III

1. *'so-seeming virtuous'*: the description of Hamlet's mother, Gertrude, by his father's ghost in the play is 'my most seeming-virtuous queen' (I.v.46).

2. *'Wave after wave ... dead shore's ear'*: William Bell Scott, 'The Wintry Sea-Shore', ll. 9–12, published in *Poems* (1854). In the original, the text is rendered in four lines rather than the two that Caird uses.

3. *'without haste and without rest'*: from Goethe's poem 'Without Haste and Without Rest', published in *Zahme Xenien* (1820–7). This seems to have been an extremely well-known poem and many writers including Thomas Hardy, Rudyard Kipling and Karl Marx use the same phrase. Caird may have been familiar with it from Thomas Carlyle who, with fourteen others, sent the poet a seal inscribed with the phrase in 1825.

4. *Bench of Bishops*: a collective term meaning all the bishops of the Church of England, it comes from the seats in the House of Lords that are reserved for them.

5. *torture that the Romans ... blazing sun*: the general was Marcus Regulus and the torture was inflicted by the Carthaginians, who defeated him in 255 BC, rather than by fellow Romans.

6. *limped*: this appears to be a misprint for 'limpid', meaning clear.

7. *Place of Stones*: Job 8:17.

8. *Druid priests ... set fire to them*: there is no real evidence that such sacrifices took place. The chief written sources are Roman, from the historian Pliny and Julius Caesar, both of whom might have wished to represent the Britons as barbaric. The sources do not mention women and children as the particular victims of these rituals, but Caird uses them to continue her theme of the sacrifice of women and the innocent.

9. *SHIRT OF NESSUS*: from Greek mythology, a shirt stained with the blood of the centaur Nessus, who had attempted to rape Hercules's wife. Nessus tricked her into believing that the shirt would guarantee her husband's love, but it was poisonous and burned Her-

cules to death. It is appropriate that the garment being referred to by Caird is Viola's wedding dress.

10. *straining at a gnat … swallowed the camel*: phrase from Matthew 23:24 which had become proverbial, 'to strain at a gnat and swallow a camel'. It suggests that it is strange to resist small things, having accepted without question something much larger.

11. *brougham*: a closed, horse-drawn carriage.

12. *Heine*: Heinrich Heine (1797–1856), German poet and essayist. Many of his poems were set to music and are characterized by a certain irony and bitterness.

13. *cynosure*: centre of attraction or admiration.

14. *gaudy monstrosity of the old place*: the restoration of churches was widespread in later Victorian England. Such restorations were frequently controversial as many disliked the new style on architectural grounds and others saw the trend towards Gothic as a symptom of Catholicism.

15. *avaunt*: archaic word, meaning be gone, go away.

16. *this case in all the papers*: this may be a reference to the Parnell divorce case. Charles Stewart Parnell, the leader of the movement for Irish Home Rule, was cited by Captain William O'Shea as the co-respondent in his suit for divorce from his wife Kitty. The scandal ruined Parnell's political career and, some argue, the hopes for a peaceful political settlement. Although Captain O'Shea did not file for divorce until December 1889 (after the publication of *Azreal*), newspapers had reported quite widely on Mrs O'Shea's relationship with Parnell before that time.

17. *"that grief stalks … each by turns"*: The lines here are slightly misquoted from Elizabeth Barrett Browning's second verse translation of *Prometheus Bound* (1850), ll. 324–5. The fifth-century Greek original has been attributed to Aeschylus. The lines in Browning read 'for Grief walks the earth, / And sits down at the foot of each by turns'. See *The Works of Elizabeth Barrett Browning*, gen. ed. S. Donaldson, 5 vols (London: Pickering & Chatto, 2010), vol. 1, p. 138.

18. chère amie: French: dear friend, here also implying lover.

19. *gay Lothario*: a seducer of women, after a character from Nicholas Rowe's tragedy *The Fair Penitent* (1703).

20. *Sybilline*: like a sibyl. Sibyls were prophetesses in classical mythology, especially associated with the god Apollo. Although they foretold the future, their prophecies were often made in very obscure and imprecise terms. There is also a pun on Sibella's name.

21. *farthing*: in the currency used in Victorian England, the coin with the smallest value: a quarter of a penny.

22. *heel of Achilles*: in Greek mythology the great warrior Achilles was invulnerable to weapons, except for a small place on his heel where his mother had held him as she dipped him in the river Styx to produce his invulnerability. The proverbial phrase refers to a person's single weak point.

23. *as Pope says … equivocating pretty genteelly*: Alexander Pope (1688–1744), poet and essayist. The phrase is found in his correspondence, in a letter of 7 August 1716, in which he was recounting his attempt to suggest that he was not the author of a controversial piece without actually having to deny it outright. See *The Correspondence of Alexander Pope*, ed. G. Sherburn, 5 vols (Oxford: Clarendon Press, 1956), vol. 1, p. 345.

24. *the Workhouse*: see note 11 to Volume I, above, p. 314.

25. *Timbuctoo or the Wild West*: emblematic of dangerous and far-off places. The west of America was its new and unstable frontier and there had been several unsuccessful expeditions to 'find' Timbuctoo in the early nineteenth century.

26. *it was the custom … every city-wall*: there is a good deal of evidence that this was the case in many societies and in many periods in history; however, the creature was much more often animal and not human.
27. *"language of imprecation"*: see note 107 to Volume I, above, p. 319.
28. *'Love not pleasure … well with him'*: Thomas Carlyle, *Sartor Resartus* (1833–4; ed. P. Sabor and K. McSweeney (Oxford: Oxford University Press, 1987), p. 146). Slightly misquoted, the original reads: 'wherein whoso walks and works it is well with him'.
29. *'I myself am … a soul on fire'*: from *The Rubáiyát of Omar Khayyám*, translated by Edward Fitzgerald, stanza lxvi, l. 4, stanza lxvii, ll. 1–2. See note 1 to Volume I, above, p. 313.
30. *première danseuse*: principal female dancer in a ballet company.
31. *harvest-moon*: the full moon nearest the autumnal equinox. Because of optical effects produced by the angle of Earth at this time of year, the moon can appear to be larger and redder than usual.
32. *Queen of the Cannibal Islands*: Frank Musgrave's burlesque opera *The Queen of the Cannibal Islands* was performed at the Royal Strand Theatre in 1865 and R. M. Ballantyne's novel *The Cannibal Islands* was published in 1869. Caird uses the figure to suggest that Harry's responses to questions about Viola are deliberately cool and might as well be referring to an unknown woman in a far-distant place.
33. *Herculean*: in a Greek mythology Hercules was a hero with superhuman strength.
34. *a problem in Euclid*: Euclid was a Greek mathematician of the third century BC. The 'problems' were mathematical tasks set in his book *Elements*, and which were widely used in education even in the nineteenth century.
35. *Carlyle*: Thomas Carlyle, from whose *Sartor Resartus* Geoffrey is reading. See note 75 to Volume II, above, p. 325.
36. *while he a tale unfolded*: Caird paraphrases *Hamlet*, I.v.15–16: 'I could a tale unfold whose lightest word would harrow up thy soul'.
37. *differential calculus*: a mathematical method of calculation, therefore much less interesting to most people than romantic notes.
38. *terra firma*: the earth, solid ground.
39. *an article of 'vertu'*: an object of fine art.
40. *Pillar of Strength*: a highly reliable person who gives support.

TEXTUAL NOTES

The copy-text is the first edition, published in London in 1889 by Trübner & Co. The book was not reprinted. Double quotes have been changed to single, except for quotes within quotes. Excepting this and the silent corrections listed below, I have retained the punctuation, spelling and word choice of the 1889 edition.

Silent Corrections

224	Mrs. Russell Courtenay] Mrs. Russel Courtenay
231	Mrs. Russell Courtenay's'] Mrs. Russel Courtenay's'
234	'Mr. and Mrs. Russell Courtenay.'] 'Mr. and Mrs. Russel Courtenay.'
242	Mrs. Russell Courtenay] Mrs. Russel Courtenay
277	Mrs. Russell Courtenay] Mrs. Russel Courtenay
287	Mrs. Russell Courtenay,] Mrs. Russel Courtenay,

For Product Safety Concerns and Information please contact our EU
representative GPSR@taylorandfrancis.com Taylor & Francis Verlag GmbH,
Kaufingerstraße 24, 80331 München, Germany

Printed and bound by CPI Group (UK) Ltd, Croydon, CR0 4YY

11/04/2025

01844008-0019